A Century of Music-Making

ROBERT K. WALLACE

A
Century
of Music–Making

The Lives of
JOSEF & ROSINA LHEVINNE

ILLUSTRATED WITH PHOTOGRAPHS

INDIANA UNIVERSITY PRESS

BLOOMINGTON   LONDON

Published in Canada by Fitzhenry & Whiteside Limited, Don Mills, Ontario

Manufactured in the United States of America

Library of Congress Cataloging in Publication Data

Wallace, Robert K.   1944–
  A century of music-making.
  Bibliography
  Discography
  Filmography
  Includes index.
    1. Lhevinne, Josef, 1874–1944.   2.   Lhevinne, Rosina, 1880–   I. Title.
ML417.L65W3   786.1'092'2   [B]   75–28908
ISBN 0–253–31330–9
1 2 3 4 5 80 79 78 77 76

To Martin Platt

Contents

CONTENTS

Part V: A World Recreated

Preface

WHEN I MET Rosina Lhevinne she was eighty-seven years old and I was twenty-three. I had heard of one of her students—Van Cliburn —but did not then know who her late husband, Josef Lhevinne, was. A year later I had become her private secretary and had married Gladys Astor Philibert, one of her students. A year after that I began work on part of this biography—as my dissertation in the "Cultural History" niche of the English department at Columbia University under Jacques Barzun and Quentin Anderson. For their consent and advice I am deeply grateful.

This book is the first biography of Josef and Rosina Lhevinne. The Lhevinnes have made their impact on the world through their achievements as pianists and teachers, and the book's main purpose is to describe and evaluate those public achievements. But the Lhevinnes' life together is also compelling on the personal level. The attempt of contrasting temperaments to achieve marital harmony seems to be a double challenge when each belongs to a gifted musician.

This book has been written with the approval and cooperation of Rosina Lhevinne, and she is principal among its primary sources. I interviewed her almost weekly for several years, but she was generous with more than her time and memory: she also allowed me to explore file cases, desk drawers, closets, and basement trunks in search of letters, diaries, photographs, recordings, tour books, contracts, and other material useful to a biographer. The friendship that developed between us has for me been one of the deep pleasures of writing this book.

For other primary source material I am indebted to Mrs. Katherine Ketchum of Toronto, who found and sent me a copy of the diary her late husband kept while studying with Lhevinne in Berlin; to Dean Gideon Waldrop of the Juilliard School, who gave me access to unpublished materials in the school's files; to E. Shibryaevskaya, who supplied information from the files of the Moscow Conservatory; to William Beller and Harold Triggs, who shared so generously their memories and notes of lessons with the Lhevinnes; and to the scores of other individuals who have spoken to me of their association with Josef and Rosina Lhevinne—especially their two children, C. Don Lhevinne and Marianna Graham. At the risk of omission, I give alphabetical thanks to Howard Aibel, Victor Aller, Cortland Barnes, Esther and John Browning, Sr., John Browning, Martin Canin, Helen Coates, Mrs. George Cranmer, Sarah Crump, Mischa Dichter, Malvina Erlich, Lawrence Evans, Olegna Fuschi, Ruth Geiger, Arthur Gold, Boris Goldovsky, Robert Grokoest, Tony Han, Stanley Hummel, Elsie Illingworth, Robert Mann, Adele Marcus, Mary Marshall, Angelica Morales von Sauer, Garrick Ohlsson, Robert Pace, Kun Woo Paik, Katherine Parker, Daniel Pollack, Sue Prosser, Joseph Raieff, Mrs. Katherine G. Rich, Maria Safonoff, Mark Schubart, William Schuman, Mary Lee Shephard, Jeffrey Siegel, Norman Singer, Brooks Smith, Izler Solomon, Lillian Steuber, Marian Szekely-Freschl, Lee Thompson, Ralph Votapek, Howard Waltz, Edward Weiss, and Eva Maria Zuk.

Apart from thousands of concert reviews, relatively little material by or about the Lhevinnes has previously appeared in print (see bibliography). I have located most of what does exist, including concert reviews from Russia, Hungary, Austria, England, France, Germany, Norway, Mexico, Cuba, and the United States. The libraries most helpful to me have been the Music Division of the New York Public Library (Lincoln Center) and the Music and Microfilm Divisions of Columbia University. Other libraries I have used include the Library of Congress, the libraries of the Juilliard School, the University of California at Berkeley, the University of Colorado at Boulder, and the Newspaper and Slavonic Divisions of the New York Public Library. My wife tracked down valuable material about Lhevinne in the National Periodical Library of Mexico City.

In the text itself, I have quoted Mme. Lhevinne in the first person where appropriate. Words attributed to her are based on our interviews, many of which were taped. Most quotes are verbatim, though I have occasionally altered syntax to help the eye understand words that made sense to the ear as spoken. The incorporation of Rosina Lhevinne's "memoirs" into this biography has involved some danger, for an octogenarian and nonagenarian mind can sometimes be loose on facts, lavish in gratuitous effects. I have attempted to minimize this danger by verifying through reviews and interviews whatever can be verified, and I am pleased to be able to confirm what many who have known her have long felt: that Rosina Lhevinne's memory is not only selectively excellent but in many ways truly extraordinary. Some things of which she speaks, of course, are known only to her; for these we must rely on her veracity and amazing memory.

In the transliteration of names from Russian to English I have not followed a rigid system. Generally I have observed the current practice of preferring "v" to "ff" but in the cases of Safonoff and Rachmaninoff I could not bring myself to alter the spellings by which these men were known while living in America. In spelling the name Lhevinne I have omitted the accent that appeared in English during the early years of the twentieth century: Lhévinne. The accent generally fell out of use while Josef Lhevinne was alive; his widow has tended to omit it. For translation of various materials from the Russian, I have been indebted to Maria Safonoff, to Mme. Lhevinne herself, and to Sosi Setian, Bruce Parrott, and Steve Baehr. For material from the Hungarian, I thank Liz Klobusicky-Mailaender; and for sleuthing in Canada, Peter Solomon. For a modest grant that allowed me to make final revisions of this book, I thank the Academic Affairs Committee of the Faculty at Northern Kentucky State College. And for help in translating from the Spanish, for having introduced me to Rosina Lhevinne, and for much more, I thank my wife, Gladys.

A final acknowledgment goes to the late Herbert Weinstock, for whose interest in this project and editorial advice I will always be grateful.

A Century of Music-Making

I

YOUTH
IN IMPERIAL RUSSIA

1

A Girl
Meets a Tradition

NOBODY THOUGHT when Josef Lhevinne died in 1944 that his wife Rosina would survive him so long or so well. But today, in her nineties, the teacher of Van Cliburn and John Browning continues to send from her studio at Juilliard many of the world's most polished young pianists. Aside from Artur Rubinstein (who is six years her junior), she is the sole surviving member of what we refer to as the Romantic Age of piano playing.

As a woman, Rosina Lhevinne has had it both ways. For forty-six years she was married to Josef Lhevinne and devotedly helped to further his career. Although she assisted him ably and at times brilliantly in his teaching and in their two-piano playing, she always insisted that his be the only solo career. Her "reward" for this devotion during his lifetime has been her own outstanding career as a teacher from 1945 to the present, beginning at age sixty-five, and a briefer but equally brilliant career as a soloist, in her late seventies and early eighties.

Rosina Bessie was nine years old when she met the man and the tradition to which she has devoted her long life. Josef Lhevinne was then fourteen years old; the tradition, the Russian School of piano playing, was about twenty-five. Only for the first nine years of her life can she be considered apart from them. During those nine years, she was exceedingly close to her mother.

Born in Kiev in 1880, Rosina Bessie was taken to Moscow about a year later. Before leaving, her parents took her to the studios of De Mezer, a photographer. He must have been one of the city's more fashionable picture takers, for on the back of his prints were words informing his customers that he had won honorable mention "à l'Exposition Universelle de Paris 1878." One of the pictures

3

he took has survived. His diminutive subject is sitting on a large elegant chair and is surrounded by pink flowers. Wearing a white dress with pink sash, and soft leather boots, she is staring unflinchingly at the camera with an expression decidedly complacent. Signs of her mother's extreme devotion are everywhere apparent.

Rosina's mother had been born sometime around 1847. She was about eight years old when Czar Nicholas I died and was in her teens when Czar Alexander II freed the serfs and established the Conservatories. We do not know what city Maria Katch was born in, nor do we know her parents' first names or occupation(s). But the family must have been relatively well-off, for Maria took piano lessons and was taught French. She compensated for the lack of a formal education by devouring the works of Dostoyevsky, Tolstoy, and Turgenev, whose first great novels came out when she was about twenty years old.

Maria Katch was short in stature and deep in passion. As befits an avid reader of novels, she fell in love at a young age with a man she was unable to marry. Rosina never learned—or today cannot remember—why her mother was not allowed to marry the man, but she does remember her mother's description of how she and the one true love of her life parted at a crossroads, the one taking a road toward St. Petersburg, the other a road toward Moscow. Whatever the reason for the painful separation, Maria overcame her disappointment enough to marry a traveling Dutchman named Jacques Bessie, settle with him in Kiev, and bear him two daughters—Sophie, sometime around 1873, and, seven years later, Rosina.

Jacques Bessie's origins, like his wife's, are known to us only through the memory of their younger daughter. He—not only we—did not know much about his parents. He was raised by an aunt in Rotterdam. His relatives were Dutch diamond merchants and he was groomed for a place in the family firm. So fastidious was his upbringing that he never in his life used soap (which he was told was too crude): creams and lotions were for him. As a boy he took piano lessons, and when old enough was sent to the University of Paris. After a few years at the Sorbonne (he did not stay for a degree), he was sent to sell the family wares in the vast provincial hinterland to the east.

Jacques Bessie never did like Russia or its people, and habitually repeated the standard phrase of his time: "Scratch a Russian and you'll find a barbarian underneath." How Maria caught the mild-mannered Russophobe (who distributed choice wines in addition to diamonds) we will never know. Most likely they were attracted to each other by their unlikely blend of background and temperament:

she passionate and aggressive and Eastern European; he restrained and refined and Dutch. One thing they did have in common was being Jewish, but if that gave them a strong bond in private they did not stress it in public or when raising their children, for Rosina did not have a particularly sharp sense of religious heritage. Her father instead stressed the broadly humanistic attitudes shared by all religions. That the Czar had a differing view does not seem to have consciously burdened her life as a child.

Kiev, where Rosina was born, was 450 miles southwest of Moscow and within the eastern boundaries of the Pale. In March 1881, a few days before Rosina's first birthday, Czar Alexander II was assassinated by nihilists, and Kiev, like many Russian cities, was the scene of fierce anti-Semitic riots. When Alexander III succeeded his father, he enacted the infamous March Laws, or "Temporary Rules," which denied most Jews freedom of movement even within the Pale. Jacques Bessie, however, because he was both foreign-born and a merchant of the first class, was allowed to take his family to Moscow sometime in 1881 or 1882.[1]

Both of Rosina's parents had strong incentives for wishing to make the move. Kiev, with its commanding position on the Dnieper River, was a good location for a merchant. But Moscow, as the hub of Russia's expanding railway system, had become an even better one. If Rosina's father was likely to find superior business opportunities, her mother was certain to find superior cultural attractions. For a provincial capital, Kiev boasted excellent cultural and educational institutions. But nothing there could compare to the Moscow Conservatory, Moscow University, the Maly Theater for drama, and the Bolshoi Theater for opera and ballet. In Moscow, Maria Bessie hoped, both Sophie and Rosina would be able to receive the formal education and artistic training that had not been available to her.

Not long after the move to that city, Maria Bessie's plans for her younger daughter were almost ruined. In 1884 Rosina contracted diphtheria. There was no vaccine for the disease then, as the diphtheria bacillus had only the year before been isolated in scientific laboratories. During the year Rosina got the disease, it also struck the Rachmaninoff family in St. Petersburg, and carried off young Sergei's sister. Rosina almost went that route too. She was about to die of suffocation, and the doctors had given up all hope, when her mother requested a tracheotomy.

Maria Bessie was an avid reader not only of novels but of Western medical journals. Obsessed with problems of health, she had a low opinion of most Russian physicians, and felt that Western journals were her only dependable source for professional advice about rearing children. In one such journal she had read that victims of diphtheria had sometimes been saved by tracheotomy (the operation in which the windpipe is pierced and a tube inserted so air can bypass the throat and enter the trachea directly). But when she requested this operation for Rosina, the doctors refused.

Their refusal was understandable, if not justifiable. Tracheotomy is a dangerous operation on the small throat of a child, because of the proximity of other organs to the windpipe. Thinking Rosina would die anyway, they preferred the disease to be the agent, not their knife in a vital organ. But Rosina's resourceful mother persisted until the doctors gave in, which they did only after she "signed with trembling hand" (she later told her daughter) a document absolving them from responsibility. The tracheotomy was successful, and Rosina was able to breathe again, but the experience left scars longer and deeper than the small one that remains today on her neck.

"After I had diphtheria, my mother brought me up exactly like a tropical plant. The winter in Moscow lasted six months, and during that time I was hardly ever allowed out of the house. Because I was kept in so much, the moment I did go out I would get a sore throat or bronchitis or laryngitis, and again I would have to stay inside. I did not go to school as a child, but instead the tutors came to me."

It was quite natural that after saving Rosina's life her mother would become even more passionately attached to her than before. And it was natural that Rosina would respond to the attention that was lavished upon her and would crave the same from various surrogate mothers for the rest of her life. Throughout her childhood she remained extremely close to her mother, whose resourcefulness and excitable temperament she seems to have inherited. Her mother "raised the roof" whenever things did not go her way; as for Rosina's father, she does not remember his ever raising so much as his voice. Their gentler relationship was characterized by a "game" they played whenever he returned from a business trip. "My father traveled a lot for the firm, and when he came back he would often say to me, 'Why did you do *this* while I was gone?' or 'Why did you do *that*?' Then always he would mention some bit of mischief I had done in his absence. I would ask, 'How did you know that?' And he would point to his fifth finger and say, 'Why, this finger knows everything!' For many years I believed that, and now I cannot remember the age at which I was undeceived."

That mild wave of her father's fifth finger was about all she ever received in the way of parental discipline.

Although Jacques Bessie left most household affairs to his wife, he did try to insist on one thing: the superiority of things Western European to things Russian. He demanded that family discussions be in French and would not allow the Russian language (which Rosina and her mother spoke in his absence) to be used at the dinner table. As domestic help was inexpensive in Moscow, Bessie employed a cook, a governess, and two servant girls. The servants were Russian but the governess was Swiss, because Bessie did not want "uncouth, indelicate" Russian girls supervising his daughters' daily activities.

When Rosina was about seven, the family moved to a comfortable apartment on Nikitzky Boulevard. Electricity had come to Moscow in 1883, but the Bessies' new apartment apparently lacked that modern convenience, for Rosina remembers reading books by the light of kerosene lamps throughout her childhood. Each room but one was heated by a large black cast-iron stove; the other room's stove was plated with porcelain of a beautiful green. Among the furnishings were several Oriental rugs, a chair that rocked sideways, and two grand pianos—a Becker and a Schroeder. The pianos were Russian makes and were considerably less expensive than the German Bechstein, which was also available in Moscow at the time —which only proves that Bessie's preference for things Western was subject to monetary modification.

The twin pianos were more than bourgeois ornaments for the Bessies' parlor, for both Rosina's parents remained active as amateur pianists. Her father enjoyed playing light tunes from operettas. Her mother, predictably, was more ambitious, and had a running battle with Beethoven's *Moonlight* Sonata. When Sophie, their elder daughter, was about twelve years old, the Bessies engaged Antonin Galli, an honor graduate of the Moscow Conservatory, to give her piano lessons. As Sophie was not particularly talented, her lessons must have been the more trying for having to endure the presence of her precocious, if not to say obnoxious, five-year-old sister. Rosina sat at the other end of the room and corrected the wrong notes. Maestro Galli suggested that the Bessies save their money for the "young one," and Rosina began her piano studies at age six.

For the next three years, Rosina spent most of her time at the piano, at lessons her tutors assigned, and at embroidery. Because

Moscow was usually snowbound from October to April and because her mother was so obsessed about health, Rosina was confined
to the apartment for half of every year. Winters spent in this fashion were restricting but were also blissfully silent. She loved to sit
at the window and watch the snow fall, and to see sleighs glide
silently by on runners. But she rode in sleighs herself only a few
times each winter. On days when it was not too cold or windy her
mother would take her along while doing errands.

Partially because of this hermetic existence, Rosina was pitiably
impressionable whenever she did leave the house. After the April
thaw she was allowed to go outside more often, but then her sensitive ears were assaulted by the noise of iron wheels grating on cob-
blestone. As a result, the arrival of rubber tires on the streets of
Moscow was one of the great blessings of her childhood.

The first opera her mother took her to was Anton Rubinstein's
The Demon, which happened to feature a scene in which devils
ran on stage from all directions. For weeks afterwards, Rosina was
terrified by the vision of the devils and insisted on sleeping in her
parents' bedroom.

This acute vulnerability to sights and sounds resulted not only
from Rosina's isolation but also from her unusually responsive nervous system and her strong and vivid imagination—both of which
were heightened by certain of her mother's preoccupations. Maria
Bessie was superstitious, and her daughter came to share her
dread not only of certain numbers but of the slightest mention of
death. In addition, Rosina's mother's concern with avoiding disease
often took the form of vivid descriptions of the aggressive qualities
of microbes. This made for a childhood filled with crises—some of
which in retrospect have a humorous edge.

"Once when I was seven or eight years old, my mother took me
walking on a spring day and we stopped at the office of a friend of
hers, who was a doctor specializing in syphilis. There was a man
in the office with a very noticeable cavity above his nose, and his
bone was deteriorating rapidly. This made a great impression on me,
but that was nothing compared to my horror and fright several
weeks later, when I noticed a small cavity above the bone of *my*
nose!

"Every day after that, I touched it, and each time it seemed to
be bigger! I was afraid to tell my mother that I had that disease,
but finally after many months the knowledge became too much
for me, and one night I ran to her bed and crawled under the covers
and cried big tears. When she asked what was wrong, I put my

finger to my nose and said, 'My nose is falling in, and I have syphilis.'

" 'But Rosina,' she said, 'I haven't syphilis, and look, my nose is falling in too. Everyone has a depression above his nose.' She kissed me, and I felt better, but still I said, 'You know, it is many months since I thought I had syphilis and still I have been afraid to tell you.' "

After spending the winter and spring months avoiding various urban microbes, Rosina would spend her summers avoiding rural ones, for the Bessies, like most Muscovites able to, left town during the hot summer months. Usually they rented a *dacha* in the country, and there Rosina got her first glimpse of rural life. She was shocked to see how the peasants lived. Their cottages had but one room, in which the whole family slept. In the room there was a big stove, with large boards surrounding it. In the winter, she learned, the peasants would put their feather beds on the boards and sleep near the heat. Their lambs slept inside too, so they would not freeze. Rosina felt sorry for the peasants, as well as for other rural creatures. She loved to see the chicks break out of the eggs, but when it came time to have them for dinner she would fall on the floor and throw such a tantrum that no one could eat. Whether or not the disrupted meals contributed, one summer her mother decided Rosina needed a more vigorous routine than the *dacha* provided.

"To strengthen me, she decided to take me to the Baltic Sea. This was to be a great affair, a big event, because we were going there alone for the whole summer—just the two of us, and no one else. She reserved a room near the sea, and when we got there it was very gray, for the Baltic Sea is not sunny. I can still see that gloomy weather today. I was depressed as soon as we got there, and kind of afraid too, because it was a new place.

"On the day after we arrived, I was supposed to learn how to swim. Mother took me to the beach, and the water was so shallow they had to take me far out into the sea with a horse and wagon. Then a man sat in a boat and put me on a hook and lowered me into the water as if he was fishing. That's how they taught swimming.

"All the other children had a wonderful time, and were screaming with joy, and laughing and splashing in the water, but I almost had hysterics there, because the whole atmosphere made such a horrible impression on me. When I got back to shore, I told my mother not only that I would never go in the water again but that

I wanted to go home. She suggested that we stay a few days more to see if I would change my mind, but I said, 'No! I want to go home immediately.'

"After a lot of begging and pleading and crying, she gave in to me. And after spending all the money and saying to everybody in Moscow, 'Good-bye, we are going to the Baltic for the summer,' she had to take me back home because I made such a scandal. She and father wanted only the best for me, but they gave me absolutely no discipline. I twisted the entire household around my fifth finger, and if there was something I did not like I would scream and shout until I was satisfied."

As Rosina grew older, she discovered more subtle and refined ways to get her way, but she never lost the basic instinct, the automatic reflex of sizing people up and knowing just how far to go with them. From what little evidence we have, her mother was also talented in this way. The cardinal rule for human conduct that she instilled in her daughter was "Never tell a lie, but nobody is pulling your tongue to make you tell the truth."

Some children who are spoiled and indulged as much as Rosina was are quickly jolted into a sense of perspective through contacts with other children. But being inside all winter and away all summer and having tutors during the school year, she had no steady companions of her own age. Her one social event each year was her birthday party on March 16 (March 28 according to the Gregorian calendar used in the West), a large and festive affair attended by her mother's friends and their children. Of these worthies, Rosina now remembers only the doctor of syphilis and a huge army colonel who dwarfed his wife. One party stands out from the rest:

"It must have been about my tenth or eleventh birthday when my mother and father bought me a little writing desk just for a child. I was tickled to have it, and when the guests came I showed them the wonderful present I got. They all made nice comments. Then one of them, a man my mother knew very well, said sarcastically, 'It's pretty early to give her a place where she can count all the money she will make from her concert career.' That comment hurt my mother so much that it completely spoiled her relationship with that man."

That Rosina's mother would sever a relationship on the basis of one sarcastic comment was indicative of her volatile temperament. Her father's attitude toward people who made such remarks was quite different: he simply said, *"Tant pis pour eux!"* ("Too bad for them!"), and forgot about it. Her own adult reactions to such comments have touched both extremes.

If Rosina's mother had never thought of counting money from her daughter's future concert career, she had most likely thought of the career itself. For Rosina, at the age of nine, had been accepted by the Moscow Conservatory. Gaining admission to the Conservatory was difficult for any child but was especially so for a Jewish one, for in 1887 Czar Alexander III had set a quota that limited Jews to three percent of the student body. Rosina's merely being admitted suggested that someday she would probably be playing concerts in public and receiving money for it.

As soon as the nine-year-old girl entered the Conservatory, she began to assimilate the principles of the "Russian School" of piano playing—some of which Galli had introduced her to in her lessons at home, but which she had not worked at perfecting in a methodical way. In addition, the Conservatory began to teach her something she had not encountered at home—discipline. Both the discipline and the pianistic principles she learned can be directly attributed to Anton Rubinstein, whose opera *The Demon* had frightened her with its devils. Then sixty years old, Rubinstein was an occasional visitor at the Conservatory. For Rosina and most of her classmates he was not only a heroic man but a musical god. Before continuing her story, it will be well to see why.

Anton Rubinstein was the first of the many Russian Jews who were born in the Pale, went to Moscow or St. Petersburg at a young age, became great musicians, and achieved international fame. Rubinstein not only set the pattern for pianists like the Lhevinnes and violinists like Elman and Heifetz but was in fact the necessary condition for the achievements of those who followed. For Anton Rubinstein established the Conservatories at which most of Russia's great musicians (Jewish or otherwise) have received their training.

Rubinstein was born in 1829. As would later be the case with Rosina Bessie, his father was a merchant, his mother was extremely eager for her children's artistic development, and he was taken to Moscow at an early age. Unlike her, he and his family had to be baptized in order to leave the Pale and he had no Conservatory to enter when he did get to Moscow. His first piano lessons were from his mother, who made him play scales endlessly and who strapped him to a chair so he would practice the required hours each day. He showed great talent, and soon began taking lessons from Alexander Villoing, a teacher of French descent who lived in Moscow (there were no noted *Russian* teachers then) and who, as soon as he realized he had a genius on his hands, took ten-year-old Anton on a three-year tour of Western Europe. The boy had great success as a *Wunderkind* during this period but received no serious musical training—a fact he was to resent later in life.

At age sixteen, Anton was about to begin the study of counterpoint in Berlin when the death of his father left the family in debt and him without funds in Western Europe. He supported himself there for four difficult years. When he returned to his homeland at age twenty, he was not allowed to enter St. Petersburg because a "musician" had no legal standing in Russia's still feudal society. Fortunately, he had made connections with members of Czar Nicholas I's court during his years as a *Wunderkind,* and he was finally allowed to live in the city, where he soon developed a friendship with the Grand Duchess Helena Pavlovna, at whose home he became Master of Music. Here he had for the first time in his life the opportunity to work seriously at becoming a mature musician. After four years of working alone, he had become the greatest pianist the world had ever known—with the possible exception of Liszt, who had recently retired.

All geniuses, the saying goes, are self-taught, but Rubinstein was more so than most. For during the four years in Russia when he developed his mature approach to the piano he did not even have an established teacher or an established school or tradition to rebel against. His great original achievement during that period was to develop a true "singing" tone at the piano. As a child the singing of the Italian tenor Rubini had impressed him as the most beautiful sound in the world. In his early twenties, as he worked at the Grand Duchess Helena's home, he tried to reproduce the sound of Rubini's voice on the piano. On a cello or a violin, whose sound is produced by drawing a bow across the strings, it is relatively easy to produce a singing (cantabile) tone. But to reproduce such a sound on an instrument whose strings are struck with hammers is something no one before Rubinstein had achieved. He knew the kind of sound he wanted, though, and by experimenting constantly with touch and with pedal taught himself to produce it. More than anything else, it was his unprecedented beauty of tone that impressed Western Europeans when he returned in triumph as a mature man of twenty-four.

In addition to the tone he produced, Rubinstein had a strong artistic temperament that found its perfect means of expression in the piano—and that caused much agitation in female hearts. His technical mastery was so strong that his instrument seemed a mere extension of his personality. And that personality was so magnetic that when coupled with his Beethovenesque appearance it invariably inspired the word *leonine*. (This was in the days before *leonine* had become hackneyed—indeed, even the *Moonlight* Sonata was hardly hackneyed then.)

At any rate, from Liszt's retirement at midcentury until his own in the early 1890s, Rubinstein was the world's great pianist, and he played throughout Russia, throughout Western Europe, and even throughout the United States (on a tour in 1871–72). By force of his playing and his personality, he, perhaps as much as any other man ever had, helped music to be recognized as a profession of the highest seriousness, not only in Russia but in the entire Western world. One of the finest tributes to his achievement in this regard is the characterization George Eliot gave of him in 1876 in her last novel, *Daniel Deronda*. Thinly disguised as a Jewish, Slavic pianist named Paul Klesmer, Rubinstein has a dramatic encounter with an English politician that illustrates both his strong character and his historical significance. The politician, on learning that Klesmer is a pianist, suggests that a man of his talents should not waste them in being a "mere musician." To which Klesmer thunders in response:

> "Ah, sir, you are under some mistake there. . . . No man has too much talent to be a musician. Most men have too little. A creative artist is no more a mere musician than a great statesman is a mere politician. We are not ingenious puppets, sir, who live in a box and look out on the world only when it is gaping for amusement. We help to rule the nations and make the age as much as any other public men."[2]

In Western Europe, Rubinstein helped to "rule the nations" and "make the age" in a figurative sense; in Russia, he did both things quite literally. His first adult tour of Europe had lasted four years, and when he returned to St. Petersburg in 1858 he became even more disturbed than before by Russia's musical backwardness. There was no systematic training available for Russians who wished to become musicians, and those who went abroad to receive it had no legal standing in the country when they came back. Fortunately, Czar Nicholas I had died while Rubinstein was on tour, and had been succeeded by the enlightened Czar Alexander II, whom Rubinstein, through his influence with the Grand Duchess Helena, was able to persuade to establish the Imperial Russian Conservatory in St. Petersburg—with thirty-two-year-old Anton Rubinstein as director.

Founded in 1862, six months after Alexander II freed the serfs, the Conservatory not only offered Russians musical training for the first time but also gave musicians legal standing in Russian society by conferring upon its graduates the title "Free Artist." The Conservatory can truly be said to have emancipated Russia's potential musicians; many of its first-year students were men who for lack of musical opportunities had already entered other professions. Among them was a lawyer named Tchaikovsky, who became one of the school's first graduates. After becoming a "Free Artist," he went to Moscow, where he was hired to teach composition at the Moscow Branch of the Imperial Conservatory, which was founded in 1865 with a program identical to that in St. Petersburg. Its director was Nicholas Rubinstein, Anton's younger brother.

Given a *carte blanche* by the Czar for determining the methods and goals of the Conservatory, Anton Rubinstein had quickly assembled a first-rate faculty, many of whom had been trained in the West. He had made it clear that the primary goal of the Imperial Russian Conservatory would be to preserve and to build upon the accepted musical traditions of the West. This brought him into bitter conflict with members of the now-famous *kutchka*—Balakirev, Borodin, Cui, Mussorgsky, and Rimsky-Korsakov—who favored the development of Russian musical traditions clearly set apart from Western ones. As several members of the *kutchka* had no formal musical training at the time and as the group as a whole had actually produced very little finished work in the 1860s, Rubinstein tended to regard its members as dilettantes who talked a great deal about Russian music but did little to further its growth, and to point to the *kutchka* as perfect examples of why the main function of the Conservatory should be to teach Russians a *disciplined* approach to the study and performance of the accepted musical masters.

The best summary ever made of Rubinstein's approach to musical education—and it is a very important one in terms of the lives of Josef and Rosina Lhevinne—is a single sentence spoken by Klesmer in *Daniel Deronda:* "Genius at first is little more than a great capacity for receiving discipline."[3] Rubinstein had resented the years of serious work he had lost while Villoing was displaying him in the salons of Europe, and he felt that the strict training his mother had given him as a child was the only thing that had preserved his potential of becoming a mature musician. Consequently, the program he established at the Conservatory was designed to give students strict and steady training from an early age. Children were encouraged to enter at age nine or ten. The first five years were spent in the lower school, where the student mastered the basic technique of his chosen instrument. In piano, this meant practicing scales and arpeggios, double thirds and double sixths, learning the proper hand position and the use of the wrists, understanding the use of the pedal, and developing a keen ear for the sounds one drew from the instrument. After completing the lower school, the student spent four years with a major professor in the upper school, where he studied the accepted masterworks of his chosen instrument. For Rubinstein, the musical masters ran from Bach through Chopin.

This program of strict and steady discipline begun at an early age, plus the example of Rubinstein's own playing, formed the basis for what has come to be known as the "Russian School" of piano playing. It features a disciplined approach to the mastery of the instrument, but does not emphasize technique for its own sake. As director of the St. Petersburg Conservatory and as professor of piano there, Anton Rubinstein set extremely high standards for technique, but even higher ones for musicality. For him the purpose of music was to communicate emotion, and learning to master the instrument was only a means to that end.

By the end of the 1860s, Rubinstein had established this approach at both the St. Petersburg and Moscow Conservatories, and was able to resign his directorship and devote his time to playing the piano and composing. It is impossible to fix the exact date at which the world became explicitly aware of a "Russian School" of piano playing, but ever since the creation of the Imperial Russian Conservatory, pianists trained in its approach have been distinguished by their powerful command of the instrument, their ability to produce a sensuous singing tone, and their preoccupation with the accepted piano masterworks, especially from Beethoven through the late Romantics. Even by 1889, when Rosina Bessie entered the Moscow Conservatory, these tendencies had solidified into a strongly felt tradition. It was a tradition which, under the force of Rubinstein's personality, had acquired the sanction of "divine right"; and a tradition which for her, among her contemporaries, was embodied by Josef Lhevinne.

"When I entered the Conservatory on Nikitzky Boulevard, the building was more or less dilapidated. My teacher in the lower school was Remesov, but after a short time he became ill. My mother went to Safonoff, the director, for advice, and he said I should take as a teacher his star pupil, the fourteen-year-old Josef Lhevinne, who soon came to our home to present himself in this role.

"On the day he arrived, one of my cheeks was swollen and I did not want to appear, but my mother insisted. He was fourteen and looked about eighteen; I was nine and looked about six. He was very big for his age, and excellently developed physically; I was a very thin and small child. With my cheek puffed out and my hair in pigtails, I was very shy and frightened, and it is no wonder he later told me what a 'pitiful' sight I had been.

"The first thing he did was to pat me kindly on the head. Then he put me on his knee and looked at my hands, and asked what I could play on the piano. I was too shy to answer, so he asked, 'Do you like music?' I nodded, and he asked if I would like him to play for me. I nodded again, and he went to the piano and played the Chopin *Barcarole*, and that piece has had a special meaning for me ever since.

"The experience of him as a teacher lasted about six weeks, until Remesov became well. After that, Josef sometimes visited my parents on the informal evenings they gave for friends of the family. But he paid no more attention to me, for I was but a child, and he a great man in his teens."

2

From Boyhood to Free Artist

WHILE ROSINA BESSIE was being "raised like a tropical plant," the "great man in his teens" was completing a very different kind of childhood. Josef Lhevinne had been born in Orel, Russia, on December 1/13, 1874. Had there been any reason to translate his name into English at the time, it would have been rendered "Levin" or "Levine." The fancier "Lhevinne" was suggested years later by Safonoff when it was apparent that Josef was to have a career in Western Europe and the United States. The additional "h" and "n" made the name unique—a distinct advantage for an artist—and also made it seem less Jewish. For Josef's father, "Levin" is a more appropriate spelling.

Arkady Levin was a trumpeter from Lodz, a city now in Poland but then within the western limits of the Russian Pale. His patronymic, Leontivich, is all we know of his parents. Short in stature, Arkady Levin was long in productivity. After fathering at least four children by his first wife, he had married the woman who was to become Josef's mother. Fanny Levin (whose patronymic, maiden name, and place of birth we do not know) had presented her husband with four daughters before Josef arrived; two more sons were to follow. As Levin added to his family, he took it slowly eastward across the Pale. Orel, where Josef was born, was halfway between Kiev and Moscow, and outside the Pale. Levin was not a university graduate or a merchant of the first class or a foreign-born Jew, but he was an excellent musician. Lacking hard information, we can only assume that he, like many Russian Jews, played his way out of the Pale by having musical talent no available Gentile had.

When Josef was a year or two old, Levin received permission to take his family to Moscow, where he was hired to play the trumpet in the orchestra of the Imperial Small Theater (also called the Maly Theater). The Imperial Small Theater was the home of state-sponsored productions of comedy and drama, and its orchestra—which supposedly did not hire Jews—played music during intermissions. Levin rehearsed with the orchestra every day, played at the theater every night, and most nights went on to work at a second job. He did his moonlighting at the Yar nightclub, where he was hired to blow his trumpet into the early morning hours. The Yar had no standard closing time. Sometimes it was nearly daybreak when Levin got home from his work there. By working two full-time jobs, he managed to support his large family in a modest way, but was unable to spend much time with his wife and children.

Fanny Levin's role in life was to produce children and feed them. This, it seems, taxed her capacities to the full, and she, unlike Maria Bessie, had no energies left with which to pamper her children or build major crises over invisible things like microbes. Her daughters were stamped in her image: they had no unusual talents and were tone-deaf. Her sons followed their father: all became successful musicians. Josef became by far the best-known of Levin's sons, but Myron made a respectable career as a composer and Theodore was a good enough flutist to become a member of Persymfans, Moscow's famous conductorless orchestra, which was organized in 1922.

The Levins' apartment was so crowded with children that Josef slept on a sofa as long as he lived at home (which was until his marriage). For the rest of his life he had an insatiable craving for space. When he was three years old, an old upright piano arrived to further clutter the apartment. It belonged to a brother-in-law of Josef's father. The man had been forced to leave Moscow and had been unable to sell the bulky, undistinguished instrument, which Arkady Levin offered to store for him.

Josef was an unusually silent boy. He was more than three years old before he spoke a word. When asked to account for that fact later in life, he said that with so many children in the house and so much trouble feeding them, no one really noticed whether he spoke or not. His father noticed though, when Josef, at the age of four, went up to the old cast-off piano and began to pick out some tunes he had heard on the street. Many children do this, but Josef began to harmonize. Arkady Levin had always been on the lookout for signs of precocity in his children and had doubtless been disappointed at his daughters' lack of it. He eagerly tested his boy and found that Josef had perfect pitch. Levin was a fine trumpeter, but knew very little about playing a piano, so he arranged for Josef to play for Nils Krysander, a Swedish-born choir director who also taught piano. Impressed with the boy's talent, Krysander offered to teach him without remuneration.

Playing the piano became easier for Josef than speaking. His attitude toward the instrument was casual, and he spent considerable time playing with other children in the streets (there was no room in the apartment). He had what Russians call a "blood and cream" complexion, and a photograph taken when he was about six years old shows a full head of light curly hair. He showed an early predilection for athletic activities of all kinds and was impressed by the sword-play when his father took him at the age of five to a Russian-language production of *Hamlet*. When his father took him to see Meyerbeer's *Les Huguenots,* he raved about the shooting-off of the guns. His childhood was not to be spent weeping over piano keys.

When Josef was about eight years old, Krysander arranged for him to play before the *Deutscher Männergesang-verein* in the Festival Hall of the Slavianski Bazaar, a popular Moscow restaurant. He played a Clementi sonata, and did it so nicely he was asked to give an encore. So he played a more difficult composition by Gottschalk, the American composer whose reputation in Russia was then at its height. Because Josef was too short to reach the nether regions of the instrument, Krysander sat next to him and operated the pedals. Krysander must have turned the pages of the score too, for he had not taught Josef to play from memory. Although the audience was quite large, Josef was not frightened about playing in public, and enjoyed himself.

The performance at the Slavianski Bazaar was followed by others of the same sort, for Krysander was eager to display the talent of his young protégé. But one such appearance spelled the end of their student-teacher relationship. When Josef was eleven, Krysander arranged for him to perform at a fashionable soirée. The host was a Jew, one of the wealthier men in Moscow, and most of the city's social elite were present. Among them was the Grand Duke Constantine, the second son of Czar Nicholas I. Like nearly all the Romanovs, Constantine was a tall man; unlike many of them, he was liberal on racial issues and extremely interested in music, being an amateur cellist himself.

Josef was dazzled by his first glimpse of "grand society." When called upon to play, he noticed that the Grand Duke had taken a seat nearby. He played the two biggest pieces in his repertoire: Beethoven's *Moonlight* Sonata and Liszt's transcription of the *Tannhäuser March.* After Josef had finished and the applause had subsided, the Grand Duke stood up and began to ask him questions. In awe of the giant man, Josef could only stammer "Yes" or "No" rather indiscriminately. But when asked if he would like to attend the Moscow Conservatory, he had the presence of mind to say "Yes." The Grand Duke shook his hand and promised to see to it that he got an education.

Grand Duke Constantine then scanned the room and discovered that the host of the party was the wealthiest man there. He walked up to the man and commanded: "*You* shall pay for the education of that boy." The man did pay, but his relationship with Josef was never a warm one. He treated him more like a servant than a budding artist, and more than once Josef was awakened late at night and ordered to go to the man's house and perform. Unpleasant as that was, it was a small price to pay for the privilege of being able to attend the Moscow Conservatory.

When Josef Lhevinne entered the Moscow Conservatory in 1886, its director was thirty-year-old Sergei Taneyev, who had studied piano with Nicholas Rubinstein and composition with Tchaikovsky. Nicholas Rubinstein had been dead for five years, but his presence was still strongly felt. He had reputedly been nearly as great a pianist as his brother, but had seldom played in public. Less austere than Anton, he had been content to direct the Conservatory, to teach a piano class in the upper school, and to enjoy social amenities. Nicholas Rubinstein had been well loved at the Conservatory, and a tightly knit cult had formed around him. Following his death, its members had remained true to his memory and to his habits, which included virtuoso bouts of drinking and gambling, a formidable and intimidating presence in front of students, and impeccable musical taste.

The piano faculty in 1886 consisted of Nicholas Sverev and S. M. Remesov in the lower school and Paul Pabst and Vassily Safonoff in the upper. Sverev, Remesov, and Pabst were holdovers from the days of Nicholas Rubinstein; Safonoff had come from St. Petersburg only the year before. Safonoff was only thirty-four years old, and was regarded as an intruder by many of the old-timers, especially Sverev. The two men had clashed from the first. Sverev's musical connections were all in Moscow; Safonoff's were in St. Petersburg. Sverev was a political liberal; Safonoff was a conservative (his wife was a daughter of Vishnegradsky, finance minister to Czar Alexander III). Sverev had never played in public, and made his musical reputation only by what his students did; Safonoff was an accomplished accompanist and had toured extensively with the cellist

Rosina Bessie at a year and a half. Kiev, 1881.

Rosina Bessie. Moscow, 1885 or 1886.

Josef Lhevinne. Moscow, 1879 or 1880.

ОКОНЧИВШІЕ КУРСЪ МОСКОВСКОЙ КОНСЕРВАТОРІИ, УДОСТОЕННЫЕ ЗОЛОТОЙ МЕДАЛИ.

VI ВЫПУСКЪ —— 1875 г.
ТАНѢЕВЪ, Сергѣй.

VII ВЫПУСКЪ —— 1876 г.
БАРЦЕВИЧЪ, Станиславъ.
КОТЕКЪ, Эдуардъ.

VIII ВЫПУСКЪ —— 1877 г.
БРАНДУКОВЪ, Анатолій.
ГАЛЛИ, Анатолій.

X ВЫПУСКЪ —— 1879 г.
КЛЕНОВСКІЙ, Николай.

XI ВЫПУСКЪ —— 1880 г.
ДАНИЛЬЧЕНКО, Петръ.

XIII ВЫПУСКЪ —— 1882 г.
ЗИЛОТИ, Александръ.

XIV ВЫПУСКЪ —— 1883 г.
ЛЯПУНОВЪ, Сергѣй.

XVIII ВЫПУСКЪ —— 1887 г.
МАГНИЦКАЯ, Елизавета.

XIX ВЫПУСКЪ —— 1888 г.
КОНЮСЪ, Юлій.
МИЛЛЕРЪ, Викторія.

XXII ВЫПУСКЪ —— 1891 г.
КОРЕЩЕНКО, Арсній.
ПѢЧНИКОВЪ, Авраамъ.

XXIII ВЫПУСКЪ —— 1892 г.
ЛЕВИНЪ, Іосифъ.
МАКСИМОВЪ, Леонидъ.
РАХМАНИНОВЪ, Сергѣй.
СКРЯБИНЪ, Александръ.

XXIV ВЫПУСКЪ —— 1893 г.
САМУЭЛЬСОНЪ, Семенъ.

XXV ВЫПУСКЪ —— 1894 г.
ИГУМНОВЪ, Константинъ.

XXVIII ВЫПУСКЪ —— 1897 г.
ГОЛЬДЕНВЕЙЗЕРЪ, Александръ.
ИСАКОВИЧЪ, Вѣра. (Скрябина)
КЕНЕМАНЪ, Ѳедоръ.

XXIX ВЫПУСКЪ —— 1898 г.
БЕССИ, Розина.
ГЕДИКЕ, Александръ.
КАРДАШЕВА, Олимпіада.
ПОПОВЪ, Викторъ.
ФРИДМАНЪ, Агланда.

XXX ВЫПУСКЪ —— 1899 г.
КАМЕНЦЕВА, Елена. (Беклемишева)
ПРОКОПОВИЧЪ, Александра.

XXXI ВЫПУСКЪ —— 1900 г.
БЕКЛЕМИШЕВЪ, Григорій.
ГЛІЕРЪ, Рейнгольдъ.

Plaque listing Gold Medal winners at the Moscow Conservatory. "1892: Lhevinne, Maximov, Rachmaninoff, Scriabin . . . 1898: Bessie. . . ."

Josef and Rosina about the time of their wedding, 1898.

Carl Davidov. Sverev was notorious for the extravagant fees he charged private students; Safonoff refused to give private lessons and gave all his energies to students at the Conservatory. Sverev forbade his students to participate in athletic activities of any kind; Safonoff strongly encouraged such participation. The differences between these two men were to influence the lives of many students, including Josef Lhevinne.

Under normal procedures at the Conservatory, eleven-year-old Josef would have been assigned to Sverev or Remesov in the lower school (and probably to Sverev, because Remesov had himself studied with Sverev and got relatively few of the most talented students). When the Grand Duke had asked Levin with whom he would like his son to study, however, Levin had given Safonoff's name. So it was Safonoff who gave the boy his first audition. Josef never forgot it:

> I played. All the time Safonoff seemed to be quietly smiling to himself as if with pleasure. Meanwhile, the Director of the Conservatory [Taneyev] had come into the room and suggested that I should be placed in a preparatory class, until I had become sufficiently advanced to study with Safonoff. Safonoff would not listen to this. He insisted that other teachers would spoil me for him.[1]

Safonoff took Josef directly into his advanced class in the upper school, thereby keeping him out of Sverev's hands.

After accepting Josef into the upper school, Safonoff gave him a lesson every day for six months in order to prepare him for advanced study. He completely overhauled the technique Krysander had taught, and Josef, after playing Beethoven, Chopin, and Liszt, had to concentrate once more on fundamentals. Safonoff had studied with Leschetizky and Brassin at the St. Petersburg Conservatory, and at this stage of his career was developing the principles that were to make him one of the world's foremost authorities on piano technique. The essence of his approach can be found in his book *New Formula for the Piano Teacher and the Piano Student* (Boston: Oliver Ditson, 1916). One of the first things he taught Josef was how to avoid stiffness in his fingers, as Lhevinne recounted later in life:

> For six years I [had been] constantly under the care of Krysander. He developed a good technique in the old-fashioned sense. That is, I could play with speed and some force. But my fingers were frightfully stiff. In fact, after a few hours' practice my fingers would feel exceedingly tired and would ache painfully. . . . Safonoff . . . told me that

the reason for my getting tired at practice was that I had never given
my muscles a chance to get strong in the right way, and that I was strain-
ing them all the time.

 He would tolerate no stiffness, but at the same time he would not
permit the slightest hand motion. He repeatedly put things on the back
of my hand, while I was playing scales and five-finger exercises, with
the injunction that I was not to permit them to fall off. . . . He was one
of the most careful and insistent teachers that one could possibly
imagine, watching every muscle as a cat would a mouse. . . .[2]

Safonoff also changed the way Josef played scales. His idea was that
"the thumb should be suspended in a natural position under the
curve of the hand in scale playing." The words were Lhevinne's,
and so is this explanation:

 With the right hand in the ascending scale of C, for example, the
thumb strikes C. The moment the next note is struck with the second
finger, the C is released and the thumb moves rapidly, lightly, and gracefully under the second finger. This keeps it in playing position all the
time and forms a habit that becomes very valuable to the player in later
years.[3]

When Rosina Bessie entered the Conservatory a few years later, she
learned the same way of playing scales. The thumb, she was told,
should stay underneath the rest of the hand "as if ashamed of
himself."

 Safonoff always emphasized that scales should not be played
mechanically, but instead with attention to tone, rhythm, and
dynamics. Because Safonoff made scales such a challenge, Lhevinne developed a love for playing them that lasted all his life.
He often said that a perfect scale was one of the hardest things to
play, and when he was nearly fifty years old he wrote that Anton
Rubinstein "could play a scale so exquisitely that it was almost
heavenly. You held your breath with the beauty of it until he had
touched the last note."[4]

 This great enthusiasm for scales had not developed, of course,
by the end of Josef's first year of study with Safonoff. The painstaking work on details was quite a comedown from the glorious
works he had played with Krysander, and demanded considerably
more time than he had ever been willing to give the piano. It was
difficult to assimilate Safonoff's methods, and even more difficult
to discard the habits he had acquired from Krysander. When his
technique became advanced enough that he could begin to learn
repertoire pieces again, he faced a new problem: memorization.
Safonoff would never allow a student to play with the music be-

fore him, and Josef, who had played with the aid of the score for six years, had to learn to rely on his memory alone.

Perhaps because of the strenuous demands Safonoff made on him, and maybe also because of the crowded conditions in his family's apartment, Josef found the cramped quarters of a practice room even more claustrophobic than most students did. Many times when he should have been working he was walking the streets of Moscow—usually with Kolya Avierino, who was studying to be a violinist. Sometimes they went to the shooting galleries. Other times they wandered aimlessly. In the Conservatory building, too, Josef found ways to avoid practicing. One of his favorite diversions was at the expense of Alexandra Ivanovna Gubert, the Inspector of the Conservatory. A severe silent woman, she was tall and thin, and wore skirts that rustled as she walked. The Conservatory building had formerly been a private mansion and had a marble staircase of twelve steps leading to the second floor. Josef would wait at the head of the stairs until he heard the familiar rustle. Then he would jump down and land at Miss Gubert's feet, just for the pleasure of hearing an involuntary shriek from a woman who did not like to show any emotion. To punish him, Miss Gubert locked him in a *karzer*, a small dark room filled with mice. In return for that lowly tactic, he pounced again at the next opportunity.

After Josef had studied with Safonoff for about two years, the great Anton Rubinstein visited the Moscow Conservatory. Rubinstein was nearly sixty years old then and had again become director of the St. Petersburg Conservatory, while continuing to perform and compose. Before making a visit to Moscow, he had informed Taneyev of his wish to hear some of the more talented students perform. Josef, in spite of his casual attitude toward practicing, was one of the students chosen. Among the others were Sergei Rachmaninoff and Alexander Scriabin, two boys several years older than he who studied with Sverev in the lower school.

Safonoff, because he had kept Josef out of the lower school in order to teach him himself, was particularly eager that his charge make a good impression on Rubinstein. He selected the following pieces for Josef to have ready: Beethoven's *Eroica Variations*, a Liszt rhapsody, three Chopin études, a Bach fugue, and a Liadov étude. Forty years later, Lhevinne recalled what happened:

> I was only fourteen and not particularly industrious. . . . My piano playing came with such ease that I felt I could leave everything to the last moment. And I always did!

The night before Rubinstein was to arrive Safonoff called me to his house. I was to play my program through to him. Always he had been very strict and severe with me. Often he had scolded me with a very loud voice, using fantastic, even bad language. But when he said nothing at all, that was worse still. And this night as I finished each piece he was terrifyingly laconic. Nothing but just an ominous "Go on!"

When at last this ordeal was over, he started to talk to me. Very gently, quietly but pointedly, he told me what a fool I had been, and how I had wasted my time and opportunities. I started to cry. Then he said: "Of course, I shall not allow you to play tomorrow. Everyone would wonder what sort of teacher I was. And in front of Rubinstein, of all people! You have lost the greatest chance of your life. Now go home. But I shall expect to see you tomorrow. You owe it to the school to hear the others play."

You can imagine the state of my feelings as I walked home. For weeks the sole topic of conversation there had been that I was to play before Rubinstein. My father was a real martinet. I hadn't the courage to tell him what happened. At least a frightful thrashing. At most . . . I could not imagine what that would be.

When I arrived home I [began] practicing with the most intense concentration. My father returned from the theater. He stood and listened to me. "You will do well tomorrow," he said. That was terrible. Early next morning I was at the piano again. I regained my confidence. That was of little use!

I went to the Conservatory. It was the first time that I should see Rubinstein. I stood near him—to me a most wonderful inspiration. Even now he remains the ideal which I am always striving to reach. He had the most wonderful personality of any man I have ever met. Safonoff passed, and pretended not to see me. Dejectedly I scanned the program pinned on to a wall. I read it again to make sure that I had not made a mistake. For my name was there, and opposite all the pieces which had been arranged for me to play! I rushed off to the Director. I asked him whether it was true that I was to play. "Of course," he replied.

Safonoff knew how to squeeze the best out of me.

I was to play last of all. The program was very long. Rachmaninoff and Scriabin, both fellow pupils, played beautifully. Rubinstein was sitting in a front seat with Safonoff, quite near the piano. He had listened to piano solos for over two hours. My turn came. I was tingling with excitement. I went to the platform and drank a glass of water, and somehow steeled my nerves. Safonoff asked Rubinstein what he would like to hear, hoping that he would ask for very little! "Let him play everything," was the reply.

I started with the *Eroica Variations*. The music absorbed me. Rubinstein was moved. "Bravo!" he cried. "Now the *Études*." I played the *B minor*. Just as I was going to commence the *C minor* Rubinstein shouted, "Make it stormy!" and shook his big head like a lion and almost roared at me. I played it with all my strength and power. Rubinstein jumped to his feet, kissed me, and wrung my hand. "You are a big, big boy," he said; "work hard and you will be a great man!"

That was the first great moment of my life.[5]

Rubinstein's advice to Josef—"work hard and you will be a great man"—may have been suggested by Safonoff, in hopes that a word from the master would inspire his talented student to take the piano more seriously. But a few minutes later, Rubinstein did something that inspired Josef even more:

> Suddenly Rubinstein decided to play and there was a hush. There was no place for me in the hall, so I sat on the stage just behind him. He tried the piano a little bit, and then he played the Moonlight Sonata. I couldn't dream it was the same piano. I forgot Rubinstein was playing. I knew he was taking me where he wanted to take me and showing me everything he wanted me to see.
>
> I couldn't tell you how he used his hands. I only remember the miracle. . . . For three days after hearing Rubinstein play I could not touch the piano for fear of committing sacrilege.[6]

The words with which Lhevinne described this incident approach the language of mystical conversion—and rightly so. For the rest of his life, he held Rubinstein in religious adoration, and could well be described as a disciple.

The most immediate result of Josef's first encounter with Rubinstein was to make him a more willing pupil for Safonoff. To use Klesmer's phrase, it greatly increased his "capacity for receiving discipline." As a result, Safonoff made a proposal he would not have dreamed of the year before: if Josef learned four Bach preludes and fugues during the four weeks remaining in the term, Safonoff would take him during vacation to his summer home in the mountains. Josef carried out the assignment with unprecedented enthusiasm, and spent the summer with Safonoff at Kislovodsk, in the Caucasus. There he discovered in himself a latent love for nature—a love that had had no opportunity to develop in the crowded section of Moscow to which his family was confined, summers and winters.

So strongly was Josef drawn to the mountains, forests, and streams that he quickly lost his new-found enthusiasm for the piano and for hard work. Safonoff had difficulty keeping track of his young protégé, and put him under the direct supervision of David Shor, a married student also spending the summer there. One day Shor and his wife went out for the afternoon. To be sure Josef would work, they locked him in a room on the second floor of the house, where his only companion was a large Bechstein.

When they returned in the evening to check on his progress, he was gone. Even the local police were unable to find him. Josef finally appeared late that night, with a guilty look on his face but glowing with enthusiasm for the surrounding mountain country. That was the first of many times during the summer that after being locked in the practice room, sometimes with his shoes taken away, he had opened the window and leaped, at great peril to his precious limbs, the fifteen feet to freedom. Shor would tell Safonoff, and Safonoff would threaten to send Josef back to Moscow. But the boy would simply say, "I love the mountains, I love the mountains," and go and do it again. Even so, he made satisfactory progress at his lessons, and each spring learned enough preludes and fugues to earn his way back to Kislovodsk. In speaking of that first summer in the Caucasus, Lhevinne later said, "I have never forgotten that first great meeting with nature. She has been my dearest friend ever since." He meant it.

In November 1889 a gala Rubinstein Jubilee was held in St. Petersburg. The occasion marked the fiftieth anniversary of Anton Rubinstein's public debut as a *Wunderkind*, and everyone of importance attended except Czar Alexander III and Mili Balakirev. The Czar, author of the "Temporary Rules," was disturbed that a man who was born a Jew should receive so much attention. Balakirev answered his invitation with the words "Rubinstein has done nothing but harm to Russian music." Balakirev, however, was the only former member of the *kutchka* who continued to resent Rubinstein—unless resentment can emanate from a grave. Both Borodin and Mussorgsky had died in the 1880s, and Cui and Rimsky-Korsakov had been reconciled with their former foe. Rimsky-Korsakov, in fact, not only had sought out the academic training he once had spurned, but was one of Rubinstein's professors of composition at the St. Petersburg Conservatory.

In Moscow, a special program in Rubinstein's honor was given at the Conservatory on November 16/28, 1889. The student choir sang a Rubinstein oratorio, and student soloists played some of his instrumental works. Sergei Rachmaninoff and another pianist played some of Rubinstein's piano compositions for four hands, and Josef Lhevinne and a cellist played the Sonata for Cello and Piano, Opus 11, No. 2. A few months later, Safonoff relayed to Josef an extraordinary message from Rubinstein.

> One day, at the end of this season, Safonoff said to me, "You bad boy, you have the devil's luck!"
> "What is it?" I asked.

"Why, Rubinstein is to conduct next season in Moscow, and he has himself asked that you should play!"[7]

This extraordinary development, of course, was as much of a windfall for Safonoff as it was for his student.

The concert Rubinstein was to conduct was the annual benefit concert for the Widows and Orphans of Musicians. This affair was one of the great events of Moscow's musical season and was always held in the Hall of the Nobility, one of Europe's largest and most impressive concert halls. This was the hall where Moscow's most distinguished musical visitors performed, and to Josef at the time it resembled heaven on earth. Rubinstein chose an all-Beethoven program: the *Coriolan* Overture, the *Emperor* Piano Concerto, and the Ninth Symphony.

The concert was scheduled for November 17/29, 1890, a year and a day after the student program in honor of Rubinstein at the Moscow Conservatory. At the rehearsal, Josef played well. For the concert itself, Miss Gubert was responsible for getting him to the hall on time. Fearing the pranks Josef might play if they went in a droshky, she hired a private coach with two horses, a driver, and a footman. When they arrived at the Hall of the Nobility, she locked Josef in the room that had been set aside for Rubinstein. When the Overture was over and she went to fetch him, she could not see him. The poor woman nearly had a stroke. Finally someone else came into the room, and found Josef slouched in a chair whose back faced the door of the room. At first it was feared he was ill. But, as Lhevinne later recalled, "the nervous tension of waiting" had simply been too much for him.

> In sheer exhaustion I had fallen asleep. It did me good, composed my nerves, and gave me strength.
>
> I remember walking on to the platform, dressed in my blue Russian blouse with belt and knickers, and feeling as full of confidence as if the playing of the solo part in a Beethoven concerto was a thing I did every day of my life. . . . I played well that day. Rubinstein was genuinely and sincerely enthusiastic. Again he embraced me.
>
> . . . It was the practice not to permit encores at these concerts. But the applause was so insistent that I was told to go on again. I [played] the stormy Chopin *Étude*. Again I had to play. Safonoff whispered to me to play [a] Rubinstein étude. As soon as Rubinstein realized what I was playing he covered his ears with his hands and ran out of the hall! Long afterwards Rubinstein confided to me that he could not bear [to hear] anyone play his own compositions but himself![8]

Rubinstein's running exit from the hall coincided with the intermission, after which he returned to conduct Beethoven's Ninth

Symphony. His interpretation of that great work was notable for its simplicity and elevation of spirit. Writing two days later in the *Russkie Vedomosti*, Nicholas Kashkin described how Rubinstein "approached the extraordinary Beethoven creation with reverent respect" and made "no deviation whatsoever from the directions given by the genius composer for its execution." Such respect for the literal directions given by a composer in a score was unusual for a nineteenth-century musician, especially for one known for his individuality and strong personality. But Kashkin's description of Rubinstein's conducting applied equally well to his piano playing. Rubinstein generally achieved his individuality not by deviating from the score but by drawing from it the genius inherent in the notes as written. Safonoff, too, insisted on strict adherence to the score, and that principle became one of the "givens" of Josef Lhevinne's musical life.

Kashkin was Moscow's most influential critic in 1890, and he had this to say about the fifteen-year-old boy who played the *Emperor* Concerto:

> The young pianist J. Lhevinne's performance of Beethoven's Fifth Concerto had a huge success. . . . One can without fear predict for this youth a very brilliant future. In his playing were united all the qualities necessary for a virtuoso: colossal technique, perfect tone, and a lot of musicality. In respect to the last, he expressed such maturity as one would never expect from someone his age.[9]

Kashkin went on to point out that Beethoven's concertos demand much more in the way of musicality than "all the new concertos after Liszt." His review concluded with a short biography of Lhevinne.

Kashkin's words were great praise for the young pianist but were not nearly so meaningful as the words Josef heard just after finishing the concerto. For family tradition has it that when Rubinstein embraced the boy on the stage of the Hall of the Nobility he whispered, "You will be my successor." Such whispered messages from great men to aspiring youths are often manufactured after the fact. Even when true they can seldom be verified. But there is reason to believe in this one. In 1913 Safonoff told a group in Copenhagen that Rubinstein had told *him* shortly after the performance: "If this youngster does not become my successor some day, you as his teacher will be to blame."[10]

Josef Lhevinne never did become Rubinstein's successor, but that was not Safonoff's fault. No pianist after Anton Rubinstein ever matched his heroic proportions. Lhevinne did become Rubinstein's leading "disciple," but that was quite a different matter. His personality, it developed, was retiring rather than engaging, and instead of courting fame he let fame seek him out. November 17/29, 1890, was to remain the greatest day of his life. Its principal was so large, he never felt the need to compound it.

"Colossal technique, perfect tone, and a lot of musicality," "heir-apparent to Anton Rubinstein"—these words described the "great man in his teens" who a year before had given Rosina Bessie a few lessons while Remesov was ill. It is no wonder that from the beginning their relationship was that of idol and worshipper:

"The first concert in my life where I ever heard an orchestra was when Josef played with Anton Rubinstein. The concert itself was in the evening, and my mother would not let me go, because it was in the middle of the winter season. But the rehearsal was in the morning, so she wrapped me in thousands of coats and furs and took me. I was greatly impressed by the colonnade of Corinthian pillars stretching the length of the hall from top to bottom. I remember not so much Josef's playing as his smart Russian blouse and his bushy hair.

"After the concert, my mother said, 'You'd better go up and shake hands with Rubinstein and kiss his hand, because you will never forget it in all your life.' She was right. Today I still have the feeling of my hand lost in his. Each of his fingers was like two of mine. After he took my hand, he bent down and kissed me on the forehead. I haven't forgotten that, either."

Naturally, Josef's appearance on the stage of the Hall of the Nobility, and his association with the legendary Rubinstein, increased Rosina's admiration for him. He continued to visit her parents' home for evenings of whist, but outside of a perfunctory kiss on the forehead paid Rosina little attention. Whenever he spoke in her presence, it was to mention all the girls he was in love with, and he told her many times how pleased he was that his high-pitched voice gave him a place with the sopranos in the Conservatory choir. She did not betray her interest in him, and one would not have thought her old enough to be thinking of him in serious terms. When Rosina was eleven, however, her mother discovered the following message in her atlas: "The man and the letter I love the most begins with L."

Because Rosina continued to be taught at home by tutors, her mother allowed her to go to the Conservatory only once a week. "I was always bundled most thoroughly in assorted sweaters, coats, and overcoats. An acquaintance of mine at the school later told me how now and then one of the doors of the Conservatory would open and a huge figure would appear. Proceeding down the corridor to the coat room, it would piece by piece diminish in size, until finally a little girl emerged, the size of a bean, who was me. Because of my mother's fears, I could not take advantage of much that the Conservatory offered. All of the students there had the privilege of going to rehearsals of the Moscow Symphony, but she never let me go. I spent most of my time at home, and when I was not at the piano I was reading. After I entered the Conservatory I was not allowed to embroider any more, because my mother said it was a waste of time.

"Remesov, my teacher in the lower school, was an unexceptional man, the kind who goes through life doing his job well but without making much of an impression on other people. Sverev, the other teacher in the lower school, was a wonderful teacher and a wonderful man. Safonoff, Pabst, and Siloti were the three piano professors in the upper school when I entered. Each of these three seemed to have a favorite among his pupils, and instead of the pupils being jealous the teachers always were. Once Josef won a competition with a student of Pabst, and for a long time afterwards Pabst would not speak with Safonoff.

"Siloti was very handsome and very young, and always wore a black velvet jacket when he taught. During my first or second year at the Conservatory, when I was still quite young, the professors had a recreation room, and the older girls would always look through the keyhole to see him. They would say, 'Siloti, *douschka*' ('Siloti, darling'). I did not know how to admire the beauty of a man yet, but I had to look through the keyhole too, and certainly I tried to imitate what the older ones did. He was really a very handsome man, and everybody regretted it when he left the Conservatory because of a disagreement with Safonoff."

When Rosina was ten or eleven years old, the family spent a summer in Switzerland. The first trip to that beautiful country was the "oasis" of her childhood and gave her many new impressions, including gardens of gravel that "made such a nice noise under the feet." The fact that it was summer vacation and she was in a strange land did not, however, sever her bondage to the piano. In Geneva, Rosina, at her mother's command, practiced a few hours a day at the Geneva Conservatory. Even for a student in the lower school of the Moscow Conservatory the business of mastering the piano was to be taken very seriously indeed.

"From the very first lessons at the Moscow Conservatory we were taught that we must possess the instrument and not let the instrument possess us. The result of this training was that we learned to work in such a way that there would be no pianistic obstacle to playing any passage. *That* was not the goal. The goal was to express the wishes of the composer. But in order to do that, we had to overcome the difficulties of the instrument. We were taught that the Greek word *techne* (technique) meant first *craft* and then *art*. We learned the craft in order to serve the art. In the course of my later life it has been very interesting to see that this approach to music and musicianship was practiced consistently at all the Conservatories in Russia. When Josef and I became friends with Mischa Elman and Jascha Heifetz, for example, we learned that they were taught the same basic approach in the violin class of Leopold Auer at the St. Petersburg Conservatory. But as I was being introduced to these basic principles, Josef was putting them into practice, and when I was accepted into Safonoff's class after three years with Remesov, Josef had already been graduated from it with the coveted gold medal."

In the summer of 1890, while Josef Lhevinne was in the Caucasus, learning the *Emperor* Concerto for his performance with Anton Rubinstein, the first International Rubinstein Prize Competition was held in St. Petersburg. One of the first of the great international competitions, it was held every five years in rotating capitals of Europe until it was discontinued because of the First World War. The competition was open to pianists and composers between the ages of twenty and twenty-six, and a first prize of 5,000 francs was given in each division. At the first competition in 1890, Rubinstein himself was one of the judges, and so was Safonoff, who had recently succeeded Taneyev as director of the Moscow Conservatory. The winner in composition (and a close second in piano) was a young Italian, Ferruccio Busoni.

Impressed with Busoni's musicality, Safonoff immediately offered him a professorship at the Moscow Conservatory. Busoni accepted, and taught there for one year. Safonoff was then gaining fame as a conductor, and when he was gone on tour for a few weeks he asked Busoni to take over his piano class. Years later, Busoni told students in Berlin that he had been impressed with Lhevinne's playing. But he was disenchanted with the atmosphere of the Conservatory as a whole, where Safonoff's promotion to the directorship had only deepened the rift between him and the Sverev faction. Busoni's fellow professors spent "their nights at the gambling-table, to return to their lessons a couple of hours late, sodden with drink but always with the grand manner of ambassadors,

their eternal cigarette only enhancing their pomposity." And Safonoff "summoned them to his chamber like a Chief of Police."[11]

Tensions between Safonoff and Sverev had been particularly
exacerbated by the appointment of Alexander Siloti to the piano
faculty. Taneyev had made the appointment before resigning as
director, and Siloti had come to Moscow directly from Weimar,
where he had studied for several years with Franz Liszt. Before that,
Siloti had studied at the Conservatory with Sverev and Nicholas
Rubinstein, and Sverev was eager that his young protégé get the
best students possible. It just so happened that Sverev had three
unusually talented students at the time, each of whom was due to
move into the upper school. Sergei Rachmaninoff and Leonid Maximov were particularly close to Sverev, for they had lived in his
home while in the lower school. They both went to Siloti's class;
Alexander Scriabin joined Lhevinne in Safonoff's.

In the fall of 1890, Michael Bukinik entered the Conservatory to
study the cello. Later he left a sketch of his various classmates, who
gathered together "either in the club room on the second floor or
downstairs in the coat room, far from the eyes of the authorities."[12]
The first student he described was "rosy Josef Lhevinne, with his
bushy, curly hair, already performing in concerts as an accomplished pianist." Also pictured was Josef's prankster friend: "Kolya
Avierino loves to attend our gatherings—he is dark as a Negro and
a great joker." Other friends of Josef described by Bukinik included
"businesslike" Modest Altschuler, a cellist, and "modest" Alexander Goldenweiser, a pianist who studied with Pabst. Lhevinne's
best friend among the piano students seems to have been "puny and
immaculate" Alexander Scriabin, for he later told friends that Scriabin's house was the first place his mother would look when she
could not find him. Sergei Rachmaninoff, whom Bukinik pictured
as "tall and gaunt, his shoulders somehow hunched, giving him a
rectangular appearance," was distant and aloof, and he and Josef
did not become friends until long after their Conservatory years.
Goldenweiser, who later became director of the Moscow Conservatory, has written of a dramatic confrontation between the two:

> Someone had told [Rachmaninoff] that nothing could be written on
> a certain Russian theme. He wrote a composition in E minor (in the form
> of variations). It was quite good music. I remember that at some benefit
> concert for our colleagues—we often arranged such concerts—Rach-
> maninoff and Lhevinne performed this piece on two pianos; it concluded
> with variations in octaves, alternating from one pianist to the other, and
> on that occasion each increased the tempo and everyone watched to

see who would outplay whom. Each had a phenomenal wrist, but it was Rachmaninoff who won.[13]

Bukinik was impressed with Rachmaninoff's talent in theory and composition, but recorded that "as a pianist, Rachmaninoff made less of an impression on us."

Lhevinne's wrist and finger control were so good that Safonoff —for fun—entered him in a competition for telegraph operators. He scored considerably higher than any of the professionals. If Goldenweiser was correct about the "battle of the wrists," perhaps Rachmaninoff would have scored even higher. Lhevinne's hands were distinguished not only by coordination but by size: at maturity his right hand could span thirteen notes—from middle C to A. As for his ears, if someone struck a cluster of notes very near each other on the piano, Lhevinne could always identify the notes that had been left out.

That Safonoff would think to enter a student in a telegraph operators' contest was indicative of the energy that he brought to the job of supervising his piano students. He had plenty of other responsibilities in the early 1890s: he was director of the Conservatory, conductor of its orchestra, director of its choir, and director of the Moscow concerts of the Imperial Russian Musical Society. Even so, Safonoff taught his piano class with great vitality and devoted an amazing amount of time to his students. Each spring before examinations he insisted that each student play his full program for the rest of the class. These sessions were held on several successive evenings at Safonoff's home and sometimes lasted most of the night. A few days before the exam, Safonoff took the entire class on an outing to the country. They would leave Moscow early in the morning and spend the whole day eating, playing games, and relaxing. In later years Safonoff liked to recall how "Josef Lhevinne jumped over stumps and ditches with the alertness of a young cub, and the frail Scriabin ran away with the speed of a reindeer from the pursuit of the wolf in the catch-play."[14] The point of the excursion, of course, was to keep students from practicing too frantically before the examinations.

The competitive atmosphere at the Conservatory created pressures not only at examination time but over the summers as well. Scriabin admired—or envied—Lhevinne's technique so much that during the summer of 1891 he tried, without Safonoff's approval, to emulate it. He spent the summer trying to play Liszt's *Don Juan Fantasy* and Balakirev's *Islamey,* and returned to the Conservatory in the fall with a slightly lamed right hand. As an immediate cure,

Safonoff gave him castor oil and Mozart concertos. But Scriabin's hand gave him trouble for the rest of his life. One of the results of the injury was that he composed the famous Nocturne for the left hand alone, which, ironically, Lhevinne was to introduce to audiences in America.

If there was any moment when competition was forgotten at the Conservatory, it was when great music was heard. Among the leading pianists who played frequently in Moscow were Eugene D'Albert, the great Beethoven interpreter; Teresa Carreño, the Venezuelan beauty who was married to D'Albert for a few years in the early 1890s; and Annette Essipova, the St. Petersburg pianist who had been married to Theodore Leschetizky. But the greatest musical experience for Lhevinne and his classmates was the series of historical concerts that Anton Rubinstein gave in the late 1880s. The first recital ran from Byrd through Bach, Handel, and Mozart. The second was all-Beethoven (eight sonatas!). The third featured Schubert, Weber, and Mendelssohn. The fourth was all-Schumann. The fifth concert included Field, Hummel, Henselt, and Liszt, among others. The sixth was all-Chopin. The last began with Chopin and ended with the music of the "modern" Russians, including Rubinstein himself, his brother Nicholas, Tchaikovsky, and three of the *kutchka*. Both Lhevinne and Rachmaninoff later claimed that no musical experience ever compared with Rubinstein's historical recitals.

As the class of 1892 neared graduation, there was considerable speculation as to whose students—Safonoff's or Siloti's—would receive the most gold medals. The highest award bestowed by the Conservatory, the gold medal was given only to students of extraordinary achievement. The winner did not actually receive a medal. Instead, his name was engraved on a conspicuous marble plaque. Many classes were graduated with no winner being named. Until 1892 no more than two had ever been named in a single year. That year there were four. All were pianists. Two had studied with Safonoff and two with Siloti—though Siloti was not around for the denouement, having left the Conservatory the year before. Today the four names remain visible on the plaque. They are listed in alphabetical order and, as it happens, from youngest to oldest: Lhevinne (17), Maximov (19), Rachmaninoff (19), and Scriabin (20). Legally, each was now a "Free Artist."

3

From
Idolatry to Marriage

DURING THE SUMMER of 1892, Josef Lhevinne was invited to visit
Anton Rubinstein in the village of Klein Schachwitz, near Dresden.
Rubinstein had moved there a year before, after resigning for a
second time as director of the St. Petersburg Conservatory. In 1867
he had resigned in order to devote himself to composing and performing; in 1891 he resigned because of pressures from Czar Alexander III. The Czar, who had limited the number of Jews in the
Conservatory to three percent, was displeased that this small group
of students had won a disproportionate share of the prizes. He let it
be known that he would like the prizes to be distributed more or less
according to the racial quotas themselves—a policy Rubinstein refused to adopt. After moving to Dresden, Rubinstein composed,
played charity concerts, and taught Josef Hofmann, his only full-
time, long-term student, for several years.

Since first taking an interest in Lhevinne, Rubinstein had never
given him an official lesson; nor did he do so in the summer of
1892. He recognized the "territorial rights" of Safonoff (who accompanied Josef to Dresden) and limited himself to musical "discussions" with the young pianist. Usually these discussions would
center on the various moods of a work, which Rubinstein would ask
Josef to describe either in words or by drawing a picture. Years
later, Lhevinne recalled that the first piece he played for Rubinstein was Chopin's F-sharp minor Polonaise.

> I played . . . and then Rubinstein asked me what I thought the mood
> of the first part of it was.
> I said, "Dramatic."
> "That's right," he replied. "Now, what is the mood of the second
> section?"

I hesitated, then said, "It is a little fantastic, a little lyrical."

"Then you must play it that way. Ask yourself always what [the mood of the composition is], and then bring out that mood. If it is sad, make people weep when they hear it; if it is gay, make them happy. If it is the Erlking, make them afraid."[1]

Because music, for Rubinstein, had to communicate emotion above all else, he was willing in very special cases to alter a composer's intentions in order to achieve a desired effect. Some time after the visit to Dresden, Josef told Rosina of further advice Rubinstein had given him with regard to the Chopin Polonaise:

"In all the editions, a certain passage was written *forte*, but Rubinstein said to play it two *pianissimo* (*pp*) because it should sound like a battalion approaching from far off and should be so faint you can barely hear it. Then gradually it increases until it becomes two *forte* (*ff*) and is interrupted by the mazurka section. The battalion then begins two *forte* again and marches off into *pianissimo*. All the editions marked it the other way, but Rubinstein insisted that this was the most effective way to play it."

After his musical "discussions" with Rubinstein, Lhevinne returned to Moscow. He had graduated brilliantly from the piano class of the Conservatory, but was still deficient in certain academic subjects. He had enjoyed classes in geography and tolerated those in history, but subjects like mathematics he found uncongenial. As he completed his final academic credits, he continued to visit the Bessies occasionally.

"When I was a child and Josef came to play whist with my parents, he would always kiss me. But when I was twelve and I came back from the summer in Switzerland, I decided that I was too big for that (or that at least it would be proper for a girl to say no). So when he came and was going to kiss me, I said, 'No. I'm a big girl now.' I can still hear his answer even today: 'Pouff! Do I care?' That hurt me for several months afterwards, because of course I had wanted him very much to kiss me."

While Rosina was smarting over the off-hand rebuff, Josef was expanding his musical connections in Moscow. Most significantly, he developed an acquaintance with Tchaikovsky, whose B-flat minor Piano Concerto he greatly admired. Tchaikovsky had long since resigned his professorship at the Conservatory, but continued to take an interest in certain of its students. He listened to Josef play the solo part of his First Concerto, and made comments that were to remain indelibly fixed in Lhevinne's mind. One comment was that the *presto* section in the second movement should be thought of as a "dream waltz"—not from a slow-motion dream but from a high-speed phantasmagorical one. Commentators were later to marvel at Lhevinne's "hair-raising" interpretation of the *presto*. Tchaikovsky also told Josef that when beginning the third movement he should think of "a man in a beer hall who has drunk all the beer and begins to hiccup involuntarily." When Lhevinne later taught the concerto and passed the composer's advice on to his students, he amended the description to that of "a drunken man staggering down the street."

One day in the fall of 1893, a few months before Josef's nineteenth birthday, he met Tchaikovsky on a street in Moscow. They exchanged greetings, and

> [Tchaikovsky] asked me to come with him to his hotel, explaining that he wished to show me a work he had recently completed. When we reached his rooms he brought out the manuscript of his Eighteen Pieces for Piano—opus 72. He asked me if I would learn three of them while he was away on a trip to Petrograd and play them for him when he returned. The three he particularly wanted me to play were "Scherzo Fantasie," "Polonaise de Concert," and "Echo Rustique." I promised to do so, and took copies with me. But alas, Tchaikovsky never returned from that visit to Petrograd.[2]

Tchaikovsky had died in St. Petersburg after hearing the premiere of his Sixth Symphony there. The title page of Opus 72 survives as evidence of Lhevinne's last meeting with the composer. It bears the inscription "To Josef Lhevinne, a talent" and is signed "P. Tchaikovsky, 22 Sept. 1893, Moscow." Unfortunately, the Eighteen Pieces are among Tchaikovsky's least-inspired compositions. The greatest legacy Lhevinne received from the composer was advice about interpreting the First Piano Concerto.

Lhevinne had little opportunity to use that advice during the years immediately following his graduation from the Conservatory, for he did not have the kind of engagements at which to play such a work. His first job after becoming a "Free Artist" was to accompany Eugenio Giraldoni, a young Italian baritone whose father taught voice at the Moscow Conservatory. Giraldoni was three years older than Josef and had about the same amount of artistic experience, having made his debut in Barcelona in 1891. Their tour of the Russian provinces was the kind politely referred to as an "artistic success." Dependent upon Giraldoni's father for expenses, they were actually stranded in one town for several days until additional funds arrived by post. Their last concert was in a town in the Caucasus. After performing there they were invited to visit the palace of the Grand Duke Michael (younger brother of the Grand

Duke Constantine), near Tiflis. Lhevinne later described the evening:

> We were invited to the palace for dinner, an affair I shall never forget, for it gave me an insight into my fellow countrymen's much vaunted "capacity" for drink. There were twenty guests, principally Georgian officers, and each a "specialist" in matters of thirst. First came the ceremony of electing the host [as the] "conductor," whereupon a servant brought him a silver plate containing three goblets of wine, each of which he emptied with scarcely a breath in between. Then was drunk the health not only of each guest, but of each member of each one's family, while at the close a huge horn with the capacity of an entire bottle was emptied by the duke as if he were just beginning.
>
> Although my friend and I drank as sparingly as possible, four hours of sipping were bound to have their effect. Consequently when after dinner the duke begged me to play I had grave doubts as to my ability to do so. Nevertheless I seated myself at the piano and began [Rubinstein's "La Valse."] But before I had gone far . . . I was obliged to stop, and bursting into laughter, said: "Your Imperial Highness must excuse me, but I [was not trained] to play on two keyboards." The host and the other guests thought the incident tremendously funny and so did I—until the next morning.[3]

The tour of the provinces did more than initiate the eighteen-year-old pianist into alcoholic mysteries. All Russian pianists knew that Anton Rubinstein had acquired his famous "singing" tone by trying to emulate the sound of Rubini's voice. Lhevinne later said that he gained many practical insights about musical phrasing by accompanying Giraldoni. Rubinstein, when teaching the piano, always stressed the importance of "singing" the phrase, of "breathing" the music. Lhevinne, in his teaching, was to do the same.

After the tour as an accompanist, Lhevinne tried to launch himself as a soloist. He played a small number of concerts in Eastern Europe and received the equivalent of $125 for each concert. At first that seemed like an unbelievable amount of money. But he had so few engagements it was barely enough to meet expenses. Josef no longer received support from the man the Grand Duke Constantine had ordered to pay for his education, and he strongly wished to give financial assistance to his parents and large family, with whom he continued to live. Later in life he expressed his gratitude to Safonoff and his father for not having allowed him to be exploited as a *Wunderkind* following his sensational success with Rubinstein. But during the difficult years immediately following his graduation he must have wondered whether it had been a mistake not to have struck when the iron was hot.

Lhevinne was not the only honor graduate of the Conservatory having difficulty making his way in the "real" world. Scriabin and Rachmaninoff, both older than Josef, were able to sell a few compositions, but each had to resort to the piano to try to make ends meet. Rachmaninoff gave piano lessons for a while, but gave up after finding himself unsuited to the task. He then went on tour with a violinist, but found the experience so unbearable that he deserted his partner before they had filled half their engagements. Scriabin made a brief European tour as a piano soloist, but was plagued by small audiences and his lamed hand. Not until Belayev, a St. Petersburg publisher, "discovered" him in 1895 did his compositions get him anywhere.

Lhevinne, unlike Rachmaninoff and Scriabin, felt no impulse toward composition. So he had only the piano with which to support himself. Either before his brief solo tour or soon after it, he teamed up with two fellow graduates of the Conservatory to form the Moscow Historical Trio. Both his musical partners had been described in Bukinik's sketch. The cellist was "businesslike" Modest Altschuler. The violinist was "tiny, alert Alexander Petschnikoff, a Conservatory celebrity who senses his own importance and pays attention to no one, but he is talented and we cannot help admiring him." Altschuler, Petschnikoff, and Lhevinne made a promising beginning as a trio, playing concerts in Russia, Poland, Austria-Hungary, and Germany. But Lhevinne did not stay with them for long. Years later, Altschuler explained why:

> I recall our earliest artistic triumphs with keenest pleasure. But it was only our great attachment for one another that prevented our growing jealous of Lhevinne. His tone was so pure and beautiful, so vari-colored and expressive of the emotional content of the work in hand, that in spite of his artistic reticence, the piano part always stood out, and we could feel that the applause was all for Lhevinne. . . . Frankly, he was too dominant a figure in ensemble playing, and he was succeeded by [another] pianist.[4]

As Josef Lhevinne was moving from accompanist to soloist to chamber musician, Rosina Bessie was trying to make a place for herself in Safonoff's piano class. At first she felt uncomfortable: "I was twelve years old when I entered Safonoff's class, and I was the youngest one there, because all the other students went to a professor when they were fourteen or fifteen. And because I was so thin and small and ugly, I felt especially out of place.

"It was very interesting, the way Safonoff taught us. He always gave lessons at home, not at the Conservatory, and he would sit at a table far away from the piano and smoke a cigar. We had to play everything from memory (which was excellent training), and when he did not like something he would call us to the table and mark in the music what was wrong. Then he explained. The comments he made about the music were priceless, but he was very excitable, and often used the words 'dourak' and 'idiotka' ('fool' and 'idiot'), even to the girls. He had a second piano there, but he very rarely got up to demonstrate at it. When he did, he had a wonderful touch.

"Every Wednesday there was a student recital at the Conservatory, and once a month the best students from the previous weeks were chosen to play a recital that was open to the public. I was not terribly nervous about playing in public—although I was certainly 'tuned up' on these occasions—but I remember being very much preoccupied with bowing, because I did it in such an awkward way. Safonoff always sat in the front row with all the dignitaries, and every time I played at one of those concerts I had to go down and show everybody the hands, because they were absolutely a child's hands."

Rosina's small hands, young age, and deft way of playing gained her a good deal of attention at the Conservatory, but her mother's protectiveness prevented her from forming many acquaintances there. She was allowed to visit the Conservatory building only to take her classes, and was not allowed to linger after they were over. She was still not permitted to attend the rehearsals of the Moscow Symphony, and stayed home while her classmates heard Safonoff and Rimsky-Korsakov and Arthur Nikisch conduct the great symphonic masterworks. Many girls her age were allowed to stay overnight with each other, but Rosina was not. She did have one friend at the Conservatory, a girl named Artsibayasheva, who was a princess from far-off Tiflis, and whose apartment she was permitted to visit on rare occasions. Now and then, she was even allowed to bring Artsibayasheva to her home. But outside of that one friend she remained isolated.

At home the pattern remained unchanged: lessons from the tutors, practice at the piano, and reading. Whenever she asked to help with the cooking or housework, her mother snapped, "That's not for you. Don't waste your time. Practice or read." Because she was not allowed to do anything practical in her youth, there were times later in life when she had to pay the superintendent of an apartment building to manipulate a can opener for her. The compulsive reading, too, left its mark: "Unfortunately, when I was about twelve or thirteen, I read a lot of Dostoyevsky. As I was so impressionable, it was the worst thing in the world for me, learning to see the world in such a gloomy way. It left a trace of pessimism that has pursued me all my life."

Living such an isolated life, her awareness of current affairs was slight, and what she did learn came in highly diluted form. "When Nicholas II became Czar, Alexandra, his wife, was granddaughter of Queen Victoria, and this brought quite an influx of Englishmen and their ways into the country. I learned about this because my Swiss governess was replaced by an English one, whose name was Miss Chance. She introduced me to the English language, and the first word I learned was 'shocking.' Everything was 'shocking' to Miss Chance—the furniture, the weather, the people. The strange thing about her was that her nose was forever running, and always had a drop under it."

Czar Nicholas II had come to power in November 1894, following the death of Alexander III. Rosina Bessie was fourteen years old then, Josef Lhevinne nearly twenty. Two days after Alexander III was buried, Anton Rubinstein died, at the age of sixty-five. In many educated circles, both in Russia and abroad, Rubinstein's death was mourned more than that of the Czar who had resented him so. Among those who missed him the most were pianists between the ages of twenty and twenty-six who had planned to enter the second International Rubinstein Prize Competition, which was to be held in Berlin in August 1895. Josef Lhevinne was among them. He was barely old enough to enter the competition and did not expect to win. But the decision to compete for the prize gave him a clear objective to work for, and helped to relieve some of the depression he felt at finding it so difficult to begin a solo career.

The requirements for the piano competition reflected Anton Rubinstein's musical interests: each contestant had to play a Bach prelude and fugue, the slow movement of a Mozart sonata, three Chopin works (a ballade, a mazurka, and a nocturne), a Liszt étude, pieces from Schumann's *Kreisleriana* or *Fantasiestück*, one of Beethoven's last eight sonatas, and one of Rubinstein's five piano concertos. Lhevinne looked through Rubinstein's concertos and chose the Fifth, in E-flat. For his Beethoven sonata, he chose Opus 106 (the *Hammerklavier*), the one Rubinstein once told him was "the Ninth Symphony of the piano."

As Josef was mastering the large program required for the competition, Rosina was preparing for her first orchestral appearance at the Conservatory. On February 5/17, 1895, not yet fifteen years old, she played Chopin's *Fantasy on Polish Airs* with Safonoff and

the Conservatory Orchestra. We do not know whether or not Lhevinne was present on that occasion, but some months later when
Rosina played Brahms's *Handel Variations* at a Wednesday afternoon concert, he was on hand. "Evidently Josef was nervous, for he
sat in the last row and put his hands over his eyes so he could not
see me. *He* did not see *me*, but *I* saw *him*, and that only made it
worse."

During the summer of 1895, Rosina and her family went to their
dacha in the country. Rosina's mother, knowing that Josef needed
a place where he could practice without interruption for the competition, gave him the key to their Moscow apartment (her father
had no say in such matters). Six days a week Josef practiced on one
of the Bessies' two pianos. On the seventh day he visited the family
at the *dacha*. There he described to an inquisitive Rosina his way
of practicing. "Josef told me that every morning he had a hearty
breakfast and then went to the apartment and worked for five
hours without any big interruption. Then he would go out and eat
a big steak, and after that would return to the apartment and practice for five hours more. For three weeks he worked in that way.
Then he went to Berlin."

Lhevinne was one of three pianists from the Moscow Conservatory who entered the Rubinstein Prize Competition. The others
were Constantine Igumnov, a student of Pabst who had been graduated with the gold medal in 1894, and Feodor Keneman, who was
still with Safonoff in the upper school. Safonoff was a judge for the
1895 competition, as he had been in 1890.

Altogether, there were thirty contestants in the piano competition and twenty-six judges to evaluate them. The pianists came
from Europe, North America, South America, and Australia. The
judges represented nearly every European country, plus America.
The most prominent among them, in addition to the Russian Safonoff, were Louis Diemer, French pianist; Charles Widor, French
organist; Gustav Holländer, director of Berlin's Stern Conservatory;
and Ferruccio Busoni, the "star" of the 1890 competition and already a renowned pianist and composer.

The contest was held in Bechstein Hall, which, having opened
only a few years earlier, was then one of Europe's most fashionable
concert rooms. The pianists began to play at nine o'clock in the
morning on August 9/21, 1895. Because each contestant had to play
for nearly two hours, they did not finish until five days later. In
the preliminary balloting, eleven pianists were eliminated. Of the
remaining nineteen, five were from Russia (including all three from
Moscow), four were from Germany, three from Holland, two from

Belgium, and one each from Bohemia, Switzerland, the United States, Peru, and Australia. In the final balloting, Lhevinne received twenty-two points, as did Staub, the Peruvian, who was a student of Diemer. Igumnov received twenty-one. Of the first-place ballots, Lhevinne received fourteen, and Staub and Igumnov four each, so Lhevinne was named the winner.

At age twenty, Josef Lhevinne had been the youngest of the thirty contestants. He had also been the only one who played Rubinstein's Fifth Concerto. Most of the others played Rubinstein's more melodic and more popular Fourth Concerto, although Igumnov and Keneman played the Second and Third, respectively. Some people thought that Lhevinne may have won because the jurors had tired of hearing the Fourth Concerto, but it is more likely that he won because of the brilliance with which he played the Fifth. Only a pianist with a most extraordinary technique can give shape to the massive clusters of notes that comprise the first and third movements of Rubinstein's Fifth Concerto. And only a pianist of extraordinary delicacy can make the notes that form the second movement pleasing to the ear. Lhevinne already possessed such technique and delicacy, and through them was able to turn an ungrateful work into an effective showpiece. He and Rubinstein himself are about the only pianists who have played the concerto in such a way that an audience would ever wish to hear it again.

A Rubinstein concerto, of course, was only one of many requirements for the competition, and Lhevinne and the other pianists were able to show their real musicality in their performances of Bach, Mozart, Beethoven, Chopin, Schumann, and Liszt. Lhevinne's performance of Beethoven's *Hammerklavier* Sonata was particularly outstanding. James Kwast, writing in the *Frankfurter Gazette*, praised the same qualities Kashkin had noted when Josef was only fifteen: tone ("splendid") and technique ("unusual"). He also pointed out that Lhevinne's interpretation of the sonata was "fully healthy." In piano performances these days, we can pretty much take for granted what Kwast meant by "healthy." But during the late nineteenth and early twentieth centuries there were many "diseased" pianists who equated excessive mannerisms and morbid sentimentality with art. Lhevinne's approach to music—from the first—was straightforward, manly, unaffected.

Kwast's most interesting observation was that Lhevinne had played the Beethoven sonata "with such perfection that it seemed to me I was hearing it from none other than Tausig, who had gone to the grave at an early age." Carl Tausig, who had been Franz Liszt's favorite piano student, had died in 1871 at the age of thirty.

Had he lived longer, he would probably have rivaled Liszt and Rubinstein as the world's greatest pianist. Tausig's interpretations were restrained and refined, as opposed to the glorious excesses of Liszt's heaven-storming approach; they could best be described as technically immaculate and interpretively pure. As Tausig stood to Liszt, so did Lhevinne to Rubinstein. Josef admired Rubinstein above all other musicians, but did not completely follow his grand manner of interpretation. Lhevinne's temperament led in the direction of purity and perfection, and his playing, even when he was twenty, showed it.

The Rubinstein Prize was the world's most important piano competition. For winning it, Lhevinne received the stipulated 5,000 francs (one wonders how he spent it), and also a contract from Hermann Wolff, Europe's leading concert manager. Before he knew it, he was engaged to play forty concerts during the 1895–96 season.

His tour began with a triumphant return to Russia. On October 15/27 he played Rubinstein's Fifth Concerto in St. Petersburg, at a special concert conducted by Safonoff. Two weeks later, Lhevinne made his return to Moscow's Hall of the Nobility. Five years after playing Beethoven's Fifth Concerto under Rubinstein's baton, he played Rubinstein's Fifth under Safonoff's. The concert was the opening event of the season for Moscow's Imperial Russian Musical Society (I.R.M.S.) Orchestra, whose third and fifth programs also featured Rubinstein concertos. The pianist for those concerts was nineteen-year-old Josef Hofmann, who was emerging from a four-year retirement (after a career as a *Wunderkind*) during which he had studied with Rubinstein. Hofmann played the Third and Fourth Concertos, and his performances, along with Lhevinne's of the Fifth, comprised as fine a tribute as there could have been to mark the first anniversary of Rubinstein's death. For the next forty years Hofmann and Lhevinne were primarily responsible for keeping Rubinstein's piano concertos in the active repertoire.

After his homecoming concert in Moscow, Lhevinne set out to conquer Western Europe. In early January he played Rubinstein's Fifth Concerto with the Concertgebouw Orchestra in Amsterdam. The large Concertgebouw Hall was filled to capacity for his performance, and many people (including one of the critics) were sitting on stage. Twenty-four-year-old Willem Mengelberg conducted, and the Dutch newspapers reported a slight mishap:

The orchestra, it is unfortunate to say, came in at one point four measures too soon. Mr. Lhevinne was so sure of his business that he immediately followed the orchestra. Otherwise, total confusion would have resulted. From this incident, one can conclude that this young pianist possesses musical brains besides his good fingers.

In addition to the concerto, Lhevinne played several solo works, including César Cui's *Causerie,* Schumann's Toccata, and the Chopin Polonaise he had played for Rubinstein in 1892.

Lhevinne's next European debut was in Paris, where he played Rubinstein's Fifth with the Lamoureux Orchestra. Safonoff conducted, and impressed Parisians with his "most rare vigor." Lhevinne impressed them with his "brilliance and delicacy." For encores, he played several of Scriabin's études. The études were well received, and their composer, who himself arrived in Paris a few days later, was pleased. In a letter Scriabin wrote on February 9, 1896, he referred to the concert in which "Lhevinne played the Rubinstein concerto and three of my études so well."[5]

One of the minor pleasures of Lhevinne's Western European tour was the opportunity to add to his stamp book—which he had begun as a little boy because of his interest in far away places. One day in Paris he absent-mindedly left the book on a park bench. After walking a few steps, he remembered it there, and went back to get it, but it was gone. Lhevinne was not the kind of person to see omens in such occurrences, but it was soon after losing his stamp book that he received word from Russia that he would have to cancel the rest of his tour. The reason was that he had turned twenty-one years old in December and was eligible for military service. Most young men in Czarist Russia were conscripted for four years; as a Conservatory graduate, Lhevinne only had to serve one year. But one year in the army was all it would take to rob his career of the impetus gained by his winning the Rubinstein Prize. He applied for a deferment, which was denied, and he had to "sign dozens of contracts with his own hand," saying he could not honor them because of military duty. After his year in the service, other young "stars" were in the spotlight and he was forgotten. Only eight of the original forty engagements he had through Wolff were renewed, and it took him five years to have as many concerts again as he had had in the fall of 1895.

Lhevinne's hitch with the army hurt his short-range pianistic prospects, but seems to have helped the budding romance with Rosina. Josef was stationed near Moscow, and he discovered that by playing popular songs at parties given by officers he could obtain some alleviation of his duties. With the freedom thus acquired, he was able to keep track of Rosina's activities at the Conservatory.

On May 12/24, 1896, about four months after Lhevinne's debut in Paris, Rosina Bessie played Chopin's E minor Concerto with Safonoff and the Conservatory Orchestra. The concerto was much more challenging than the *Fantasy on Polish Airs* which she had played the year before, and it has remained one of her favorite pieces of music. Likewise, the day on which she played it has remained one of the most exciting of her life:

"On the day of the concert, Josef came in the morning to give me courage. When he glanced at my hand, he saw a black-and-blue mark. 'Look,' he said, 'your middle finger is black-and-blue. Doesn't it hurt?'

"I hadn't felt any pain before, but when he said that, I looked, and immediately I felt a sharp pain. 'Yes! Oh! Oh! Oh! Oh!' I screamed. 'It's terrible! I can't stand it!'

"Josef was really worried when I said how terribly it hurt. But before doing anything else, he put his finger to his lips, moistened it, and touched the black-and-blue spot. Immediately I felt all right again.

"For the rest of my life, I regretted that that episode had happened. For a man as well balanced and 'normal' as he was, it was impossible to understand how I could feel pain just by looking at my finger, or how that pain had disappeared just because he had touched it. After we married, there were many times when I really had big pains, but each time I would complain about them he would say, 'Do you remember the black-and-blue finger?' It got so he never believed me."

Lhevinne may have become skeptical about the black-and-blue episode later in life, but for the day of the concert he suspended disbelief. When Rosina stepped on stage, she wore a pink chiffon dress with a mauve velvet belt. Lhevinne did not sit in the last row this time, nor did he cover his eyes. He later said in an interview that that was the day he fell in love:

I fell in love with her very suddenly. It was when she was fifteen [actually, she had just turned sixteen] and I heard her play the Chopin E minor Concerto in Moscow, with Safonoff conducting the orchestra. She was so pretty and she played so beautifully.[6]

She learned of his love a little later:

"One day the wife of my tutor in history had gone to visit her mother, and I was asked to be hostess at a bridge party where Josef would be. I was delighted and very proud of this honorable position that I would have as a hostess, and I was especially excited about it because Josef would be there. The party went well, and afterwards I was in the kitchen cleaning up some beautiful glasses we had used, because I didn't want the maid to break them. Josef came in and said, 'What are you doing?'

" 'Just cleaning these beautiful glasses,' I replied.

" 'Please, may I help you?' he asked. 'I'll wipe them for you.'

"So he began to wipe the dishes and I, being a rascal, asked him, 'Who are you in love with now?'

"He replied, in his nonchalant way, 'Oh, I am passionately in love with a girl who is a student at the Conservatory, with brown hair and brown eyes, who is very vivacious and talented. . . .'

"At this point, I realized by the look in his eyes that he was describing me! It was the only declaration of love he ever made to me (and the only time he ever helped with the dishes). As for me, I never said that I was in love with him. It was always, 'Josef, I am very fond of you.' "

Although Josef made no formal proposal, he and Rosina were seen together quite often following the tacit declaration of love. She was invited a few times to his parents' home for dinner, and remembers Fanny Levin's complaints about the difficulty of feeding a large family. And sometimes Josef would take her to a soirée at which he was invited to play. The most impressive were those given by Professor Lev Tikhomirov, a world-famous historian.[7]

"The first time I was in the social world was when I was sixteen and Josef took me to a soirée at Professor Tikhomirov's home. He had very distinguished guests, not only in music but also in theater and drama, and later we met Chekhov and Gorky there. At one of these soirées they asked me to play too, and when we were leaving a woman came up to me in the coat room and said, 'You know, I liked your playing more than Josef's.'

"I'll never forget the face of that society woman or the anger I felt when she said what she did. For me it was a monstrous thing to compare my playing with Josef's. I really think her comment had a lot to do with my decision not to have a solo career if we married."

In some ways it is hard to believe that the talented, headstrong teen-ager could have resented the praise of her own playing. But Rosina's worship of Josef's, it seems, canceled out the pride she took in her own.

Rosina's sixteenth year should have been one of the happiest of her life. But her success at the Conservatory and with Josef was overshadowed by anxiety about, and confrontations with, her mother. The anxiety resulted from her mother's health. Maria Bessie suffered from what was euphemistically known as "female trouble." Moscow doctors wanted to operate. Distrusting them, she went to a specialist in Berlin, who said the operation would not be necessary. Her condition worsened. Again the Moscow doctors said yes, the Berlin man no. Rosina went to Berlin both times. When the specialist for the second time said there was no need to operate, Rosina gratefully kissed his hands. Yet the anxiety remained.

The confrontations with her mother resulted from the time she spent with Josef. They argued bitterly over how late Rosina could stay out, for which today the daughter still feels guilty, in view of her mother's physical pain at the time. At least they could agree, though, about parties given at home. There was the annual birthday party for Rosina which, now that she was older, featured a hired musician who played waltzes and polkas for the guests to dance to. In addition, her mother gave parties of a more informal nature. Many guests at these would be from Moscow University.

"Most of the students who came were very poor. I don't remember where we met the first one, but when the others learned that they could go to a house where they could fill their stomachs and be in a warm room, they immediately came. They would arrive around eight o'clock for the little party. There was no radio or television or records to dance to then, so we would invite them right to the table. There was a big samovar and I would pour, and there would be sandwiches and all kinds of cookies, and maybe cake. The arguments at those parties were so intense that if a stranger entered the room he would think personal insults were being exchanged. But really these students were arguing abstract ideas about the condition of the country. The youth of my time was very interested in the future of Russia and cared intensely for its welfare. Not until the 1960s did I see young Americans take a similar interest in the fate of their country.

"Some of the guests were nihilists, and they especially would get very hot as they expressed their ideas. One student almost drove me crazy because when I said 'Please pass the zwieback' he would always ask, 'How do you know it is a zwieback?' Those parties always lasted until about midnight, with constant talk and smoking of cigarettes. Everyone had ideas about how to save Russia from that horrible regime."

Josef Lhevinne was not always at these parties, but even when he was not, Rosina could proudly display a little present he had given her—a small silver holder for her tea glass, which perfectly matched his larger holder.

Rosina Bessie enjoyed the political discussions at her mother's parties, but her own intellectual interests tended toward the purer fields of mathematics and music. Her tutor in math told her she had a "good head" for the subject, and wanted her to take more courses in preparation for a career in that field. She liked mathematics very much but enjoyed music more, and music, she decided, was to remain her major interest. Her courses at the Conservatory were not limited to the piano. Like all students there, she had to choose a course in painting, sculpture, or architecture. She chose the latter, and though she remembers very little from it, she thinks it was good such a course was required because "even a superficial training in the different arts might strike the right chord in a student and awaken a genuine interest.

"In my courses in theory and harmony I was given eight bars of a fugue and then would have to complete it, sometimes with orchestration too. Once they gave me Beethoven's *Waldstein* Sonata to orchestrate. Arensky was my teacher for composition (he had also been Josef's), and I always remembered him as being shy and rather weak. It was obligatory for pianists to accompany then, and also to sing in the Conservatory choir. I was assigned to accompany the students of Hřimaly, who was the best violin teacher in the school, and hearing his comments was a great inspiration. Safonoff conducted the Conservatory choir, and I remember singing in Beethoven's Ninth Symphony five different times in the Hall of the Nobility. Safonoff was a wonderful conductor, and that experience gave me a deep love for the symphony."

By the time Rosina entered his class, Safonoff's duties as choir conductor, conductor of the Conservatory Orchestra, director of the Conservatory, and director of the I.R.M.S. apparently made him too busy to be able to take his piano students on picnics before their final examinations. But he still made each student play his full program before the rest of the class, and this caused Rosina's mother great concern. "These classes took every evening for a week before the examinations. There were no intermissions, and we had to sit still the whole time. Even so, each session usually lasted until about two in the morning. This petrified my mother, not because she would have to come and get me, but because she thought something bad would happen to me from going to bed so late.

"At one of these pre-examination sessions, I think in 1897, the year before I graduated, Josef was present, probably to hear me play.

I played Chopin's Nocturne in E major, and after I had finished, Safonoff told Josef to go to the piano and show me how it must be played. When he had finished, Safonoff said to me, 'If you could play the beginning and the end, and Josef the middle, it would be a perfect nocturne.' I was amazed that he would say that. But I was not delighted. Although this was great praise for me, I always reacted strongly when anyone compared our playing in that way. Even Safonoff, a man I admired."

Safonoff and the woman at the soirée were not the only people who compared her playing to Josef's. Lhevinne himself thought there were some things at the piano she could do better than he. "There is a piece by Liszt, *Au Bord d'une Source,* where the fingers must stay very close together, and this was extremely difficult for Josef to play, because his hands were so large. Everything involving octaves and chords was easy for him, but not this. He always said how beautifully I played it, and many times would say, 'Come and play again that Liszt.' He would stand by the piano and look at my hands, and say, 'How I wish I could do something like that.' "

Rosina, of course, had difficulty playing pieces that required unusually large hands. Her glove size during her last year at the Conservatory was five-and-a-half. Somehow she managed to get through the opening of Beethoven's Opus 106, and she loved play-ing that work then, but today she would not want to hear how it sounded. She also studied Beethoven's Opus 109 at the time, though she did not play it in public. The most difficult work (in terms of technique) that she played in public at the Conservatory was the last movement of Henselt's F minor Piano Concerto, which is a real knuckle-breaker. She played it at a student concert on February 5/17, 1898, after a girl named Friedman had played the second movement. At the same concert, another girl, named Kardasheva, played two movements of a Rubinstein concerto.

As Rosina was enjoying her last year at the Conservatory, Lhe-vinne was trying to regain some of the momentum he had lost during his year in the Imperial Army. In February 1898 he re-turned to Paris, and played Saint-Saëns's Third Concerto with the Lamoureux Orchestra. A month later he and Safonoff were in St. Petersburg, where he played Rubinstein's Fifth Concerto again. But in May he was back in Moscow, awaiting Rosina's graduation.

As Rosina Bessie took her final examinations at the Conserva-tory, she was not—she claims today—expecting to win a gold medal. And it must have seemed unlikely that many would be awarded. In the five years since 1892, when Lhevinne and three others had won, there had been a total of only five winners. There had been one in 1893 (Samuelson, a student of Pabst), one in 1894 (Igumnov), none in 1895, none in 1896, and three in 1897 (Keneman, Goldenweiser, and Vera Isaakovich, who married Scriabin shortly after her graduation). The class of 1898, however, produced more gold-medalists than any in the history of the Conservatory. There were five winners in all, among them the pianists Bessie, Friedman, and Kardasheva. Rosina Bessie was the fifth girl ever to win a gold medal and, at eighteen, the youngest.

A week after Rosina's graduation, she and Josef were married. Before the ceremony, they received instruction from a Dutch Reform minister, for, like many Russian Jewish musicians before them, beginning with Anton Rubinstein, they had been baptized. As "Free Artists," Josef and Rosina Lhevinne would have received most of the privileges of Russian citizenship even had they not been converted (though they would not have been granted full citizenship itself). But even Jews who were "Free Artists" were subject to harassments—sometimes subtle, sometimes not so. This had been particularly true since the Grand Duke Serge had come to power in Moscow in 1891 and vowed to "run every Jew out of town." Rosina remembers that her entire family had been baptized sometime before she and Josef married—she does not or will not remember exactly when. And it was determined, by her parents we must assume, that Josef would be baptized too. In his case, as in hers, it was a matter of expediency.

"We were not baptized out of conviction but rather because life in Russia was easier that way. My parents had never stressed the importance of being Jewish. Josef's parents had given him the *bar mitzvah*, but he had left the synagogue by by the time he was fifteen and did not take organized religion seriously. Before we married, the minister insisted that we take some religious instruction from him, and I remember how interested Josef was. He viewed the lessons as something to add to his knowledge.

"Even today, I can see the face of that man who married us. He was Dutch or German, and his face was very red, and he was very nice to us both."

The wedding was on June 8/20, 1898. Arkady Levin was not present, for he did not approve of his son's baptism. Rosina wore the simple dress she had worn at her graduation a week before. After the ceremony, her parents took the newlyweds to L'Hermitage restaurant, which had been a favorite of Tchaikovsky's. Attending the party were about a dozen of the Bessies' friends, including the doctor of syphilis whose patient had frightened Rosina many years before. After dinner and champagne, the doctor said to Rosina, "I would like you—not Josef—to play something for us." She went to an upright piano and played Schumann's "In der Nacht." Following that, the other guests asked Josef to play, but the doctor pleaded with them that Rosina's be the only playing. With that the party ended. Rosina Bessie had become Rosina Lhevinne.

II

NEW BEARINGS

4

Retreat
and Rededication

IMMEDIATELY following the dinner at L'Hermitage, Rosina Lhevinne donned a bright red hat and boarded a train with her
husband. Their destination was Pushkino, a resort town about
twenty miles north of Moscow, where her parents had rented and
furnished a honeymoon *dacha* for them. At the *dacha*, Lhevinne,
who had slept on a couch while living with his parents, was to
have the everyday luxury of a bed, as well as a wife to share it
with. He was also to have a dog, a piano, and a vegetable garden—
everything he thought he needed in order to be content during a
long summer's honeymoon. But easy contentment was not to be
a hallmark of the Lhevinnes' marriage. Their honeymoon ended
prematurely, and three events suggested the shape of things to
come.

Lhevinne loved to fish, and soon after settling in the *dacha*
asked his bride to spend a morning with him on a lake:

"In Russia, Josef always went fishing at sunrise. Before we
married, I had always thought how romantic it would be to go
with him and read some poetry and discuss it. So one day we got
up at dawn and went out on the lake, and I brought out a book and
began to recite. 'Shh! Rosina,' he whispered, 'the fish will hear.'
From four in the morning until noon we were on that lake, and
except when we ate our little meal not a word was spoken. I never
went with him again."

Lhevinne's passion for fishing had dated from his first summer
in the Caucasus, and he was not about to let Rosina's literary no-
tions about what was "romantic" on a lake deter him from the
business at hand. He was equally serious about stargazing:

"One Sunday my parents invited us for dinner at their *dacha*

55

on the other side of Moscow. On the way home, we were riding in
a droshky, and it was a very humid night. We were sitting in the
open carriage, and Josef, as usual, was looking up at the sky (he
found the constellations there and tried to teach me, but I was very
stupid, because all I could remember were the Big and Small Dip-
per). As we were riding, he said, 'Look, Rosina, there are millions of
mosquitoes!' I looked, and the sky was full. Then he said, 'You
know, we are one of them.'

"That remark was absolutely the turning point in my life. As a
child the whole household had revolved about me, and until this
moment I had assumed that the rest of the world did too. To hear
my own husband say that I was nothing, that I was one of those
mosquitoes, was something I was totally unprepared for. When I
later came to understand this statement, I saw simply that I was
one person in millions and that there was nothing special about
me. But at that moment, I was terribly humiliated."

It is hard to believe that an offhand remark about mosquitoes
could trigger an identity crisis, but such was the nature of Rosina's
upbringing that it was actually the case. As she has put it, "I
was a child and then a married woman. There was nothing in between." The pain and humiliation she felt on that humid, sultry
evening was the first of a series of extremes she went through in
which, finding she was not everything, she felt she was nothing.
That duality has haunted her ever since.

"We had a dog at the *dacha*, and one morning after we had been
there for several weeks, I got up and saw him under the bed. He
looked at me with eyes that I will never forget, and their wildness
put me in terror. I screamed and ran to Josef and then ran out of
the house. Those eyes made such an impression on me that I did
not want to go back. I told Josef that I would never return to the
dacha, and he, who was not a strong person in that way, did not
force me. We lived for the rest of the summer with my parents, and
I would not even return to help move our things. I still do not
know how they got the dog, which was rabid, out of the house."

That the sight of a dog's eyes actually ended the Lhevinnes'
honeymoon was both a legacy from Rosina's past and a precedent
for the future. As a continuation of her childhood, it was another
in the series of Dostoyevskian impressions (the man with the
crumbling nose, the devils in the opera) that her mind could not
subdue. As a forecast of the future, it established the pattern
whereby her husband, when she was in an excitable state, accommodated himself to her demands. He was no more willing to make

her stay at the *dacha* than her mother had been to keep her at the Baltic Sea.

Three episodes do not speak for a full five weeks, nor do the above-mentioned difficulties speak the full truth of the Lhevinnes' honeymoon. Among their intimate discoveries was seeing how the other approached the piano. One day Josef said, just for fun, "Let's see how long it will take each of us to learn the E minor Mendelssohn *Étude*." So she worked on it and he worked on it and two or three days later she told him she was ready. She played the whole piece accurately and without stopping, and was quite pleased with herself.

It was about ten days later that Lhevinne announced he was ready. "He played it so fast and so wonderfully that I did not even recognize it. He found so many inner voices and countermelodies, and he made the melody sing out so much, that it was an entirely different piece. That, by itself, was impressive enough. But about six months later he said to me, 'Rosina, let's play that *Étude* together.' And I had to say, 'Josef, how does it start? I don't remember.' That showed how superior his way of learning was to mine."

Her husband's honeymoon performance of the Mendelssohn *Étude* strengthened Rosina's instinctive sense of his pianistic superiority. By the time they abandoned the *dacha* to join her parents and the larger world, she had made an amazing decision: she would not pursue a solo career. Everyone who knew her was astounded.

"When we married, our friends speculated on us almost as on horses that we would last a year at the most." One reason for skepticism was a belief that Lhevinne, who had always been strongly drawn to members of the opposite sex, might pursue other women to the detriment of the marriage. The other reason was a belief that Rosina, with her ambition and drive to become a concert star, might pursue her career to the detriment of his.

As a pianist, Lhevinne then seemed to be three years past his prime—at the age of twenty-three! He had no talent or inclination for self-promotion, and the difficulty he was having in rebuilding his career was all the more bitter after the brief taste of glory he had had in the fall of 1895. Rosina, on the other hand, was fresh out of the Conservatory as its youngest female gold-medalist and had every reason to think that she could build a career for herself. The world then had two great female pianists, both of whom she had heard. Her own pianistic potential could not compare to the thundering talent of Teresa Carreño, who played the Tchaikovsky Concerto with the force of a man, and who looked so regal at the keyboard, with medals from all over the world draped on her breast. But it did compare with the delicate art of Annette Essipova, who played Schumann and Chopin with such exquisite touch and pedaling.

In the eyes of their Moscow friends, Rosina's marriage to Lhevinne would only enhance her own prospects, as Carreño's to D'Albert and Essipova's to Leschetizky had enhanced theirs. If it ended in divorce or separation, as the other two had, that still would not hurt her career. But Rosina knew her own competitive nature as well as her so-called friends did, and she knew how she felt whenever anyone dared to compare her playing to Josef's. Buoyed by her first intimate exposure to her husband's pianistic craft, she decided to be content to be a wife. By doing so, the eighteen-year-old girl, who had shown her youth on the honeymoon, revealed an instinctive shrewdness well beyond her years.

After living out the rest of the summer with Rosina's parents, the Lhevinnes moved in with her sister and brother-in-law in the fall. Sophie Bessie had recently married Leonid Mindowsky, a young man who had come to the family parties and had once seemed to be courting Rosina. His family, which was wealthy and conservative, disapproved of the marriage. So the Mindowskys and the Lhevinnes, aided financially by the Bessies, lived together in a small Moscow apartment. Lhevinne, who was used to crowded living conditions, added a St. Bernard dog to the household—perhaps as a shield from all the in-laws.

The crucial event of the year for him was his recital in the Hall of the Nobility on December 17/29, 1898. It was the first solo recital he had scheduled in Moscow since serving in the Imperial Army, and his musical future there seemed to depend upon how it was received. The program he prepared was strenuous and serious —perhaps a bit too serious for a town whose playgoers expected to be serenaded during intermissions and whose concertgoers expected piano soloists to share the stage with popular singers. Lhevinne built his program around Beethoven's *Hammerklavier* Sonata and Brahms's *Variations on a Theme of Paganini*, works which make little concession to the pianistically uninitiated; he also played shorter works by Mendelssohn, Chopin, Schumann, Liszt, Rubinstein, and Borodin. By all accounts, the recital was one of the finest heard in Moscow in a long while. Technically and interpretatively, Lhevinne handled all difficulties with ease. By the time he had completed his final piece, the elaborate Schulz-Evler arrangement of Strauss's "Blue Danube Waltz," numerous admirers were surrounding the stage. Then the encores began. One reviewer left after counting seven.

Unfortunately, the handful of people who surrounded Lhevinne at the end of his recital comprised the bulk of his audience. Artistically successful, the recital had been a fiasco financially. Newspaper accounts pointed out that solo recitals by young pianists were uncommon events in Moscow, and suggested that giving one in the Hall of the Nobility had been rather quixotic. There *had* been the extraordinary exception of Josef Hofmann, who a few years before had given seven recitals in the space of a few weeks. But he had come to Moscow with a glowing reputation from Western Europe. Lhevinne, it was suggested, would be better off to try his luck abroad.

It was little consolation to Lhevinne that his recital had been an "artistic" tour de force. If his concerts were not financially successful in Moscow, he would have to continue receiving financial assistance from Rosina's parents. Nor did it help much that other talented Moscow musicians found themselves without a public. Rachmaninoff played a series of concerts in London that season, in hopes of making the reputation and money he could not earn in his homeland. Successful in London, he found things unchanged upon returning to Moscow, and fell into a deep depression that lasted two years. His companions during this time were three St. Bernards, as compared to Lhevinne's one.

Scriabin, like Lhevinne, had a wife to support. Unlike Lhevinne, he had a steady income, for Safonoff had appointed him to a professorship at the Conservatory in 1898, a year after he had married Vera Isaakovich. After six years during which his concert tours and compositions had netted him only the most erratic returns, Scriabin had finally achieved some financial security in his native land. He took an interest in Lhevinne's December recital, and went with him to Jurgenson's (a leading publisher and dealer in music) in order to choose an instrument. "All they showed us," in Scriabin's words, "were sluggish and uneven."[1]

Moscow was a booming operatic and theatrical town in 1898–99, which only compounded the difficulties of a young pianist trying to gain recognition. Mamontov's Russian Private Opera, with its imaginative staging, superlative casting, and its willingness to produce operas of the *kutchka*, was mounting a dramatic challenge to the state-sponsored Bolshoi Opera. Ten days before Lhevinne's recital, Feodor Chaliapin made his celebrated debut in the title role of Mussorgsky's *Boris Godunov*. Chaliapin was then twenty-five years old and had been with Mamontov's company for two years, but it was his performance of Boris that made him a star.

In drama, the season's great rivalry was between the Maly Theater, where Arkady Levin continued to blow his trumpet during intermissions, and the Moscow Art Theater, which had been preparing for its first season at Pushkino when the Lhevinnes were spending their honeymoon there. The Moscow Art Theater "arrived" in Moscow on the night of Lhevinne's recital, although its season had begun a few months earlier. As Lhevinne played to the empty seats at the Hall of the Nobility, a small crowd at the Moscow Art Theater was witnessing the world premiere of Chekhov's *The Seagull*. Literally overnight, Stanislavsky and Nemirovich-Danchenko, the company's directors, had become prophets of a new theatrical style. One of their many innovations was to let the play itself entertain the audience. The Moscow Art Theater had no orchestra.

As Josef Lhevinne did not have many concerts with which to compete with Moscow's dramatic and operatic events, he had plenty of time in which to enjoy those events. He took Rosina quite often to Moscow's theaters and music halls, attending not only the Mamontov and Stanislavsky productions but those of the Imperial Theaters as well. As Rosina had seldom been allowed to go out in the evenings when living with her parents, this was her first opportunity to attend not only the new productions but also the standard ones that had been in Moscow for years. On their evenings at the theater the Lhevinnes were usually accompanied by the Mindowskys.

At home Rosina and her sister gave an occasional small party. Leonid Mindowsky had studied at Moscow University, and most of the guests came either from there or the Conservatory. Sometimes when guests were over, and less often when they themselves were visiting, the Lhevinnes played the piano together. For Rosina had not stopped practicing just because she had decided not to have a career. When Josef was away from the piano, she worked on her favorite solo pieces, which at this stage of her life were mostly works by Chopin. With Josef, she began to learn music for four hands. They played some duets at a few private gatherings, and soon after one such occasion César Cui presented his card at young Mme. Lhevinne's door. Cui was one of the three surviving members of the *kutchka*, and a lieutenant general in the Imperial Army. He was a musical miniaturist in comparison with his more illustrious associates, but his compositions—many of them for the piano—were then thought to possess great charm:

"Cui entered the room in full military dress—his gray coat lined in scarlet, a sword at his side, and wearing spotless white gloves. 'I hear with great respect,' he said, 'that you have decided to withdraw from professional life and dedicate your career to that of Mr. Lhevinne. But I am at the head of an important charity concert for widows and orphans, and I would be very pleased if you and Mr. Lhevinne would play there Arensky's newly written Suite for Two Pianos.'

"As Cui's request was so delicately phrased, and as Josef and I had both taken classes from Arensky at the Conservatory, we accepted. So at that benefit concert, held in the Hall of the Nobility, we made our first public appearance together. The success was a very unusual one—not because of our playing, and not because of the composition, but because of the monstrous idea of having two pianos on the stage."

The appearance of two pianos on the same stage certainly was an anomaly in Moscow in 1898–99. It was not very common in Western Europe either. James Kwast—who had compared Lhevinne to Tausig in 1895—and his wife Frieda had been one of the first professional two-piano teams in Europe, and Carreño and D'Albert had played a few duo-concerts during their tempestuous marriage. But the day of the full-time professional two-piano team was still a long way off. One reason for that was the scarcity of good compositions available. Arensky's Second Suite was to become one of the staples of the twentieth-century repertoire, as was Rachmaninoff's Second Suite, also composed in 1898–99.

Following the performance of the Arensky, many people, including several respected critics, urged Rosina to reconsider a solo career for herself. "But in spite of the strong temptation, I did not give in. It is a decision I have never regretted. For today as I look back on my youth I find in this decision and in Josef's career as a soloist the basis for the richness of our musical life together."

During the first year of marriage, her husband's career as a soloist had not progressed very far. He had only one more important engagement that year: a performance of Beethoven's *Emperor* Concerto, the work he had played when fifteen. Safonoff conducted Moscow's I.R.M.S. orchestra, for the one-hundredth time.

By the end of the season, it was clear that Lhevinne, even with his wife's moral support and her parents' financial support, had been unable to win a secure place for himself in Moscow's musical world. To live another year with Rosina's sister and brother-in-law, and to educate the Moscow public at her parents' expense (and thus at the cost of his own self-esteem) was hardly an inviting prospect. Abroad he was likely to find audiences more appreciative of his playing. But to take Rosina to Paris or Vienna or Berlin would make him even more dependent upon her parents for financial support.

The answer to his dilemma came from the unlikely place of Tiflis (now Tbilisi), where the local branch of the Imperial Conservatory offered him a professorship. There, at last, he would have an opportunity to be self-supporting. As a bonus, he would be able to live near his beloved mountains. In late August or early September 1899, the Lhevinnes set out for "The Pearl of the Caucasus."

Tiflis, situated on the banks of the Kura river between the Black and the Caspian Seas, was then a city of 160,000 Russian, Georgian, and Armenian inhabitants. The Lhevinnes' trip from Moscow took four days—two to get to Vladikavkas (now Ordzhonikidze) by train, and two more to cross the Caucasus by horse and buggy.

"At Vladikavkas, we climbed into a large coach and were pulled by two horses. We went up and up and up, and every four hours they changed the horses. Then, after going all the time up, we came to a peak and began to drop down. Suddenly, down in the valley we saw something so stupendous that we thought we were dreaming: there, at the foot of a broad panorama, was the magnificent city of Tiflis. Even now I can visualize that first impression: there is the town and the streets, and the houses are just like little spots. I experienced nothing like it until the first time I flew in a plane [fifty-six years later]."

After arriving in Tiflis, the Lhevinnes caused some visual excitement of their own. The officers of the Conservatory had hired Lhevinne sight-unseen, and when they saw him they demanded that he grow a beard, thinking he looked too young. The director of the Conservatory was "a wealthy young bachelor" named Archipov, who rented the Lhevinnes a guest apartment in his house. It consisted of an antechamber, a small dining room, and one larger room, which housed a piano and a convertible double bed. Soon a cot was added to the antechamber.

"There were no women servants in Tiflis, and I was too young to have a manservant, because Josef was away from home most of the day. But finally we found a little girl of fifteen whose parents said they would be glad to have her keep me a little company and help with a few things."

With the young girl as her personal maid, and with Archipov's cook preparing all their food, Rosina was free to discover why Tiflis was known as the cultural center of Transcaucasia. In addition to its Conservatory, the city had a Russian theater, an Armenian theater, an opera house (where Chaliapin had begun his career six years earlier), a symphony orchestra, and a theological seminary (from which Josef Stalin, four years younger than Josef Lhevinne, had recently been discharged). There was not enough musical talent in Tiflis for Lhevinne to have much competition, but there was enough musical appreciation for him to be recognized as a brilliant virtuoso. As local celebrities, he and Rosina were mightily entertained. There were dinners and parties and balls, as in any other city. And picnics peculiar to Tiflis:

"With four couples we went by horse, with an expert Georgian leading us. He rode a beautiful horse with leather saddlebags—on the one side was food, on the other, wine. He led us through forests and fields to a beautiful place, where we dismounted. There he prepared *shaslik*. First he took the branch of a tree and peeled off the bark, revealing wood of the purest white. Then he built a fire, and one by one placed medallions of mutton on the long white stick. With wine and salad, barbecued mutton in the heart of the Caucasus! What an experience that was!"

Young Mme. Lhevinne's legs were dreadfully stiff after her first experience of riding a horse, but she soon managed to take that and all other social events in Tiflis easily in stride. She loved any occasion where she could be with other people and exchange opinions. Such was her character, however, that she remembered none of the partying in Tiflis as vividly as this event, which followed a night out on the town:

"Whenever we went out, we always made sure that the little girl was in bed, and we locked the door to make sure that she was safe there. One night when we came back, she was not in her bed. We called and called, but she did not answer, and we were very frightened. Just as we were about to notify the police, we saw her crawl out from under the bed. When she saw me, she ran and kissed me, and clutched me in fear.

" 'Dear,' I asked, 'what is the matter? Why are you frightened?'

" 'Look!' she cried. 'There is an animal there. I was afraid that it would eat me.'

"She pointed to a chair. There was my fur boa, which had big eyes. She had thought that it was a real animal, and she had stayed, poor thing, all the time under the bed while we were away."

Between the excitable fifteen-year-old girl and the impressionable nineteen-year-old Rosina, there was always some kind of crisis in the small apartment. The two of them were usually together there in the daytime, while Lhevinne was at the Conservatory. He taught about twenty students and usually left home early in the morning, returning in time for dinner. The pattern worked well enough—as long as he came on time.

"Sometimes it was nine or ten at night and still I had not heard from Josef. There was no telephone, no way to inquire. Being of such a nervous nature, I could not understand what had happened to him. I always knew when he had come back, because he would knock on the door very timidly. I was a real spitfire then, and as I ran to the door I would be happy that he was safe; but I would also be ready to express my great disappointment that he had not sent word to me.

"When I would open the door, my excitement would quickly diminish, for there would always be a certain student there, standing in front of Josef. With the boy there, I had the tact to hold my tongue, and by the time he had gone I had already cooled off. So many times Josef did the same thing. He loved to play billiards."

At the billiards hall, Lhevinne seems to have been particularly adept at a version of English billiards, the game played with three balls on a pocketed table. He and his friends called it by the French-derived word *carambole*. He must have taken Rosina to the billiards hall once, or she, impatient, had gone there to fetch him, for she still remembers the way he held the cue stick and how the balls caromed off each other before dropping into the pockets.

In the concert halls of Tiflis, Lhevinne was immediately recognized as a pianistic wizard. The special quality of his playing was said to be the way he drew such warm and clear sounds from the piano, along with the way he achieved powerful effects without "pounding." On December 11/23, 1899, he played a Rubinstein trio with some local musicians and impressed his listeners with the "airy lightness and crystalline clarity" of his playing. On the next day, he gave a recital consisting almost exclusively of works from the Romantic period (the composers were Brahms, Schumann, Schubert-Tausig, Chopin, Mendelssohn, Schubert-Liszt, Rubinstein, and Borodin). The pieces he played were warmly received, but the newspaper *Kavkaz* chided him for not including Bach or Beethoven. This was the first suggestion that he might not be taking his artistic responsibilities in Tiflis seriously enough.

At Christmas, Lhevinne had a two-and-a-half week vacation from the Conservatory, and he and Rosina decided to make the difficult trip to Moscow. "It is remarkable how with age it is not the things you enjoyed in life that you remember with pleasure, but the things that were difficult. We did not enjoy it much then, and Josef was on a very small salary, but in spite of all the gaieties in Tiflis and the tempting holiday invitations there, we went to Moscow to see our parents.

"In the winter, it was extremely dangerous to cross the Caucasus by horse and carriage. Josef liked that part of the trip because it was an adventure, but I was not the kind of person for that. The wind blew the snow so hard I thought it would push us over. Then, at a certain place in the road, the driver stopped the carriage and told us that in the year so-and-so the carriage had stopped at this same place and an avalanche had come and killed all the people. Being so impressionable, I screamed, 'Why do you stop here? Go! Go! Go!' And certainly all the other passengers, who were quite calm, laughed at me.

"I did enjoy it when the carriage stopped at the inns, but only because it was so warm inside, where there was always an open fire and Caucasian food and wine. The trip over the mountains took two days up and two days down, and then two days from Vladikavkas by train, so we had only a few days in Moscow before we had to start back. My mother was so ill, though, that it was only right to have gone to visit her."

The musical highlight of the Tiflis season came soon after the Lhevinnes returned from Moscow. Josef Hofmann came to town. "That first year we were in Tiflis, Hofmann played seven concerts. He did not know anyone there, so he spent almost all of his free time with us, and Josef's students had the opportunity of meeting him. On the evening of his first concert, he was having dinner with us, and before eating he noticed that my Josef had left his copy of the 'Lorelei' among the other music on the piano [Lhevinne had played Liszt's arrangement of Schubert's "Lorelei" at his December recital]. He had never seen it. He looked at it carefully for a few minutes, but did not try it at the piano.

"The concert was sold out, and when we arrived at the hall we found many chairs placed on stage. Hofmann asked us where we were sitting, and we told him the orchestra. 'I would feel more comfortable,' he said, 'if you, and not strangers, were closest to me on the stage.' So we took the seats nearest the piano.

"At the end of the concert, he played several encores. Then he looked at us with a twinkle in his eye and started the 'Lorelei.' Our hearts sank, and I grabbed Josef's hand. But Hofmann played it with such assurance that he continued to glance at us with the eye! After the concert, he told us what pleasure he had had in seeing our frightened faces.

"Hofmann always had a prodigious memory; but that year his playing, too, was as stupendous as we ever heard it. He was still fresh from Anton Rubinstein's inspiration, and I cannot exaggerate the impression he made on us. His impeccable technique left him free of any worry about the difficulties of a composition, and he could concentrate completely on its musical content. His playing was expressive without being sentimental. And he was able to preserve excellently the style of each composition. Hearing him then was a musical experience not to forget."

The musical and personal friendship formed that winter lasted throughout the two Josefs' careers. Before leaving town, Hofmann presented the Lhevinnes with a photograph in which he pokes his head through a pasteboard setting to become one of three armed Cossacks guarding a Georgian mountain pass. The inscription, written in German, is addressed to "Frau Levin."

Aside from Hofmann, the only artist of stature the Lhevinnes saw in Tiflis was Feodor Chaliapin, who came through for an occasional opera performance. They had heard him sing in Moscow, but had not know him personally there. "In Tiflis, he came several times to our apartment. He was huge, six-foot-six or something like that, and he had a big chest like Van [Cliburn]—but a giant Van. He loved to tell stories, and he told them so magnificently that everybody loved him not only for his singing but for his magnificent spirit as well. He also had interesting ideas on interpretation. Once when we were with him in Tiflis someone asked, 'How much do you actually experience that you are Boris Godunov when you are playing the role?'

" 'That theory is nonsense,' he replied. 'You have to study the part you are playing so thoroughly that you identify yourself completely with the *role* and do not connect yourself with the *person* you represent at all. If I felt that I was Boris Godunov every time I played the role, I wouldn't survive.'

"For anyone who had seen him play the role of Boris, it was impossible to believe that he did not feel it. You were so taken with the suffering—especially at the end, when the hero chokes himself. Each time, he did it so realistically that you trembled. But he even used that scene to support his theory that the actor must remember who he is even while performing. One time, he said, his dissimulation was so convincing that a member of the chorus called out, 'Feodor Ivanovich, are you sick?' He remembered so much who he was that he told the man, 'Go to the Devil.' "

The brief visits of Chaliapin and Hofmann were the Lhevinnes' only links with the larger musical world they had left behind in Moscow. Two of Rosina's personal friends lived in Tiflis, though. One was the Princess Artsibayasheva, her first friend at the Conservatory. The other was Count Toumanov. "He was one of the students from Moscow University who had come to the little parties that my mother used to give. He was a Georgian prince from Tiflis and was very handsome, and during his four years of study in Moscow we had been very good friends. I do not think that he was in love with me, and I know that I was not in love with him, but he danced beautifully and came to many of those little parties. Then he left.

"When Josef was invited to teach in Tiflis, Count Toumanov wrote to say that his mother (he had no father) would be so glad if we would consider their home our home, so that she could repay all the kindnesses my mother had done for him while he was a student in Moscow. So we went there very soon after arriving in Tiflis, and many times she invited us for dinner. He came also to visit us, sometimes in the evening for dinner, sometimes in the daytime.

"There were no automobiles then, but he had a carriage with horses, and a driver. I was all day alone with the little girl, so, many times he asked me, 'Wouldn't you like to go for a ride?' And I would say, 'I would be delighted.' So, many times he took me.

"Then one day I received a letter:

> Having such a wonderful husband, aren't you ashamed at having a lover and going almost every day riding with him?
> Mr. Lhevinne is such a noble man, how can you be so superficial as to take another man as a lover just because he is a count?
> If we see you once more with him, we will write Mr. Lhevinne about it.

When I read the letter, I could not sleep, and I cried, and I showed it to Josef. He was upset, too, but his first reaction was to say, 'It's evidently a good-for-nothing person who wrote this, why trouble yourself about it?' Then he suggested, 'Why don't you show the letter to Toumanov, and have him take you riding several days in succession. Then maybe they will write me and we will know who it is.'

"So I showed Toumanov the letter and we went almost every day riding. Before I had had great pleasure, but now I took that letter very close to my heart. Every person I saw, I wondered: is that the one who wrote the letter? So we went riding—but nothing happened. Josef never heard from them.

"As time passed, we thought about the incident a little less, but whenever we remembered it we always said how much we would give to know who had written such ugly things about me."

Aside from the poison-pen letter, Rosina Lhevinne's first year in Tiflis had seemed to her "365 days a carnival." She and Josef spent the summer of 1900 in Moscow and then returned to Tiflis in the fall for another year. The comfortable pattern repeated itself —the spirited social life, the outings in the forest, the good cooking (Archipov's cook told the Lhevinnes he used a pound of butter a day on their food alone), the billiards and concert halls, the Christmas trip to Moscow, and the spectacular natural surroundings. The winter trip to Moscow was easier this year because a railroad line between Tiflis and Vladikavkas had been completed in 1900, skirting the Caucasus Range via Baku on the Caspian Sea and eliminating the necessity of crossing the mountains by horse and carriage. Apart from that, the only measurable difference between the first year and the second was the passage of time. In the twentieth century the difference between the Julian and Gregorian calendars became thirteen days, so it was on March 16/29, 1901 that Rosina Lhevinne celebrated her twenty-first birthday.

"For my birthday, Josef had arranged that we would go out to dinner and then to the theater. At four or five in the afternoon, Archipov rang the bell and said that he would appreciate it if Josef came for a few hours to replace someone at the poker table. Josef was rather sorry to leave me on my birthday, but he did not want to disappoint him. So he went. About three hours later, he returned. 'Dear,' he said, 'I'm so sorry that I had to leave you, but now we can really celebrate in a glorious way.' He had won two hundred rubles."

The Lhevinnes spent the second summer in Moscow too and planned to return to Tiflis again in the fall. The third year promised to be even more rewarding than the other two:

"One day during the summer, the contract came from Tiflis. When Josef brought it into the room, he was radiant. They had doubled his salary and invited me to be on the Conservatory staff; in addition, they invited us to play two-pianos with the symphony orchestra. But I was very cool, and for a long time I did not say a word.

" 'What is the matter?' he asked. 'You ought to express appreciation for all that they want to do for us.'

" 'I cannot feel that,' I said, 'because I think all our friends were completely right in saying that by marrying me you killed your career. Because if you had not been married, you would never have gone to Tiflis in the first place. You would probably be in Europe concertizing. You can go back to Tiflis, but I won't go with you.' "

She had been gathering the courage to say this for months.

Characteristically, it had all stemmed from a single sensory impression:

"Josef was playing Brahms's *Paganini Variations* during our second year in Tiflis and I was in the audience. I was thrilled by his beautiful playing, for he played magnificently, as usual. But from my seat in the audience, I could see something between him and the piano—his stomach! When I saw that, I decided that we must leave Tiflis.

"Financially, we were comfortable, and socially, well established. And Josef was near his beloved mountains and stars. But I suddenly realized that this was not the right atmosphere for his artistic development. With the exception of the one short visit by Hofmann, my Josef had absolutely no pianistic rival in Tiflis. When he should have been competing with and learning from the world's best artists, he was merely growing fat in a comfortable environment.

"I thought about it for a long time and finally decided that we should go to Berlin, then the musical capital of the world. But I did not know how to tell him what I thought."

When the contract arrived, she found the words to tell him.

"I asked Josef if he didn't think it might be wiser for us to go to Berlin, where he would have the opportunity of further developing his prodigious God-given talent. I said that I was sure my parents would be very glad to help us financially for a little while and that he would very soon be able to give concerts there and to occupy the position that he deserved. Life in Tiflis, I said, was hospitable, but basically it was a life of luxury. It would ruin his career to remain there.

"It was only after a long conversation that we finally decided it would be best to go to Berlin. It was a difficult decision for us both, but neither Josef nor I ever regretted it."

In his wife's words, twenty-six-year-old Josef Lhevinne heard his artistic conscience speaking, and he willingly ended what was to be his longest retreat from the responsibility of developing his artistic powers. In the imagery of his childhood summers in the Caucasus, he once more traded the mountains, streams, and stars for the claustrophobic practice rooms of the North. This time, the transaction was terminal. The Lhevinnes were on the high road—for good.

The geographical shift from Tiflis to Berlin was accompanied by severe changes in status. The "local celebrity" in Tiflis was now an "aspiring artist" in Berlin; the self-supporting husband and wife were once more youngsters dependent upon her parents for support. The Lhevinnes' awareness of their diminished status was heightened by the kind of reception they got in Berlin.

Their most immediate problem was to find lodgings suitable for intensive practice, for if Lhevinne was to regain his eminence as a pianist he would have to get quickly down to work. Many landlords allowed only upright pianos, and it was quite a while before the Lhevinnes found a pension where they were allowed to install a concert grand. They divided the day into practice times, and Rosina, who needed only an hour or two a day, took the period from two to four in the afternoon. Not realizing that many Berliners were in the habit of napping then, she practiced quite strenuously.

After four days on this schedule, she went to a concert. Lhevinne, tired after practicing all day, stayed home. Upon returning, Rosina discovered she had forgotten her keys. The porter opened the door for her, but on seeing who she was, he slammed it in her face. The ensuing conversation was carried on through a keyhole:

"I live on the third floor," I shouted. "I have forgotten my keys. I want to get in."

"You cannot come in," he cried back. "It is you who own that devil-piano that plays when decent folks want to sleep. I will not let you in."

"But I must get in," I expostulated. "This is where I live and I have no other place to go and it is late."

"You can no longer live here, you who do not play either Strauss or Offenbach! No more can you live here!"

"But my husband is here," I said, "and my things are here."

"We will pack up your things and send them to you," was the obdurate reply. "I will not let you in. So go away."[2]

She did go away, to a police station across the street, but the officers refused to intervene. She had to wait there until Lhevinne finally realized she was late, and wandered out to hunt for her. They had to bribe their way back into the building.

The porter's rudeness was soon compensated for by the hospitality of Ferruccio Busoni, who invited the Lhevinnes to visit his studio. Busoni had witnessed Lhevinne's performance with Rubinstein in 1890 and also his Rubinstein Prize victory in 1895, and he was curious to know how the young Russian had developed since then.

"Certainly Busoni was by then one of the great and well-known pianists, and we were quite flattered when he wrote to ask us to spend an evening with him. I cannot exaggerate the impression he made on us when we entered his studio. There he was, with his tremendous head of hair and a crooked black tie, sitting on a high armchair as if it were a throne; and there, sitting on colored pillows at his feet, were some of his students, most of them girls, who seemed to admire him as if he were a saint. The guests were various well-known pianists.

"When Busoni saw us, he stood up and greeted us warmly. All the rest stood up, too. Then, after about ten minutes of social conversation, Busoni said, 'Lhevinne, I've heard so much about your playing, will you play for us the Schumann Toccata?'

" 'Well,' Josef began to answer in his quiet and unassuming way, 'I didn't practice it, but—'

" 'Oh well, play it anyway.' So he played the Schumann Toccata.

"When it was over, Busoni said, 'Lhevinne, play the Paganini-Brahms.' He played the Paganini-Brahms.

" 'Lhevinne, play now the *Feux Follets*.' And he played the *Feux Follets*. And then Rubinstein's Octave Étude, Chopin's Octave Étude, and Chopin's Étude in Double Thirds.

"He played them all, and I remember it like yesterday, with Busoni and the others standing around the piano. When it was over, Busoni complimented him, but not in such an exceedingly warm way. Refreshments were served, and we left.

"On the way home, Josef was in a pensive mood, and he asked, 'Do you really think Busoni liked my playing?' And I said, 'Of course. Of course he did. How could he not?' But Josef never really knew what impression he had made.

"I found out about fifty years later. I was teaching a master class in California and had gone to a party. A man came up and introduced himself as Mark Ginsburg. He turned to my daughter Marianna and said, 'I have something to tell you that maybe your mother does not know.' Then he asked, 'Mrs. Lhevinne, do you remember the time that Busoni invited you and your husband to come, and he played?'

" 'Yes, yes,' I said. 'I remember.'

" 'I was studying with Busoni then. The next day we had a class, and Busoni said to us: "Yesterday I heard a young Russian pianist, and if I put you all in one pot you would not make one Lhevinne." ' "

Busoni, a member of the jury, remembered the young man who had won the Rubinstein Prize in 1895. But Berlin's general musical public had not remembered Lhevinne. In a city glutted with pianists, the six years since his victory were comparable to six generations. Whenever Lhevinne was not practicing, he and Rosina were scouting the competition. Among the pianists who marched through Berlin that season were Rosenthal, Sauer, D'Albert, Carreño, Busoni, Godowsky, Schnabel, Gabrilowitsch, Lamond, Risler, Pugno, and Paderewski. Among violinists, Lhevinne's former classmate Alexander Petschnikoff had quite a following, as did Eugène Ysaÿe and Fritz Kreisler. As for conductors, the Lhevinnes heard Muck, Weingartner, Nikisch, and Richard Strauss.

In such a challenging musical atmosphere, so different from that in Tiflis, or even Moscow, Lhevinne was able to work with great dedication. By January 1902 he felt ready to express his growth on the concert stage. Early in the month, he played in Warsaw, where a critic immediately included him with Busoni, Godowsky, Hofmann, and Rosenthal in the "family of pianistic giants." Lhevinne had been a mere "technician" when he had played in Warsaw three years earlier, the man wrote. But now he had "descended into himself," he was "exploring the depths."[3]

Rosina had traveled with him to Warsaw, where they stayed in the Hotel European. The reviewer's praise did wonders for Lhevinne's appetite, for on the morning following the concert Rosina had to watch, horrified, as he put away nine consecutive fried eggs. Later in the month, they went to Paris, where they gave a joint recital in Salle Erard. After Lhevinne played a long list of solo works, in which the French found a "finesse absolument délicieuse," he and Rosina played Arensky's Second Suite. This was her Paris debut, and *Le Figaro* found her playing "intelligent, energetic, and remarkably rhythmic."[4] *Monde Musicale* called it "elegant, gracious, and charming," and expressed a wish to hear her as a soloist. But as Rosina's only goal was to aid her husband's career, Parisians never did hear her without him.

After Lhevinne's success in Warsaw and Paris, he felt ready for Berlin. A concert with the Berlin Philharmonic was arranged for March 22, 1902. He was allowed to play two concertos, and he chose the two associated with his past glory: Beethoven's *Emperor* Concerto and Rubinstein's Fifth. In addition, he decided to play Weber's C major Sonata, with its famous *perpetuum mobile* finale, which he had played in Warsaw and Paris. The concert was one of the most important of Lhevinne's life, and one of the more curious. Dr. Paul Ertel, distinguished critic of the *Berliner Lokal-Anzeiger*, described it:

> First, Lhevinne played Beethoven's Fifth Concerto with the Philharmonic Orchestra. It was technically good (one could hardly expect differently after the distinguished build-up), but with a certain lassitude of expression. All who already knew Lhevinne shook their heads and

spoke of indisposition. And so it was in fact. Even so, in the next piece, Weber's Sonata, the magician at the keyboard demonstrated such an eminent ability, such an uncommon creative power, and such a harmonious grasp of style, that all who were present at this memorable concert broke out in frenzied applause, calling Lhevinne again and again to the stage. With this incontestably brilliant performance, he had immediately won himself a secure position. His good disposition carried him to the end.[5]

Lhevinne's "good disposition" carried him through Rubinstein's Fifth Concerto, which ended the program, but not to a large reception that had been planned for after the concert. He and Rosina had asked that it be canceled, and the reason they did that was the probable reason for his "indisposition" at the beginning of the concert:

"My mother's condition had gotten steadily worse in Moscow, and again the doctors there wanted to operate. So she went to Berlin to consult the specialist once more. This time he agreed that an operation was necessary, but by the time he did, it was too late.

"The operation was on the morning of Josef's concert with the Berlin Philharmonic. As soon as it was over, the doctor knew that my mother did not have long to live. He did not tell her, but he told the rest of us, and when I heard the news I was absolutely hysterical. Josef could do nothing with me, and it was only my father who could finally calm me down. In spite of this, Josef played the concert so that my mother would not know that anything was wrong, and I managed to go to the Singacademie and hear him."

Maria Bessie died not long after Rosina's twenty-second birthday. Even today, the daughter feels acute pain when speaking of "that terrible operation" and of the doctor who had delayed it for so many years. The pain of her private bereavement in the spring of 1902 continues to cancel out the joy she would have felt in her husband's public achievement under different circumstances.

Under the circumstances, the amazing thing was not that Lhevinne played the Beethoven with "a certain lassitude of expression" but that he was able to concentrate on the music during the rest of the program. The "secure position" he won for himself with his brilliant performance of the Weber included a contract from Hermann Wolff and an offer to teach at Berlin's Stern Conservatory. The teaching position was offered by Gustav Holländer, who had been on the jury for the Rubinstein Prize Competition in 1895. The management contract was not offered by Hermann Wolff himself, who had managed Lhevinne's short tour in 1895–96, for he had died in 1901, the year before the pianist made his sparkling comeback.

But Louisa Wolff maintained her late husband's firm as Europe's leading concert management and was able to secure Lhevinne excellent engagements for the coming season.

His success had certainly justified Rosina's insistence the summer before, that they go to Berlin rather than return to Tiflis. He was about to accept Holländer's offer and settle a while longer in Berlin, when Safonoff wired from Moscow, inviting him to return to his alma mater as a full professor. After being assured that he would be allowed to honor his engagements in Western Europe, Lhevinne accepted Safonoff's offer.

Four years (and two cities) after beginning their married life in Moscow, the Lhevinnes returned to their hometown. They were accompanied by Rosina's father, who was to live with them during his twenty-odd years as a widower.

5

Alma Mater
and the New World

LHEVINNE RETURNED to Moscow in full possession of the two things he had left it for the lack of: a Western reputation sufficient to win him Moscow's respect, and an income sufficient to support himself and his wife. This allowed him to take a large apartment in a "tall" five-story building. "It had a beautiful dining room and a beautiful music room, and Josef and my father—he had exquisite taste in such matters—bought very luxurious furnishings for it. We had our bedroom and my father had his, and there was one extra room."

Even so, the Lhevinnes' "homecoming" was not particularly pleasant. First, there were many associations that painfully reminded them of Rosina's mother. In addition, they were running their own household for the first time and found certain social customs not to their liking. "We hired an excellent cook and a private maid for me, whose name was Masha. We paid them the standard wages (about five rubles a month) and soon learned first-hand what idiotic rules there were for the treatment of servants. First of all, the servant had to bring his own feather bed. Even today I shiver when I think of all the microbes and filth in those feather beds that were dragged about from one place to another. Another rule was that the servant could not drink the tea of the master. The servant had to buy his own tea.

"Further, we found that people in our building followed a very strict code in the feeding of the servants. Every night for dinner the servants were given *schi*, the soup made from cabbage. With it every night, they had either buckwheat or fried potatoes. On Sundays, as a special treat, they were given meatballs in their *schi*.

" 'Certainly,' I said to the cook and Masha, 'you will eat what we eat.' So one day I received a letter signed by all the women living in the building. It requested that I come that day to a very important meeting. When I got there, they all began to shout at me: 'What are you doing? We have a small revolution here! All *our* servants know that you give *your* servants the same food that you eat. *Nobody* does that! *Nobody!*'

" 'It is very easy for you to remedy the situation,' was my reply. 'If you just give your servants the same food that you eat, there will be no discontent.'

"Needless to say, they continued in their ways. And these people were not the wealthy ones. Like us, most of them probably earned about 350 rubles—or 180 dollars—a month. Their narrow views, and the views of people like them, played their own small part in creating the mood for real revolution."

The Lhevinnes were never political crusaders, but they generally did what they could to improve the conditions of those less advantaged than they—including the hired help. This, it seems, set them apart from most of the people in their apartment building, as did the fact that they were converted Jews, and thus regarded with reserve by both their Jewish neighbors and their Russian Orthodox ones. Only at the Conservatory did they truly feel at home.

"Josef was twenty-seven and I was twenty-two when he took the position there. In Russia, it was the custom for all the professors to have seats together in the best locality of the hall, and when we entered the new hall and saw that row of comfortable red plush armchairs, it made an unforgettable impression on us. Josef, as full professor of piano, had his own personal chair. And I, as his wife, had the one next to him. I must admit that we were very proud of them. It was not so many years before that we had been trembling students giving recitals at the Conservatory, and now it was a big change to be on the other side."

The hall which housed the Lhevinnes' impressive chairs was not the one in which they had given their student recitals, for, a year before inviting Lhevinne to join the faculty, Safonoff had installed the Conservatory in a massive new building (still in use today). During the 1902–03 academic year, Lhevinne had nineteen students, eighteen of whom were beginning their first year in the upper school. In a small black book he recorded their names and the compositions they studied. The works he assigned are interesting primarily for their similarity to works assigned today. Each of his students had to learn two or three Bach preludes and fugues and one or two Beethoven sonatas. Nearly all of them also studied works by Scarlatti, Mozart, Mendelssohn, Chopin, and Schumann. The only name conspicuous by its absence is that of Haydn. Otherwise, the compositions he assigned from the Baroque, Classical, and Romantic periods would seem quite familiar to today's teacher.

Of his nineteen pupils, one had studied with him before. "Soon after we had arrived in Moscow, one of Josef's students from Tiflis wrote that she would like to come to Moscow for further study. She asked if we would help to find a room large enough for her and her sister. We liked them both very much, and Josef suggested that we put them in our extra room. 'I will be at the Conservatory all day,' he said, 'and this will give you a companion.' As I never liked solitude—it was always like punishment for me to be alone—I was easily convinced. So we wrote her a very nice letter and said that we would be delighted to have them in our apartment. They came, and Marusha enrolled in Josef's class at the Conservatory. They became just like members of the family."

Most likely, Lhevinne's suggestion that they invite Marusha and her sister to live with them was an attempt to keep Rosina occupied so she would not dwell obsessively on the loss of her mother. He may also have talked Rosina into accepting a concert engagement that winter for the same reason. On December 5/18, 1902, Rosina Lhevinne played Henselt's F minor Concerto with Arthur Nikisch and the Moscow Conservatory Orchestra. Nikisch was the Lhevinnes' favorite conductor, and Rosina's appearance with him v·as her first solo performance since her marriage. By insisting that his wife suspend her scruples about playing alone in order to perform with Nikisch, Lhevinne was encouraging the best possible therapy that Rosina could have had.

Nikisch, a handsome, bearded Hungarian, was then forty-seven years old. Thirteen years earlier he had gone to America to conduct the Boston Symphony Orchestra. After that he had become conductor of the Leipzig Gewandhaus. A frequent visitor to Moscow, by the turn of the century he had become not only the Lhevinnes' favorite conductor but the favorite of most of their Russian contemporaries. Rachmaninoff admired Nikisch greatly, and Scriabin —who did not—chose him to conduct the world premiere of his *Divine Poem.* Another Nikisch admirer was Serge Koussevitzky, who in 1902 was a double-bass player at the Bolshoi Theater. A few years earlier, Koussevitzky had been an impoverished young musician who came to some of the parties the Lhevinnes and Mindowskys gave. A few years later, he would be the wealthy husband of Natalya Ushkov, daughter of Moscow's most affluent tea merchant. Koussevitzky was to make use of his wealth by following Nikisch to Berlin, where, for four years, he taught himself the rudiments of conducting by studying Nikisch's public performances.

The Lhevinnes' high opinion of Nikisch had increased during their year in Berlin, where they were able to compare him with most of the world's best conductors. Just how or why Rosina was chosen to play with him during their first year in Moscow, we do not know. She only remembers that Safonoff was partially responsible for the arrangements and that he had told her she must play Henselt's F minor Concerto (the third movement of which she had played during her last year at the Conservatory).

Strangely, the concert was hardly advertised and was billed only as a "Nikisch Concert." The soloist, the program, and the orchestra were not listed in the announcements. Even so, the Great Hall of the Conservatory (where the Lhevinnes' red plush armchairs were) was sold out. Rosina Lhevinne's performance of the Henselt was "successful," according to the *Russkie Vedomosti*.[1] But she did not enjoy playing it. The concerto is not only demanding but freakish technically, and it is a wonder she could train her small hands to play all the notes. She may have been one of the last pianists to play the work before the recent Romantic revival, for it disappeared from the active repertoire "around the turn of the century."[2] Even Anton Rubinstein, who could take on any concerto, had thought the Henselt "ungrateful," and Mme. Lhevinne has always regretted that she was not allowed to play a more interesting work during her one appearance with Nikisch.

Josef Lhevinne did not play an important concert in Moscow until March of that season, when he performed Saint-Saëns's Third Concerto with Safonoff and the I.R.M.S. Orchestra. He had spent the fall and early winter preparing for his Western European concerts, which were scheduled for January and February. Lhevinne's Vienna debut was on January 12, 1903. Safonoff conducted for his former student in Vienna, as he too was developing a Western reputation. Then fifty years old, Safonoff was at the peak of his conducting powers and was taking to Western and Central Europe a good deal of Russian music that had never been heard there. (Diaghilev did not give his famous series of all-Russian concerts in Paris until 1907.) Three days before Lhevinne's debut, Safonoff conducted a concert that included Tchaikovsky's Sixth Symphony, music by Ippolitov-Ivanov, and Rachmaninoff's Second Piano Concerto, with Rachmaninoff at the keyboard. The Viennese enjoyed the *Pathétique* Symphony, but found the Russian "novelties" that

Arthur Nikisch, 1902. Inscribed to "Mme.
Lhévinne."

César Cui, 1905. Inscribed to "R. B.
Lhevinne."

New York, 1906. A note on the back of this photograph reveals that a certain Mr. S. remarked to Josef, "I don't envy you so much how you play the piano but I envy you for your wife."

Early American publicity picture. Photo by George Maillard Kesslere.

followed too tiring. The Russian novelty that Lhevinne played three days later caught them off guard.

Lhevinne's first appearance in Vienna was like his wife's with Nikisch in Moscow in that the pianist's name was not mentioned in the advertisements. It was billed as the "Kubelik Concert" because of the great popularity of Jan Kubelik, the violinist who played on the same program. Few of the people who filled the Grossen Musikverein-Salle on January 12 had come to hear a pianist, and none of them, we may assume, had come to hear Anton Rubinstein's Fifth Piano Concerto. When Lhevinne walked on stage to join Safonoff and the Concertverein Orchestra, there was absolute silence. The audience met the "unknown commodity without applause" was the way a critic from Odessa put it. "But after his first few chords the public perked up and was taken in by his powerfully sonorous—and at the same time tender—tone. By the end of the concerto's first movement, he had become the favorite of the public, and [afterwards] was made to give several encores."[3]

To judge from the rest of the Odessa man's review, Lhevinne had taken the whole town by storm. Lhevinne, the man wrote, was a Russian national hero. Just as Russia's great novelists had taken her literature to the Western world, so had Lhevinne taken her music. Certainly the people in the hall had been impressed with Lhevinne's performance. But the average citizen of Vienna remained quite oblivious of the fact that his town had been so overwhelmed. The *Neue Freie Press,* having heard Kubelik before, did not even review the concert.

When Lhevinne returned to Vienna a month later to play Liszt's E-flat Concerto, the press and the city's music lovers were out in full force, and he was well received. But the most interesting stop on his winter tour was, not Vienna or the German cities he visited, but Paris, where he played in Salle Erard on January 27. Rosina went with him to Paris and again joined him in a two-piano work (this time the Scherzo from Anton Rubinstein's Fantasia, Op. 74). But it was Lhevinne's solo playing that stole the show. "I doubt if even Chopin himself ever interpreted the *études* and the poetic Ballade in F minor with such finesse and soft melancholy," wrote the critic of *Le Siècle.* "Lhevinne is a perfect pianist," he continued, "and more than that, he is a perfect musician. So rare is this combination that he can feel assured that the Parisian public will always be ready to welcome and to applaud his wonderful art."

During their stay in Paris, the Lhevinnes saw the composer

Maurice Moszkowski, who inscribed a photograph "À l'excellente artiste Mme Rosina Lhevinne." That photograph was added to her "Frau Levin" from Josef Hofmann and her "für Madame Lhevinne" from Arthur Nikisch (inscribed one week after the concert in Moscow). A few months after the Lhevinnes returned from Paris, *he* received a large likeness of Anton Rubinstein from his first class at the Moscow Conservatory. The Lhevinnes never parted with this meaningful gift, which has been hanging in their various studios ever since.

When the academic year was over, Lhevinne completed a busy season by making his London debut. On June 25 he "warmed up" at an informal musicale attended by King Edward VII and Queen Alexandra; on the next day he gave his first full recital. The audience was small, but the *Times* wrote that it was "most favorably impressed with the player's many admirable qualities. His touch is always beautiful, and in his execution of rapid passages a rare strength of finger is displayed, the quickest notes being often as full of tone as if they were solid chords." Unfortunately for Lhevinne, the *Times* could not write about much more than his amazing finger technique. He had played an unaccountably unbalanced program, consisting of works by Bach–d'Albert, Weber, Henselt, Anton Rubinstein, Schloezer, Cui, Borodin, and Strauss-Schulz-Evler.

Warsaw, Paris, Berlin, Vienna, and now London: Lhevinne had finally made a name for himself in the major European capitals. The hard work of the last two years was clearly beginning to pay off, and the easy living of the two years spent in Tiflis was becoming more and more a thing of the past. "I had begun to make my way again," Lhevinne recalled three years later, "until I was riding a bicycle one day in London and had a bad fall that broke my leg."[4] The accident occurred the day after his London debut. Once more his concert career had come to an unexpected halt.

Maria Alexieff (who liked to be called Masha) was born in 1874—the year of Lhevinne's birth. Young Josef had shown his precocity by performing with Anton Rubinstein at age fifteen; Masha showed hers by marrying at that age. Every day for six months, Masha went home so her mother could comb her hair. Then her husband died, making her a sixteen-year-old widow. After consulting a Russian Orthodox priest, Masha decided never to marry again. She devoted the rest of her life to religion and, from 1902, to the Lhevinnes.

"Masha came to us a beautiful girl of twenty-eight, with blue eyes and blonde hair and the most kind face. She told us that all the education she had had was a few months with a priest, who slapped the hands of anyone in the class who made a mistake. But the best-educated person could not have had the common sense that she had. If you asked her for advice, she never hesitated, and immediately came out with the right answer. Officially, she was my maid, but Josef did not have time to worry about domestic affairs, and I was not prepared to make decisions because my parents had given me no responsibility in that way. So I asked Masha's opinions very often. She was outspoken, but was always very just. Even in those early years, she gave us the feeling of being a saint."

At that point in life, Masha's spiritual stature greatly exceeded her physical. Never a tall woman, she was then thin as well, and "on Sundays, the only day Masha went out much, she always put a towel underneath, so she would look bigger." The Lhevinnes went out on Saturdays.

"Because there were no bathtubs then, we went with other pairs of young friends to the open bath institutions on Saturday afternoons. The women went to one side and the men to the other, and we sat on some benches while women almost naked washed us. Some of us had Turkish baths. Then we dressed and made up, and usually wore nice clothes, and if there was not some concert or play that night, we stayed right in the beautiful dining room of the bath house and had supper. That was always a must on Saturdays."

"If there was a play that night," it was most likely at the Moscow Art Theater, for the Lhevinnes had come to prefer its productions to those of the Maly Theater. Mme. Lhevinne remembers Stanislavsky as "not young, tall, with a lot of hair, and very handsome." His theater was "a real revelation. Before him, the plays were very traditional and quite stiff." Now that Lhevinne had a teaching position and a decent income from concerts, he and Rosina could afford a subscription.

"We saw six or eight plays a year, and always had the same neighbors. Gradually, we began to talk with them. Many times after the performance we all went somewhere for a glass of beer or a cup of coffee. The debates were so hot you would think we were quarreling for the last penny. Many of the plays were so problematic—especially those of Ibsen, Tolstoy, and Chekhov—that everyone had a different opinion. We could hardly wait to see the papers in the morning to know who was 'right'."

The play that made the strongest impression on Mme. Lhevinne was Chekhov's *The Cherry Orchard*, which had its premiere in

1904. Her brief impressions of a performance given six decades previously suggest both the "ensemble" and "feeling" qualities for which Stanislavsky's "style" became famous:

"They were in the country and having guests, and it was a sign of being common if the hands were not absolutely swan-white; so the servant girls before the guests arrived were shaking their hands over their heads so that the blood would run down and they would not appear so common.

"Then at the end, the family decides to leave and they have the coach there, everything ready to go, and they lock the door and you see the carriage go away, and then you notice that they forgot the old man, the poor old man who sits there alone, and whom I will never forget."

It is significant that Mme. Lhevinne remembers these particular fragments from *The Cherry Orchard*. Always concerned with the unwritten codes by which society operates, she has often performed the equivalent of "shaking the hands to make them appear white" herself. And while she has always been extremely demanding of the people working for her (perhaps because her mother had been so unnaturally attentive during her childhood), she has always inspired remarkable loyalty. Masha, who joined the Lhevinnes in 1902, was to stay with the family until her death sixty-two years later. Sarah Crump, who was to join the family in 1921, lived and served until 1972.

If Rosina Lhevinne's favorite play was *The Cherry Orchard*, her husband's was Gorky's *The Lower Depths*, which had its premiere at the Moscow Art Theater on the night Lhevinne was making his Vienna debut. Such a preference is no surprise in view of the teeming, scrambling nature of Lhevinne's childhood home and in view of his life-long interest in people of all social levels. He had been able to develop that interest most strongly during the two years he and Rosina had lived in the multilayered society of Tiflis, which happened to be the town in which Gorky had begun his writing career in 1892.

During the fall of 1903, as Lhevinne was recovering from his broken leg, his class at the Conservatory grew from nineteen to twenty-three students. During the same time, Rosina, who was then twenty-three years old, took her first teaching job. She taught at one of Moscow's finishing schools for the daughters of noble families, but her students refused to take their lessons seriously, and her patience ran out before the school year did. During the next season, she began to build up a class of private students at home. Her only significant memory from the experience at the finishing school was that Rachmaninoff, who was general inspector, came by each month to see what progress was being made.

For Rachmaninoff, the token job of inspector was not so vital as it once had been. With the success of his Second Piano Concerto and with his marriage in April 1902, his life had reached a new stage of equilibrium. Just the opposite was true of Scriabin. He had grown impatient with teaching and had resigned his position at the Conservatory about the time Lhevinne accepted his. He taught only a few students the next year, after which he left Moscow for a period of ferment that was creative artistically, but trying personally. Not long after leaving Moscow, Scriabin left his wife and family in order to live with Tatyana Schloezer, who was a niece of Boris de Schloezer, one of Lhevinne's colleagues on the piano faculty of the Moscow Conservatory. As for Leonid Maximov, the fourth gold-medalist of 1892, he died in 1904, at the age of thirty-one.

By late January 1904, Lhevinne's leg was sufficiently sound for him to accompany a child prodigy—eleven-year-old violinist Franz von Vecsey—in a Moscow recital, but he was not able to go on tour until March. In Berlin, Lhevinne's recital fell during a week in which Risler, d'Albert, Schnabel, and Carl Friedberg also played; in the Russian provinces, his playing fell upon a musical wasteland. In Kazan, his performance of Brahms's F minor Sonata, Op. 5, was the local premiere of that work, and his listeners found it too "diffuse in form and too difficult to understand." Even so, Lhevinne seemed to enjoy his playing that night, and he achieved one of the goals for which he always strove: "such art in playing legato that in places it seemed as if you were hearing the sound not of a piano but of a stringed instrument."[5]

A week later in Yalta, where Anton Chekhov was living, Lhevinne gave the local premiere of Chopin's F-sharp minor Polonaise. Hofmann and Gabrilowitsch had played the "massive" Polonaise in A-flat major there, according to the *Crimean Courier*, but Lhevinne was the first to bring the "more psychological one" in F-sharp minor "to our forgotten Yalta." His recital, heavily slanted toward the Romantics, was appreciated, but the provincial critics continued to prick him. A sixteen-paragraph review concluded with a request that he bring some Beethoven next time.

While Lhevinne was away on tour, Rosina experienced one of the greatest shocks of her life:

"One night I was home alone. It was dark in my bedroom, and somebody knocked on the door.

" 'Who is it?'

" 'Marusha.'

" 'Of course. Come in.'

"So she came in and she kneeled before the bed and she had hysterics. She kissed my hands and she kissed them again. 'Do you remember anything about a letter written to you in Tiflis?' she asked.

" 'Yes! Yes!' I cried. 'What do *you* know about it?'

" 'I was the one who wrote it. I loved you so much and I loved Mr. Lhevinne so much and I had no respect for Count Toumanov and I did not want him to achieve what I thought was his design of getting you to live with him.'

"At first I could not believe my ears. For some reason we had always thought that a man had written that terrible letter. To learn that it was not only a girl, but this girl whom we both loved and who lived in our house, was a dreadful blow to my nervous system.

"After a few minutes, however, I began to feel relieved that the mystery was over. As soon as I realized that she had done it out of devotion to him, I forgave her. Marusha was two or three years younger than I, so when she had written the letter she was about sixteen. It was understandable that at that age she might think a handsome man was my lover after seeing me go for some rides with him. Because of the 'romantic' feelings in Russia and because of the literature she had read, she simply thought that writing that nasty letter was the way to defend the man whom she adored.

"It was very noble of her to admit what she had done, and finally I convinced her that she had taken a great burden from my heart. She was afraid that we would never want to see her again, but we kept her with us and maintained the same relationship. We continued to go shopping together, and when Josef was gone, she went with me to concerts and the theater. She remained a wonderful companion in spite of what had happened."

Rosina Lhevinne has a certain magnanimity, and that was one reason she was able to forgive Marusha so speedily. But she also had a need for Marusha's companionship. Throughout her adult life, she has managed to surround herself with people younger than she, people grasping for the cultural awareness she might help provide. Because Marusha fit that requirement so nicely, her startling revelation was smoothly assimilated into Mme. Lhevinne's everyday life.

Aside from the cracking of the poison-pen mystery, the mending of Lhevinne's leg, and the cutting short of Rosina's first teaching venture, the Lhevinnes' second year in Moscow had been rather routine. During the summer, they decided to return to Pushkino, where they had spent their honeymoon five years earlier. With the Toumanov episode finally settled, Rosina had a strange encounter with one Sascha Alexandrovich. He had been a regular at Mrs. Bessie's "little parties," and with Toumanov and Mindowsky, it seems, had formed a troika of young men who had shown an interest in Rosina before she was married.

"It is like one in a million that in my whole life I was never in love with anyone but Josef for a single day. From the age of nine, it was as if the whole world was populated by many creatures but only one of them was a man. The rest could have been mules or something.

"Sascha Alexandrovich (in Russia when somebody was born illegitimate he was given the patronymic of the Czar) was one of the students who had come to Mother's little parties. He had asked me out a few times before I married, and I think I may have gone with him once or twice. His way of thinking was very close to mine, and I enjoyed being with him, but I did not take it very seriously because I knew in my mind that for me Josef was the only man.

"When Josef and I married, Sascha remained one of our friends, and one night during the summer that we returned to Pushkino, he came to have dinner with us. Josef had played a concert that afternoon and had one the next day, so he went to bed early. He slept upstairs.

"There was a drama that night in a small town about an hour and a half away by train, and Josef and I had wanted to see it very much, so Josef told me to go, but not to wake him up when I came back. Sascha left after dinner and I went with somebody else. We had an enclosed porch surrounded by little trees and it was a very warm day, so Josef and I had decided that I could sleep on the porch when I got home. I got back about two o'clock and went to bed. Then suddenly I saw somebody creeping there in the trees, and I thought it was a burglar. But when he came closer I saw it was Sascha, and I asked, 'Sascha, what is the matter?'

"He came to the bed and he kneeled and he said that it was six or seven years since he had come to our parties and that he had met many, many girls, but that he knew it was only I who could make him happy. Then he said, 'I know you are not happy either. You and Josef are wonderful together, but you are so different in your thinking. Your approach to the important questions in life is obviously the opposite. The easiest time to separate is now and you can stay best friends, and I will marry you. You and I have so many things in common that we look on things with two eyes instead of four. Don't be offended, but I want to know why you do such a wrong thing for him and such a wrong thing for you by staying together.'

"I was furious. 'Who are you to judge?' I said. 'Go away!' So Sascha went creeping away through those little trees.

"At the time, I thought that Sascha had said those things only because he was infatuated. But when I recollect it now, I realize that he had been observing Josef and me very carefully, and that what he said was really true. He was very fond of us both, and he had looked at all sides of our life and into the future, and he had said to me, 'No matter how much you love him and are devoted to him, I assure you that you cannot be happy and neither can he, because you are so different.' Once later in life, I told Josef what Sascha had said, and he said, 'You know, maybe he was right.' That hurt me very much, and it was not until much later that I realized there was some truth in it."

During the fall of 1904, Josef Lhevinne began his third year as a professor of piano at the Moscow Conservatory. In November, two weeks before his thirtieth birthday, he gave a recital in Moscow that has seldom been duplicated: every work was by Anton Rubinstein. The purpose of the recital was to commemorate the tenth anniversary of Rubinstein's death, and Lhevinne's tribute was well received. But in St. Petersburg, less than two months later, an event occurred which gave the subjects of the Czar more recent deaths to think about. On January 9/22, 1905, dozens of workers were shot to death by government troops as they marched to present a petition at the Imperial Palace. "Bloody Sunday" marked the beginning of the Revolution of 1905, and before the year was out its repercussions had shaken the lives of Russians throughout the Empire—musicians included.

Several students from the St. Petersburg Conservatory had witnessed the shootings and were quick to express their outrage. When the Conservatory directors suspended one of the students for "voicing political opinions," Rimsky-Korsakov protested. He was summarily dismissed from the Conservatory staff. In sympathy with him, many professors resigned. The Conservatory was closed for the spring term, and the dissident professors taught at home for the balance of the school year.

In Moscow, the Imperial Conservatory remained open during the spring of 1905, but many students abandoned their studies. According to Lhevinne's black book, he began the year with thirty students and finished it with twenty-three. Among those who remained were eighteen who had entered his class in 1902, for they were scheduled to be graduated in the spring of 1906. But the 1905–06 academic year never really got under way for Lhevinne. One reason was the general strike that paralyzed Moscow during the late fall and early winter, disrupting the normal operations of the Conservatory. The other was connected, oddly enough, with Russia's humiliating defeat at the hands of the Japanese.

The Russo-Japanese War had been settled at the Portsmouth Peace Conference during the summer of 1905. Following the deliberations in New Hampshire, certain members of the Russian Embassy in Washington had decided to sponsor a tour of the United States by the Russian Symphony Orchestra in order to give a boost to their country's image. The Russian Symphony—which was mainly composed of Jewish immigrants from Russia—had been established in New York in 1903 by Modest Altschuler, Lhevinne's cellist friend from the Conservatory and former chamber-music colleague. Its tour was to begin in January 1906, and Safonoff, who was already scheduled to be in America during December and January as guest conductor of the New York Philharmonic, was named conductor for the tour. Josef Lhevinne was invited to be the piano soloist, and a manager, John Warren, was chosen to make the necessary arrangements. Safonoff, as director of the Moscow Conservatory, was able to promise Lhevinne a leave of absence from his teaching responsibilities.

Lhevinne was overjoyed at the prospect of an American tour, for both financial and artistic reasons. All Russian pianists knew about Anton Rubinstein's tour of America in 1872, in which Rubinstein had played hundreds of engagements and made mountains of dollars. Tchaikovsky's B-flat minor Piano Concerto, which Lhevinne admired so much, had received its world premiere in America in 1875 and was still more popular there than anywhere else in the world. Josef Hofmann had told the Lhevinnes about his tour of America in 1888 as an eleven-year-old prodigy, and of how a businessman there had given his family thousands of dollars so he could stop playing concerts and begin the business of becoming a serious musician. Many Europeans had heard that audiences in America were hopelessly uncultivated, but Safonoff, who would be returning to New York for the third time as one of the Philharmonic's guest conductors, assured the Lhevinnes that that city's concertgoers were as responsive as those anywhere. Finally, many of the pianists Lhevinne admired most—Busoni, Hofmann, Godowsky, Gabrilowitsch—had already played in America. If Lhevinne really wanted to validate his membership in "the family of pianistic giants," he could do it by giving a successful New York debut.

Rosina, always eager for her husband to test his art against the world's best audiences and pianists, was totally in favor of his trip to the far-away country. And not just for professional reasons. She knew that Josef loved to travel, and she knew that he shared her simple idealism about the United States. "From our earliest childhood in Russia, we had both heard only the most wonderful things about America. I still remember reading in my primer about the great freedom there, the liberty, and the lack of poverty. In later youth, I read the novels of Cooper and Mark Twain, and Josef never forgot the adventurous frontier novels of Captain Mayne Reid.[6] The ideals of liberty and equality, along with an intense love of nature, were an essential part of Josef's being, and he was eager to see the country which embodied them."

During the months of September and October, plans for the trip were going well enough despite rising political tensions in Moscow. One day in October the Lhevinnes joined a group of friends for an evening at the Moscow Arts Club. While they were there, an actor burst into the room with news that Czar Nicholas II had granted a new constitution. The room was the scene of wild rejoicing, and the Lhevinnes, like many there, hoped that a new day of political freedom was about to dawn in Russia. But disillusionment came soon. The constitution was modified and the hopes extinguished. Following a protracted general strike, fighting broke out between soldiers and revolutionaries on the December day on which Lhevinne's leave of absence was to have begun.

For the next week, because of the intense fighting on the streets outside, the Lhevinnes were virtual prisoners in their own home. Eager to prepare for the coming tour, Josef tried to practice whenever the sounds subsided—until informed by the authorities that his piano was disturbing the public peace! He did not know how long the fighting would last or whether he would be able to leave for America in time for his tour. The physical ordeal of sitting out the siege was compounded by the uncertainty of what its political results would be. We do not really know to what degree Lhevinne sympathized with the revolutionaries. He had little love for the Czarist government, but probably did not advocate that it be overthrown by bloodshed and physical violence. In a detailed account of the fighting that he later gave to the *New York Times,* he showed a great fascination with the way the revolutionaries operated, but took pains to disassociate himself from their activities.[7]

As Lhevinne was waiting for the fighting to end, he and Rosina discovered that she was two months pregnant. Even so, they remained determined that he should try to leave for America as soon as the streets and railways were reasonably safe.

"It was seven years after our marriage, and now we knew that we were to have our first child. I had always told Josef, 'The day that God chooses to bless us with children, they will be first and not you.' And he had always responded by saying that he wanted a few more years in the spotlight. But now that we knew we were to have a baby, we were terribly excited, even though Josef would soon be leaving on a dangerous journey.

"When he left for the station, I was unable to accompany him. For several weeks, I knew nothing of his fate. Finally, a letter came from America. Imagine my shock when I read the first line: 'When you read this letter I will be in the middle of the ocean on the way home.' Because of poor management, his tour had been canceled. There was nothing he could do but return.

"A short time later, I was shocked again, this time by a cablegram that said: 'I have a contract with four zeros in it!' A debut had been arranged at the last minute, he had received a huge contract for the next season, and they wanted to keep him for another two months.

"The four zeros did not impress me at all, for I was never greatly concerned about money; but about Josef's success I was ecstatic. Even today I cannot believe the answer I sent in response to this wonderful news. In condensed form, it went something like this: 'I'm so happy—It's so wonderful—But what about me? Will you really be gone for ten weeks more?' "

Lhevinne, who loved to read adventure stories, had one of his own to tell soon after leaving Moscow. Two days after arriving in New York, he gave the *New York Times* an account of the departure from his hometown. As he knew little English at the time, the *Times* must have used a translator:

At last, on the evening of December 29, I was able to leave the house. I had heard that the trains were running and the revolutionists had been driven from the streets, and had telephoned for a sleigh to take me to the station. None of the drivers was anxious to serve me, but when I promised $125 [did the translator mix his rubles and kopeks here?] to the one who should make the drive I got a driver.

It was pitch dark when we started. It would have been too dangerous to start in the daytime. All the lampposts had been taken up by the revolutionists for barricades. Entanglements which the troops had not had time to remove, and often bodies, were lying about, and it was hard work to make the horses pass them.

Four times on the way to the station we were halted by the military parade. I know some of them had been tempted to take no chances against bomb throwers and to shoot us before investigating.

We were carefully searched by the soldiers, all our papers scrutinized, and what luggage I had taken with me was pulled apart and gone over piece by piece, in search of arms or incriminating matter. It was by merest chance that I escaped being taken to prison.

When we arrived at the station we found great confusion. I had intended to take the seven o'clock train, but in spite of my delays I found myself in plenty of time to catch the train scheduled to leave at four o'clock.

Finally we did get away, and went very slowly. At Tver [a city between Moscow and St. Petersburg], however, we came to a stop. It was hard to learn what had happened, but firing on ahead at times showed that fighting was going on. I learned that the revolutionists had torn up the railroad line and that the troops had not had time to repair it. I was told it would be best to remain under the protection of the military, but decided that as I had risked everything in Moscow and come through I would take the further risk and go on.

After much difficulty, I found one of the mail sleighs which go between the villages. It was to carry the mail to the next station. I paid double rates and was taken. We drove out and made a wide detour, now and again stopping when we heard firing or other suspicious sounds. We met no revolutionists, and the troops were satisfied with the credentials of the mail driver. In a few hours we came to the next wayside station and learned that the line from there was open and that I could go through.

It was not all without difficulty after that, of course, but I finally got to Berlin and was able to cable my American friends that I was on the way.[8]

Lhevinne's cablegram from Berlin arrived in New York on January 3. Warren and Safonoff had been awaiting word from him since December 20 and were fearing not only for the fate of the concert tour but for Lhevinne's life. They had sent telegrams to Berlin, Vienna, Hamburg, and Moscow, but had learned nothing of his whereabouts. On New Year's Day, 1906, this headline had appeared on the front page of the *New York Times:* "Moscow Pianist Missing." When Lhevinne's cablegram finally arrived, Warren made the final arrangements for the tour. Lhevinne, Safonoff, and the Russian Symphony Orchestra were to open in Boston on January 27 and then proceed to give twenty concerts in ten major cities.

On the day that Lhevinne's cablegram was received, the newspapers reported the arrival of a young Polish pianist—the nineteen-year-old Artur Rubinstein. His was a typically bizarre New York reception. First, there were all the people at the pier who thought he would be Anton Rubinstein (dead eleven years, and no relation). Then there were the famous New York reporters, who asked his opinion of America before he had stepped off the boat. The *Herald* informed its readers that Artur Rubinstein "has quantities of hair, but not so much as Mr. Paderewski, his fellow countryman, or even Mr. Kubelik." The *Times* ran a long article describing how the young virtuoso had been painfully initiated into the game of poker en route.

By contrast, Lhevinne's reception was like a bad joke. On Sunday, January 14, the French steamer *La Savoie* passed through the narrows and entered the harbor of New York. As soon as Lhevinne stepped off the boat, he was met with the news that his tour had collapsed for lack of funds. As he had never asked Warren for an official contract, he had no legal grounds upon which to collect for damages; nor did it seem likely that any public appearances could be arranged before he sailed back to Russia. Reporters sought him out, but they were interested in the political conditions he had left behind in Moscow. No one seemed overly concerned about the possibility that he might have to return there without having had a chance to perform. To add to his distress, his raw nerves—still worn from their ordeal in Moscow—were assaulted by the jarring sounds of New York City. Several reporters were surprised to see the husky but bewildered young Russian jump or become startled in response to sounds they took for granted.

Fortunately, Altschuler and Safonoff were able to salvage Lhevinne's trip. Altschuler wisely suggested he make the rounds of the major piano houses, in hopes of receiving a contract. He did, and each house fairly raved about his playing. But each told him, in effect, that before making an offer it must have an opinion from Krehbiel, Aldrich, Henderson, and Finck (not a law firm, but the four most formidable New York critics). For that, of course, a debut was needed. Altschuler obliged, inviting Lhevinne to perform at the next concert given by his orchestra. He could offer no fee and could not afford to advertise, but there was nothing to lose. Lhevinne decided to play Anton Rubinstein's Fifth Concerto—with which he had startled the unsuspecting Viennese. Safonoff, whose duties with the New York Philharmonic ended January 20, agreed to conduct the Rubinstein—as he had in Vienna.

The concert was cheduled for January 27, 1906, which happened to be the 150th anniversary of Mozart's birth. Usually the Russian Symphony Orchestra played only Russian music, but for this special occasion, Altschuler opened the program with Mozart's Symphony in A major. In the effort to pay tribute to Mozart he had on stage a plaster bust of the composer, which, as Henderson quipped the next day in the *Sun*, "stared with a fixed expression of yearning towards the doors leading out to Fifty-Seventh Street."

The duty done to Mozart, Safonoff appeared on the Carnegie Hall stage. He was by then well known in New York, and received considerable applause. When Lhevinne walked on stage, New Yorkers saw "a somewhat sturdily-built man with a stock of brown hair and a pale, serious face." It was then the custom for a pianist to do a little posturing or posing before sitting down to play, but Lhevinne would have none of that. He "came out from the side door, made his way quietly to the piano, and after he had bowed to the audience took his seat without any fuss or circumstance whatever."[9] When he began to play, the audience was stunned— but not into submission. Many years later, a fireman who had worked at Carnegie Hall that night told Mme. Lhevinne of a phenomenon he had never witnessed before or since: as soon as Lhevinne began to play the concerto, many people got up from their seats and moved toward the stage, in order to see whether one man with two hands was really producing the driving, penetrating piano sounds that were filling the hall.

By the end of the concerto, a mass of admirers had pushed to the very foot of the stage, where they wildly recalled Lhevinne again and again. Finally, he returned to the piano. First he played Chopin's Octave *Étude*; then Scriabin's Nocturne for the Left Hand. The encores increased the swarm surrounding the stage, and many more recalls were necessary before Lhevinne's fans would return to their seats. With difficulty, the hall was restored to order for the rest of the program.

Early the next morning, Lhevinne was called to the offices of Steinway and Sons. There he was offered $10,000 plus expenses for making an extended tour during the 1906–07 season. To the young professor then earning 350 rubles a month at the Moscow Conservatory, the offer seemed unbelievable. During its distinguished history in America, Steinway and Sons had undertaken the exclusive personal management of only two pianists. The first, in 1872, was Anton Rubinstein. The second, in 1891, was Paderewski. By signing "the contract with the four zeros in it" on February 2, 1906, Josef Lhevinne had joined very exclusive company. In addition to the extensive tour that would begin in the fall, Steinway and Sons arranged for him to make a short tour in February and March, before returning to Moscow.

Steinway and Sons' enthusiasm was matched by the critics, all of whom marveled at the way the thirty-one-year-old pianist had brought the Rubinstein concerto to life. Henry T. Finck's comment is probably of most interest to the modern reader. He measured Lhevinne against the two Rubinsteins: Anton, whom Lhevinne worshipped above all other musicians; and Artur, whose own Carnegie Hall debut had occurred just three weeks earlier.

> What's in a name? An attempt has been made lately to introduce a new Rubinstein to local audiences; but the real Rubinstein II is Mr. Lhevinne. He has the great Anton's technique, his dash, his bravura, his brilliancy, and a good deal of his leonine power. He can make the piano sing, too, as he showed in the slow movement.[10]

The point, of course, was not to denigrate Artur Rubinstein's abilities, for they were already acknowledged as formidable; the point was, rather, that Lhevinne's American debut invited comparison with only the established and the legendary. Even the man from Odessa (who had overestimated the impact of the Vienna debut) would have been hard put to exaggerate the impression Lhevinne had made.

Once accepted by Steinway and Sons and the New York critics, Lhevinne found all the doors of hospitality thrown open to him. A dinner in his honor at Charles Steinway's home was followed by a series of lavish suppers, parties, and balls such as he had never experienced. On Sunday, March 11, the *New York Times* printed an interview which treated Lhevinne as a full-fledged celebrity. He gave his opinions about composers and composition, spoke of his reverence for Anton Rubinstein, and talked of his hobbies—tennis and fishing (telling how once near Moscow he set a record by fishing nonstop and without food for eighteen hours—no wonder Rosina "never went with him again"). He was even prevailed upon to discuss his way of protecting the cracked skin of a finger: by applying collodion and covering it with a thin layer of cotton.

Shortly before his debut, Lhevinne had split the skin of a finger while practicing. The injury did not seriously affect his playing that night, but many observers had wondered what he was doing between movements of the concerto (i.e., smoothing out a wrinkled layer of cotton with a small pair of scissors). "Split skin" is a minor occupational hazard of most piano virtuosos, and Lhevinne became so adept at treating himself with collodion and cotton that Rosina often pretended one of her fingers was hurt so he would attend to her hands with the same delicacy he showed toward his own. As for more serious occupational hazards, Americans were surprised that Lhevinne, unlike other virtuosos, had not taken the precaution of insuring his hands against major accident or injury. They did not realize that before coming to America he could hardly have afforded the premium.

The momentum of Lhevinne's New York debut carried him through the short tour arranged by Steinway and Sons. In a letter to Safonoff, who had returned to Russia, he described the tour:

> I played twelve more times, including two recitals in New York, two in Chicago, one in Cincinnati, and one appearance in New Haven (Rubinstein Concerto) with the [New York Symphony] Orchestra of [Walter] Damrosch, whose accompaniment, to my regret, in no way resembled yours. But the success was nevertheless grand, as everywhere, everywhere.[11]

Lhevinne's initiation to America had proceeded like a fairy tale. Unknown and in a strange land, he had arrived in New York only to see his substantial prospects vanish. Ten weeks later he departed, the musical sensation of the season.

In accepting the brief tour of five American cities, Lhevinne had knowingly overstayed his limited leave of absence from the Moscow Conservatory. Before returning to Russia, he was forced to resign his teaching position. The resignation did not affect his plans for the 1906–07 academic year, for he would have to be in America in October to begin the long Steinway tour. As for the spring term of 1906, Lhevinne had no way of knowing (when he made his decision) whether the Conservatory would again be in operation. He sailed from New York on April 5.

By the time Lhevinne did return to his troubled city and his pregnant wife, fractious disputes at the Conservatory had resulted in the removal of Safonoff as director. In the aftermath of the strikes and political protests, Safonoff, a staunch defender of the Czar, had wanted to punish dissident students. Taneyev, then a respected professor of theory and counterpoint, threatened to resign. After a bitter controversy, Safonoff was forced to relinquish the position he had filled with distinction for more than fifteen years. The ouster was painful emotionally, but left Safonoff free to sign a three-year contract as permanent conductor of the New York Philharmonic.

Before returning to Moscow, Lhevinne had decided that the entire family would accompany him on the next season's tour. This surprised Rosina, for her husband had never shown such decisiveness in domestic matters: she had always been consulted on

such questions and had often had the last word. In addition, Lhevinne had made plans for the summer without consulting her.
Paris, not Moscow, he decided, was the city in which their child
should be born. Otherwise the baby would have to travel in un-
hygienic Russian trains before boarding a ship to America, which
he knew would upset his microbe-fearing wife. May, when Rosina
would be in the sixth month of pregnancy, would be the ideal
month in which to leave town. The necessary arrangements in
Paris, he decided, could be made by Dr. Jean Goldman, a distant
relative who ran a *maison de santé* there. As for the family's ac-
commodations en route to America, he chose a *cabine de luxe* on
the best French steamer, paid for by Steinway and Sons.

Before the Lhevinnes left Moscow, their friend César Cui, who
was then seventy-one years old, dedicated to them his first compositions for four hands.[12] A year before, he had presented Rosina with
a photograph of himself in full military dress, upon which he had
jotted two bars of music in 2/4 time and penned this tantalizing
inscription: "I remember a supper . . . Be happy: and do not forget
about me." She has forgotten about the supper, but not about Cui,
to whom she remains ever grateful for having helped to launch
her and Josef's two-piano career in 1899.

"As we prepared to go to Paris, we asked Masha if she would
come with us to help with the baby and with our settling in America. 'As much as I love you,' she answered, 'and as much as I know
I would adore the child, I cannot go with you.' She was a strict Russian Orthodox and truly believed that God would not forgive her
if she left her native land. We felt very badly, and we cried and
she cried, and we left.

"Soon after arriving in Paris, we received a short message,
roughly to this effect: 'If you do not change your mind, I hope God
will forgive me, but I am coming to Paris. I cannot live without
you.' Several days later, Josef set the alarm and got up early in the
morning to meet the four o'clock train from Moscow. Masha was
there as expected. By coincidence, the same train brought an old
spinster language teacher from the Moscow Conservatory. That
woman was one of the many who had said eight years earlier
that our marriage would not last because we would compete at
the piano and because Josef was such a flirt. Seeing him meeting a
beautiful blue-eyed blonde at four in the morning in Paris was all
she needed in order to start the stories going again. But Masha
outlived all the rumors."

To await the birth of their child, the Lhevinnes moved into an apartment three doors from Dr. Goldman's *maison de santé* in the Auteuil suburb of Paris. The room was not hygienically equipped for childbirth, and when Rosina began her labor, Lhevinne quickly notified Dr. Goldman, who sent several husky young men marching down the street with a sanitized bed. Rosina gave birth to a son on July 21, 1906. He was named Constantine, in honor of the Grand Duke who had arranged for Josef's admission to the Conservatory. In a letter asking Safonoff to be the boy's godfather, Lhevinne wrote proudly: "I hasten to share our joy with you. A healthy baby boy was born to us whose hands are particularly exquisite, I find." Seven weeks later, under the pressure of the coming tour, he wrote again:

> At present I am practicing strenuously, at times 7–8 hours a day—and frequently to the baby's accompaniment. But this does not create any dissonance. A baby is a great joy in the family. The structure of your godchild's little hands makes us really think that he is destined to be a pianist.[13]

It was natural for the Lhevinnes to give particular attention to their son's "little hands." Genetically speaking, few couples in history have been more likely than they to produce a child of great pianistic gifts.

As Josef prepared for the tour, Rosina had the opportunity and duty of living up to her earlier words that "the children will come first." At first, she lacked knowledge about how to carry out her new responsibilities. In that she was not alone. "Masha was a very serene influence on the children, but at first she was as inexperienced as I was. For two months after the baby was born we had a trained nurse. But after the nurse left, Masha was afraid to bathe him and I was afraid to bathe him and Josef would not even enter the room. By the time we were on the boat, though, Masha and I were having a wonderful time."

As the October departure approached, Lhevinne had good reason to be practicing "7–8 hours a day." During the summer, his scheduled engagements for the coming season had soared from twenty-eight (June) to forty (July) to more than sixty (September). He had never played that many concerts in a single season, and in order to have an adequate repertoire on hand, he had to learn many new works and relearn dozens of old ones. In the letter to Safonoff announcing the birth of his son, he had listed five possible recital programs, consisting of more than fifty individual compositions. When he wrote Safonoff again in September, he was working under the additional strain of an upcoming concert in London and a piano-roll session in Leipzig. Still, the letter closed on a happy note: "Rosina and I send you our cordial greetings, and Cocoschka— his most bewitching smile."

On October 6 Lhevinne was in Leipzig, where he apparently visited the studios of Welte and Sons, the firm that two years earlier had introduced the world's first commercially successful "player" pianos. Lhevinne made several piano rolls for Welte in 1906, including two excellent performances that are now available on LP discs (see Discography): Scriabin's Nocturne for the Left Hand and Czerny's Octave Study, Op. 740, No. 5. His performance of the latter communicates an infectious joy seldom associated with Czerny's studies. Doubtless, most of the recording's buoyancy derives from the uncanny ease with which Lhevinne could negotiate octaves; but perhaps part of the buoyancy can be attributed to the happy state of the pianist's personal and professional fortunes in October 1906.

Three days before sailing for America, he played a demanding concert with the London Symphony Orchestra. Safonoff conducted Beethoven's and Rubinstein's Fifth Piano Concertos; unaccompanied, Lhevinne played four solo works. This was his first appearance in London since breaking his leg there, and his program left the audience wanting more. Americans then paid close attention to English and European reviews, and it was somewhat of a gamble to play such a demanding program just before his first extensive tour of the United States. But the gamble paid off, as the British press praised him highly.

On October 13, 1906, Josef and Rosina Lhevinne, their son, her father, and Masha sailed from Le Havre on *La Savoie*. The date was no accident, for Lhevinne, unlike his wife, took pleasure, during certain expansive moods, in defying superstition.

6

America before the War

WHATEVER QUALMS Mme. Lhevinne may have had about the October thirteenth departure date (and those, to be sure, were not insubstantial) were temporarily put out of mind by the excitement of sailing for America. For her husband, veteran of two Atlantic crossings, the experience was old hat; for the rest of the family it was high adventure. Weather conditions were ideal, and seven days on the open sea were too few for twenty-six-year-old Rosina. Her two-month-old son was soothed by the motion of the ship, and caused her and Masha less trouble than he had on land. As for Lhevinne, he was constantly practicing on an upright piano he had had rigged up in a state room, which left Rosina free to mix with those wonderful creatures who peopled ocean liners before the Great European War. She remembers that she once stopped talking long enough to give a recital for four hands with her husband. They were afterward invited to the captain's table for dinner, where champagne was served. Because she had not yet learned to drink it, she sipped slowly until Josef finished his. Then when no one was looking, they secretly exchanged glasses.

Her first view of Manhattan was dominated not so much by the impressive skyline as by the scores of reporters eager to interview her husband. In January, Lhevinne had arrived in New York to find his tour cancelled; in October, he learned upon arriving that Steinway and Sons had scheduled more than a hundred concerts for him. Herein lay the year's first disappointment. A careful reading of the contract he had signed in February showed that he was guaranteed no more money for playing a hundred concerts than if he played only forty. He had bound himself to Steinway like an indentured servant, promising to play every concert scheduled for him between November 1 and April 1. For playing at least forty concerts, he was guaranteed $10,000; but for the additional sixty concerts now planned, he was guaranteed not a penny more. Lhevinne was never a man of business, and when negotiating had been handicapped by his lack of English. Before signing another contract to come to America, he would get better advice.

The Lhevinnes took an apartment on Fourteenth Street, near Union Square, the Academy of Music, Luchow's, and Steinway and Sons. Therein was their second disappointment. "We had taken the rooms on Fourteenth Street because we were told it was a good part of town. On the first nice day, Masha and I took the baby in a carriage and went out to sit in a park. It was crowded and it was hard to find a bench where we were alone, and after we finally did sit down we saw that all the poor men came there to chew tobacco and spit it on the ground. With my obsessions about microbes and disease, you can imagine the impression that gave me. When several times the tobacco just missed the baby's face, I decided that Fourteenth Street was not for us.

"The next day a man from Steinway came to help me look for a new apartment, because Josef was busy practicing. We got on the tramway, and Masha came too. We rode for a while and then all of a sudden she exclaimed in Russian, 'Mrs. Lhevinne! All these Americans have a contagious disease! Their jaws are walking!' We were both terribly frightened until the man from Steinway explained the custom of chewing gum.

"Finally we found an apartment and began to get accustomed to New York and its ways. The only thing wrong with the apartment was that it had steam heat, which Josef could never get used to. He always loved the fresh air, and all our life he would sneak and open the windows and I would sneak and close them. But at least the neighborhood was better. Before we left Fourteenth Street, someone had stolen my father's coat, which had a big fur collar. Josef had immediately gone out and bought him a new one, in the 'modern' style, and Father seemed very pleased with it. But one day when Josef was gone on tour, and Father and I were walking, he said so gently, 'You know, it's a wonderful coat you bought me, but sometimes I do miss my fur collar.' My God, how I wish we had gotten him a coat like the first one. Certainly it was not a question of money. But he, of course, had been too delicate to suggest it."

The first outsider's glimpse we have of the Lhevinnes in America comes from a reporter for *Musical America* who interviewed them for a story to appear November third. They must have been at Fourteenth Street, for Lhevinne greeted the reporter with the words, "My wife—she look for an apartment—excuse her for a few minutes, yes?" Lhevinne was always extremely courtly and deferential to his wife—and to most women. The next words catch his style.

> . . . Suddenly, quickly crossing the room, he put his hands behind him and his head through the portieres, calling softly, "Madame." There was an exclamation, a laugh, Lhevinne drew back pleased as a schoolboy, and "Madame," a dainty little brunette in a maroon gown and dark furs, entered the room.

The interview that followed was America's introduction to the young woman who fifty years later was to become its "Dean of Piano Teachers." It reveals her rambling garrulity, her high maternal expectations, and her transparent quickness of mind:

> "I look for an apartment, but I cannot find. It is *très-difficile, très-difficile.* I want one near [Central] Park—on account of *le bébé,* you know. We are going to stay in New York this Winter while my husband makes his concert tour. I cannot travel so much with *le bébé,* he is only three months old. I was so afraid to take him across the seas, but he was splendid. He met a little girl, just his own age, and they were such good company."
>
> "Do you think he is going to be a musician?"
>
> "Oh, yes!" And Madame's eyes grew big. "It is astonishing. When he is bad and cries, if my husband or myself goes to the piano he stops—at once. *C'est vraiment étonnant!* And the doctor who has examined the hands of 2,500 babies says the formation of the little one's is absolutely remarkable.
>
> "I am so glad to be in New York this Winter. Last Winter was so dreadful for me. I was in Moscow at the time of the bombardment. After four o'clock one could not go out at all. And I think New York is splendid. It is the prettiest city I have seen—and I have traveled all over."
>
> "Even the skyscrapers?"
>
> "Skyscrapers?" Madame looked blank but on learning what skyscrapers were said:
>
> "Why not? I find these immense twenty-story structures very inspiring."

In the fall of 1906, the New York Philharmonic was beginning its sixty-fifth season. Twice the age of any other American orchestra, it nevertheless faced stiff competition from "upstart" groups in Boston (twenty-five years old) Chicago (fifteen), and Philadelphia (six). The Boston Symphony Orchestra had during its short history attracted some of Europe's leading musicians and conductors, including Austria's William Henschel, Hungary's Arthur Nikisch, and, in 1906, Germany's Karl Muck. The Chicago Symphony, whose founder, Theodore Thomas, had died in 1905, was now in the capable hands of youthful Frederick Stock. Under Fritz Scheel's direction, the young Philadelphia Orchestra was already one of America's best. While these orchestras were growing, the Philharmonic had been floundering. For three years, it had hired four or five visiting conductors a year, looking for the man who could restore the orchestra to its once predominant position in America's symphonic life. In Safonoff, its directors thought they had found the right man, and in the fall of 1906 he was beginning a three-year contract as the orchestra's permanent conductor.

On a Friday afternoon, November 16, the Philharmonic opened its season before a dazzling capacity crowd at Carnegie Hall. Safonoff chose Josef Lhevinne as his piano soloist, and Lhevinne, for his debut with the Philharmonic, chose to play Rubinstein's Fourth Concerto, the one most of his competitors had played in 1895. He and Safonoff received warm, thunderous ovations. But the next day, when the leading critics had had their say, it became known that the concert had been only a qualified success.

Before evaluating Safonoff's musical interpretations, the critics all pointed out that he continued to conduct without a baton. "He still conducts without a stick," Richard Aldrich wrote in the *Times*, "and he still clutches, whirls, stirs, and pokes the atmosphere with his hands in a way that is disturbing to the eye." William Henderson in the *Sun* (who must have had one of his eyes on Aldrich) said, "it is a pity that instead of becoming absorbed in the music some persons were deeply occupied in trying to trace the effect of Mr. Safonoff's aerial graphics on his musicians." H. E. Krehbiel of the *Tribune*, after discussing the pros and cons of the matter, dismissed it by saying that Safonoff would have done no better or worse with "a dozen sticks" in his hands. Heated differences were expressed concerning Safonoff's interpretation of Mozart's *Eine Kleine Nacht-musik*, Henderson calling it "a ruthless onslaught on Mozart's inoffensive little work for strings," Krehbiel praising the conductor for his poetry and inspiration. All the critics agreed, however, that Safonoff conducted Tchaikovsky's Fifth Symphony with a strength and vigor unprecedented in New York.

As for Lhevinne's performance of Rubinstein's Fourth Piano Concerto, only Finck accepted it without reservation. To the others, Lhevinne's playing seemed less dramatic, more reserved than in January. Krehbiel praised the "beautiful clearness and lusciousness of his cantilena" in the second movement, but Henderson found the first two movements "singularly dull." For Aldrich, Lhevinne's playing was that of a conscientious artist burdened with an "over-heavy accompaniment." The fairy-tale aura of Lhevinne's American debut had clearly dissolved; from now on he would have to re-establish his reputation with each performance.

It is inconceivable that Mme. Lhevinne would have missed her husband's debut with the Philharmonic or their former teacher's as its permanent conductor, but today she does not remember the concert. Her memory is selectively excellent, and its failure on this point is most likely due to the fact that her husband played another Rubinstein concerto. While she always revered Anton Rubinstein as a pianist and a personality, she has never admired his compositions. From the day as a little girl when Rubinstein's *The Demon* frightened her with its devils to the last time her husband would perform one of the mammoth piano compositions, she would never be able to hear Rubinstein's music with enthusiasm. As she often helped Lhevinne plan his programs, we can be sure they had more than one quarrel over whether to include his music. Recently, Mme. Lhevinne was astounded to learn that she had joined her husband in playing a Rubinstein scherzo for two pianos at their Paris concert in 1903. She had been sure she had never collaborated in playing one of his works.

Anyone checking the next day's newspapers for an account of the opening concert of the New York Philharmonic would have noticed that the prime space in some musical columns was given over to an incident that occurred simultaneously a few blocks northeast of Carnegie Hall—at the Central Park Zoo. Just before five o'clock that same Friday afternoon, an officer named Cain had seen a "stout man of very dark complexion" pass his hands over the body of a woman "standing in front of the marmosets' cage."[1] The man was Enrico Caruso and the court case which followed the bizarre incident held the headlines for weeks. Ever since Caruso had joined the Metropolitan Opera Company in 1903, any incident involving him had been "hot" copy in the New York press. But this was particularly true in 1906, the first year of New York's dramatic opera "war."

The Metropolitan Opera Company, founded in 1883, child of "The Gilded Age," was the proud possessor of the best voices money could buy. Not only did it have Caruso, but it could surround him with Emma Calvé, Emma Eames, Lillian Nordica, Olive Fremstad, and Marcella Sembrich. Challenging the Metropolitan was Oscar Hammerstein, who created the Manhattan Opera Company in

1906, built a hall for it, and despite dire predictions that New York would never support two opera companies, successfully competed with the Metropolitan for four years (until the latter bought him out in 1910 on the condition that he not produce any operas in New York during the next decade). Caruso's monkey-house antics occurred during the first weeks of Hammerstein's challenge to the Metropolitan, but the publicity certainly did not hurt attendance at the hall he sang in. Hans Conried, director of the Metropolitan, called the charge against his tenor "preposterous" and defended Caruso on the grounds that "he could have any woman he wanted in New York."

Rosina Lhevinne was not greatly concerned about who won the opera war. She was simply thankful for the opportunity of listening to so much wonderful singing during the weeks her husband was away on tour. Among all the singers she heard that year, Caruso impressed her the most. "I will never forget hearing Caruso for the first time. Even today I remember the ecstasy I felt when I heard him holding a note. He would hold it and hold it and hold it until you thought you would lose your mind. He combined this supernatural ability with so many qualities of musicianship that he was one of those artists who could never be replaced, just as there was never another basso to replace Chaliapin."

Pianists and conductors might rightly complain about the attention given to the private doings of opera stars in New York in 1906, but the opera war had a few peripheral benefits even for them. For the two houses did not limit their competition to opera. Every Sunday, for example, they presented informal musical programs in which various artists performed and in which an instrumental soloist was often thrown in with the vocal ones. On Sunday, December 23, Moritz Rosenthal played several piano compositions in a program at the Metropolitan Opera House while Lhevinne did the same at the Manhattan. It is interesting that Lhevinne, who later in his career suffered terribly from nerves before playing in public, sat calmly and prominently in a box during the performances which preceded his.

That occasion was neither the first nor the last time during the season that the two pianists competed for audiences. Like Lhevinne, Rosenthal had arrived in America on October 20 and was to play more than a hundred concerts. A famous disciple of Liszt, he carried himself "in the grand manner." In referring to him today, Mme. Lhevinne invariably speaks first of his colossal technique, and then of his sang-froid before playing a concert.

Once he went into a restaurant before his concert, and asked for three steaks. For a long time he was waiting for the steaks. "Where are my steaks?" he asked the waiter. "I am waiting for your guests," the waiter said. "But the steaks are for me," said Rosenthal. Nobody these days eats before a concert. They are too nervous. But not Rosenthal.[2]

The assertive Rosenthal and the self-effacing Lhevinne provided a perfect contrast in personal style. Gabrilowitsch, Scriabin, and Saint-Saëns also played in America during the 1906–07 season, but Lhevinne and Rosenthal dominated the scene.

Six days after his concert with Safonoff and the Philharmonic, Lhevinne returned to Carnegie Hall for the first of four New York recitals. The program was typical of those he played before the war—

Beethoven	Sonata, Op. 27, No. 2 ("Moonlight")
Brahms	Intermezzo, Op. 117, No. 1
Mendelssohn	Spinning Song
Chopin	Barcarole
Chopin	Valse in A-flat, Op. 42
Schumann	Carnaval
Brahms	Paganini Variations
Czerny	Octave Study, Op. 740, No. 5
Balakirev	The Lark
Rubinstein	Valse, Le Bal

—and the critical comments established a theme Lhevinne was to hear over and over again. Invariably there was high praise for individual pieces (after this concert, especially for Schumann's *Carnaval*). Then came the chilling qualifications (in this case, by all the leading critics but Finck):

Mr. Lhevinne is a great technician and has a fine command of tone, but does not yet disclose profound insight. (Henderson)

[Lhevinne] has an exceedingly beautiful tone, variety of touch, an exquisite feeling for tonal color and subtle dynamic gradation . . . [but] his playing in respect of sentiment, poetical feeling or deep emotion is singularly uneven. (Aldrich)

However lacking in poetic depth of feeling Mr. Lhevinne's playing was, it wooed by its tonal elegance and chastity. (Krehbiel)

The "buts" and "howevers" were cause for dismay but not despair. In those days, every European virtuoso who toured America knew that each suitcase stuffed with dollars would be matched with a stinging remark from a New York critic. It was part of the price one paid. Lhevinne may have been disturbed that his inward and restrained type of musical poetry was not fully appreciated, but these were the days when Paderewski and De Pachmann were thought to be highly poetic. Lhevinne knew his day would eventually come. In the meantime, he could only continue to be himself—no mannerisms, no posing, no musical exaggeration.

A few days after the Carnegie Hall recital, Lhevinne left for his first extended tour of the Midwest. Five days after his departure, his wife attended a concert billed as "the only piano recital by M. Camille Saint-Saëns." The French composer-pianist was then seventy-one years old, and Rosina found his performance notable mainly for the fact that "he came on stage wearing long white gloves, which he delicately removed before playing."

"Josef was gone a lot that year, and sometimes on very long trips. But I kept very well occupied while he was away. When I was not at home practicing or spending time with the baby, Father, and Masha, I was discovering the cultural life of New York. In Europe, where attitudes were very different, it was perfectly natural for a married woman to go to concerts and other events with a man who is a common friend of hers and her husband's. Americans thought it strange, but in this way I think I went to more concerts and artistic events during that year than at any other time in my life. I drank in everything New York had to offer—opera, theater, museums. And while Josef's many absences often left me alone in New York City, they also made possible the numerous reunions with him—each one like a new honeymoon."

When Lhevinne returned from his first extended trip, Rosina's "new honeymoon" had to be postponed for at least one evening, for her husband attended a stag dinner party given for Alexander Scriabin. On December 20, Scriabin made his American debut by playing his First Piano Concerto with Altschuler and the Russian Symphony. Lhevinne, who had played the day before in Janesville, Wisconsin, must have arrived in New York barely in time for the concert. The midnight-to-dawn party afterwards was given by William Steinway. Aside from Ernest Urchs, a member of Steinway's staff, the invited guests had all been at the Moscow Conservatory during Safonoff's term as its director. In addition to Lhevinne and Scriabin, Safonoff was there, and so were Modest Altschuler and his brother Jacob.[3]

A few months before the stag party in New York, Scriabin had written Lhevinne from Geneva, apparently in response to a letter from the pianist. The composer's two-part reply, previously unpublished, sheds interesting light on his attitudes toward making dedications and toward certain of his own piano compositions.

2, chemin de la Fontaine
Servette, Genève
[9/10/1906]

Dear Ossia [shortened form of Josef],

   I received your nice letter and was very glad to learn of your success in America. I would of course be very happy to dedicate to you one of my compositions, if it were not for the promise I gave myself never to do that. It will be easy for you to convince yourself of the fact that I never in my life broke this rule. I am certain that you will understand me and not feel hurt. I will be very glad to hear something more from you. In the meantime I ask you to accept the assurance of my sincere devotion.

A. Scriabin

   Forgive me for not replying right away but I received your letter on the eve of my concert in Geneva when I was very busy.

   I also forgot to write you with regard to my compositions. As an author I would be of course very agreeable to acquaint the public with the most colorful of my works, which because of their difficulty are inaccessible to average pianists (I mean the four sonatas, *poëme satanique, poëme tragique,* and the most difficult of the preludes and études). Accept, dear Ossia, my great appreciation for your feelings toward my creative art and my wishes for everything best.

A. Scriabin

Lhevinne did play "the most difficult of the preludes and études" occasionally during his career, but I have yet to find evidence that he ever played the other works the composer suggested.

   Scriabin's letter to Lhevinne, though cordial, was certainly not effusive. Shortly after the stag party, and shortly before his first American recital, he wrote a letter to Tatyana, who was about to sail from Europe to join him in New York. The attitude expressed there toward Lhevinne was not, shall we say, keenly sympathetic:

   My recital is tomorrow. I am quite unsettled in mood, worried, in fact. I am readier for concerts than I was even in Brussels; but still the demand here is for technique and technique to be better than Rosenthal, Lhevinne and all that ilk of tightrope walkers.

   My soul, it is already 10 and I haven't eaten yet. I practiced for 3½ hours non-stop. . . .[4]

Scriabin's fears proved well founded. His first recital in New York failed to meet the technical standards then taken for granted in that city. His right hand never did fully recover from the summer of 1891. That same lame hand, because of Lhevinne's success with the nocturne at his debut the year before, had been "shot" by clamoring photographers as soon as Scriabin had arrived in New York.

At the end of February, the Russian musicians who had attended Steinway's party collaborated in a concert at Carnegie Hall. Altschuler led his orchestra in a typically Russian program: music by Mussorgsky, Scriabin, Rubinstein, and Ippolitov-Ivanov. Safonoff and Scriabin sat prominently in a box, and Lhevinne introduced another obscure composition by his idol Anton Rubinstein: the *Caprice Russe* for Piano and Orchestra. The fact that "it seemed to be Rubinstein himself at the piano" interested only Finck. Scriabin received an ovation after the performance of his First Symphony, but the critics panned it in the next morning's reviews.

Several weeks later, Scriabin's tour ended in disaster. Shortly after his *Divine Poem* was presented to the American public, word got out that Tatyana, who was then living with him, was not his wife. The year before, Maxim Gorky had suffered public disgrace under similar circumstances, so Scriabin fled the country before a scandal broke, taking Tatyana with him.

Following Scriabin's hasty departure, Lhevinne continued to play and to defend his former classmate's music. In May he wrote words which have recently begun to come true: "Scriabin . . . is a man of ideas, new ideas, and when he is more thoroughly understood he will be accorded the high place which he deserves."[5]

The first time Mme. Lhevinne left New York and her baby was in late January, when she accompanied her husband to Washington, D.C., where he played with the Philadelphia Orchestra. The morning after the concert, the Lhevinnes were summoned to the White House and introduced to President Theodore Roosevelt, the First Lady, and their son-in-law and daughter, Mr. and Mrs. Nicholas Longworth. For nearly an hour, Lhevinne played for them on the 1,000th piano built by Steinway and Sons—a special ornate model featuring gold-plated eagles with widespread wings. What did the Roosevelts request? Among other things, the Schulz-Evler arrangement of the "Blue Danube Waltz"—which was already being demanded of Lhevinne wherever he played in America.[6]

From the White House, Lhevinne went to the Midwest again, while his wife returned to New York. She had been afraid of leaving the baby for even a few days and was eager to consult again with Dr. Holt, the pediatrician who every three weeks gave her a new formula for Constantine's food. Now, however, she had more than the baby to worry about. On February 17, she was scheduled to play a two-piano recital with Josef in Chicago. She caught a bad cold as she prepared for it (temperatures were in the low teens in New York early that February) and a week before the concert sent her husband a postcard (c/o Empire Theater, Quincy, Illinois). So far as I have discovered, it is the only surviving piece of correspondence from her to him:

February 10, 1907

My Dear,

With great impatience I await a letter from you to find out how you are. Although I still have a big cold and cough, I have started to go out, and I was today at Welte's Studio, remembering their invitation, and afterwards they took me to lunch at the Waldorf-Astoria. Tomorrow they are going to go away. I drank a lot and therefore have a big headache because I am not accustomed. The weather changed today and is 2 above [freezing]. Now it is terribly windy.

I weighed Koka, our dear son, today, and he weighs 12.380 [kilograms]. Thank God, that's very good, don't you think! How nice he is—so charming and playful. He rolls from the pillow with his little hands and makes wonderful gymnastics. "Give me, Give me" he repeats, before you give him something.

We kiss you and hug as hard as we can.

Devotedly,
The Cat and the Kitten[7]

Peering from the upper left-hand corner of the postcard is a head-and-shoulders photograph of Lhevinne, dressed according to the Paris fashions of 1906. In his cape, hat, double collar, tie, and pleated shirt, the pianist looks young, gallant, and unconventionally handsome.

The Lhevinnes' American debut as a two-piano team followed the pattern they had established in Europe: the program consisted largely of solo works for him. He opened the recital with a novelty for Chicago: Brahms's F minor Sonata! Lhevinne was far ahead of most of his Russian contemporaries in the extent to which he played the music of Brahms, and in 1906 was far ahead of Chicago. W. L. Hubbard wrote in the *Tribune* that the Sonata was "not easy to grasp either by performer or listener." The next compositions were more familiar: a Chopin nocturne and waltz. Hubbard thought the latter (in A-flat, Opus 42) was "given even more brilliantly than Rosenthal recently played it here, with more fleetness and with finer grasp of its poetic and musical content." Then came the two-piano numbers:

> Mme. Lhevinne is a dark-haired, petite young woman, who plays the piano unusually well, as far as could be judged. She and her husband thoroughly understood each other so far as musical intent was concerned, and their performance deservedly found warm approval at the audience's hands.[8]

The music listed for two pianos was Chaminade's *Le Matin* and Raff's Gavotte. After the Lhevinnes played the Arensky Suite as an encore, he returned to his piano (at which he had seated her for the ensemble playing) and completed the recital with works by Liszt, Scriabin, and others.

A month later, the Lhevinnes played together for the first time at Carnegie Hall. Their performance was on the evening of March 14, only a few hours after the premiere of Scriabin's *Divine Poem* in the same hall. That afternoon, Constantine, whose "wonderful gymnastics" had delighted his mother in February, caused her excitement of a different sort by scratching the spot on his arm where he had been vaccinated. The wound bled profusely, and the commotion that ensued is better imagined than described. But the bleeding was at long last stopped, and Mother and Father repaired to Carnegie Hall, where, in a long program, only one of the listed works was for two pianos:

> The Suite by Arensky is a pleasing and brilliant piece in three movements, of which the couple gave a finished performance of the most accurate ensemble and perfect cooperation with each other. Mme. Lhevinne has a graceful and fluent style; how much more was not to be ascertained from her playing on this occasion. The performance pleased the large audience much, and the couple were called upon to play again.[9]

Aldrich's words were echoed by his colleagues; fine reviews all, but hardly enough to launch two serious artists on a full-time two-piano career in 1907.

After the brief appearance with her husband, Rosina Lhevinne was approached, as at the time of her marriage, by friends and admirers eager for her to play a solo program. Today she would like to think she had resisted their importunities. The record shows she succumbed. In New York on April 2, the day her husband made his Montreal debut, she played what may be the only solo recital she has ever given in America (she "previewed" the program in New London, Connecticut). The concert was in Mendelssohn Hall

on West Forty-first Street, five days after her twenty-seventh birth-
day. The program included Chopin's B minor Sonata, Schumann's
"In der Nacht" (which she had played at the wedding supper), a
Scriabin étude (which she played for the composer before he left
New York), and one of the two études attributed to Boris de
Schloezer (Scriabin's Tatyana's uncle and onetime professor of
piano at the Moscow Conservatory). Krehbiel reported that

> the lady's technical equipment is far from impeccable, and her poetic
> fancy is not yet capable of lofty flights, but in music which does not exact
> too much in respect of these things she plays interestingly.

Aldrich wrote that

> her style is somewhat small, somewhat restrained in power and scope of
> expression, but she has nice taste, a fluent and rippling technique, and
> commands a beautiful tone, not without variety in its color and character.

While Aldrich and Krehbiel made critical use of their ears, the man
from the New York *American* was fixing his eyes on the "plump,
pretty little Russian. . . . Madame Lhevinne the pianist, like Madame Lhevinne the person," he wrote, "has good tone, an ingrati-
ating style, and [an] abundance of vitality."

We will never know how Rosina Lhevinne might have compared to her husband as a soloist had she not subordinated herself
to his career, but one thing is certain: she would have enjoyed being on stage much more than he did. When she stepped out before
an audience, its members immediately could identify with her as a
person as well as an artist. Her exuberance and vitality when in the
spotlight contrasted sharply with her husband's characteristic
reserve.

In spite of the interest shown in her recital, and in spite of the
fact that she returned with her husband for another long season in
1908–09, Rosina Lhevinne did not appear again on an American concert stage until after the First World War. That she made
no more solo appearances is not surprising, in view of her resolve
not to pursue a solo career. But the Lhevinnes' self-imposed mora-
torium on two-piano playing was a different matter. "That next
year we did not play more together because I knew that in his
heart Josef hated to play two-piano music. We always performed
without the score, and the repertoire was then so small and the
transcriptions so poor that for him to take the time to memorize
it was really a waste of time. And I myself hated to learn this repertoire, too." Lhevinne did not want to "waste time" on two-piano

works because his first complete season under the auspices of Steinway and Sons, though successful, was not overwhelmingly so.

In November, Safonoff had opened the sixty-fifth season of the New York Philharmonic with Tchaikovsky, Rubinstein, and Lhevinne; in April he closed it with the same three principals. Apart from opera singers, Safonoff and Lhevinne had probably been New York's most-talked-about musicians during the year, and Safonoff's interpretation of Tchaikovsky's Sixth Symphony concluded what for him had been a highly successful season. Lhevinne, in the final Philharmonic concert, played Rubinstein's Fifth Concerto. His performance of that work—by then recognized as his "war-horse"—was brilliant enough; but Finck politely suggested that in the future he use only the last movement, which is "wholly good from every point of view."[10]

As Lhevinne played out the season with various out-of-town recitals, he and his managers at Steinway and Sons began to evaluate the season's achievements and to plan for the future. Obviously, his tour had not been the financial success that Rubinstein's and Paderewski's Steinway tours had been. In New York, he could fill Carnegie Hall time and time again, for that city had no shortage of cultivated music lovers. Even the occasional carping of the critics did not keep the crowds away. Outside New York, however, the pattern was reversed. There Lhevinne received ample praise, but often played to half-filled halls and auditoriums.

The year before, critics in Chicago had diagnosed his major "pianistic" problem as the lack of a pose. This year that analysis was expanded:

> Lhevinne lacks all the qualities that the uninitiated public craves but possesses everything that the musician demands. He is authoritative, sincere, unaffected. As a great artist he is the peer of any; as a poseur he is a failure. . . . Lhevinne is too great an artist for his own good.[11]

If not "too great an artist for his own good," he was certainly too great an artist for the good of his management. A little showmanship, a few distinctive mannerisms, would have helped to fill the halls in provincial communities. In the same small towns where bankers, barbers, and most ambulatory females turned out to see Paderewski's private Pullman—and his flaming hair—and to bathe in his "mystique" while hearing a little music on the side, Lhevinne appealed almost exclusively to those who loved music. He was not only unable but unwilling to make himself a marketable commodity, and in that was a pianist ahead of his time. Such were the expectations of the day concerning the "pianist as poseur" that one writer chided him not only for bringing his wife to America but for admitting that he had one! Mme. Lhevinne recalls that they were asked to perform as a two-piano team without disclosing that they were married, in order to draw larger crowds.

Although Lhevinne did not bring Steinway and Sons the kind of windfall profits Rubinstein and Paderewski had, the company offered him another exclusive contract, this one for a seven-month tour in 1908–09. From Lhevinne's point of view, the conditions were much improved. He was guaranteed $15,000 for playing the first seventy-five concerts, and for each additional concert would receive at least $200. (We do not know exactly how much Lhevinne did earn on his early Steinway tours, for in addition to the money guaranteed he was promised a healthy percentage of the net profits: 50 percent the first year, 60 percent the second.) As before, Steinway and Sons was to pay his personal and traveling expenses, but this time the company limited the amount ($750) it would pay for his trans-Atlantic passage. The *cabine de luxe*, it seems, had been too much.

Lhevinne signed the new contract on May 20, 1907. A few days later, the family sailed for Europe. After a brief visit to Moscow, they decided to spend the intervening year in Wannsee, a suburb of Berlin.

In 1906, the Lhevinnes had sailed for America on October 13; in 1908, they arrived on that date. Because Cleofonte Campanini, the conductor of the Metropolitan Opera Company, was superstitious, he slept overnight on the ship. Josef Lhevinne, who had no such scruples, led his family ashore without delay, telling reporters he was eager to find an apartment without steam heat. Six days later, he began his tour.

February and March were the most successful months for Lhevinne, for then he was conquering new territory, first in Mexico, then on the West Coast. As before, he created an absolute sensation in any city where he played for the first time. But the rest of the tour followed the pattern of the preceding one: high praise from critics, low enthusiasm among nonmusicians; full houses in New York, mediocre ones elsewhere. In November, he filled Carnegie Hall twice in three weeks, and at the second recital achieved a phenomenal success with Anton Rubinstein's difficult and little-known Variations, Op. 88. But during this season, as during the previous one, his devotion to the music of his idol probably detracted from his success more than adding to it.

When New York critics had called Rubinstein's Fifth Concerto his "war-horse" in April 1907, they were more accurate than they might have imagined. For in ten orchestral appearances during that season, Lhevinne had played Rubinstein works at no less than eight. The exceptions were with Frederick Stock and the Chicago Symphony (Beethoven's *Emperor* Concerto) and with Walter Damrosch and the New York Symphony (Tchaikovsky's B-flat minor). When Lhevinne returned to America in 1908, he announced that he planned to add variety to his orchestral appearances by playing a Mozart concerto and a work by Liapunoff. He played neither. Whether his intentions were vetoed by management or dropped of his own volition, the record shows that during this season he played a Rubinstein work at *every* appearance with orchestra (with the New York Philharmonic, the New York Symphony, the Boston Symphony, the Philadelphia Orchestra, the Minneapolis Symphony, and the Seattle Symphony).

Lhevinne's debut with the Boston Symphony Orchestra in December 1908 parallelled those with the Concertgebouw Orchestra in January 1896, Vienna's Concertverein in January 1903, and the Russian Symphony in January 1906: he played Rubinstein's Fifth Concerto and captivated his audience.

> The concerto . . . sounded like the stammerings of a giant. . . . Economical and terse of motion, [Lhevinne's] heavy paw descended upon the keyboard, bringing forth growls of the Russian bear that would have delighted the ear of Rubinstein. Never were heard such maelstroms of tone from mere scale passages. Taken by surprise, one scanned the orchestra to see what engine of aural destruction Richard Strauss had invented now and smuggled into the Rubinstein concerto. But it was only Lhevinne playing a scale. . . . His delicate scales were crystalline, and his staccato passages clean and crisp as electric sparks. . . . He made Rubinstein's thoughts stand out from their setting like Alberich's golden hoard from the rocks of Nibelheim. . . .
>
> I saw Lhevinne later in the evening, boarding his train at the South Station. He looked like any other man.[12]

Such hero-worship had also greeted Lhevinne when he had first played a Rubinstein concerto in Philadelphia. But a month after the concert in Boston, his decision to play Rubinstein's Fantasy in C major with the Philadelphia Orchestra cost him many admirers. The audience did not openly reject the work, but the critical opinions were summed up by the phrases "strenuous virtuosity" and "good, if you like that kind of thing."[13]

Following the Philadelphia concert, Lhevinne left his family and the East Coast for one of those long extended tours that are both the bane and the blessing of the piano virtuoso's life. Two days after the Philadelphia concert, he played in Montreal. From there he went to Ottawa and Toronto, and two days after that was in Tennessee. Less than a week after concerts in Chattanooga and Nashville, he played in Mexico City. Lhevinne traveled by train, and while he appreciated the material comforts of trains like the *Twentieth Century Limited*, he found the "constant noise and nervous fatigue involved in traveling at so rapid a rate" disconcerting.[14] In more ways than one, he would have enjoyed a more sedentary life than that of the traveling virtuoso; on more days than one, he must have privately cursed the day he agreed to leave Tiflis.

Only a handful of people showed up for his Mexico City debut, but among them was the critic of *El País*, who immediately began a ten-day campaign devoted to informing his readers of the quality of Lhevinne's art and the necessity of attending his concerts. After the pianist's fifth recital in Mexico City, the critic really had something to write about. He took obvious delight in the task:

> The triumph obtained by Lhevinne in the concert of Friday is simply indescribable. How to make known the enthusiasm of an audience that applauds to the point of frenzy? That waits outside the theater until the great magician who has touched them with the magic wand of his sublime art, of his overwhelming genius, comes out? That lifts up the artist in an embrace of five hundred people and carries him bodily to his carriage? And that pushes the great and inimitable artist toward his lodgings in an imposing triumphal procession?
>
> That was what happened *outside* the theater Friday night after the concert of the illustrious Lhevinne was finished. *Inside* the theater ovations fell in torrents at the end of every number he played, and boomed like salvos. It was as violent as a hurricane. The vibrations of the applause and the bravos made the old theater [Teatro Arbeau] tremble, and even threatened its collapse. And all of this with no more than five hundred people in the theater (that is, about one-fifth of its capacity). If it had been as full as it should have been, I do not know what might have happened.[15]

No pianist—not Hofmann, not Paderewski—had ever had such a reception in Mexico City. Lhevinne reportedly showed his gratitude with tears of happiness as his carriage was being pulled through the streets.

After Mexico City, Lhevinne played in Redlands, California, then took a five-day "vacation" to explore the Grand Canyon, which he had wanted to see ever since studying geography as a boy. When he arrived in Los Angeles for the first time, he was appreciatively described as a "rugged, virile man-type of artist." When asked to compare the West Coast to the East, he called California a "paradise" because of its warm weather. Winters on the East Coast bothered him, he said, not so much because of the cold and the confinement as because of the insufferable steam heat, which he claimed "deadened all his sensibilities and killed his inspiration."[16]

The salubrious effect of California's climate on his sensibilities was evident in San Francisco, where his playing was described as "so spontaneous, so full of meaning and always so full of beauty" that it "seems as one apart from the academic art of other virtuosos."[17] Farther north, in Seattle, however, his performance of Rubinstein's Fifth Concerto prompted this unpleasant comment: "He clings in the face of severe criticism to a senseless old concerto and drags forth its dry bones to rattle them wherever he can."[18]

While Lhevinne was on tour, Rosina was again enjoying New York's cultural life. She heard Mary Garden at the Manhattan Opera House and two new conductors at the Metropolitan—Arturo Toscanini and Gustav Mahler. Mischa Elman, the spectacular seventeen-year-old Russian violinist, made his American debut that year, and Lhevinne's leading pianistic rivals were also Russians: Emil Sauer (who had returned to America after an absence of nine years) and Ossip Gabrilowitsch (who was about to marry Clara Clemens, Mark Twain's daughter). Josef Hofmann was in America too, but was not playing the piano; he was in North Carolina, the home of the woman he had recently married, building an automobile.

Like their compatriots Hofmann and Gabrilowitsch, the Lhevinnes were tempted to settle in America. Being married to each other, they did not have an American spouse to attract them, but there were other temptations. "Josef had been very pleased with the orchestras and audiences in America, and we were surprised to find that there an artist was considered of first importance. Whenever he was in New York, we were invited to wonderful parties and balls and treated as royalty, and he was always placed on the right of the hostess, instead of wealthy persons or those prominent in business. One day, after one of those fancy parties in New York, we were driving down Broadway and we saw a great black mass filling Columbus Circle. I'll never forget our shock when we learned that those dark figures were people waiting in a bread line. Because we had heard such idealistic things about America in Russia, until then we really thought there was no poverty there.

"So we learned that in America there was a great difference between the rich and the poor. But certainly it seemed to us a very advanced country compared to Russia. Nothing in America could compare with the gap that separated Russia's small group of wealthy intelligentsia from the great mass of peasants, who lived in the most abominable conditions."

Attractive as they found America as compared to Russia, the Lhevinnes decided to make their permanent home in Berlin, which was then the musical center of the world and the obvious base for Lhevinne's pianistic globe-trotting. On May 25, 1909, they left New York on the *Kaiser Wilhelm*, with Lhevinne carrying a contract for still another Steinway tour, to begin the following January. Mme. Lhevinne recalls the passage as fast and smooth, the skies as clear. Every night her husband took her out to look at the constellations. Their new friends, Mischa Elman and his father, who sometimes joined them, were amazed that a musician could know so much about the heavens.

III

GEMÜTLICHKEIT
AND *ANGST*

7

Europe
before the War

"ONE DAY in the month of May, Josef came home and began to eat his soup. After he finished he said with a twinkle in his eye: 'By the way, I bought the Chinese House today.'

"We all about fainted, especially Masha, who said, 'All those windows, who will wash them?' Masha was told not to worry about the windows.

"Then I said, 'Darling, do you know what it all will mean?'

" 'Oh—Oh—,' he sighed, slipping into one of his dreamy states, 'all that room, all that space—.' Then, coming back to earth, he said, 'Listen, no more discussion about the house. It's all signed for. But about the furniture I want to ask you, because it is an unbelievable bargain.'

"After dinner we went to see the furniture. It was beautiful cherry wood, each piece engraved with a little crown. He liked it and wanted to keep it. But I said, 'Josef, isn't it enough that our friends from Moscow will see such a big house? For them to have to sit on furniture engraved with a crown would be too much!' On that point, I finally convinced him.

"The next day he telegraphed his bank in Moscow to send 20,000 marks for the down payment on the house (it was the onlly money we ever got from our savings in Russia) and then we called the *Kunstgewerbe Haus* to help us plan the furnishings. The *Kunstgewerbe Haus*—that is the combination of the artist and the craftsman. The craftsman came and measured between the windows and walls. The artist came and looked me over to see my colors for the bedroom. Josef and I had a gay time choosing the furniture and being interviewed, and soon we placed our order."

The time was May 1914, the place Wannsee, a Berlin suburb

located on one of the lakes that stretch southwest to Potsdam. The house had belonged to the Chinese Ambassador to Germany, and all the residents of Wannsee knew that its walls were hung with rich damask. The largest "villa" in the area, it stood at the end of Bismarckstrasse, a street where the Lhevinnes had lived for several years. As Lhevinne had always yearned for additional space, he had long had his eye on this particular house. When it was suddenly for sale, he bought it outright—without consulting Rosina. Two months later, when the outbreak of World War I turned their lives upside down, their vast new home seemed a mockery. But for eight weeks, they enjoyed it as a natural culmination of six happy years in Wannsee.

The Lhevinnes had returned to Moscow after their first year in America, but had not stayed long. Socially, they were uncomfortable there. And musically, Lhevinne, like Chaliapin, felt Russia unappreciative of his talent. They arrived in Berlin just in time for Constantine's first birthday, and the baby helped determine where they settled. Because his mother feared the city microbes, they looked for a place in the suburbs. As soon as they saw Wannsee—"a beautiful place right on a lake with a big forest around, and you would never know you were only forty minutes from Berlin"—they rented a "villa" for the season.

Lhevinne, exhausted after his American tour, had also liked the idea of a place outside the city.

> "I hid myself in the 'villa' without seeing anyone," [he recalled in an interview a few years later] "and was successful in avoiding obligations until I was careless enough to go to a concert. . . . There I bumped into an American student who said he had been looking for me with great determination in order to deliver a letter. He asked for lessons, and I had no other remedy than to accept him as a student. The damage was done. In the space of a week, my hiding place was discovered, and an avalanche of students—Americans in the majority—invaded my 'villa.' The result was that I ended my season of 'complete rest' giving lessons to more than fifteen students."[1]

Because Lhevinne had to prepare for his next Steinway tour, Rosina was for the first time pressed into service as his assistant. After the 1908–09 tour, a new wave of followers crossed the Atlantic:

"Before we knew it we had forty students. Each one had one lesson with me before Josef would see them, and those needing work on fundamentals took almost all of their lessons with me. When someone wrote to Josef and asked for lessons, he had to write that he could not accept them for fewer than ten, because some came for one lesson and went back and said they were a pupil of Lhevinne. I still remember the name of one girl who had enough time and money for nine days and ten lessons, having two on the last day. Such was the demand for study with him."

Of Lhevinne's first students at Wannsee, most were long on money and short on talent. Berlin was then the mecca for young Americans wishing to make a career in music—as well as those making a career of wishing to make a career. So many were in town that one of David Hill's major problems as ambassador (1908–11) was to find housing for them. One of his solutions was to sponsor a benefit concert at the Hotel Adlon, the proceeds of which went toward building a dormitory. Appropriately, Lhevinne was among the artists who donated their services.

Lhevinne played very little in public in 1907–08, and he turned down another invitation to join the faculty of the Stern Conservatory. The reason was that he had to prepare for the next American tour. Even so, he and Rosina found time to sample Berlin's cultural life. "That first year in Berlin we had a wonderful time. We saw Max Reinhardt's productions of Ibsen and Hauptmann. We went to art galleries and took courses. We went to Wagnerian operas, saw the first half from six to eight, had dinner from eight to ten, and saw the rest from ten to twelve. We went to Dresden for Richard Strauss's conducting and heard Schnabel and his wife Therese Behr, who did not have much of a voice but whose interpretations were wonderful.

"We also saw Artur Rubinstein quite often, and spoke with him about America. He told us of his mistake there: thinking Americans would be 'uncultivated,' he had not worked very hard at preparing for his concerts. Strauss's *Salome* was then a success in Berlin, and Rubinstein was so enchanted by the production he went three days in a row. After the third time, he came raving to us about it, sat down at our piano, and played most of the score by heart.

"Although we enjoyed living near Berlin, some things about Germany shocked us. Even in 1907, the military officers, with their pinched collars, got into line in front of everyone else in restaurants. And it was surprising to see a man and a woman returning from the market with the woman carrying the heavy baskets of food. But after a while we took those things for granted."

The Lhevinnes were soon well known in Wannsee, and because of Josef's American success they received numerous invitations to dinners and parties, most of which he insisted they decline. The *Herr Professor* (as he came to be known) refused to take his newly won esteem too seriously, and continued to enjoy simple pleasures—gardening, fishing, stargazing. Shortly after arriving in Wannsee, he was walking down a road and saw some roses. Stepping across a lawn to admire them, he was confronted by the woman of the house, who, a sign in the window showed, gave piano lessons. She asked if he was interested. He asked the price and was led to her studio. After ten minutes she was taking lessons from him.

During each of the five years beginning with 1909–10, Lhevinne played concerts from October through June, in Europe and America. At the same time, he kept a large class of private students whose lessons Rosina took over while he was on tour. She sometimes went with him on his travels, to listen to his concerts or to join him in performing two-piano works. But never during this period did she leave home long enough to go to America with him. Her life fell into an irregular but satisfying pattern: caring for Constantine and the students, playing an occasional concert, and adjusting to her husband's busy schedule of arrivals and departures.

In January of 1910 Lhevinne sailed into New York's harbor for the fourth time. After consulting with Steinway and Sons, he left with Ernest Urchs, his Steinway manager, for another tour of Mexico. Two months before he had arrived in New York, the *Delineator*, a magazine published there, had printed an article in which he explained his approach to Chopin's Octave *Étude*. Lhevinne stressed the work's emotional content and analyzed each section by "mood"—as Anton Rubinstein had made him do in the summer of 1892. Characteristically, his advice to American readers included two basic principles of pianistic restraint: Do not "sentimentalize a melody already overripe"; keep a "reserve force" when approaching a musical climax.[2]

Judging from the mad receptions Lhevinne got in Mexico, one would hardly think him a practitioner of restraint. The year before, he had been alarmed when students tossed him into the air. This time, according to Mme. Lhevinne, he was armed with a clause in his contract prohibiting such demonstrations. It was impossible to enforce.

Arriving in Mexico City on January 12, he was met by a raucous brass band. At his first recital, the audience picked up where it had left off the year before, lifting him onto its shoulders and parading him around the hall. A few days later in Guadalajara, he was bounced all the way to his hotel in the same fashion. Back in Mexico City, his recital at the *Academia Metropolitana* set off a demonstration which, in the words of our friend from *El País*, "could only be compared to the frenzy of a bull fight." Lhevinne, perspiring heavily after two hours' work, offered encore after encore to the "victims of the special delirium tremens of the moment, who were satisfied only by new libations of the delicious nectar that had disturbed their sanity" (the delirium, it seems, had touched the critic, too).[3]

Lhevinne's Mexican engagements were to have lasted two weeks, but such was the demand to hear him that he stayed one week more. Two additional concerts were arranged—one with orchestra, the other a gala farewell recital. Such was the interest in Lhevinne's playing that President Porfirio Díaz—then eighty years old and seldom seen out after dark—attended both concerts and remained until the close of the program.[4]

At the orchestral concert, the *El País* critic, who normally raved about everything Lhevinne did, thought his performance of Beethoven's *Emperor* Concerto well below par. Searching for an explanation, he noted this strange behavior on the part of the pianist:

> While the master was in front of the piano, thinking distractedly about something, he took a pair of scissors from his vest and began doing the toilette of his nails. This carelessness would really be unpardonable if we did not suppose that the artist was deeply worried about something.

If the critic had read the *New York Times* interview following Lhevinne's American debut, he would have realized that the pianist was not trimming his nails, but cutting a new layer of cotton with which to cushion a throbbing finger. With concerts almost daily for three weeks, it was no wonder he had split the skin.

The puzzled critic gave a second example of Lhevinne's "strange behavior," and it, too, unknowingly confirms that the pianist's fingers were hurting. After Lhevinne had played Tchaikovsky's B-flat minor Piano Concerto, it was expected that, with his usual "gallantry," he would give some encores. But, we are told,

> in spite of the fact that such respectable hands as those of the President of the Republic, the Señora Carmen Romero Rubio de Díaz, the Señora Raigosa de Díaz, and others equally respectable were applauding him, he returned to the stage, yes, but always shaking his head in a negative sense.[5]

The possessors of respectable hands evidently were not offended by the lack of encores, for Díaz and his family invited Lhevinne and Urchs to the presidential palace after the concert. Two days later, Lhevinne dedicated his farewell recital to Díaz (who not long afterwards was overthrown by the Revolution of 1910).

Lhevinne loved Mexico not only for its musical enthusiasts but for its sky. That country was the farthest south he had ever been, and as an amateur astronomer he was delighted with the new stars and constellations he could see there. On his first visit to Mexico City, he had climbed the stairs of his hotel every morning to see the Mexican sunrise. This year, he took a room on the top floor so he could view it through his window. A man from *El Mundo Ilustrado* interviewed him there. Lhevinne was exhausted from all the concerts, but the interviewer was nonetheless impressed by his "soundness of body, soundness of mind." So impressed, he was moved to declare that with Lhevinne as an example, the pianists of the world would be freed from the necessity of neurasthenia! Lhevinne spoke of many things, including his family awaiting him in Wannsee. About Rosina he said, "Oh, she is a true pianist. But her style is not like mine. Her interpretations are more romantic."

As the interviewer was about to leave, Lhevinne looked out of the window and uttered a short paean to the Mexican sky, with its "wealth of stars and unlimited space. . . . For us, the sons of the north, the inhabitants of snow and fog," he declared, "this winter sky is a beautiful absurdity . . . a detail from a fairy tale."[6]

The "son of the north" was home all too soon. After working his way from San Luis Potosí to Monterrey, from Memphis to St. Louis, and from Louisville to Milwaukee, he reached Troy, New York, for a recital on February 17. The next day he was scheduled to give a concert in Ithaca. Years later he recalled the terrible trip between the two cities:

> All that day a blizzard had raged. The train by which I traveled became snowbound twelve miles from Ithaca. Wading through the snow drifts, I tramped along the ties, reaching finally a farmhouse, whose owner was at last induced to drive me to Ithaca to keep my engagement.
>
> Not until nine o'clock did I appear before my waiting audience. . . . Without stopping to change my [clothes], I stepped out before a welcoming audience, played some massive chords with all my strength to start my almost congealed blood into circulation, and proceeded with the program.[7]

Lhevinne not only played with tingling fingers that night but, after his heroic exertions in getting to Ithaca, discovered that the piano's damper pedal failed to work. He was glad, when the blizzard subsided, to move on to the larger cities of Baltimore and New York.

For his orchestral appearances during his fourth American tour, Lhevinne chose to play Beethoven and Tchaikovsky concertos rather than those of Rubinstein. His most interesting concert was in New York, where he ended the tour with a performance under the baton of Gustav Mahler, who had succeeded Safonoff as permanent conductor of the New York Philharmonic. Mahler, whose conducting had been poorly received by New Yorkers all year, bravely offered an entire program of Safonoff's former specialty: Tchaikovsky. The critical reaction was predictable. Writing of the program as a whole, Krehbiel stingingly referred to Mahler's "confounding of passionate expression and noise"; even when referring to the Piano Concerto, the dean of New York critics could not resist a final stab at Mahler:

> Mr. Lhevinne, who [has] just returned from a tour in Mexico, played the solo part of Tchaikovsky's Concerto in B flat minor with superb rhythmical incisiveness and a brilliancy that has had few parallels in our concert rooms this season; and Mr. Mahler and his men accompanied him valorously—sometimes too much so.[8]

Preceding Lhevinne in New York's "concert rooms" that season were Rachmaninoff, who made his first American tour in the fall, and Busoni.

Following the concert with Mahler, Lhevinne returned to Wannsee in time for Rosina's thirtieth birthday. If an entry in his tour book can be relied upon, he brought with him a tidy profit of $7500 for two months' work. But overseas success was followed by domestic conflagration:

"That year we had taken another villa, this time on Bismarckstrasse, a long street that ended in a forest, where Josef and I had often gone for walks. This house had beautiful furniture, silver, and china, and belonged to an American millionaire who had never rented it out before. The owners left a pony and a cart at the villa, and we hired a young man whose job was to take the cart to the train station to pick up the students, because it was a fifteen-minute walk from our villa. He wore a dark maroon uniform with gold buttons, and after bringing one student he would take back the one who had finished. Then he would wait for the next train. When a student arrived, Masha opened the door and my father sat with him until we were ready. My father loved meeting the students and talking with them, and took a great interest in all their problems.

"One day Rudolph Ganz came to visit us and, as usual, we sent the wagon. He has always been a great wit, and I will never forget his reaction to the ride in the cart. 'Now I know!' he exclaimed. 'We should all move our studios to Wannsee—Godowsky, Busoni, Hofmann, and myself. We could each have our own boy with a cart and a hat bearing our name. And we would compete with Lhevinne just as the great hotels compete with each other!' But before Rudy could try out his beautiful idea, the villa burned down.

"We were sound asleep on the first floor and my father was on the second. He was very much like Josef—the calmness he had—and I think he even hesitated to wake us, knowing how impressionable I was. Very quietly, he knocked 'tic, tic, tic' on the door, and said, 'Rosina, I think there is some strange smoke in my room.'

" 'Josef! Josef! Fire!' I screamed. Immediately he ran upstairs, and when he got there the flames were so high he had to call the firemen. My only thought was to grab Constantine and carry him out. I wrapped him in a blanket and went to the neighbors and said, 'I hope you will allow me to put my baby down to rest.' I stayed there with Masha and Father and the baby, and rather expected Josef to come, as the fire was so big it eventually burned the house all the way to the ground.

"Finally he came, and I learned from the firemen what had happened. Josef had rushed into our studio and bedroom and taken all our things—clothes, books, music—and instead of throwing them out the window had moved them from one side of the house to the other! He had worked so hard at this that he hadn't even noticed the increasing flames until one of the firemen told him there were cinders in his hair and pushed him out the door. He nearly lost his life, but he didn't save a thing."

The Lhevinnes lost many treasured possessions in the blaze, including documents and letters that would have been useful for this book. But income from concerts and lessons meant that, financially at least, the fire was only a temporary setback. Soon they were able to take another villa on Bismarckstrasse, where they lived until the purchase of the Chinese House. During those four years, Lhevinne's reputation in Europe and America rose rapidly.

According to Mme. Lhevinne, her husband's many absences, often for months at a time and often overseas, contributed to the strength of the marriage. Absence not only made the heart grow fonder but provided a respite from the clash of opposing temperaments. There were certain difficulties, however. One of the more curious occurred during the above-mentioned tour of Mexico. Soon after Lhevinne left, the pony-and-cart boy, all of seventeen years old, burst into Rosina's room and declared his love in the most passionate terms. She properly rebuked him—and did not see how they could keep him on. But Josef saw no reason not to let the boy stay—which he did until the fire caused the family to move.

Lhevinne's response to this incident paralleled his reaction to the Count Toumanov and Sascha Alexandrovich episodes. With his powerful masculinity and his wife's single-minded devotion, he may never have doubted her loyalty a single day. And in this case he probably sympathized in part with his employee. For Josef there were sins far worse than a young man's hankering for a woman—even if that woman was Josef's wife.

This being so, it was probably mere coincidence that during the season that followed the fire and the horseman's indiscretion Lhevinne played only in Europe. He was by now a fixture in Berlin's concert halls, having established himself as such on December 10, 1909, just before leaving for the United States and Mexico, when he had played Anton Rubinstein's Fantasy for Piano and Orchestra. Berliners appreciated the work more than Philadelphians had. In fact, the ability to enjoy Rubinstein's music seemed to depend on whether one had heard the composer play it himself. Forty years had passed since Rubinstein had last played in America, and to perform his work there was to invite speedy oblivion. Only twenty years had passed in Germany, and whenever Lhevinne played a Rubinstein work there, an important critic would be on hand to compare his interpretation with the composer's own.

Following this concert, Lhevinne played several times a year in Blüthner or Beethoven halls—as did Busoni, Godowsky, Rosenthal, and Sauer. At first, American students resident in Berlin formed the bulk of his audience; before long, as many Germans as Americans came to hear him. During the 1910–11 season, his stay-at-home year, Lhevinne played four times in Berlin and four times in Vienna, and traveled to France and Spain, to Budapest and Bremen and Barmen. His first Blüthner Hall recital of the season was typical of his repertoire at the time: works by Beethoven, Scarlatti, Mendelssohn, Schumann, Liszt, Chopin, Rubinstein, and Liapunoff. On tour, he restored Saint-Saëns's Third Piano Concerto to his repertoire and made several forays into the chamber-music field. In Vienna, he played Brahms's G minor Piano Quartet with members of the Prill Quartet. In Budapest, he played Beethoven and Rubinstein trios with the well-known team of Eugen Hubay and David Popper. And in Berlin he collaborated with his wife:

> Madame Lhevinne proved to be a remarkable pianist; she has an exquisite touch, a clear, pearly technique, and her delivery revealed a very musical as well as a warm, sunny nature.[9]

At his Berlin recital in March 1911, their only two-piano works were the Arensky Suite and two encores of the "salon" variety. A month later, however, they gave their first public performance of Mozart's E-flat Concerto for Two Pianos.

Besides her own Berlin debut that spring, Rosina had a student's to worry about: Daphne Hilmers, one of the few Wannsee students to study only with her, gave a Choralian Hall recital at age twelve. In addition, Rosina had to plan the annual spring soirée in the large music room on the second floor of their new "villa" at 60 Bismarckstrasse (that was where *she* practiced and taught—Josef's studio was on the first floor overlooking the lake). The Lhevinnes' best students played there twice a year. The winter recital was usually near Christmas, the spring one near May Day, and students competed fiercely for a spot on the program. This year the spring recital was on April 30, and Lhevinne accompanied one of the students at a second piano in Rachmaninoff's First Concerto. Before the concert, Masha served cookies and candies, cakes and chocolate, and assorted Russian goodies. Afterwards, pictures were taken and the whole group went for a picnic on the lake (this year, Lhevinnes plus students equaled forty-one). Following what in those days was a thrill—a motorboat ride—they all disembarked at a pleasant spot and swam and ate some more.

The annual spring soirée and picnic marked the end of the season's activities, and soon the Lhevinnes began to prepare for those of the next. Summer months unfailingly brought more Americans to Wannsee for lessons, and July always brought a birthday party for Constantine. The guests his mother invited were mostly students and professional musicians, and the little boy did not feel much a part of it all, but in a way that was fitting, for those were the people he gaped at and talked with most of the year. His Aunt Sophie's visits were more to his liking, for her son was about his age. As for Lhevinne, he got away each summer for a short period of rest, as he had once explained while in Mexico:

> In my time of rest, I devote myself solely to hunting and fishing. These sports are an absorbing passion for me; surrendering to them, I am able to forget about the piano and . . . future obligations.[10]

After his solo vacation in the summer of 1911, he and Rosina spent a few weeks in the Austrian Tyrol.

Franz Liszt was born on October 22, 1811. One hundred years later a festival was held in Antwerp, among other places, to celebrate that fact. Lhevinne, whose repertoire had lately included an increasing amount of Liszt's music, was soloist for the opening night's program and played the Piano Concerto in E-flat, *Robert le Diable*, a *Soirée de Vienne*, and an étude. He then returned to Wannsee and took Rosina to Russia.

Their destination was St. Petersburg, where Safonoff was conducting a series of concerts for the Imperial Russian Musical Society. With their former teacher providing the accompaniments, the two Lhevinnes played contrasting concertos in E-flat—Liszt's for one piano and Mozart's for two. Perhaps because most Russians tended to take a condescending attitude toward Mozart's music, the Lhevinnes' performance of the Double Concerto came as a real revelation.

> . . . One hears [this music of Mozart] so rarely that it can be classed as a novelty. It seems to present no particular difficulties; nevertheless, its interpretation cannot succeed unless the artists are endowed with a very high degree of musical sensitivity and unless they are by temperament of the highest musical taste, eschewing any tendency toward producing an effect. Madame and M. Lhevinne were truly in harmony with these demands, and the result was a purity of transmission that made a deep and profound impression. They played with that rare simplicity which shuns any attempt to draw attention to itself. Certainly the absence of the acrobatic *tours de force* that certain contemporary virtuosos use in their playing did not detract from the interpretation of this concerto. This work demands to the highest degree the art of possessing the instrument; it demands that the artists be able to give to their playing a character corresponding exactly to the character of the work itself; and it must be performed with the requisite elegance and finesse. From all these points of view, the artists had every right to the acclaim which was passionately and endlessly lavished upon them.[11]

Following the splendid debut in the Great Hall of the Nobility, the two-piano team disbanded for the season—Rosina returning to Wannsee, Josef going to Moscow and the provinces for a solo tour. If the one piece of evidence is representative, the tour of the provinces was disappointing. In her diary of 1911, Josef Hofmann's first wife recorded that Lhevinne, Rachmaninoff, and her husband played in the city of Rostov within a few days of each other. She claims that only Hofmann was a financial success there and that his friend Lhevinne, after being guaranteed 800 rubles for two concerts, made only 150 and 40 rubles.[12]

Mme. Lhevinne, after returning from St. Petersburg, had resumed the teaching of their students. But she was not able to teach for long, as she underwent major surgery in a Berlin hospital on December 12. Lhevinne had to play recitals in Beethoven and Blüthner halls a week before the operation; a week after it, he left Berlin for his fifth American tour. So during her long convalescence, his wife had only his letters to console her. As usual, his trip to America produced a number of diverting incidents.

This year Lhevinne was greatly annoyed because his new manager, Loudon Charlton, made him wear a bright green felt hat "so he would be recognized at small-town railway stations." He had never had difficulty being recognized before—this was obviously a ploy designed to satisfy the American appetite for "eccentric" pianists. Lhevinne also complained of "chicken salad coming out the ears." That dish, he wrote, was served at every reception across the land. Then there was Joseph Stransky, Mahler's comparatively inept successor at the New York Philharmonic, who, Lhevinne wrote his wife, stuck tape to appropriate places in the concerto score so he would know where the solo entrances were! Finally, Rosina read of how her husband played Liszt's E-flat Concerto for four thousand people in a huge structure in New York called the Hippodrome. His was the first in a long series of "popular" concerts there, and the demand for the Strauss-Schulz-Evler *Blue Danube* was so great that the stagehands had to wheel the piano back on stage.

In less than three months in America, Lhevinne earned $12,400. Rosina was in much better health by the time he returned, and in June went with him to London, where he played with Safonoff and the London Symphony Orchestra. Lhevinne had not played in London for nearly five years, and he presented an ambitious program: Beethoven's *Emperor* Concerto, Liszt's E-flat Concerto, and Tchaikovsky's B-flat minor. The morning after the concert, he and Rosina were ready to leave on a two-week vacation to Switzerland. As they were eating breakfast in the Savoy hotel, the room was filled with a wonderful perfume. A footman called out for "Mr. Lhevinne" and brought him a letter from the Marchioness de Ripon. She wrote that she had heard his concert with Safonoff and had visualized all night how wonderful it would be if he would play Weber's "Invitation to the Dance" at a soirée she was giving that afternoon for the Russian dancers Nijinsky and Karsavina, for whom she had built a special stage.[13] She asked him to play some solo pieces too, and offered a substantial sum.

"Josef, when he received this letter, was quite upset. We had made our reservations in Switzerland, and this would cause us to lose a whole day of our short trip. He said he didn't think we should accept it. I told him that I had heard that the concerts one gives in London are not nearly as important as the people one meets there, and urged him not to miss this opportunity. But he would not be convinced. He wrote Lady Ripon that he appreciated her offer very much, but that we had already made our reservations for Switzerland. Hoping to close the matter once and for all, he added that 'we couldn't stay unless you would give me double what you offer.'

"Imagine our astonishment when, fifteen minutes later, the man returned with Lady Ripon's reply: 'I am more happy than ever that you are willing to change your plans in order to play for me. I hope you will bring your wife with you.'

"Soon after we arrived at Lady Ripon's, we spoke with Nijinsky and Karsavina, and then they all rehearsed for the performance of the 'Invitation to the Dance.' Nijinsky asked Josef to play a little slower in the first 'leap' passage so that he could jump into the air and stay in the air and be at the highest point just when the highest musical note was being played.

"At the performance, Josef began the 'Invitation' and the stage opened and Karsavina was in a chair asleep. Suddenly Nijinsky came over the stage with that marvelous leap to the music, and I couldn't help gasping 'Oh!' with the rest of the audience. I could not believe that he could hang in the air so long, and was not at all surprised to hear after his death that the structure of his body was in some ways found to be more like a bird than a human being. When Nijinsky landed, he woke Karsavina and they began their dance together. But nothing could erase the impression of that incredible soaring entrance of his.

"After the performance, Lady Ripon gave a supper for the artists and some of the guests. My table partner was the Aga Khan, a very handsome young man, and on the other side of him was Karsavina. Nijinsky was extremely thin, with a pale complexion, but Karsavina was a real beauty and the Aga Khan seemed very much taken with her. He had been impressed with Josef's playing, and at dinner said to him, 'I am having a large party and musicale at the Hotel Ritz tomorrow, and will pay you whatever you ask if you play for me there.' Josef was reluctant to lose another day of his precious vacation, but finally accepted, I think for twice the amount of money Lady Ripon had paid him.

"I had a tremendous cold the next day and couldn't go, so Josef went alone and played. Dinner was served with plenty of champagne, and the Aga Khan wore his native costume, complete with turban. He sat on a throne, and Josef could hardly recognize the man he had seen the day before in black tails. He later said that he had never seen so many naked women, dressed only in jewelry, but that if you took all the jewelry the women wore it would not have touched what the Aga Khan had in precious stones in his turban alone.

"The next day we left for Switzerland, and visited Geneva, Vevey, and Chillon. Then we went to Zermatt for the three-day expedition of climbing the Matterhorn. It is hard to believe, but years later Josef never remembered the wonderful concerts in London or the money he had made, but only how much he had missed the places he could have seen if we had not lost those two days."

Little Constantine Lhevinne was six years old in the fall of 1912. A stocky old man visited the family for several weeks then and played quite often with the boy. The visitor tended to sweat, and whenever he needed to he took his shirt to the room with the bathtub, washed it, and hung it in the sun to dry. Arkady Levin's personal habits contrasted sharply with those of the boy's other grandfather: Jacques Bessie liked to walk and talk with Constantine, delivering "pearls" of wisdom, but he never played with the child, and seldom was seen to perspire.

Since moving his large family from Orel to Moscow nearly forty years before, Arkady Levin had hardly left the city for a single day. On a pension from the Imperial Orchestra, he had decided to visit Wannsee after his son's Russian tour the year before. His father's visit was Lhevinne's only respite that year from an endless succession of concerts. As the season before, he played in Europe in October and November, in America from December through April, and in England in May and June.

When Lhevinne arrived in New York for his sixth American tour, he was expected to bring his family with him. Before returning to Europe the year before, he had complained of such loneliness that he publicly vowed never again to cross the Atlantic without his wife and child. Constantine, however, was then old enough for school, and a stream of tutors had begun a steady flow up Bismarckstrasse. As for Rosina, she held firm to her pledge that "the children will come first." She stayed home with their young son and taught the students, whose lessons had been irregular, at best, during her illness the year before.

In leaving for America, Lhevinne purposely defied superstition once again: he sailed on the *Lusitania* on December 13. A storm whipped up the English Channel, however, and the ship had to turn back. Slightly chastened, he sailed a few days later on the *George Washington,* and was afterwards more tolerant of Rosina's numerical "reasonings."

According to records Lhevinne kept of his earnings, Loudon Charlton, his new American manager, had not superseded Steinway and Sons, but rather served as their proxy. Charlton handled the publicity and arrangements for his tour, but Steinway, whose piano he continued to play, paid him his profits. On the "green felt hat" tour Charlton had arranged the year before, Lhevinne had played Rubinstein's Fifth Concerto in six cities with the New York Philharmonic. One wonders how the tour had been such a success, with the combination of Stransky and that concerto. But Lhevinne had played thirty-four other concerts, including a performance of the Tchaikovsky Concerto with young Leopold Stokowski in Cincinnati and a performance of the Brahms G minor Piano Quartet with members of the Kneisel Quartet. On that tour, Lhevinne's recitals had shown more refinement than in earlier years. After he had played in Boston, the *Christian Science Monitor* had grouped him with Busoni and Hofmann as representing the "modern" school of piano playing. The reviewer felt that they achieved more sensitive and subtle effects than did the "highly colored" De Pachmann and Paderewski "school." Still, some of the old reservations had lingered. Reviewing the same Boston recital, H. T. Parker had praised Lhevinne for having "sloughed the excesses" of the days when he used to "rock the walls of Steinert Hall," but had argued that the pianist was still in need of "a new skin of warming personality."[14]

This year he brought with him that "new skin," and on a cold, bitter winter afternoon all reservations about his playing seemed to dissolve. The date was January 13, 1913 (it was not a Friday); the place was Aeolian Hall, a new hall near the New York Public Library seating 1,000 people. No one was surprised at the way Lhevinne's recital charmed the overflow crowd, for that happened whenever he played in New York. But the nearly unqualified praise it received from the city's tough-minded critics was astonishing. Aldrich openly revised his assessment of Lhevinne, adding "warmth of feeling" and "poetic touch" to his catalogue of the pianist's "extraordinary excellencies." Krehbiel and Henderson both took for granted the sheer virtuosity of Brahms's *Paganini Variations,* and reserved their highest tributes for the way in which Lhevinne "brought out beautifully the poetic spirit" and the "noble depths" of Beethoven's *Les Adieux* Sonata.

The sole reservations were expressed by Finck, who was normally Lhevinne's most enthusiastic supporter. He attacked the pianist for not pausing after the first work in the program—thus leaving a hundred latecomers out in the cold for nearly forty minutes. "There should be legal redress for such an outrage," Finck fumed. His felt concern for the plight of those people (of whom he was most likely one) cost him the "honor" of having his words included in an unusual leaflet soon printed by Charlton. Measuring eight inches by twenty-two, it contains twelve full-length "rave" reviews of the concert. Reading it today, one is bewildered to find the comments of the *New York Times* surrounded by those of the *Mail,* the *Press,* the *Tribune,* the *World,* the *Sun,* the *American,* the *Evening Journal,* the *Evening World,* the *Globe,* the *Evening Sun,* and the *Brooklyn Sun* (but not, thanks to Finck, the *Evening Post*).

Lhevinne's tour ended with his second trip to the West Coast. After playing in California, he crossed the continent by train and the Atlantic by ship and met Rosina in London. The year before, while he was preparing the three concertos with Safonoff, she had to rely on one of their students to choose some entertainment. The result was what the student—years later in a letter to her—called "one of the great *faux pas*" in his life.

> One afternoon when Mr. Lhevinne was busy practicing, you asked me to get tickets for a matinee, the one condition being that it should be nothing tragic. What did I do but get tickets to *Oliver Twist,* and in the very first act poor little Oliver was forced to break into a house and was shot and wounded! This was too much for both of us, and we left the theater to seek a happier scene![15]

This year she chose a *musical* matinee. During a week in which Lhevinne played three times, Londoners could also hear Paderewski, De Pachmann, Petri, Hambourg, D'Albert, Edwin Fisher, or Guiomar Novaës.

"In the hotel where we were staying, everyone said not 'Are you going to hear De Pachmann play?' but 'Are you going to *see* what De Pachmann will do?' Out of curiosity, I went too. In the middle of the sonata he completely forgot where he was in the music. Without any hesitation, instead of going behind the stage he went forward and up the aisle. He walked like a lunatic, staring straight ahead, and slowly went to the very back of the hall. There he jumped up on a chair, reached up and stopped a clock, and said in a loud voice that the ticking of the clock had disturbed him. Then he returned to the piano and resumed playing."

The De Pachmann matinee she attended was probably his Queen's Hall recital at 3 P.M. on May 31, 1913: the London *Times* chided him the next day for his asides to the audience. It is a moot question as to whether he "forgot" the sonata on purpose or actually suffered a memory lapse from which he extricated himself brilliantly. What is certain is that Lhevinne's playing featured no antics such as those of the legendary "Chopinzee." His two recitals in Steinway Hall simply demonstrated his own brand of self-effacing and aristocratic musicianship. The recitals were preceded by a performance of the Tchaikovsky Concerto with Willem Mengelberg and the London Symphony Orchestra. This was the first time Lhevinne and Mengelberg had collaborated since their appearance together in Amsterdam at ages twenty-one and twenty-four. One observer found the pianist "rigid," another "nervous," at the beginning of the concerto. But both considered the performance as a whole very powerful, and notably free of sentimentality or false display.

The 1912–13 season turned out to be the most peripatetic of Lhevinne's life. After playing in London, he celebrated his fifteenth wedding anniversary with Rosina, visited Moscow for a month to see his father and deposit the year's earnings, vacationed for two months with Rosina in the Harz Mountains, and went hunting with a friend in the Thuringian forest. Lhevinne's seemed a life to be envied.

Josef and Rosina Lhevinne were thirty-eight and thirty-three years old as the 1913–14 season began. On November 1, Vassily Safonoff, then sixty-one, conducted a concert of the Berlin Philharmonic. Lhevinne played Tchaikovsky's First Concerto and Rubinstein's Fifth; he and Rosina played Mozart's Double Concerto in E-flat. This was to be their last orchestral appearance under their former master's direction, and all three made it a concert to remember.

Safonoff's conducting was as strong and fiery as ever, but age was beginning to take a toll on the double-fisted "aerial graphics" that had fascinated New Yorkers in 1906. He still conducted without a baton, but *Die Musik's* critic noted that "the stout conductor kept his left thumb buried for the most part in his vest-pocket." Concerning the Lhevinnes' performance of the Mozart, the critic offered his own variation on the standard praise for duo-pianists: "A greater precision of execution and a purer harmony of spirit can hardly be conceived." A man with a sharp eye for appearances, he also noted the relative positions of the pianos, which were placed against each other in opposite directions. That arrangement he recommended to his readers, pointing out that it allows the pianists to look into each others' eyes, rather than sneaking sidelong glances at the fingers.

Music critics were highly esteemed in Germany; the more so the older they were. That night in the artist's room, Lhevinne received unusual tributes from two real veterans. Karl Klindworth, aged eighty-four, had been among the judges who awarded the Rubinstein Prize in 1895. Lhevinne's performance of the Fifth Concerto set him to reminiscing:

> "As soon as I heard you play, I remember saying to myself that here was the probable winner, and although there were many other contestants still to be heard, my premonition proved to be correct. If you will remember, you played the same Rubinstein concerto you played tonight. While your performance even then was extraordinary, it fell far short of today's achievement, for I tell you frankly that I did not imagine that the difficult work could be given so faultless a rendition as we have just heard."

A few minutes later, Dr. Paul Ertel walked up to Lhevinne, shook his hand, and said simply:

> "In my work as a critic I have heard the Tchaikovsky Concerto played many many times, but you have given me my first real hearing of it. It was a sensational revelation to me."[16]

That tribute was considered particularly meaningful because Ertel, wishing to remain strictly impartial as music critic of the Berlin *Lokal Anzeiger,* seldom spoke with artists. With this performance, just twenty years after Tchaikovsky's death, Lhevinne became recognized as perhaps the world's greatest interpreter of the concerto he had admired so much in his student days.

He and Rosina repeated the same program two weeks later with the Tonkünstler Orchestra in Vienna.

When they returned to 60 Bismarckstrasse, a young Canadian was waiting to ask for lessons. Lhevinne accepted J. Davidson Ketchum as a student and gave him lessons for nearly a year. A diary Ketchum kept gives the most complete view we have of the Lhevinnes at Wannsee. After the audition, he described Lhevinne as

a funny little man . . . clean-shaven, and not at all inspiring to look at.
Speaks pretty good English and was not so terrifying as I had imagined.[17]

Before taking his first lesson, Ketchum attended the annual winter
soirée. Sunday, December 14, broke wet and windy in Berlin, but
the weather had improved by the time Ketchum arrived at the
Wannsee station for the mile-long walk to the villa.

Reached the Lhevinnes' at 4.30, and was among the first there. After a
few minutes spent in talking with Mrs. Lhevinne's father, went upstairs
with some of the others into the big hall, where Mrs. L. does her teaching. . . . Met Mrs. L. for the first time; she is very nice . . . and a great
pianist, too. After a while Josef came in. He has just returned from playing with the London Philharmonic. Also Constantine, their son, a bright
little kid of about 7 who knows English, German, and Russian! I talked
with several of the pupils, who are nearly all Americans, and very nice.
. . . First we had chocolate and all kinds of cakes and candy, and then
after some time, the music began. Mr. Basset Hough is the organist of the
American church here, but not much on the piano. But the thing he
played was so rotten that it was hard to tell [Hough was the student who
had taken Mme. Lhevinne to *Oliver Twist* in London]. Miss Selby was
very good indeed, tho' not exciting. Seitz played very well, but not nearly
as well as I expected, seeing that he soon expects to go on stage. . . . Lastly,
Miss Weiskopf, who is a Minneapolis girl, played two movements of
[Beethoven's] C minor concerto in fine style. She is one of his best pupils.
Lhevinne played the orchestral part on a second piano, and little Constantine turned [the pages] over for him. . . . I like both the L's very
much, and they have a charming home and atmosphere. The pupils are
a nice sociable bunch, and I am sure I will enjoy my time here to the full.

Three days later, Ketchum arrived for his first lesson. The gate,
fifty yards from the house, was shut.

. . . Seeing a bell, I pressed it, and immediately the gate . . . was unlocked,
and I opened it and went in. I was quite surprised, for while all the
doors do that here, I had never seen it on a gate before. Whenever you
go into one of these huge houses, you just ring the bell and press against
the door, and in a minute the *Pförtner* releases the catch from his room,
and in you go.

Had I known Lhevinne, I might have had a long walk before my lesson, for he was running 45 min. slow. After saluting young Constantine,
who was out in the yard, I went in at 4, and waited, reading *Musical
America* and listening to a girl playing the Beethoven C minor concerto
upstairs, until 4.45. Then Lhevinne comes in, very merry and hot after
his lesson, greets me warmly, and after seeing the young lady off takes me
into his room downstairs. I show him the music I have brought, and he
says, 'SO-O, let me see this F# prelude and fugue.' I play it as well as I

can, he meanwhile walking about like a young lion in a cage, stopping short now and again when I do something that either pleases or displeases him. Having got rid of his lady pupil, he lights a big cigar with evident enjoyment. At the end he comes to the piano, thinks a little, and then [plays the piece] carefully from beginning to end, commenting on everything I have done in it. 'Thees sounds chust a leetle too cherky!' 'Don't force the tone here.' '*Mooch* more pianissimo here.' 'A leetle quicker, you must not tire se audience.' Then, usually, I play it once more, correcting the mistakes as much as possible. Sometimes, when he is very pleased, he sings aloud. In the middle, in comes a lady [Masha, most likely] and has a little talk with him about coming to dinner, and then goes upstairs to see Mrs. L. It is the most curiously arranged house I ever saw. L's studio is a kind of general thoroughfare, for you cannot get to the front door without going thru it. It does not worry me at all, but nervous pupils must find it very trying. After the Bach I tell him that I have been having trouble with octave work, so then he comes, puts down his cigar, and sits beside me, and for half an hour we work hard at his way of playing octaves, which is quite unusual and at first sight, impossible. But he has the most marvellous octave technique I have ever heard, so I am going to put all my energies toward grasping his method.

Lhevinne used a high wrist to play octave passages that alternated between black and white keys, rather than the low wrist favored by most pianists. He explained why in the article he had written for the *Delineator*.

If the reader will play octaves alternately on black and white keys he will find that with the level wrist the hand and forearm continually move backward and forward for the changing positions required. This looks and feels awkward, and is apt to sound so. By raising the wrist high the hand swings as from a pivot and accomplishes the rapid changes of position without arm movement. This facilitates matters and enables us to obtain the utmost speed and breadth of tone. In continuous white-key passages, I do not employ the raised wrist, as the need for it does not exist.

Ketchum's account of the first lesson concluded with these words:

In explaining a thing, he is *most* careful and painstaking, and never impatient yet. After the hour is up, we arrange for the next lesson, and then go out, to find the next pupil, a fellow named Cole, apparently asleep on the sofa, having been waiting since 5. Lhevinne cracks a joke with him, says goodbye, and I am out on the Wannsee rd. again, with a billion stars shining through the pines. It is pretty cold, and I walk fast to the station.

Although first promised only biweekly lessons, Ketchum was soon taking one a week, as did most of the students. In addition to

Married a decade.

Constantine with his parents in 1913.
Wannsee.

Constantine with his mother and Masha.
Wannsee.

Lhevinne with Constantine and Marianna.
Wannsee, 1918.

"Villa" on Bismarckstrasse, and pony and cart. Wannsee.

Lhevinne with his pupil Homer Samuels. Wannsee.

"The magnificent stormer of the keyboard." Photo by Becker and Maass.

all the teaching, Lhevinne played with eight major orchestras that year and gave one, two, or three recitals in each of twenty European cities. Sometimes he took the more advanced students with him on his tours. In January, when he played with Arthur Nikisch in Hamburg, Rosina and several students went along. The day before the concert they went to Hagenbeck's Zoological Park, where the pianist persuaded a keeper to lift two lion cubs from a cage. Lhevinne fondled them with evident pleasure until his wife intervened, in fear that the animals might scratch his precious hands.[18]

"We had gone to Hamburg a day early because Josef had never played with Nikisch and they had planned to rehearse and discuss the concerto. But when we arrived there, there was no Nikisch, no rehearsal. On the day of the concert, we couldn't find him either, so finally Josef had to dress, and I too, and we went to the concert hall.

"Even for the concert itself Nikisch was nearly late. But finally he arrived in a fur coat, and hurriedly kissed my hand (he had a little beard and moustache). He said that he had heard from others that Josef had been frantically trying to find him, and asked: 'Lhevinne, why you wanted to see me? You didn't want to play the Tchaikovsky in B minor instead of B-flat minor?' Then he kind of laughed and said, 'That would be the only reason to see me before the concert' and walked away to begin the program.

"I was kind of worried about how the performance would go, but when they played the concerto together it was not to believe: the communicative and sensitive relationship they had from the first note was absolutely spellbinding. Josef said afterwards that if he'd had half a dozen rehearsals with any other conductor he still couldn't have had an accompaniment like that one." Nikisch returned the compliment, telling friends he had never heard any concerto played more beautifully than Lhevinne had played the Tchaikovsky.[19]

A day after the concert with Nikisch, Lhevinne was back at Wannsee giving a lesson to Ketchum, who gave this account of it:

The walk from the station to the Lhevinnes' was beautiful, but it was pretty cold, and I was not sorry to get in. Josef appeared 15 minutes later, clad in a sweater coat, and with his skates over his shoulder! He had played in Hamburg the night before and only arrived 2 hours before my lesson, but [had] immediately skated away from the end of his garden, for these Berliners prize their ever-shortening winters very much. He was in good spirits, and said that "everything was fine" at Budapest and Hamburg. First I played him the Bach Prelude and Fugue, which he said was very good, and finished. But then came the Moszkowski Étude, which I thought was pretty nearly finished too. But when we had spent exactly an hour on it alone, I changed my mind! He simply revolutionized the whole thing, and made me utterly ashamed of my stupidity in not getting all those ideas myself. He certainly is a *master-teacher*, giving me in that hour more ideas on tone-color, technique, phrasing, and general interpretation than I would have got in a month of work with other teachers. He raised his voice sharply a couple of times, but never got at all angry, but was only fearfully *persistent*, and determined to give you his idea of the thing, if it took all night. [Schumann's Symphonic] Études [which] I had been working at, we did not touch at all, and even so were 20 minutes over time. I hurried back to the station, feeling as if I had been severely mauled by a prize fighter, and with my brain whirling with things to remember. . . .

A month later his performance of the Moszkowski had improved enough that Lhevinne told him he could play in the spring soirée —an honor seldom accorded (Ketchum proudly recorded) a first-year student.

On the first of February, Lhevinne was in Scotland, at the end of the month in Budapest. In between, he played in London and Paris. In March, after concerts in Hamburg and Berlin again, he took Rosina (and some students) to Russia. It turned out to be their last visit to the country in which they were born.

"Josef was engaged as soloist with the Moscow Philharmonic under Rachmaninoff. He had just learned Beethoven's First Concerto and was going to play it in public for the first time. In the night, after we arrived, he asked, 'Rosina, do you think I ought to tell him that I have never played the concerto in public, and see what he thinks about the *tempi*?' And I said, 'Of course. Certainly you must discuss it with him.'

"So we went to the Rachmaninoffs' for dinner, and Josef told him. Both he and his wife started to laugh and laugh, and Josef and I were very uncomfortable. Finally they stopped, and Rachmaninoff said that *he* had awakened *her* in the night and said, 'You know, the Lhevinnes are coming for dinner today. Do you think I should tell him that I don't know the concerto?'

"We all felt relieved after he told us that, and that was actually the beginning of his and Josef's friendship, for they had never been close at the Conservatory. After conducting the concerto for Josef the next day, Rachmaninoff came to like it so well that he later played it all over America.

"When we were ready to leave Russia, we went to get our passports verified. Usually you gave five rubles under the table and the clerk gave you the passport immediately. But this time, to our astonishment, they told us to come back the next day. So the next day Josef went and waited and waited, and when he presented his credentials they again told him to come back the next day. He had a concert scheduled very soon in Budapest, so finally he went to the head commissioner for those things, and his passport was issued.

"Technically, Josef was still an officer in the Russian Army, and we should have suspected that there was some political reason for the delays. Unfortunately, we thought nothing more about it."

Had the Lhevinnes been more suspicious, they might have returned to Germany with more than memories of the concert with Rachmaninoff. Ever since his first American tour, Lhevinne had kept all his savings in Moscow banks, and instead of withdrawing the money, he blithely deposited the proceeds from the current season as well. Thus unencumbered, he and Rosina returned to Western Europe—she to be with Constantine and the students, he to complete his concert season in Budapest, Luxembourg, and the German provinces. The students gave their recital near May Day, the class went for the traditional picnic on the lake, and Lhevinne came home to say, "By the way, I bought the Chinese House today."

Mme. Lhevinne's recollection that the Chinese House was purchased in May of 1914 is confirmed by a letter Arkady Levin wrote his son on June 10, congratulating him on "this rare occurrence in our family." The letter gives a touching picture of Levin in his old age, and suggests that Josef Lhevinne's capacity for viewing himself with detachment may have been in part acquired from his father:

> All my heart-wounds heal when I reread your nice letter. Thank you, dear fate of mine, that this act has been accomplished during my life. I pray thee to let me live until the completion of this event and to see with my own eyes the property of my beloved son—and then it may be "finita la comedia"! In a few months I complete my seventh decade and enter into my eighth decade on my back. It's time to go. And what if fate makes a joke on me and gives me on my spine another five years? Maybe I will gain in stature by my name because you rise higher and higher in the art and I as your father will profit by the happy opportunity to accompany you in your glory. I congratulate you and dear Rosina and Jacob Jacobovich [Rosina's father] and esteemed Masha on this housewarming. May God send you in your new home good health, joy, and good times for many years to come.

Levin's letter also expressed joy at news that his son would be playing in Moscow again in the fall, at a concert with the Moscow Philharmonic on November 22. He closed by asking Josef to "work on the broadening of your repertoire: Beethoven, Chopin, Brahms, and Schumann—more of these composers."

Back in New York, Loudon Charlton and his publicity men were busily compiling reports of the recent European successes, for Lhevinne's seventh American tour was scheduled to begin in December 1914, a month after the concert in Moscow. But the "guns of August" were to change those plans, and many more.

8

Enemy
Aliens in Berlin

WHEN THE Czar and the Kaiser went to war on August 1, 1914, life became dangerous for Russians living in Germany. German civilians were eager to display their patriotism by harassing the enemy, and for the less imaginative the government manufactured the "Geld-Auto" scare, spreading the rumor that a large quantity of gold was to be smuggled from France to Russia via Germany by automobile. The gold shipment was never found, but the sight of peasants, police, and other patriots (some armed only with pitchforks) stopping suspicious vehicles on roads large and small gave a good boost to the nation's war morale. More imaginative Germans enlisted the support of friends and neighbors in tracking down Russian spies—an activity with more tangible results. Throughout Germany, thousands of Russian civilians were arrested and confined to concentration camps. During the early weeks of the war, there was no national policy concerning the treatment of a suspected spy. Each case was left in the hands of local officials.

In Munich, where Ossip and Clara Gabrilowitsch were living, anti-Russian sentiment was particularly strong. Soon after war was declared, Gabrilowitsch was accused of being a spy and was taken to Meisbach, a prison camp where, rumor had it, some civilians had already been executed as enemy agents. Only the intervention of Bruno Walter rescued the pianist from imprisonment and possible death. After he was released, Gabrilowitsch was told he could remain in Munich only on the condition that he report daily to the authorities. Wisely fearing continued harassment, he and Clara took the earliest train out of the country, making their escape to Switzerland. From there they went to the United States,

143

where he resumed his concert career. In the summers, they joined the famous wartime musical colony in Bar Harbor, Maine—whose members included Josef Hofmann, Walter Damrosch, Harold Bauer, Carl Friedberg, Olga Samaroff, and her husband, Leopold Stokowski. For these musicians, the First World War was a time of great artistic development.

In Loschwitz, near Dresden, Leopold Auer, the sixty-nine-year-old teacher of the St. Petersburg Conservatory, was holding his annual summer camp for violinists. As Mischa Elman and Efrem Zimbalist had already passed through his hands, Jascha Heifetz and Toscha Seidel were then his two most brilliant protégés. Auer was interned in his villa, ordered to report periodically to the police, and asked to obey a 7 P.M. curfew. But it was only a matter of time until his repatriation was arranged, for he was well beyond the arbitrary age limits established for possible military service—seventeen and fifty-five. In October 1914, Auer (too old) and Seidel (too young) were allowed to take a special train to the Baltic, where they boarded a Swedish ship and sailed to Russia. But Jascha Heifetz, also too young, had to remain in Berlin with his father, who was of military age. In December, however, they too were allowed to return to their homeland. Three years later, in 1917, Heifetz, then seventeen, made his spectacular debut in New York. Soon afterwards, Auer and Seidel arrived in America—escaping this time not from the Kaiser but from civil war in the former land of the Czar.

In Wannsee, the Lhevinnes' neighbors celebrated the outbreak of the war with their own variation on the "Geld-Auto" theme:

> The office telephon[ed] every resident and request[ed] all who had arms to go out and try to stop the mysterious car, with the French loan to Russia on board. All the residents went out with their guns, but after three hours wait concluded that the Russians had dodged them.[1]

The first few days of the war were particularly harrowing for the Lhevinnes because of the possibility they might be denounced and taken to a prison camp. Repatriation was completely out of the question for the family, for Lhevinne was thirty-nine years old and a reserve officer in the Imperial Russian Army. But soon after the declaration of war, the pianist received a document from Kaiser Wilhelm that spared him the kind of anguish Gabrilowitsch had suffered at Meisbach. Because of Lhevinne's musical talent, the document declared, he and his family were to be interned only in their villa, and not in a prison camp.[2] The conditions of their civil internment were these: they must report to the police regularly;

they must obey an 8 P.M. curfew; and they must not give concerts or earn money as long as Russia and Germany were at war. The prohibition on income was the harshest condition, for they had no access to their savings in Russia.

Even had they been allowed to teach, they would not have kept many students for long. For on the fifth of August, England declared war on Germany. This surprising move released an animosity for English-speaking people equal to that which for four days had been reserved for Russians. James Gerard, the American Ambassador to Berlin, reported that two secretaries of his own embassy were slapped in the face because they dared to speak the English language on the streets of Berlin. With the distinction between British and American clearly too academic, Gerard advised all Americans to leave the country. Passports (which had been unnecessary before the war) were issued quickly, and special trains were chartered to carry American citizens beyond the German border. On these trains departed all the Lhevinnes' students save two: J. D. Ketchum and Sarah McKeen.

Ketchum had been out to Wannsee for a lesson on the day before England declared war. His diary for August 4, 1914, records great admiration for the German people ("I am sure they will win, for right is on their side and they know it"). It also suggests the Lhevinnes shared his sentiments. In spite of the fact that mobilization had reduced passenger trains to the suburbs from 150 to 6,

> I reached Wannsee fairly easily. Lhevinne was surprised to see me, as no one else had tried to get there during the train dislocation, but after a chat over the war he gave me a splendid lesson of nearly two hours on the Chopin [concerto] which was much improved. He is a Russian, but has lived here so long that he has not been arrested like all the rest. His sympathies are entirely with Germany, he says he hates the Russian government worse than any German does. It is the most cruel, tyrannical, and corrupt in the world.

A day later, when England declared war, Ketchum, a Canadian citizen, became an enemy alien too. Jailed and interrogated, he was soon released on conditions similar to those governing the Lhevinnes' civil internment. He continued to practice the piano, and on August 25 went to Wannsee for another lesson.

> Had a long talk with the Lhevinnes and a very good lesson, the concerto being much improved in spite of the war. It was very nice out there, playing in the big music-room with the family having tea out in the garden.

The peace was deceptive. Ketchum never returned to Wannsee. Three days later he was re-arrested—this time permanently. Until the Armistice of 1919 he lived at Ruhleben, a race track on the outskirts of Berlin converted into a prison camp for British civilians. The aspiring pianist was turned into a practicing sociologist. Ketchum's study of life at Ruhleben was published posthumously in 1965.[3]

During the month of August, when Ketchum had come for lessons, the Lhevinnes' spirits had been somewhat buoyed by the possibility that the German government would allow the pianist to visit America for his tour. A few months later, however, Lhevinne was informed that he could not go. He sent Loudon Charlton the disappointing news:

> At the time of the first hostilities of this deplorable war, I was unable for a while to tell whether or not it would be possible for me to go to America. After a few weeks of suspense I was definitely informed that the German government (the attitude of whose officials has been most courteous) would permit me to leave, and I notified you accordingly. I was told, however, that it was unwise to leave Berlin until definite arrangements for sailing were made, for, if by any chance I left the city and found it impossible to embark, I would not be able to return to my home in Wannsee. The difficulties of securing passage were innumerable, and I was compelled to wait much longer than I had anticipated. Suddenly an order was promulgated that no more alien residents of Berlin belonging to any of the warring nations would be permitted to leave Germany. I exerted every influence through governmental and business friends, but all to no avail, for I was quite unable to secure the necessary passport.[4]

Josef Lhevinne's wartime trip to America would not have been the escape to freedom that those of Gabrilowitsch, Heifetz, Seidel, and Auer were. But it would certainly have provided money and new impressions with which to help buoy the spirits of the family for the duration of the war.

At least the Lhevinnes had their physical safety to be thankful for. They were also thankful for having been able to communicate the news of that safety to Josef's parents. Writing to Charlton in New York was no problem, but in August 1914 for a Russian in Germany to write openly to Moscow was impossible. Word was sent through intermediaries. Josef's father never actually saw the letter. The husband of the woman through whom the letter was sent "had been constrained to destroy it," he wrote. "He gave me the contents of the letter by word of mouth." Arkady Levin was eighty years old, and he responded to news of his son's family's safety with this moving sentence:

> Believe me, my dear, that I and mother have not kissed each other for a long, long time, but on this happy occasion we threw ourselves on each other's necks as if by electric shock and we began to kiss each other sincerely with tears in our eyes.

His letter was also sent through an intermediary—an old orchestra crony who is "my only heart-to-heart friend among the Russians." Signed "Arkady and Fanny" and dated September 12, 1914, it is, so far as we know, the last time Josef Lhevinne heard from his parents.

In the Chinese House there was now very little of the "joy and good times" Arkady Levin had asked God to send his son after learning, in June, of its purchase. When war was declared, the only money the Lhevinnes had on hand was that with which they planned to furnish the new villa. They immediately called the *Kunstgewerbe Haus* to cancel their order. That firm's artists and craftsmen must have been busy meeting the demands of mobilization, for the order had not yet been processed. With the money they were to have spent on custom-made furnishing, the Lhevinnes supported themselves for the better part of a year. The sudden turn of events meant that their main concern was now with the basic necessities of life: food, clothing, and shelter. Of clothing they had enough; of food too little; of shelter too much.

The extravagant Chinese House was transformed by the declaration of war into the proverbial white elephant. On the first floor were an entrance hall, a music and a living room, a dining room, a den, a large kitchen, and a parlor. A long straight staircase led to the second floor. Here were Constantine's bedroom and his studio-playroom, his mother's practice room, his father's study, his parents' bedroom, and Grandfather Bessie's bedroom. On the third floor were two guest rooms; on the fourth, an attic. The basement had a living room, a bedroom, and a small kitchen for gardener and chauffeur. Altogether, the villa had four, five, or six bathrooms— no one remembers exactly.

With so much space, the Lhevinnes desperately needed *some* furnishings, and they met the problem with ingenuity if not with style. "When Josef bought the villa from the Chinese man, he did not buy the furniture with the crown engraved on it, but he did pay 300 marks for a lot of junk in the attic that the man wanted to throw away. With that we furnished the villa. In the music room, with the damask walls and two Ibach pianos, we put an old green sofa. In the dining room, which had beautiful oak paneling and wallpaper of a beautiful raspberry color, we put the garden furniture: a big white table with white chairs that we used for picnics outdoors! It was really very funny."

Not only was the furniture ludicrous but the upkeep on the place was staggering. To keep all its rooms warm during the winter, to supply current to all its electric lamps, to keep water running in all its faucets—this was a large drain on the family's dwindling resources. Lhevinne kept daily records of his expenditures during the war, and in each year's accounts electricity, the waterworks, gas, and coal occupy a prominent position. He was so meticulous that in May he entered the small amount paid to the *Shornsteinfeger* (chimney sweep).

The basement had to be kept as warm as the rest of the house, because the gardener and chauffeur were replaced by "two German soldiers who slept downstairs. They were there not so much to guard us as to guard the railroad tracks to Potsdam, which were opposite our villa. Every day we had to give these soldiers and two others sandwiches from our rations, and we always gave them the best of what little food we had, for we feared they would have stomach-aches and report 'the Russians' for poisoning them." The "two other" soldiers were watchmen the Lhevinnes apparently hired for their own protection—and paid 27 marks a month.

Surplus of shelter was matched by scarcity of food. For the food supply was limited by more than inability to pay—which would have been limitation enough. As the Allied blockade became increasingly effective, foodstuffs were rationed out in ever-decreasing quantities. The Lhevinnes were allowed to buy as much food as Germans were; even so, a person's weekly portion sometimes amounted to a quarter pound of meat and a quarter pound of butter. The bread was made half of flour, half of birch tree bark. Vegetables, jams, and marmalades all had one source—the turnip. And even for food of such poor quality, Mme. Lhevinne remembers, "you had to take a suitcase full of money." The typical breakfast in the Chinese House during the war was bread spread with turnip marmalade, and coffee made from acorns that grew in the yard. Even when sweetened with saccharine, the coffee and marmalade left a bitter aftertaste.

Such a limited food supply had to be supplemented, and the Lhevinnes, with their excess of space, did the obvious. "The villa had a marvelous garden with magnificent flowers, and the next summer we decided to make a vegetable garden out of it. Among the first things we grew were strawberries, and it was a tremendous joy to eat them. Later, we had radishes and carrots and corn. A man continued to help us in the garden, but gradually Josef did more and the gardener less. By then, Don was big enough to help, too. As the war went on, we all spent more and more time in the garden. Without it those years would have been much more difficult than they were."

Don shed the name Constantine about the time he began to work in the garden—and about the time the Grand Duke Constantine's Romanov relative declared war on Germany. He remembers that the family became so tired of turnips that he and "Daddy" cut down a few of the acorn-bearing oak trees and expanded the garden to include potatoes. During the summer months, father and son could often be found high above the ground, vying with ravenous birds for the spoils of a new cherry crop. As an alternative to turnip marmalade, Masha made cherry and strawberry preserves.

Lhevinne also used his angling skills to supplement the family diet: every month he spent several marks to renew his *Angelkarten* (fishing licenses). In addition, Don remembers that his father shot an occasional fowl. In 1917, Lhevinne paid thirty-two marks for a *Luftgewehr* (air rifle). Like all good woodsmen, he not only hunted and fished but also learned to identify edible plants.

"There was a real forest at the end of Bismarckstrasse, and we went there almost every day to walk. One day we found a place where hundreds of mushrooms grew, and we were so hungry we were temped to eat them. There were two kinds—both a beautiful brown color on top and white underneath. They were absolutely identical except that one had a little red line underneath. We knew from the forests in Russia that the one without the line was wonderful and the other was poisonous. But we were afraid that with the different soil it might not be the same. So just to be sure, Josef went in to Berlin and bought a book on mushrooms, and verified that the white one was safe. After that, we ate them whenever we went walking, and they were wonderful.

"One day it looked like it would rain, and we had the brainstorm to fill our umbrellas with mushrooms and take them home. The next day we went again, and brought back big umbrellas and baskets full. Josef especially liked mushrooms, and it was really a God-sent gift to have them right there in the forest. Masha fried them and cooked them and made soup from them, and whenever we got enough eggs, she chopped them and made omelettes. For the winter, she would marinate them with vinegar.

"When our neighbors first saw us carrying mushrooms from the woods, they expected never to see us again, because they thought they were poisonous. But when we came out of the forest day after day, they finally got the courage to ask: 'How do you eat them? Aren't they poisonous?' So we explained to them what we knew. The result was that in the last years of the war we had to get up very early in the morning for the mushrooms, and even then we seldom found more than a dozen, for everyone in the village knew one from the other. In a way, we were sorry for ourselves that we had told everybody, but we rejoiced that it was a help for so many families."

Rations, gardening, fishing, and mushroom picking—from these sources the Lhevinnes managed to obtain a meager supply of food. Fortunately, one additional line of supplies became available to them. This was thanks to the generosity of their one American student who stayed in Berlin:

"Before the war, Sarah McKeen was the worst student of all, and she took her lessons from me. When her lesson was over, I always had to take an aspirin and go to bed, and each time Josef would say, 'Rosina, that is the last time you give her a lesson,' because he saw how difficult it was for me. But always the next week she would come back and say, 'Mrs. Lhevinne, I lived the whole week looking forward to the lesson with you,' and I could not say no. That went on for about two years.

"When the war was declared, Ambassador Gerard advised her to return to America, and so did we. But she said, 'As long as Mrs. Lhevinne is in Berlin, I am in Berlin.' By chance, she happened to share an apartment with a secretary to the Dutch Embassy. The war did not bother things so much in Holland, and every so often the Embassy would receive a large package of food. Of what the secretary brought home, half went to Miss McKeen. And she would not take a bite of it, but insisted on giving all of it to me.

"That changed things completely. Before long, both Josef and my father began to say, 'By the way, when is Miss McKeen coming for a lesson?' On the appointed day, they both sat by the window and waited for her to come up the walk, her arms full of bacon and coffee and chocolate and half heads of Dutch cheese. With a hungry family of five, this food did not last long, but it certainly helped our morale."

On August 4, the day before he became an enemy alien and a few weeks before he became a prisoner of war, Ketchum had written:

Indeed, it seemed impossible to believe that there really was war, out there in Wannsee. . . . The sight of the smooth lakes lying quietly between their pine-clad shores, the twittering of the birds, the stillness of it all, made one's thoughts turn inevitably to peace and rest.

For the Lhevinnes "the sight of the smooth lakes lying quietly between their pine-clad shores" lasted throughout the war. But that did not guarantee thoughts of "peace and rest." Shortages of food and money, serious as they were, were no more difficult than the artistic and social deprivations, than the "stillness of it all." They could use their ingenuity to increase their food supply; they could not alter their forced isolation. Rosina suffered from this the most.

"Because Josef was both a gourmet and a gourmand, he suffered physically from not having enough food. But I became almost sick mentally, because there was no possibility to exchange ideas or to be with other people on those long evenings with nothing to do. The Germans were nice to us, and a few even invited us to come and see them, but we were afraid, because if you said anything at all they could denounce you as spies. We preferred to say nothing, and were therefore forced to see no one. With my love of people, I suffered terribly during those years."

Although Lhevinne did not miss the daily companionship of other people as much as his wife did, he felt the musical deprivation as strongly as she. When his trip to America was canceled, it looked as if he would have no chance at all to perform during the war. In 1915, the German government allowed him to play at a few charity concerts in support of the war effort, but at these he played only one or two solo works. The only significant performance he gave in Berlin during the war was on November 19, 1915, when he played Liszt's E-flat Concerto at a benefit concert of the Berlin Philharmonic. According to Arthur Abell's review of the concert, the first year of internment had done little to diminish Lhevinne's interpretative powers. Abell had heard him many times in Berlin before the war, but had never witnessed so great an ovation for him, nor had he ever "heard Lhevinne play so magnificently. His reading of the . . . concerto was big, broad, authoritative, masterful."[5] The program as a whole was well calculated to stir up patriotic sentiments. Besides the Liszt Concerto, there was music by Weber, Berlioz (from *The Damnation of Faust*), and Wagner, plus a recitation from Goethe's *God and World*. The famed soprano Lilli Lehmann (then aged sixty-seven) closed the program by singing the "Immolation" from *Götterdämmerung*.

A few weeks later, Rosina joined her husband for one of the

last of his handful of benefit performances. It was her only public appearance during the war. "That one concert we were allowed to play was at Philharmonic Hall in Berlin and was sponsored by the Crown Princess. She sent an officer in a wonderful carriage to take us to the concert, but when we got to the hall we clearly had the feeling of being enemies. The audience was completely German and the performers were too, except for us. After the concert, the Crown Princess asked all the performers to her box and thanked them for their contributions. She invited us too, and was very cordial and shook our hands, and said that she liked our playing. But then the officer took us home, and the next day at eight in the morning we reported as usual to the police station, where they always stamped our books with the image of an organ grinder. It was the only way they had to indicate musician."

The "completely German audience" appreciated the Lhevinnes' contribution as much as the Crown Princess did. After a Bruckner symphony, the delicacy and grace of Mozart's E-flat Concerto for Two Pianos was a welcome contrast.

That Rosina Lhevinne played a Mozart work at her only public performance during the war was significant: every morning during the conflict she read through at least one of his sonatas at the piano. Playing Mozart every day helped to give some meaning to the confusing void with which civil internment had brought her face to face. But aside from that, there was very little musical stimulation. There were relatively few concerts in Berlin during the war, and it was both expensive and inconvenient for the Lhevinnes to go to them, for each time they had to go to the police station and have their books stamped with the "organ grinder." As there were no commercial recordings to speak of, the only music they heard in their home was the music they made themselves. "So instead of hearing symphonies every evening, we played through them with four hands at two pianos and in this way became thoroughly acquainted with a great deal of the orchestral literature. That gave us great pleasure, and in some ways compensated for the lack of concerts."

There was enough music in the Chinese House during the war for Don to remember habitually falling asleep to the sound of the piano. He was eight years old when war was declared, and at that point became totally isolated from children his own age. As a child of enemy aliens, he was not allowed to attend German schools, but continued to receive his formal education from a series of strict tutors. To some degree, however, the absence of playmates was compensated for by the fact that his father now spent more time at home. They not only worked in the garden together but took daily advantage of the fact that Germany's toy industry was almost as advanced as her armaments industry. Their favorite products were little house kits made of miniature bricks that were assembled according to plan and stood two or three feet tall. They worked on these for hours at a time and finished each one in a few weeks. Don's mother also remembers "railroad tracks that went from one room to another in the Chinese House. There was a very complicated switching system, and Josef would sit on the floor all day long demonstrating it to Don. I would say, 'My goodness, he's so young he can't understand what you are doing.' And he would answer, 'Yes, but I didn't have any of this in *my* childhood, and *I* enjoy it very much.' "

Lhevinne also read to his son a great deal during the war. Usually he chose adventure stories about the Americas by James Fenimore Cooper or Karl Friedrich May. Lhevinne knew May and was amazed that he could write such exciting stories about South America without having been there. May had acquired his material only by reading and using his imagination.

For Rosina, one of the few diversions on winter afternoons was to watch her husband skate. "The lake was frozen right in front of the bedroom window, and it was so elegant the way he went with that rhythm, making the 8, the 8, the 8, the 8. It would stay in the ice a week, he cut it so deep." The "figure eight" itself sums up all too neatly the monotonous and self-enclosed existence she led during the war.

Lhevinne liked to skate on the lake because there were not the confines of a rink. Once each year, he was allowed to escape the confines of civil internment and spend a few weeks in Budapest. The extent to which his physical and artistic health came to depend on this annual journey cannot be exaggerated.

The visits to Budapest were arranged by Gustav Bárczy, a concert manager and member of the Rózsavölgyi publishing house, which in 1914 had published Lhevinne's edition of Tausig's transcription of Schumann's *El Contrabandista*. Bárczy and Lhevinne had been prewar friends. Regulations prohibited travel by enemy aliens between allied cities, but Bárczy's brother István was mayor of Budapest. He was able to allow Lhevinne to come once a year from Berlin to play charity concerts. This arrangement literally gave the pianist a new lease on life.

His first wartime concert in Budapest was in March 1915. Although his playing had been thoroughly appreciated in that city before the war, this recital came as a new revelation. The account printed in *Pesti Naplo* deserves to be quoted at length, both for its description of the atmosphere of the evening and for the questions it raises about the pianist in the last sentences.

> Those by whom the Auditorium of the *Musik-Akademie* was packed to the limit gladly forgot that Lhevinne had been born in hostile Russia; which is not surprising, considering the intelligence of the Budapest public. We mention this because it happens to be such an opportunity for calling attention to our public's good sense. Only he who comes armed against us is considered our enemy. He who brings art and music is our good friend.
>
> Josef Lhevinne is primitive force itself. We have the feeling that among the living masters of the piano he is the greatest. For him nothing is impossible on the piano, and his technique, dynamics, tempo, and rhythm differ from those of the best virtuosos by an inimitable naturalness and matter of course. Even the most prominent of them do not come up to him in supreme mastery of the instrument. Lhevinne is something absolutely new, something unique and unprecedented, something one can only marvel at, and about whose existence one must rejoice.
>
> As he sits at the piano, it dawns upon us that what is being given is the highest measure of human achievement. After each number there was a tumult of applause. The faces in the overfilled hall beamed, strangers smiled to each other—it was in the air that something extraordinary was taking place. Lhevinne, however, looked straight before him, quietly unconcerned, as if his art were the most natural matter-of-course thing in the world. If the masterfulness of his art struck us, we were equally struck by his calmness of manner. What thinks this magnificent man about music, about the piano, about himself? And what about us, his hearers, we who pay homage to him and whom he scarcely seems to notice?[6]

Lhevinne's seeming aloofness increased each year that he returned to Budapest; and so did the reverential awe with which Hungarians regarded his playing. Marian Szekely-Freschl, the noted voice teacher at Juilliard, was then a student in Budapest. She remembers that Lhevinne concerts in that city during the war were like Horowitz concerts in New York during the late 1960s: whenever one was announced, the next day it was sold out, even if it was a month before the performance.

"Josef Lhevinne was my great idol during the war. I first met him at a party given by my uncle after my graduation from the Royal Academy of Music. When my uncle introduced me, it was like being introduced to the Lord. But Lhevinne was very kind, and at my uncle's request he agreed to look after me when I went to Berlin to begin my vocal career."[7]

Lhevinne was always a bit reluctant to leave Budapest during the war, because there he found in abundance at least two things he lacked in Berlin—food and money. Hungary did not have the food shortage that Germany did, and Mme. Lhevinne remembers "a comical little episode" connected with that fact:

"Josef always took his dress suit to Budapest, of course, and when he came back Masha would take it to the attic because he wouldn't use it again until the next year. Then, when he was invited to return, she would bring it down from the attic as if it were a sacred garment. But when he tried it on, it hung on him like a hanger because he had lost so much weight. So he would quickly take it to the tailor and the tailor would make it smaller, and Josef would go to Budapest. There he would play and play and eat and eat, and before he left for home they would have to enlarge it again."

Like his waistline, Lhevinne's bank roll bulged in Budapest and receded quickly in Berlin. Each year after the charity concert in the Hungarian city (which one year benefited Alsace-Lorraine), Bárczy carefully arranged several private concerts for the pianist. The proceeds from these private engagements represented almost the only money Lhevinne earned during the war, and for a few months after the annual trip to Budapest he would be able to buy a few "delicacies" in Berlin's markets. But the money never lasted long. A prosaic incident suggests the extremities of Lhevinne's financial and gastronomical plight. One day he had a little extra money and took the train to Berlin, where he found and purchased a large chunk of wurst. Riding a crowded train back to Wannsee, he had placed the meat on an overhead rack, and when he got off the train he absent-mindedly left it there. Many years later in America he told a friend that was the worst moment of his life.

The money that was to have gone to the *Kunstgewerbe Haus* ran out in 1915, and each year after that Lhevinne had to write Bárczy for cash advances against the concerts he was scheduled to play in Budapest. In addition, he was forced for the duration of the war to take large loans from Bárczy and from Ibach (the company whose piano he used for his wartime concerts). At the end of 1916 he summed up the family's income and expenses for the year:

Income:	Ibach, Budapest, Bárczy	12,178 M.
	Lessons	3,500 M.
		15,678 M.
Expenses:		15,317 M.
Balance:		361 M.

The year's balance of 361 marks (the equivalent of $90) shows that every *pfennig* counted—and most of the money came from Budapest. That was even true of the 3,500 marks the Lhevinnes made that year from teaching. Technically, they were not allowed to teach for money. But it seems the German authorities looked the other way as long as the money they received did not come from German pocketbooks.

The 3,500 marks earned in 1916 compared with 31,500 marks in 1910–11. If Lhevinne continued to teach at the prewar rate of 40 marks per lesson, that amount could have come from as few as two students. Two students are known to have studied with him in 1916. One, Miss McKeen, was American. The other, Piroska Hevesi, was Hungarian. Miss Hevesi had discontinued her studies with Béla Bartók in Budapest in order to prepare for a concert debut in Berlin, and evidently had followed Lhevinne home after hearing him play. She studied with him during the 1915–16 season, and that spring, at age twenty-two, made her first orchestral and recital appearances in Berlin.

The annual trip to Budapest, then, brought Lhevinne concerts, food, money, and one female student—in addition to a brief respite from the monotony of civil internment. There was only one unpleasant aspect to it. "Every summer this wonderful friend Bárczy would write to Josef on the letterhead of a musical society. 'Josef,' the letter would say, 'we can arrange several concerts again for you here, but this time the Beethoven Society would like you to play such and such sonatas.' On the list would be maybe one work that he knew and three or four that he did not. He would write back asking to substitute sonatas already in his repertoire. But Bárczy always had to reply that it would be impossible to change the program, that the society insisted that if he wanted to play in Budapest he would have to play what the society wanted to hear. So, hungry and tired and discouraged, he would roll up his sleeves and learn the four sonatas and go there and play. Each year the same thing happened with a different composer, and he had to learn many new works. But that inconvenience was a small price to pay for the great opportunity of being able to play."

Because of Germany's submarines, America entered the war on the side of the Allies in April 1917; despite the submarines, the Allied blockade of Germany became increasingly tight. As the size of their rations dwindled, the Lhevinnes grew more and more food in the garden, a fact that shows in their expenditures for the year: increased amounts were allotted for garden tools, seeds, and fertilizer. They also had to borrow more money from Bárczy and Ibach, but as they muddled along from month to month they at least had the security of knowing that at the war's end they would be able to use their savings and investments in Russia to pay off their debts. That security, of course, vanished in November 1917.

"When the Revolution began in Russia, and Lenin came to power, we soon learned that all our money had been confiscated by the Russian government. I am still surprised at our reaction to the news. Because we were both idealistic persons, we thought that with all the money of the rich divided among the poor there might not be any more poverty in Russia."

The Lhevinnes could be philosophical about losing tens of thousands of rubles to which they had no access at the moment, but when the German war machine ran out of rubber and confiscated their small household supply of *that* item, their living conditions were changed dramatically. Without small rubber rings, Masha could not make cherry and strawberry preserves, and the family had to put up with the tiresome turnip marmalade. And without tires for their bicycles, they had to walk to the police station. They also went walking at night, for at least the stars were dependable.

"One night the sky was unusually clear, and Josef became extremely excited. 'There is something in the Aquila constellation that doesn't belong there,' he said. I tried to persuade him to go to bed—not only because of the curfew but because we usually retired early, before we became too hungry to sleep. But he insisted on staying outdoors and he took his telescope to confirm what he had seen. He spent most of the night with his books and maps of the heavens.

"The next morning, the newspapers announced the discovery of a star of the first magnitude in another constellation. Josef insisted it was in Aquila. On the next day the newspapers printed a correction. Josef was right."

Nova Aquilae III appeared in the heavens on June 8, 1918, attained a brightness only slightly inferior to Sirius, and then faded away as mysteriously as it had come. One month later, the Lhevinnes' second child—a daughter, named Marianna—came into the world. The human constellation into which she was born was hardly as serene as the one into which Aquila's *nova stella* was accepted.

"A few months before Marianna was born, Josef and I were out walking and a young boy on a bicycle struck me accidentally in the back. After that, we had been terribly afraid that the baby would come too soon. But Marianna was born right on time in July, and in spite of the difficulties of our living conditions, the hunger and privation, she was a most wonderful addition to the family. She was delivered at a hospital in Berlin, and I must say that they treated me very well there. My doctor was an exceedingly nice woman who didn't consider me as an alien at all. She was very fond of music, and looked at me from this angle.

"The nurse from the hospital came home with us and stayed for about twelve days, but it was definitely a mistake to send her away so soon. Masha stayed with Marianna after the nurse left, and Masha—saint that she was—was still inexperienced with babies. Marianna would cry, and I would tremble and Josef would tremble, and we were a frightened family.

"I was so excited about having a daughter that I said to my father, who had a nice room facing the sun, with a terrace overlooking the garden, 'I know you will not mind, but I think it would be best for Marianna to be in the room with the sun.' So Marianna and Masha moved into that wonderful room, and my father moved into one of the guest rooms upstairs. Although it was one of our great pleasures in life to keep Father with us after Mother died and to care for him in his old age, it is interesting how in *my* old age I think not of the good we did, but think instead with bitterness of what we could have done but did not do for him. I am glad that Marianna had the room with the sun and the terrace, but I regret to this day that in that huge house we did not find a more comfortable place for my father."

So during the first few months of Marianna's life, as American re-enforcements reversed the balance of power on the Western Front, revolution swept Russia, and the Aquila constellation (known as the Eagle or, sometimes, the Vulture) perched unmoved in the heavens, benignly neglectful of its *nova stella*, the members of the Lhevinne family, in the self-enclosed world of the Chinese House, celebrated, and adjusted to, their new indisputable evidence of the miracle of birth.

The Armistice of November 11, 1918, ended the war for J. D. Ketchum and more than two thousand British civilians interned with him in the Ruhleben prison camp. French and American subjects who had been interned in Germany were also freed at once. But for the citizens of Germany, and for Russian aliens interned in that country, the Armistice did not bring peace. For more than ten months the victorious Triple Entente (England, France, and the United States) maintained its economic blockade against Germany; and for more than four years, two hundred thousand Russians who had been interned in Germany were denied repatriation.

The reason, of course, was the civil war in Russia. A week after the Armistice ended the First World War, General Kolchak emerged as the leader of the "White Russians" who were attempting to overthrow the Bolshevik government. Germany, having difficulty enough feeding its own people, would gladly have sent its Russian prisoners home. But the Entente was more concerned with seeing Lenin's regime overthrown than with freeing the men who had been its own allies at the beginning of the war. Fearing that if the Russian prisoners were freed, they would support the Bolsheviks rather than Kolchak, the victorious nations not only forced these people to remain in Germany but insisted that the German government feed and clothe them.[8]

Because the Lhevinnes had not been sent to a prison camp with the rest of the Russians, they were spared being used as pawns in these postwar maneuvers. Even so, they were not allowed to leave Germany until September 1919. Because of the civil war in Russia and the war-ravaged state of Europe, Lhevinne had decided to take his family to America. For nearly a year after the Armistice they lived for the day their passports would be approved. Although the food shortage continued, they no longer had to report each day to the authorities. And Lhevinne at last was free to play whatever concerts could be arranged in Europe's depressed musical world.

In September 1919 he played in Berlin. He was a different man from the one who had played so magnificently at the charity concert three years before. Despite a warm welcome from the audience in Beethovensaal, he seemed unable to concentrate on his pianistic task. With each successive composition, he projected more the mood of the music, but not until he played Brahms's F minor Sonata at the end of the program did he seem to approach his full powers.[9]

October took him to Breslau, Ratibor, and Zagreb; November, to Budapest, where he played three times. His return to that city must have brought mixed emotions, for it was on his previous visit there in March 1918 that he had read in a newspaper of Safonoff's death at his home in Kislovodsk in the Caucasus (where, incidentally, Alexander Solzhenitsyn was born several months later). Safonoff had not been able to communicate with the Lhevinnes during the war, and was one of several Russian friends and relatives they would never see or hear from again.

When Lhevinne played four concerts in Christiania (Oslo) in January 1919, the effects of internment were strikingly apparent.

He played with "a wealth of emotional intensity," one reporter wrote; but the same man added, after accompanying Lhevinne and the composer Christian Sinding to the Park Hotel after one of the concerts, that

> it would be hard to recognize Lhevinne as the same person of before the war. His features are now drawn, he is much thinner, and there is an unforgettable look in his eyes which grazes a bit too closely the boundaries of melancholy. [Both] the actual physical deprivation . . . [and] the continual worry and hopelessness of [being] a quasi-prisoner . . . have left their marks.[10]

A former enemy alien's freedom is ever less than complete.

The postwar concerts brought Lhevinne obvious emotional and financial relief, but perhaps more important to the rest of the family's well-being was the fact that their isolation was now over. For the first time in his life, Don was allowed to attend school, and every morning but Sunday he walked with a German friend named Fritz to the Real Schule in Zehlendorf (a suburb near Wannsee). Rosina could now display her daughter to friends, and again felt free to exchange opinions with Germans without fear of reprisal. Once more, the Chinese House opened its doors to students and friends. Among the friends was Marian Szekely-Freschl, who had arrived from Budapest to begin her vocal career:

"In that magnificent villa at Wannsee, I would sit in the corner of the huge practice room and watch Lhevinne prepare for a concert. Rosina would come into the room carrying the infant baby in her arms, and I thought Rosina was just beautiful. She was slim and small and very attractive.

"One day I was walking with Mr. Lhevinne in the garden, and I said, 'Ah, your wife is so beautiful,' and he said, 'Oh?' He was very quiet when other people were around, but when I was alone with him he was usually very talkative. He became another person when he sat at the piano."

Although the Lhevinnes enjoyed their new life in the Chinese House, they were actually marking time until they received permission to leave for America. Their passages were finally arranged through the American ambassador at Copenhagen. They were to sail from that city on September 12, 1919, on the *Frederick VIII*. When September 12 arrived, the Lhevinnes were in Copenhagen and so was the ship, but they were not able to sail. A longshoremen's strike prevented the liner from leaving.

The strike delayed departure for four weeks. For Don, who was thirteen years old at the time, the extra month in Klampenborg, a suburb of Copenhagen, provided a swarm of interesting impressions. Even so, he realized how agonizing this period was for his parents. As Lhevinne waited for the strike to end, he wrote Loudon Charlton words which he and many others sincerely felt in the early decades of the twentieth century:

Oh, that tantalizing line of the western horizon. I look at it every morning and every evening from our hotel window, for I know that America lies beyond. Only those who have gone through the experience of internment can know the real meaning of the last four years or can realize my yearning for your country.[11]

Actually, Klampenborg (and the Lhevinnes' hotel window) was situated on the *east* coast of Denmark. But surely in his mind's eye, the pianist saw the western horizon.

Before carrying the Lhevinnes to America, the *Frederick VIII* had deposited on European soil a man who resented the United States as much as they yearned for it. Dr. Karl Muck had good reason. The distinguished conductor had begun his tenure with the Boston Symphony Orchestra in 1906, the year the Lhevinnes had first sailed to America. In 1917, after America had entered the war, he was arrested in Boston and interned for two years in a Georgia prison camp. His crime: allegedly refusing to begin a symphonic concert with "The Star-Spangled Banner."

Muck was only the most prominent of many "enemy" musicians who were casualties of the psychological fury with which America had entered the Great European War. Ernst Kunwald, conductor of the Cincinnati Orchestra, was also interned, as were other German members of his orchestra. Even Fritz Kreisler, Austrian violinist and humanitarian, was advised not to play in America during the hostilities. All his engagements were canceled, and neither the Armistice (November 1918) nor the Treaty of Versailles (June 1919) was sufficient to allow his safe return to concert life. He had to wait until October 1919, when a separate peace between Austria and the United States was signed.

Some Americans were not satisfied with purging concert halls of German bodies. In several major cities "German" music was prohibited as well (which, needless to say, severely limited the repertoire). The words with which Lhevinne had been received in Budapest—

Only he who comes armed against us is considered our enemy. He who brings art and music is our good friend.

—found no echo in the New World.

For non-Germans and non-Austrians, of course, the musical climate was most stimulating (except in cities where German music was *verboten* for them, too). Russian musicians, especially seemed to thrive in America during the war. The most quoted anecdote of the period involves three of them. When Jascha Heifetz made his Carnegie Hall debut in 1917, Leopold Godowsky and Mischa Elman were sitting in a box. After hearing a few notes, Elman whispered, "My, it's getting hot in here." To which Godowsky replied, "Not for pianists."

Heifetz was the instrumental sensation of wartime America, just as the voice sensation was an Italian soprano whose story is connected indirectly with the Lhevinnes. Homer Samuels, a young American, had come to Wannsee for piano lessons in 1910 and had studied with Lhevinne for several years. At the time the war broke out, Samuels was on tour with violinist Karl Flesch. When Flesch returned to his home in Germany, Samuels had to find another job. The next year he accompanied violinist Arrigo Serato, who then returned to Italy. The year after that, he toured with singer Emmy Destinn, who was interned in Bohemia during the summer. Again without a job, Samuels agreed to accompany an unknown soprano on her first American tour. By the end of the season, Amelita Galli-Curci was a celebrity. The Chicago Opera Company signed her immediately, and when she appeared in *La Traviata* at the Lexington Theater in New York in 1918, more than seven thousand people tried to enter the small East Side theater. One of the larger musical riots of the war ensued, but at least in this case most of the venom was directed at fellow spectators, not at the performers.

As the Lhevinnes contemplated the "tantalizing line of the western horizon" from Copenhagen, they were quite unaware of America's mistreatment of "enemy" musicians (Dr. Muck would gladly have enlightened them, had he bumped into them when he stepped off the *Frederick VIII*). Nor did they realize that the America awaiting them in 1919 was a nation considerably more complex and problematical, musically and otherwise, than they had found in 1906. But even had they known, they would have had little doubt that America was to be their permanent home. For during internment, memories of the America they had known before the war had become increasingly idyllic. That alone made them terribly eager to cross the Atlantic.

A more immediate cause of restlessness was the tour Loudon Charlton had arranged. It would begin October 24. By sailing on

September 12, Lhevinne would have had time to get settled in New York before embarking on what was certain to be a grueling season of concerts. With the four-week delay he feared he would lose not only the time to readjust to America but several engagements as well. Nothing could be done, though, so the family made the best of it.

"Just before we were finally able to leave, Gustav Bárczy came from Budapest to see us off. It was only then, when he came to say good-bye, that we learned the secret of the Budapest music society. It had not been the members of the society who had demanded that Josef play specific works, but Bárczy himself. He knew they were not in Josef's repertoire and that having them assigned was the only way he would work while interned in the villa. It is with great thankfulness that I think of this wonderful friend, whose goal was always to keep Josef working in order to maintain his morale.

"Soon after we were in America, there was terrible inflation in Hungary, and we were able to help Bárczy when he really needed it. Josef and I had many disagreements and differences in character, but we always agreed that that is the only way to live: to take and to give."

In America, each would have ample opportunity to do both.

IV

AT HOME IN AMERICA

9

Kew Gardens
and Points West

THE LHEVINNES steamed into New York on October 22, 1919. To celebrate, the family devoured crates of oranges in an attempt to revitalize their famished bodies. Before-and-after-the-war photographs of Lhevinne show the body-building process in reverse: he was decidedly paler and thinner. Yet there was no time for leisurely rejuvenation. During the first day on shore, he installed the family in a downtown Manhattan hotel. On the second day, he gave a recital in Connecticut. On the third day, he prepared for the fourth —his "homecoming" concert at the New York Hippodrome.

The Hippodrome accommodated five thousand spectators for circuses and all-Tchaikovsky programs. It was nearly filled when Lhevinne came on stage. After the spacious dome had swallowed the last notes of the B-flat minor Piano Concerto, the general public gave him a great ovation. But the many musicians present were disappointed, and not only because of the poor acoustics. The orchestral accompaniment had been "villainous."[1] And Lhevinne's own performance was below his prewar standards. Politely, the *Tribune* proclaimed him "perhaps not yet fully recovered" from his wartime ordeal.[2] But then, neither was America.

On the same day, Fritz Kreisler returned to Carnegie Hall. In New York, the Austrian violinist was warmly received. But in a dozen other cities, he was abominably baited by the American Legion. In Louisville, Kreisler's concert was billed as a clear-cut "test of the Americanism of everybody. One [is] either for the Legion and what it represents, or for an Austrian on tour."[3] It was as if a diplomat, after two years of concessions to the enemy, had been pistol-whipped on leaving the conference room.

New Yorkers, who had tolerated Kreisler's return, directed their postwar spleen at Otto Gorlitz. Violent crowds at the Lexington Theater actually stoned his opera company for daring to sing German opera *auf deutsch*. But such shoddy displays of extended warfever were only temporary. By the next season, Kreisler could play where he wished and German could be sung without riot.

The aftereffects of the war on Lhevinne, though subtler, were longer lasting. A few days after the Hippodrome concert, he set out on an eight-month, forty-city, fifty-concert tour. Greeted by large, friendly crowds in every city, he seemed to recover his prewar form. But in slight, unmistakable ways, the war's "acid mark" (as one writer put it) showed through. If Kreisler was a diplomat disserved, Lhevinne seemed a soldier slightly shell-shocked.

A week before Christmas, he played in Montreal. There, as in most cities, he opened his "homecoming" recital with Beethoven's Sonata *Les Adieux, l'absence, et le retour*. He played it with "such inescapable pathos that at times it was almost unbearable to listen to." Throughout the program, he evoked "fantasy and magic and the touch of genius." But he was "greatly changed." He played the entire recital "as if in a dream," and hardly seemed aware of his auditors. Once "there thundered so strident a burst" of applause that it seemed "he momentarily felt their enthusiasm." But he quickly escaped again into the privacy of the music.[4]

"One never knows how the artist's mood will develop," Lhevinne often said, and this was certainly true of him after the war. With time, however, the dreamy, reflective side of his personality came to predominate over the objective and direct, even to the point where one student voiced the fear that "when he came out on stage he might not find the piano." Whether this vagueness was a result of wartime isolation or was a natural development of the artist's temperament, no one can say. Whatever the cause, the change was plain to see.

Lhevinne worked off his wartime torpor on a strenuous concert tour; his wife shed hers in Manhattan's thriving musical colony. No better antidote to the musical and social deprivations of the previous five years could have been prescribed. The Rachmaninoffs, the Hofmanns, the Godowskys, the Stojowskis, Elman and Heifetz, Ganz and Gabrilowitsch—these musicians and many others either lived in New York or stopped over regularly. Because of Rosina's gregarious nature, the Lhevinnes soon took a place among them. But theirs was a place twice removed: he, as always, remained socially aloof; and they soon bought a house in the suburbs.

The house was on Richmond Hill Avenue in Kew Gardens,

Queens. Lhevinne chose the place for its spacious lawns and hill-top location—and much to the consternation of his wife, who had wished to find out about the neighborhood first. They soon did. Interested in joining a nearby club in order to play golf, they were astonished to learn that Jews were not allowed. ("In Russia we had learned with our mother's milk that America was free of such prejudice.") They were also surprised to discover the low esteem in which artists were held. One spring day, Mme. Lhevinne was pushing Marianna in a carriage down a neighborhood street. Another woman was pushing her baby and they began to chat. Soon came the inevitable American question:

"What does your husband do?"

"He is a concert pianist."

To which the other replied—as if dropping a trump card on the poor five of clubs—"Mine is a broker."

Perhaps the lady on the street should have had a look at Lhevinne's tour book for the year:

Concerts	$20,850
Steinway	3,000
Welte	2,500
American Cons.	6,700
	$33,050

The first figure appears to be his income after deducting Loudon Charlton's fee; the second sum he received for his use of and testimony to the Steinway piano; the third was royalties received from piano rolls for Welte and Sons; the fourth was his salary for teaching a summer master class at the American Conservatory in Chicago.

In signing up Lhevinne for the summer of 1920, John Hattstaedt, the director of the American Conservatory, had landed the big catch needed to match the attractions of the rival Chicago Musical College—Leopold Auer and Rudolph Ganz. As soon as Lhevinne's name was announced, applications flooded in, and by the time he arrived to begin the session, there were more students than the school could handle. The class had to be housed in a large and stuffy basement totally without ventilation. Even so, Lhevinne was glad to teach there, for he found a fishing hole not far from the city to which he could escape on weekends. With it as a lure, he was to spend ten consecutive shirt-sleeve-in-basement summers at the American Conservatory.

In June and July, Josef made brief visits to Kew Gardens to celebrate Don's fourteenth and Marianna's second birthdays, setting a tradition he kept as long as he taught in Chicago. By the time he returned home at the end of the session, a presidential election (Harding's, as it turned out) was in full swing, and he and his wife were eager to observe American democracy in action. He on his tours and she with her friends had heard much of its wondrous workings, including the two political parties, but so far could hardly say what the difference was between Democrats and Republicans. The revelation came on a weekend trip to the country—where they *were* allowed to play golf. Josef had ordered special left-handed clubs which had not yet arrived, so Rosina found herself on the fairways with a doctor of law who was also a judge.

"Here is my chance, I thought to myself, and I said to him, 'You know, I cannot deny myself the opportunity of speaking with a judge, who can certainly solve a big problem of mine. We have many friends in this country, and they get into these heated conversations—one for the Democrats and one for the Republicans. I listen to these disputes, but I still cannot formulate what is the difference between them, and what is the point of getting so excited.'

" 'My lady, I can tell you in one phrase,' he said. 'The one is there and the other wants to get there. It's as simple as that.'

"At first, I was shocked by this cynical statement. But until Franklin D. Roosevelt became president, we really saw no reason to think it false."

Political and neighborhood disillusionments aside, the Lhevinne family had much to be thankful for as the next concert season approached. Josef had overcome his wartime torpor, regained his concert reputation, and repaid part of the debt to Bárczy; Rosina again had access to the concerts and the social life essential to her mental health; and Don, having suffered the last in a long succession of tutors, could look forward to entering the Kew Forest Private School in the fall. The basement was filled with crates of vodka and caviar; delicatessen items replaced turnips and mushrooms as the staples of Masha's cooking; and a new automobile (of which Lhevinne was fiercely proud) was soon parked in front of the house. Grandfather Bessie and Marianna were the oldest and the youngest in the household, and he—as if the new home were lacking in Old World discord—gave his granddaughter a toy xylophone, which she liked to "play" on the kitchen floor. The Lhevinnes had settled in.

As Lhevinne crisscrossed the continent after the war, he found that America's musical axis had shifted slightly westward. Musical life had improved across the nation, but the most notable growth had come in the Midwest, where Chicago was the musical hub. Less than a week after the unhappy Hippodrome affair, Lhevinne played the Tchaikovsky Concerto with Frederick Stock and the Chicago Symphony Orchestra. Their accompaniment was as sublime as the other had been ruinous.

> There come moments in the life of the concert-goer when a performance is met with, which is so complete, so perfect, so satisfying that it becomes golden in experience and memory. From that time on his musical life is richer, his spiritual sensibility finer, his appreciation of the beautiful truer. These are the moments really worthwhile in life, the ones that positively count. For by them music exerts its true power and mankind grows bigger through its beneficent ministrations.[5]

For W. L. Hubbard, who had reviewed the first Lhevinne-Stock collaboration in 1906, this performance of the Tchaikovsky Concerto rounded out an era; he was serving his last year as music critic for the *Chicago Daily Tribune*. For pianist and conductor, it was the first of many highly satisfying postwar ventures.

The Chicago Symphony compared with any in the world at the end of the First World War, and the Chicago Opera Company rivaled the New York Metropolitan. But they were not the Midwest's only outstanding musical institutions. Lhevinne found improved orchestras in St. Louis, Minneapolis, and Cincinnati, and excellent new ones in Cleveland and Detroit. In 1919–20 alone, he played five times with Midwestern orchestras, and in the last four appearances insisted on dragging out his patented musical millstone—Anton Rubinstein's Fifth Concerto.

In Detroit, Ossip Gabrilowitsch provided a superb orchestral accompaniment for the work, for he too had come under Rubinstein's personal spell while a student in Russia. But in St. Louis, Lhevinne's special pleading for the work was likened to "Rabbinical ministration"—which, however edifying, is not what most people go to concerts for.[6] In Cincinnati, Eugène Ysaÿe provided an "inexcusably ragged" accompaniment and actually missed several orchestral entrances.[7] In Chicago, the performance itself was excellent, but Hubbard found the work "uninteresting, ineffective," and unworthy of Stock and Lhevinne.[8] At last Lhevinne got the message. For the rest of his career he favored concertos of Beethoven, Liszt, Chopin, and Tchaikovsky. The few times he did revert to Rubinstein, he chose the more melodic Fourth Concerto.

Even on the West Coast, to which he returned in late 1920, Lhevinne found surprising musical growth. In fact Boston and New

York were the only major cities he visited whose orchestras had not improved during the war. Colonel Higginson, founder of the Boston Symphony, had been so angered by the internment of Karl Muck that he disowned the orchestra in his will (he died in 1919). In New York the situation was not so much declining as stagnant: the two major orchestras were still in the hands of Stransky and Damrosch. Nor was Manhattan the opera town it had been in 1906. Any decline in its orchestral or operatic life, though, was more than made up for by the soloists who streamed through the city.

Besides Lhevinne, pianists included Hofmann, Rachmaninoff, Bauer, Godowsky, Gabrilowitsch, Rosenthal, Paderewski, De Pachmann, Siloti, Backhaus, Grainger, Hutcheson, Ganz, Cortot, Artur Rubinstein, Guiomar Novaës, and Olga Samaroff. Among violinists, Heifetz, Elman, Kreisler, Thibaud, Zimbalist, and Spalding were supreme. And for every established virtuoso there were many dozens more trying to make the grade. Among the pianists who made New York debuts shortly after the war were Artur Schnabel, Benno Moiseiwitsch, Serge Prokofieff, Clara Haskil, and Myra Hess. Significantly, of all the artists listed above, the only native Americans were Spalding and Samaroff—and they had been trained in Europe. The Menuhins and Kapells were still a short generation away.

In 1921, to help accommodate the growing number of recitalists, Town Hall was opened at Forty-third Street near Sixth Avenue (only a block from Aeolian Hall and the Hippodrome). The new hall relieved Carnegie of some of its burden but took away none of its glory. Then thirty years old, Carnegie Hall was one of the world's most important concert stages, and the only threat to its position came from real-estate men, who already wanted to demolish it to make way for office buildings. (See *Musical America*, February 14, 1925, when Isaac Stern, latter-day savior of the hall, was four years old.) Lhevinne gave three Carnegie Hall recitals in 1919–20, and at least one in each of the twenty-four subsequent seasons. Until Krehbiel's death in 1923 (after which Aldrich and Finck soon retired), the powerful four continued to appraise his art. Their accounts were often disturbingly contradictory. But such diversity of opinion would be welcome to some of today's musicians whose careers have been stunted by single and unchallenged reviews in the *New York Times*.

A case in point was the Carnegie Hall recital of April 18, 1920. In many ways it was a typical Lhevinne concert. A capacity audience, consisting largely of musicians and students, filled the hall on a warm Sunday afternoon. They demanded several encores during the program, and crowded around the stage at its close, making him play even after the stage lights were dimmed. The next day, Finck praised his interpretation of the Schubert-Liszt "The Linden Tree" and welcomed his performance of Anton Rubinstein's Prelude and Fugue in A-flat, a work that is "too much neglected." But only for the excellence of these pieces did he "pardon" the pianist for playing the "immature sonata, Opus 5, of Johannes Brahms." To Krehbiel, on the other hand, "The Linden Tree" was not sufficiently songlike and the Rubinstein sounded like "a faint reflection of Bach." The pinnacle of the recital was the pianist's performance of "one of the loveliest and most fragrant blossoms of musical romanticism"—Brahms's Sonata, Opus 5.

Critics might disagree about specific Lhevinne performances, but certain aspects of his pianism were beyond dispute. His technique was unsurpassed (as his colleagues Hofmann and Rachmaninoff freely admitted). So were his tone and his range of dynamics (Finck called him "the Heifetz of the piano" in this regard).[9] He also showed unusual deference to the composer. His modesty, complete lack of mannerisms, and cultivation of the "art that conceals art" invariably drew attention to the music rather than to himself. So much so that critics, in those days of subjective piano playing, sometimes expressed the wish for more Lhevinne in his interpretations and less unadulterated Brahms or Beethoven.

A peculiar aspect of his playing in the early 1920s was what the *Sun* called the "lash of contrasts." The contrasts were twofold: between Lhevinne's dreamy appearance and his authoritative playing; and between a crashing fortissimo and a pianissimo so gentle that "to analyze it was but to thrash a dream."[10] The *Sun's* use of such violent language to describe his playing was by no means atypical. At a San Francisco recital, he played "both massively and tenderly, swinging the hammer of Thor with mighty blows, or letting it fall as lightly as a wand."[11]

Any concertgoer could feel the "lash of contrasts" in Lhevinne's playing, but other aspects of his art were more esoteric. So highly developed was his technique that it "ceased to amaze any listeners save those who thoroughly understood the secrets of the piano."[12] This brought students and pianists to his recitals in droves, and it also inspired the phrase "a pianist's pianist."

When H. T. Parker applied that label to Lhevinne after a 1920 Boston recital, he meant it in a partially derogatory sense. Lhevinne, he wrote, is not capable of pleasing "miscellaneous hearers."

Acknowledging that many students came to hear the Russian play, Parker gave a slightly perverse reason as to why. The argument ran like this: If a student hears a great pianist—such as Hofmann, Bauer, Gabrilowitsch, or Rachmaninoff—he will be made so aware of the pianist's genius and his own lack of inspiration that he will despair. But if he hears the note-perfect Lhevinne, he will go home and work a little harder on his scales, with the hope that someday he will play just as well himself. For "given a like technical skill, a like musical and pianistic intelligence, a like experience of the concert hall [this is a lot to take for granted] and any pianist could have played . . . as Lhevinne played."[13] Parker's argument reduces to the old prewar complaint that Lhevinne's playing lacked emotion, passion, and the spark of individuality.

Some who heard the pianist went along with Parker's reasoning. Others gave the same facts a different twist. The latter usually made the vital distinction that Harold Schonberg emphasized in an article on Heifetz: Musical "coldness" is one thing; the musical "reserve" that results from a great artist's "discipline" is quite another.[14] New York's "formidable four" noted that Lhevinne's playing lacked the outward intensity of some of his colleagues, but they found in it a clarity and calm distinctly individual. In St. Louis, he was thought to be "not so much lacking in emotion as superior to it."[15] In Los Angeles, he was recognized as "the *inward* poet of the piano" (italics mine).[16] After the recital about which Finck and Krehbiel disagreed so sharply, this comment was overheard as Carnegie Hall emptied: "Other artists bring out the beauty, the passion, the human, but Lhevinne's interpretations are spiritual."[17]

Did Lhevinne fail to project the fleeting, transitory moods of the human heart? Or did he transcend them, transmute them into something higher? About this, his partisans and detractors argued as long as he lived.

Students, students, students—they swarmed to Lhevinne's recitals, they sweltered in his summer master class, they flocked to his Kew Gardens home hoping for auditions. In the early 1920s they came to him more for his concert reputation than for the disciples he had produced. Of the many Americans who had studied with him before the war, only Homer Samuels and George MacManus had made more than a local reputation—and they were both accompanists. In 1921, Samuels, after supporting Amelita Galli-Curci at the piano for four years, finally married the famous coloratura. MacManus accompanied Pablo Casals.

While Lhevinne was on tour, attracting more students, Rosina taught those he had already accepted. With the advanced pupils, she merely "filled in" in his absence; those not so advanced, she trained until they were ready for him. In 1921, Harry Stevens and Bomar Cramer came to the Lhevinnes. They were the first students sent them by the Juilliard Foundation.

Augustus D. Juilliard, a millionaire wool merchant, died in 1919. In his will he left a considerable portion of his wealth for the benefit of music in America and appointed a foundation to oversee its distribution. The news of his bequest shocked both the music world (which had not even known of the man) and his survivors (who had not known of his intended generosity to the cause of music). Legal efforts on the latter's behalf reduced the amount made available to the foundation, and delayed for two years its use. But after the lawyers were through, about $14,000,000 remained for music.

The director of the Juilliard Foundation was Eugene Noble, a former Methodist minister. He decided the best way to use the money was to offer young musicians fellowships for study with recognized artists, the latter to be chosen by the foundation. Josef Lhevinne was one of the first artists so designated, and the arrival of Messrs. Stevens and Cramer marked the beginning of the Lhevinnes' still unbroken connection with the name Juilliard. Although they and other leading musicians received many private students in this manner, the air soon was thick with complaints about how Juilliard's bequest was being handled. But more of that later.

One student who began study with the Lhevinnes about this time recorded her impressions of the first visit to Kew Gardens. She was met at the door by a "Negro woman—afterwards known as Sarah"—who led her into the living room. Lhevinne, whom she had never met, was practicing.

> He did not stop or look up when I came in. I felt rather apologetic, almost as though I were eavesdropping. But soon I became fascinated by the way he would repeat a passage, adding perhaps only a note or two each time, or playing a single measure, always over the bar line, or repeating a tricky passage that sounded perfect to me at least three or four times more. After fifteen minutes or so he stopped and said, as though resuming a conversation: "I just wanted to show you how I practice."

She soon learned firsthand that he taught with the same painstaking thoroughness with which he practiced. At first that depressed her. But

> even when you felt he was "picking" on you and demanding an almost transcendental quality of perfection, you realized, after weeks of struggle and discouragement, that suddenly you were blossoming out and

had gone a long step forward. What at first had seemed like a near-sighted concentration on a detail suddenly opened a vista for you.[18]

Students generally were patient with Lhevinne's "near-sighted" attention to detail. They hoped later results would justify it. But his wife sometimes felt obliged to come to their rescue.

"Once Josef was teaching Beethoven's Sonata in E-flat, Opus 31, and I was upstairs. Without exaggeration, I heard the student play the first two chords twenty-five times. It got so much on my nerves that I simply had to call down to him, very gently, 'Josef, I cannot hear anything that he does wrong. Please tell me what you want from the boy.' And he called back, 'Maybe you cannot picture it from upstairs, but if you were here you would see that he holds the finger on the note too long.' "

The student that day happened to be Arthur Gold, now of the Gold and Fizdale two-piano team, but everyone who studied with Lhevinne had similar experiences. So thorough was his approach to the keyboard that he invariably gave as much attention to releasing a note as to striking it. A decade after Kitty Hawk, he used an interesting figure of speech to express his idea. In melodic passages, he wrote, "the finger [must] leave the key like an aeroplane leaves the ground."[19]

The young woman who met students at the door was Sarah Crump, who joined the household in 1921. She took over that task from Grandfather Bessie, who had suffered a stroke shortly before her arrival and was partially paralyzed. Instead of sending him to a rest home—as their American friends recommended—the Lhevinnes hired private nurses so he could stay with the family.

The arrival of Sarah caused some problems for Masha. "One day Masha ran up to me with her eyes popping out, and she said to me in Russian, 'That new girl has no respect for me. I told her to put *salfetken* on the table, and she didn't pay any attention to me.'

"In Russian, *salfetka* is napkin, and Masha wanted to say it in German, so she said *salfetken*. Certainly there was no way for Sarah to understand."

Sarah, a native of Virginia, spoke only her native language, whereas Masha's broken English contained fragments of Russian, French, and German. As soon as they were able to understand each other, though, they became an incomparable team. Sarah cooked and cleaned; Masha ran the household and was in effect the children's mother. That Masha assumed the latter role was not entirely for Rosina's lack of trying. "I always wanted to put the children first, but in some ways I did not know how to do it. In Russia, there is a proverb—fish against ice. He sees where he wants to go, but he cannot get there."

The "ice" that blocked Rosina Lhevinne from a warm relationship with her children was the residue of her own childhood, for she was still possessed by the fears her mother had drilled into her. In moving to Kew Gardens, she left behind Manhattan's big-city microbes but not those of the Moscow of her youth. Not wanting Don and Marianna to fear germs and disease as she did, she admonished them without giving the reason: "Wash your hands before eating—Don't touch animals—Wear your galoshes—Eat this, not that." The children knew what not to do but they did not know why. Naturally, that made it difficult for them to relax with her.

Lhevinne went along with this as much as he could, and a few of his actions were quite touching. "Josef did not believe in germs and such things, but out of regard for me he used to eat his dinner at a little table in the corner if he had a cold." Certain policies, however, he could not adhere to—like the rigid approach to what the children were allowed to eat. And no wonder. With his haphazard childhood diet, he had emerged a perfect physical specimen; his wife, after a pampered childhood, had developed innumerable physical complaints. She visited Dr. Holt every three weeks to get a formula for Marianna, as she had for Don. Her husband's mild form of sabotage was "to slip Marianna, under the table, salami"—or herring, or whatever delicacy he happened to be eating. Even today Mme. Lhevinne feels it was unforgivable of him to do this, and worries that printing the incident here might reflect unfavorably upon him.

Out of her love for the children, Masha, too, sometimes undermined the excessive concern about diets and microbes. When her mistress was away from home, she seldom insisted that the children obey all the rules. One day Marianna came in for lunch after being outside. She was surprised when Masha insisted she wash her hands, and went reluctantly to the washroom. There she found a puppy that Masha had bought in the Bronx and smuggled into the house. Faced with a *fait accompli,* Mother made no complaint.

Tours are the bane and the balm of every virtuoso's existence. Or so it was until technology made possible a career like that of Glenn Gould, who performs mostly in recordings. As early as 1921, Lhevinne caught an envious glimpse of the hermetically sealed pianist of the future.

On November 29 he played in Madison, Wisconsin. At the end of the recital, the standard balm was profusely applied: "No artist here has received a greater ovation" reported the local press. But

Lhevinne was more interested in reports later relayed to him from eighteen states and Canada. The concert had been transmitted over the University of Wisconsin's "radiophone," and was picked up over a thousand-mile radius—from Palmette, Georgia, to cities in northern Saskatchewan. In Freeport, Illinois, a large audience heard the recital at the local fire station. When Lhevinne learned that the reception had been good, his head filled with visions of how he could play throughout the country while sitting in a studio. Years later, his dream briefly materialized during some network radio broadcasts. But nearly to his dying day he carried music to the American people by traveling from city to city.

The repetitive nature of this kind of life threatens all traveling virtuosos with insufferable boredom. Sometimes the threat comes on a wholly mundane level—such as the aversion Lhevinne developed to chicken salad during his early American tours. At other times it involves the very essence of what he is doing—making music. Not long after the Madison concert, Lhevinne discussed this problem:

> Under constant repetition, interpretation tends to become a habit rather than something made alive at the moment, as it should be. I have almost reached the point where I am determined never to play the same program twice in succession. The freshness of mind with which a concert artist approaches his performance is a great factor toward gaining the interest of the audience.[20]

To avoid constant repetition, he prepared three to five recital programs for each season's tour. He always asked his wife to help him choose his repertoire, and she remembers how irritated he was with the managers, who wanted him to repeat the same program for the whole season so the cost of printing would be less. She claims he sometimes paid for additional printing from his own pocket so he could play the variety of programs he felt was necessary.

Lhevinne's postwar programs were similar to his prewar, and occasionally identical. He continued to play the recognized masters. Although his repertoire had not broadened significantly, it had deepened, thanks to Bárczy's wartime efforts. Between 1919 and 1922, for example, he played six Beethoven works for the first time in America.[21] But unlike Artur Schnabel, who sometimes played four Beethoven sonatas in one recital, Lhevinne never played more than one at a time. Lhevinne always wished to entertain as much as educate. "A public program should be like a good meal," he told one student. "Not too many beefsteaks, nor too much frothy dessert."

The one significant postwar addition to his repertoire was negatively forecast by Philip Hale in 1920. On the day Parker told his readers about "a pianist's pianist," Hale told how unlikely it was that Lhevinne would ever turn to the works of modern composers —such as the French Impressionists. In 1922, four years after Claude Debussy's death, Lhevinne began to play that composer's music. By the 1930s he had become somewhat of a Debussy specialist. But Hale was essentially correct. Debussy's music was the limit of Lhevinne's modernism. As for Prokofieff, someone once asked Lhevinne whether his works were more difficult to play than those of preceding composers. "No," he replied, "only more uncomfortable."

Lhevinne put his multiplicity of programs to good use when he returned to Mexico City in 1921. He played six recitals in less than two weeks. Only three had been scheduled, but the Mexicans were just as enthusiastic as before. The *Excelsior* printed multiple-column reviews of four of the recitals and came to these conclusions: Before the war Lhevinne was more pianist than artist—now these roles are perfectly balanced; before, he "persuaded" his hearers— now he "convinces" them; and now his most distinctive qualities are "sobriedad, seriedad, discreción."[22] His Mexican admirers showed no such *cualidades*; again they tossed him into the air and paraded him on their shoulders. At age forty-seven, he found these antics even more disconcerting than he had a decade earlier, and was in fact quite exhausted by the time he recrossed the Rio Grande. A photograph aptly documents Lhevinne's last Latin journey: he is being ferried across a river on a fantastic flower-strewn barge, and appears a bit bored and bewildered by the excessive adulation.

Like all traveling artists, Lhevinne was warmly received in some cities, coolly in others. Mexico City was the most exuberant of the "warm" ones; others included New York, Budapest, Chicago, Denver, Pittsburgh. Among those generally "cool" were Boston and Philadelphia. But nowhere was his reception more consistent than in Milwaukee's Pabst Theater, which seemed to be enchanted territory for him. He was always relaxed and spontaneous there, and invariably played in his warmest, most intimate style. At his recital on February 26, 1922, the audience reportedly went "music mad." But more interesting was the way in which Lhevinne, who was easily distracted after the war, overcame a rude interruption:

Only one unfortunate happening marred the recital of Sunday. This
was when some insistent individual demanded to converse with someone off stage and the telephone was rung feverishly for some moments.
Mr. Lhevinne finally was forced to cease playing and silence the jangling
instrument. To be roused from commune with Chopin to deal with the
discord of Alexander Graham Bell was an experience little relished by
the pianist, but his vexation was quickly subdued.

Lhevinne finished the recital with a string of encores nearly as
long as the listed program; as he played them, he

wore what, worn by lesser men, would be called an infectious grin.[23]

After the war as before, Lhevinne's tours gained variety by the
occasional appearance of his wife at a second piano: Rosina played
with him three or four times each season. Because of her concern
for the children, she left home only for tours limited in time and
distance, and refused to take the five-day train ride to California
until the children had grown up. The Lhevinnes' two-piano jaunt
often followed his West Coast tour:
"When Josef went to the Pacific Coast, he was usually gone for
two or three months, and I would meet him in Chicago on his way
back. I remember a big hotel there, and it was like a new honeymoon each time. We had dinner together, and the next morning
we went to rehearse. We played together like children, and then
began our short tour." One year they played in Chicago, Rochester,
and Boston; another year, in Cleveland, New Orleans, and New
York; another, Chicago, St. Louis, San Antonio, and New York.
On these brief excursions, much of the excitement they created—as in Moscow at the turn of the century—was due to the
mere presence of two pianos on the stage. Despite efforts of Maier
and Pattison to popularize the medium, most Americans (critics
included) knew little more about two-piano performance than
they had in 1907, when the Lhevinnes had last played together
here. From reading the reviews you would think they were three-
ring magicians rather than two-piano musicians. Words like "wiz-
ardry," "magic," "miracle," "telepathy," "uncanny," and "com-
munion of spirit" predominate.[24] When reviewers did not use the
language of hocus-pocus, they used the quasi-scientific language
still in use today: "unanimity of phrase," "precision of ensemble,"
"synchronization." Even so, it was the theatrical aspect of two
pianists playing on the same stage that attracted the most attention.
Loudon Charlton's advertising tactics helped to "Barnumize"
the Lhevinnes' two-piano appearances, and considering the pub-

Grandfather Bessie, Don, Marianna, and Rosina. New
York, 1921. Photo by Klim-Check.

Kew Gardens, New York.

A good catch.

With Stanley Hummel, 1932.

Kew Gardens, mid-1920s. Photo by Bains News Service.

Two-piano team, early 1920s.

Moszkowski Benefit, 1921. Back row, from left: Ernest Schelling, Sigismond Stojowski, Alexander Lambert, Walter Damrosch, Robert Braun, Percy Grainger, Ignaz Friedman. Middle row: Harold Bauer, Leo Ornstein, Germaine Schnitzler, Ossip Gabrilowitsch, Elly Ney, Alfredo Casella, Josef Lhevinne. Front row: Ernest Hutcheson, Ernest Urchs.

Dr. Rosina congratulates Josef on his receiving an honorary
Doctor of Music degree. University of Colorado, 1940.

Married forty-four years. Washington, D.C., 1942.

lic's lack of familiarity with the repertoire, perhaps that was necessary. In San Antonio, even Mozart's great Sonata in D major for
Two Pianos was unknown, and the concert was billed in this
fashion:

Mr. Josef Lhevinne: World's Greatest Pianist
Mme. Rosina Lhevinne: Russia's Greatest Woman Pianist[25]

Aside from Mozart's D major Sonata and Rachmaninoff's Second
Suite, "Russia's Greatest Woman Pianist" remembers very little of
the two-piano music she played under that label soon after the
war. Her most vivid memory is of the trip to New Orleans, where
she saw the legacy of slavery for the first time. "Everywhere in the
stores were Blacks, and where the whites of the eyes are, they had
red. It was frightening, and I began to understand why there was
so much antagonism in the South. But at that time I didn't have
the wisdom to understand that it was the white man who had
made them that way."

One musical experience was memorable. On Friday, March 31,
1922, two days after Rosina's forty-second birthday, the Lhevinnes
played Mozart's E-flat Concerto for Two Pianos with Stokowski
and the Philadelphia Orchestra in Pittsburgh. On Saturday, they
repeated the program, which had included Lhevinne's performance of Liszt's E-flat Concerto. On Sunday, they were to have given
a two-piano recital, but owing to the demand for seats it had to
be shifted to Monday night and a larger hall.

Although the reviews of the three Pittsburgh concerts give little indication of the Lhevinnes' distinctive pianistic qualities, a
few excerpts do give a sense of the phenomenon their joint appearance represented shortly after the war. Their collaboration
with the Philadelphia Orchestra was in many ways "the performance of the season" and "demonstrated that as an accompanist-
conductor Leopold Stokowski is without a peer." In their performance of the Mozart Concerto, "there was synchronization plus
virtuosity in every note and phrase," and "they made two pianos
speak with but a single thought." ("Then why play *two* pianos?"
was Lhevinne's private response to that.) His playing of the Liszt
Concerto "electrified" the Pittsburghers, and revealed these interesting characteristics: "He has fire in his blood and velvet on his
finger tips."

At the Monday-night recital, their performance of the Mozart
Sonata inspired: "two butterflies, darting, loafing, and floating in
the sunlight." In Rachmaninoff's Suite, there was "no primo and
no secondo, just one Steinway speaking a gorgeous language." Lhe-

vinne in his solos came "precious near being the perfect pianist."
He closed the program with Balakirev's *Islamey*, and our reviewer
left after "hearing him whang the Asia Minor out of the Balakirev
opus major."[26] So much for Pittsburgh, 1922.

Rachmaninoff's Second Suite had been composed in 1899, when
the Lhevinnes were living in Moscow with the Mindowskys. Their
performance of the work twenty-two years later constituted its
American premiere. Audiences were surprised to discover such a
gay, delightful work from the pen of the somber Rachmaninoff,
and the *Valse* and *Romance* movements were particularly successful. The composer was interested in their performance of his work
and gave them some good advice about the *Romance*. "Skip from
here to here," he said, passing over two pages of the score.

Upon immigrating to America in 1918, Rachmaninoff had resumed his career as a virtuoso, after devoting the previous twenty
years to composing and conducting. The transition was difficult
at middle age, and in spite of his great talent he had to work hard
at acquiring a repertoire. He and Lhevinne had become closer
since their mutual dinner confession in 1914, and Rachmaninoff
consulted his former classmate. "Whenever he and his wife invited us for dinner, Josef and I knew just what to expect. During
the meal, Rachmaninoff talked and joked and said nothing about
music. Then, after dinner, he took us to the living room. 'Sit
down,' he commanded. 'I will play for you what I want to use in
my next program. If it is too far from the standard attitude toward
the work, I will not play it. But I will not change. I will not alter a
single note to meet convention.'

"Josef always told him exactly what he thought, and Rachmaninoff appreciated it, but he never changed a thing. He had no
peer in playing his own compositions, but when he played other
composers it often came out Rachmaninoff."

Although Rachmaninoff played solo works by other composers, he seldom played another composer's concerto. One of the
very few exceptions was Beethoven's First Concerto—the one Lhevinne had played under his baton in 1914.[27] Lhevinne played Rachmaninoff's solo works, but never his concertos. Whenever he
proposed one to his managers, they either asked him for a more
popular work or pointed out that Rachmaninoff himself was playing it soon in the same city. When Lhevinne did play Rachmaninoff, he usually chose a group of preludes, among which the notorious one in C-sharp minor was sometimes, but not normally,
included. Rachmaninoff, however, had to play that work as much

as Lhevinne did the "Blue Danube," and he once told the Lhevinnes he was ashamed of having composed it.

Rachmaninoff honored Lhevinne by asking his advice. Did Lhevinne follow suit? His wife thinks not. In fact, she cannot remember his eve rasking any colleague for advice. Did he ask *her?* "No.
But he didn't have to. I always butted in with my opinion." Colorful legends have grown up about her tenacity in this regard. According to one, she coached him from the wings at his Carnegie
Hall recitals. But surely that is apocryphal. She always eyed him
from a box (as a recollection from William Shore indicates):

> He was playing one of the Chopin Impromptus—I forget its number
> or key—its movement is in triplets—and at the end of the first move-
> ment preparatory to the slow middle movement there is a down-running
> scale—a simple scale—certainly no difficulties involved—and for no
> reason at all—he stumbled—missed fingering or something—and in his
> embarassment he immediately glanced up to the box where you were
> sitting. He looked like a little boy whose mother comes upon him with
> his little hand in the cookie jar. And as I recall you looked back at him
> and did not even smile—but no matter—no one else paid any attention
> to it and the balance of the recital was a glorious success—as always.[28]

It was unusual for her to frown at him in Carnegie Hall, but
elsewhere it happened frequently enough. For in both their teaching and their two-piano work the Lhevinnes invariably disagreed,
especially about tempo. She generally wanted the fast movements
faster, the slow slower; he held out for subtler contrast. Like Rachmaninoff, however, he thought out his musical interpretations by
himself and seldom changed a note, even under the most determined onslaught. Each year, he did his most serious musical thinking during a month of perfect isolation. His favorite point west
of Kew Gardens was Portage Bay, Wisconsin.

"The Great Good Place," a short story by Henry James, is a
fable that addresses the needs of all creative artists. George Dane,
the novelist-hero, breaks down under the social and literary pressures he has to meet in order to hold his place as a leading man
of letters. Suddenly he is swept off to a mysterious retreat. Here no
demands are made upon him; an unseen benevolent agent provides everything necessary for his mental and physical comfort.
After an unspecified time, his creative faculties are wholly rejuvenated. He returns to society and rededicates himself to his
artistic mission.

Dane's retreat, it turns out, existed only in a dream; but his rejuvenation was nonetheless real. Josef Lhevinne was fortunate in having a "Great Good Place" in the real world. Every summer, he re-enacted Dane's drama at a Wisconsin retreat called Bonnie Oaks. He first heard about the place when teaching in Chicago. A woman walked up to him, said she heard he was "a passionate fisherman," and offered him the use of her home. She pointed out that it was only an overnight ride on the train and that he could fish all day Saturday and Sunday and be back in Chicago on Monday for his class. "Josef had never seen the woman before, but because he loved to fish so much he accepted her offer without hesitation."

Mildred Greene's offer was particularly inviting because of the hot and humid teaching conditions at the American Conservatory. Josef's annual summer master class consisted of ten to fifteen playing students and forty to fifty auditors. Four times a week they all crowded into the basement, where the advanced students played works from the standard repertoire. Lhevinne commented after each performance and often demonstrated at a second piano. By Friday afternoon, he was eager to board the train for Portage Bay; by Sunday evening he was reluctant to return.

Lhevinne not only commuted to Bonnie Oaks while teaching in Chicago but always managed each year to spend an uninterrupted month there. He lived in "Josef's tower"—a three-story water tower altered exactly to his specifications. On the third floor was his observatory, complete with telescope and astronomy books. The second floor was his bedroom, where he kept his fishing gear, a rifle, and a photograph of Rosina and the children. His studio was on the first floor, with a Steinway concert grand sent from Chicago. Here he prepared his programs for the coming season, working as the spirit moved him. On a particularly inviting day or night, he might spend all his time fishing or stargazing. Other times, he chopped wood, tended a garden, built things with his hands. And sometimes, he sent music reverberating through the woods all day long. Don occasionally stayed with his father at Bonnie Oaks, and remembers hearing the piano ring out over water and fields— seemingly from miles away.

The annual retreat to Bonnie Oaks became almost sacred— Lhevinne let nothing interfere with it. Once he was asked to tour Australia. He refused point-blank—Australia's winter concert season and Wisconsin's summer fishing season were mutually exclusive. Even in the 1930s, when he did his summer teaching elsewhere than Chicago, he always spent at least a month (usually May) at Bonnie Oaks. Without this refuge—where he could escape into himself, where he could cast his spirit out over sky and water, where he was entirely free of domestic pressure—he could never have sustained the breakneck pace of teaching and performing that he kept up to the end of his life.

In the early 1920s Lhevinne not only taught and performed music but wrote about it. Specifically, he wrote a series of short essays for *The Etude* magazine that were gathered up in 1924 and reprinted under the title *Basic Principles in Pianoforte Playing*. Primarily of value to students and professional pianists, these essays also illuminate certain aspects of Lhevinne's professional life at the time he wrote them.

Any reader of *Basic Principles* will sense his deep dismay with the superficial musical training then given to America's talented young pianists. He had encountered too many "musical parrots" who could rattle off the notes of a Liszt or Tchaikovsky concerto but "who barely knew what key they were playing in."[29] At the time he was writing, America was groping toward a long-range solution of the problem—with the creation of the Eastman School (1921), the Curtis Institute (1924), and the Juilliard School (1924). But even with these additions, America's patchwork system of musical education always seemed pitifully inadequate to the Russian-trained Lhevinne. He continued to teach the best students who came to him—turning a few into concert artists, many into excellent teachers. But to see the day when America could really turn out pianists of quality in quantity, he would have had to live as long as his wife has.

That Lhevinne wrote of his irritation with his students' lack of preparation is no surprise. But it is curious that the fifty-year-old master also wrote of deficiencies in his own musical training. The confession came in a section on "Velocity":

Personally, I was always able to play with great rapidity. One of the serious mistakes that Safonoff made with me was that when he found that I could do a thing unusually well he would indulge me in it. He never gave enough of the works in which there was no occasion for bravura, virtuosity, and velocity.[30]

This statement was not born of ill-will against Safonoff; rather, it sprang from a certain dissatisfaction with his current pianistic reputation. He was simply tired of being known as "a pianist's pianist."

"It came rather gradually," Mme. Lhevinne recalls. "More and more he became tired of reading in the papers about his phenomenal technique, his phenomenal octaves, everything phenomenal but the musicality. After every concert he played in New York, Sarah went in the morning to buy all the papers, and she put them at the top of the stairs. He would never take them himself, but when I got up I certainly took them with great interest and read him the reviews. I was gradually told not to read about technique. If it said something about musicality or understanding, then I could read it."

On February 12, 1924, she could read him every one. For on the night before at Carnegie Hall, his musical personality had seemingly changed. It was a recital unlike any he had ever played. Parker might even have recommended it to "miscellaneous hearers." There was not a single sonata. The program was a "box of inarguably pretty trinkets," a "flower garden of simple familiar delights."[31] Many nonmusicians were present. They heard "echoes of the young, impetuous Lhevinne." They demanded encores after each piece, and got them—"scintillant as stars among his native Caucasus mountains." Henry T. Finck was there. He gave his final blessing to a pianist he had always found poetic: "He can sing . . . on the piano better than most vocalists can with their throats." Then the seventy-year-old indulged in a bit of rhapsody: Lhevinne "can dramatize a song like Liszt's 'Lorelei' till you seem to see the maiden on the rock combing her golden hair with a golden comb and making the boatman so crazily enamored that he almost comes to grief in the squall."

The recital's popularity, however, did not prevent the praise of Lhevinne's technique. Even in a program of short works poetically played, his amazing dexterity showed through. Moreover, Lhevinne was not really satisfied with such a light-weight program—and it showed.

> There were times last night when he seemed to be a giant gently and patiently waiting for a sonata worthy of his contending.[32]

In later recitals, whenever he did "contend" with a sonata on its own terms, he could not help making full use of his technical powers. Praise of the "phenomenal" automatically followed.

The reader can test this for himself by playing Lhevinne's Ampico piano roll recording of the Liszt-Busoni *La Campanella* on an Argo disc. Lhevinne made this roll in the 1920s, and I defy anyone to listen to it without marveling at the superhuman dexterity. Mme. Lhevinne remembers that he actually played this work at a slower speed in the 1930s, hoping to disguise some of the technique that came to him so naturally. Surely the attempt was self-defeating: the exhilaration that comes from hearing him play it is a direct result of the daring with which he negotiates the notes. The fact that he later tried to play it slower, however, shows the degree to which he tried to hide the virtuoso flair indulged in, in his youth. (For a "short work poetically played," be sure to hear the Chopin nocturne that follows *La Campanella* on the Argo disc.)

The reader is certainly as tired as I am and Lhevinne was of reading about his technique, so we can leave the final word to Samuel Chotzinoff, who first reviewed the pianist in 1925. "Technique in our age is taken for granted," he wrote, "like the possession of bathtubs." Even so, Lhevinne's "virtuosity is so phenomenal that nothing else seems to matter." And that is too bad. For "if [it] were less perfect, one would become aware of a sense for beautiful phrasing, a fine feeling for form and a certain unostentatious nobility of line."[33]

The 1923–24 concert season was Lhevinne's fifth in America after the war. It began with a tour of the West Coast (where he previewed the "flowers and trinkets" program) and ended with his first visit to Havana. As he drifted on stage, he struck Cubans as "una figura rara." The press gave this curious sketch of him:

> With his badly-rumpled jacket, his white vest, and his mussed-up hair, you could take him for one of those hopeless *bohemios* who frequent the coffee-houses, declaiming verses or painting with their finger-tips on the marble humidity of the table tops.

As soon as he sat down, however, he "dominated the piano despotically" and made it "express all the feelings, all the emotions, all the states of excitement that can be expressed through music." He "made out of the instrument a living and sensitive thing: he humanized it."[34]

Three days later, Lhevinne straightened his jacket, shed the role of the "hopeless bohemian," and introduced his wife to the Havana public. They played the same two-piano program they had given a few weeks earlier in Indianapolis, and in both cities the praise rose from the technical to the musical to the personal:

> There was never a slip, never a blurred note or phrase. . . . The ensemble of the two players was flawless. It was a supreme example of the beauty possible when two human beings are coordinated well-nigh perfectly.[35]

The Lhevinnes had by this time been married twenty-five years.

When they returned to Kew Gardens that spring, they returned to a life as comfortable as they had known in Germany before the war. Their house in Kew Gardens lacked the splendor of the Wannsee villas, but in it they had food and shelter and clothing in abundance. Aside from Lhevinne's growing dreaminess, he and Rosina had left behind the unhappy signs of their five-year internment. Sarah and Masha's domestic efficiency allowed them to devote almost all of their energies to music, and the only thing they seemed to lack was time to develop their role as parents as fully as their roles as recitalists and teachers.

In spite of all the concert-giving, lesson-giving, and concert-going, however, they managed to establish certain family traditions. At Easter they always gave a party *à la Russe* for students, family, and friends, complete with *pasha, kulich,* eggs, veal, and ham. They celebrated Thanksgiving American style, with Sarah doing the honors. Lhevinne's annual spree at the Schwarz toy store on Fifth Avenue set the tone for Christmas. New Year's Eve, too, was a family affair, with Masha baking raised doughnuts and serving raisins, nuts, and hot punch. No matter what the musical demands upon them, the Lhevinnes tried to enjoy at least these family traditions.

The only event in the early 1920s that threatened to disrupt this rhythm was the death of Grandfather Bessie. For a long while afterwards, Rosina made wide detours around the chair her father had used in the living room. But one day when she was standing in the middle of the room, Josef walked up to her, put his hands gently on her shoulders, and said, "Rosina, you *will* sit in that chair." She did, and from that moment on was able to mourn in a more private fashion.

As the summer of 1924 approached, Lhevinne could look forward to the master class in Chicago and the weekends at Bonnie Oaks, to Don's eighteenth and Marianna's sixth birthdays, and to another concert tour in the fall. Not long before Josef left Kew Gardens for Chicago, the telephone rang. "That was Eugene Noble," he told Rosina. "Now they have decided that to execute the will of Juilliard they must form a school, and I am the first one they have approached for the faculty."

10

The Juilliard
Graduate School

IN NOVEMBER 1924, Calvin Coolidge was elected to his one full term as President of the United States. Fittingly, the austere, taciturn New Englander presided over the middle years of America's Prohibition; ironically, he ruled during the "roaringest" years of the twenties. A similar paradox governed the original years of the Juilliard School, which opened two weeks before Coolidge was elected. Eugene Noble matched Calvin Coolidge in austere demeanor; under his leadership, the school enjoyed its most exuberant, spendthrift days.

Augustus D. Juilliard had not specified in his will that his fortune be used to create a school of music. But by 1924 Noble and the other directors had decided that that would be the best way to make use of the bequest. Artistically, the lessons the Foundation had been underwriting with Lhevinne and other musicians were successful enough; but the operation was not sufficiently visible to inspire the public's confidence. For that, Noble deserved a large part of the blame. For three years, the press had queried him as to how the Juilliard millions were being spent, and his standard answer was this: "I would be delighted to tell you what the Foundation is doing with its money, but I am so busy deciding just that that I cannot spare the time to tell you." Moreover, many people who did find out how the money was being used objected to the fact that fellowship winners were told with whom they must study. That went against the American grain.

On October 5, 1924, news of the creation of the Juilliard Graduate School broke in the *New York Times*. Two weeks later, the school opened its ornate doors at the Vanderbilt Mansion at 49 East Fifty-second Street. The faculty of ten was distinguished:

189

voice, Marcella Sembrich, Léon Rothier, Francis Rogers; piano, Olga Samaroff, Ernest Hutcheson, Josef Lhevinne; strings, Felix Salmond, Paul Kochanski, César Thompson; composition, Rubin Goldmark. Some patriots were piqued that Rogers, Goldmark, and Mme. Samaroff were the only Americans on the staff, and likened Noble to the wealthy American who acquires treasured European paintings while ignoring, say, those of the Hudson River School. But they could not complain on those grounds about the student body: it was all-American. Two of the first-year students were Negro—a fact that greatly pleased the Lhevinnes, who had been members of a minority in Russia:

"Juilliard was a very liberal man for his time, and carefully specified in his will that the money be used without regard to race, religion, or color. The school was wonderful during those first years. The cooperation and complete lack of envy among the faculty was remarkable. Every student was given a full scholarship, and we were in that magnificent mansion, with its chandeliers, carpets, and silk draperies. The teachers were paid by the hour, not by annual salary. Marcella Sembrich got $100 an hour, and so did Leopold Auer when he joined the faculty. Josef got $40 and I got $25. Olin Downes, music critic for the *Times*, was one of the examiners, and he got $100 an hour for that."

The students' practice rooms at the Vanderbilt Mansion were in the former servants' quarters on the top floor. Each was equipped with a new Steinway upright. Because there was racial equality at the school, students were segregated only by sex: the girls were to practice on one side, the boys on the other. But they did not remain separated for long. Not with Rosina Lhevinne on the faculty. "I was never exactly a matchmaker, but if I felt that a certain boy and girl would understand each other, I would encourage them to get together, especially during the first year at the school, when it can be very lonely." A former Wannsee student recalls that she showed this kind of solicitude for her students even before the First World War. No statistics are available.

The Lhevinnes' studio was the former drawing room on the second floor of the Vanderbilt Mansion. Because he continued to tour, she gave his students many of their lessons, and sometimes a pupil did not know whether Josef or Rosina would be there. Sometimes they both were, and discussed the playing in Russian. This was disconcerting for students who knew only English, but even worse for one who knew Russian and did not let on: the remarks were not always complimentary.

Some students remember her as the more efficient and articulate teacher. If she could not explain a point one way, she would try a dozen others until she was understood. William Beller, one of their first pupils at Juilliard, characterized her manner as "a kind of severity tempered with grace, a kind of formality tempered with humor."[1] Lhevinne, on the other hand, was insistent in a gentle way. He often ran out of words altogether, and sat at the piano to demonstrate, giving marvelous illustrations that some students felt were worth a thousand pedagogical·words. Each approach was effective in its way, for musical concepts can be taught both with words and with tones.

Lhevinne had tended to emphasize technical matters when teaching at Wannsee, for most of his students there were poorly prepared. At Juilliard, the students were of much higher caliber, and he had them for several years. This meant that he could teach technique and interpretation in tandem. In *Basic Principles*, he wrote that the business of the pianist is "to communicate human sensations and emotions" to the audience, not merely "to play the notes." But in practice it is difficult to separate the two. In a few sentences, Lhevinne summed up how the mental, emotional, and technical elements of piano-playing are related:

> The player can actually think moods and conditions into his arms and fingers. His mental attitude means a great deal in the quality of his playing. Just as the voice immediately reflects in its quality the emotions of great joy, pain, sorrow, meanness and horror, so do the finger and the arm in somewhat similar fashion respond to these emotions and represent them in playing. . . .

The clause that ends this passage shows what Lhevinne (and the Russian School) took for granted:

> . . . for those who have mastered the technique of playing so that they are not concerned with details which should become automatic.[2]

The day after the Juilliard School opened, Lhevinne took part in another inauguration—that of Chickering Hall. For during the previous season, he not only had turned to a more poetic and lyrical repertoire but, like a gambler trying a new system, had dropped the Steinway piano for the Chickering and traded Loudon Charlton's management for that of Evans and Salter.

Lawrence Evans and Jack Salter were new to the management field, and their great aim was to be "exclusive." That goal was clearly reflected in their first list of artists: Lhevinne, Galli-Curci, and Tito Schipa. Later they expanded to six, adding Tibbett, Rethberg, and young Yehudi Menuhin. But their idealistic enterprise was short-lived. By the end of the decade, most managing power was in the hands of the conglomerates: NBC Artists, Arthur Judson, Columbia Artists. Lhevinne switched to Judson in 1928 and to NBC three years after that. He stayed with the latter for the rest of his career.

As his wife tells it, he left Steinway because he was left-handed. "In his youth, that was the hand he always hit other boys with. The bass of the Steinway is so strong, and Josef's left hand was so overdeveloped, he never could get the balance he wanted." Lhevinne used the Chickering for a relatively brief period of time, then switched to the Baldwin, which he played to the end of his life. Until the Depression he was one of the few pianists provided with both a private tuner and a number of pianos scattered across the land. After he left Steinway, the tuner was Emil Neugebauer. They traveled together and became close friends—so close that in Kew Gardens they sometimes carried out the old Tiflis ploy. Don remembers that "Daddy often went to play billiards with Neugebauer, and when he left the house he told Masha to be sure not to tell Mother. They usually came back very late, and Daddy pushed Neugebauer through the door first."

From Chickering's point of view, there was one special event during Lhevinne's brief tenure with them—his Carnegie Hall recital on October 31, 1927. That night no stage lights were used, and the pianist performed under three dim shaded overhead lamps. After playing the listed program on his customary instrument, Lhevinne moved over to a "somewhat ornate brown piano" and played Liszt's *Liebestraum*. The piano had been one of Liszt's own Chickerings. Its tone was surprisingly strong and mellow, and the *New York Times* wrote that "the gentle sonorities of the 'Dream of Love' may well have sounded much as they did half a century ago when Liszt himself played." Lhevinne's feelings about the promotional gimmick are unrecorded.

Actually, performing on Liszt's own piano was an accurate (though crude) symbol of Lhevinne's conscious artistic goals. While men like Prokofieff and Ornstein were stressing the percussive possibilities of the instrument, Lhevinne continued to uphold the lyrical traditions he thought would never die. For him, the piano was always a singing instrument, and the song to be sung that of the composer's time, the composer's mood, the composer's intention. As long as he played, he felt that his real artistic role was that of a "middleman" between composer and audience.

The two Carnegie Hall recitals he gave during his first year on the Juilliard faculty exemplified that philosophy. The programs were more demanding than the "flowers and trinkets" program of the previous year, but were still skewed toward the lyrical and poetic. Each time, the hall was filled to capacity, including chairs on stage. Yet in spite of the large surroundings, he continued the previous year's effort to create a mood of intimacy:

> Last night he seemed to take his audience deep into his confidence, not for self-aggrandizement, but only to lead them to the composer. He was eager, with authority but self-effacement, to make his hearers aware of [the] beauty that stirred him, and he recreated that beauty with a sincerity and mastery that more than compassed their ends.[3]

In summing up the second recital, the *New York Times* summed up the man as well. "Lhevinne's contribution to the sum-total of present-day pianism springs from an individuality which is far removed from the clangors of the market-place; he is an idealist, a dreamer, whose quests have led him in the direction of perfection, polish, and refinement. He seems almost to have abjured the strenuous methods of many instrumentalists today and to have taken refuge in a contemplative philosophy."[4]

Lhevinne's "contemplative" nature, his removal from "the clangors of the market place," and his reluctance to try to impress people his wife might find "interesting," were perfectly illustrated by his first postwar encounter with Serge Koussevitzky, his friend from student days in Moscow. Koussevitzky's arrival in Boston in 1924 had restored that city to its prominent place in America's musical life, and the new conductor made his much-heralded New York debut with the Boston Symphony Orchestra a month after the Juilliard Graduate School opened. The Lhevinnes apparently missed that concert, as they played a two-piano recital in Grand Rapids, Michigan, on the following day. But they were on hand when Koussevitzky returned with his orchestra during the following season:

"We sat in a first tier box at Carnegie Hall, and Koussevitzky could not help seeing us. He conducted beautifully at that particular concert but did not make much of an impression on Josef. After the concert I suggested that we go backstage, but he hesitated, because he did not feel that he could compliment him sincerely. But when I insisted that it would be extremely awkward if we did not go, he said, 'All right.'

"There are two flights of stairs to the artist's room at Carnegie Hall, and that night they were so crowded that the line moved very slowly. By the time we reached the entrance of the room, there were still many people in front of us, and Josef must have thought there was plenty of time to think of something nice to say. But as soon as we put our heads in the door, Koussevitzky left the people he was with, ran to Josef, and embraced him warmly in the Russian manner. And my poor Josef, having no time to prepare himself, sincerely said what had struck him the most: 'My, do you look elegant tonight!'

"For many years after that, Josef's managers wondered why the Boston Symphony was the only major orchestra that never invited him to play, and so did we. Then one day the management phoned to say that Koussevitzky wanted him to play at a Tchaikovsky Festival in Boston. We were overjoyed.

"The rehearsal went very nicely, and at the concert Josef was delighted with the wonderful accompaniment. Afterwards, there was a big party at Koussevitzky's house, and we were invited. When we came and announced our names, the doorman said, 'Mr. Koussevitzky left word that he would like to see you both for a moment in the library.' So we waited there, and he came soon. After a warm greeting, he asked Josef, 'Lhevinne, do you remember what you told me ten years ago, after the first time you heard me conduct in New York?' And Josef said, 'No. Not at all.'

"So Koussevitzky repeated the exact phrase Josef had used, and said, 'I am really ashamed that in all these years I could not conquer the terrible shock I felt when you told me only how elegant I looked. Every year since then, I have been asked if I wanted you as a soloist, and I must admit that each time I was on the borderline of asking you when I thought to myself, "If that is what he really thinks of me, I will not ask him to play." After hearing you play so beautifully tonight, I am sorry that I waited so long, and I ask you to please forgive me. Let's be old friends again.' "[5]

Lhevinne was amazed that Koussevitzky had taken his comment so seriously, and thought the whole episode rather silly. Close friends say that in later years he told the "Koussevitzky story" in a spirit dangerously approaching that of a naughty child recalling a prank. But Rosina took the episode very much to heart and resolved never again to insist on anything to which he answered "all right" in the tone of voice he had used that night. Their differing reactions indicated a deep split between husband and wife.

"I loved to be with musicians and to talk music and ideas, but Josef generally preferred doing something else—like playing Ping-Pong or bridge or billiards. He worked at the piano endlessly and thought about it a lot, but once he left the piano he would not talk about it. He kept everything inside, kept his ideas to himself, and in some ways this created a false impression with fellow artists.

"One night when we came home after an evening with friends, I asked, 'Why were you so quiet? Why didn't you say anything?' And he replied, 'I would have, if you had given me a chance.' But our differences went deeper than that. He always thought I enjoyed being with other people because they were 'important' or powerful socially, when actually I enjoyed them because they were interesting."

The one musician whose company they enjoyed equally was Felix Salmond, the great English cellist. Two years after his 1922 New York debut he was named to the original faculties of both the Juilliard Graduate School and the Curtis Institute. For all his expertise as a cellist, his favorite instrument was the piano, and he and his second wife, Helen, became perhaps the Lhevinnes' best friends. "We taught them to play bridge, and they showed their appreciation by beating us almost every time. Sometimes, when we went there for dinner or they came to us, Josef would be learning something new and Felix would ask him to play and would make comments afterwards. I would not say that Josef always accepted the comments, but in the car on the way home he would say, 'Isn't he really a wonderful musician!' Felix was the only musician for whom Josef ever played a new piece."

Though Lhevinne generally kept his interpretive ideas to himself, he did not entirely avoid other musicians. He and Rosina often joined the informal musicales at Leopold Godowsky's apartment, and many a Friday night found them playing chamber music at Mischa Elman's. Lhevinne joined his colleagues in informal concerts at the Bohemians Club and the public performances of the Beethoven Association, and he also participated in many of the benefit concerts given in the 1920s for worthy causes or weary musicians. The most interesting of these was the Carnegie Hall program in 1921 for the benefit of Moritz Moszkowski, who, like many a well-known musician, was almost penniless in his old age. Fourteen pianists participated, playing various works for single and multiple instruments. The highlight of the evening was a performance of Schumann's *Carnaval* by Lhevinne, Gabrilowitsch, Bauer, Hutcheson, Grainger, Backhaus, Friedman, Schelling, Stojowski, Lambert, Casella, Ornstein, and Mmes. Ney and Schnitzler. They all played the final march together after taking the preceding parts singly.

For the solo sections, they had drawn lots to determine who

would play what. Lhevinne told his wife that Bauer got "Reconnaissance" and came to him and asked, "Lhevinne, will you
change with me?" "Josef said, 'Fine.' Then Gabrilowitsch got 'Paganini' and asked Josef to play that, too." Technically, "Paganini" and
"Reconnaissance" are the most hazardous parts of the *Carnaval*.
But surely Gabrilowitsch and Bauer were capable of playing them.
It is evidence of the fine camaraderie among these men that they
preferred to take more comfortable sections and had no compunc-
tions about asking Lhevinne to switch with them.

For all his concern and fair-mindedness with the people he associated with, Lhevinne's imagination was often somewhere else.
He once told a friend, "The more I meet people, the more I like to
fish." He was a communist in the universal sense of the word and
often said that one should love the man on the street as well as
one's best friend. Rosina was always more of a particularist.
Whereas his favorite writer was Rabindranath Tagore, the mystic
philosopher and poet, her favorite reading has always been of the
topic or personality nearest her at the moment. Her attentiveness,
like his expansiveness, took in all sorts and conditions of man.

"One day I was not feeling well, but I felt it my duty to go to
the school and teach. Before leaving, I said to Sarah, 'The chauffeur
will take me to the school and bring me back. Then I must rest.'

"So I went to the school and came back, and while riding
home I felt myself already resting in bed. When I saw Sarah, she
said with her wonderful smiling face, 'Mrs. Lhevinne, I hope you
don't mind, but Mrs. So-and-so will be here to see you in half an
hour. She says she will only be in town one day.'

"I was still somewhat of a spitfire then, and I am sure it was in
a loud voice that I said, 'Sarah, didn't I tell you not to make *any*
engagements for me?'

"She was very calm, although her lips trembled a bit, and she
said quietly, 'Mrs. Lhevinne, my mother was not an educated person, but she always told me never to raise my voice when I was
excited.'

"In my whole life, I do not remember being so humiliated. I had
had governesses as a child, I had traveled with my parents before
my marriage, and I had always lived in a so-called cultured environment, and now a girl with comparatively little education had
given me such wonderful advice. I sat down, and then I took her
by the hands and said, 'Sarah, as long as I live, I will remember
what you said, and I will really make an effort to reform
completely.'

"That same night, we were invited to play bridge with some

friends, and I told them what had happened. The man, who was very liberal, said, 'Bravo, Rosina.' But his wife, who was an American with conventional racial ideas, said, 'Rosina, I don't understand you at all. How can you accept advice from a servant?'

"But I certainly did accept Sarah's wonderful advice, and now the angrier I am the lower I go with my voice, and my students know *that* is when to watch out."

Some of the Lhevinnes' best friends could not understand why Josef was so impolitic before Koussevitzky or why Rosina felt so humiliated before Sarah. But each action was perfectly in character. He cared not a whit for the "main chance"; she grasped insights from whatever the source (and does still).

By 1926 the Lhevinnes' two-piano repertoire was wearing thin, and they had to work up some new pieces. He particularly disliked this task, as he cared very little for two-piano music. But knowing how much Rosina enjoyed playing in public, he was glad to cooperate. They chose four new pieces, which she memorized in her unique manner. "Although I did not enjoy memorizing this music any more than Josef did, we always played by heart. Whenever I had to learn something new, I took Masha and the music, and we went to Jones Beach. We would walk along the boardwalk and I would memorize with my eyes. Then we would sit on a bench and I would hear the music in my ears. We would walk some more, have lunch, and then I would come home and sit at the piano and play it. It was a present from God to be able to memorize in this way."

Lhevinne always had difficulty remembering the notes, and he dealt with memorization (and with his wife's methods) in Chapter VI of *Basic Principles*. Most likely, he remembered their honeymoon contest of learning the Mendelssohn étude as he wrote:

> Do not place too much stress on those who memorize readily. Some people seem to be gifted with a kind of mental glibness. They make their mental photographs with a kind of cinematographic rapidity; and the impress is likely to disappear quite as rapidly. If you memorize slowly, do not let it bother you. . . .
> The thing to remember is the thought, not the symbols. When you memorize a poem you do not remember the alphabetical symbols, but the poet's beautiful vision, his thought pictures. So many students waste hours of time trying to remember black notes. Absurd! They mean nothing. Get the thought, the composer's idea; that is the thing that sticks.[6]

His thinly disguised diatribe against those with photographic memories is perhaps unfair to his wife and to others blessed with the ability to remember "black notes" with facility, but his emphasis on the thought behind the symbols is an excellent corrective to the literal-minded attitude with which most students approach the task of memorizing. Although Mme. Lhevinne, in her teaching today, continues to stress the usefulness of the visual memory (especially when *combined* with the aural, the tactile, and the analytical), she now agrees with her late husband that the analytical memory is the most valuable of all.

Of the four new works the Lhevinnes had chosen for their Carnegie Hall recital of January 1926, the central piece was Schumann's Andante and Variations. They produced a "resonant, sensuous and finely finished legato" that one writer described as being "as soft as velvet on the surface, but possessing beneath this sheen of color the dignity of some unruffled limpid stream whose current is both broad and deep."[7] Again, Rosina was asked to give a solo recital. But she never obliged. A few months earlier in Carnegie Hall, she and her husband had given their first New York performance of Mozart's E-flat Concerto.

Lhevinne's solo recitals, which had featured the "lash of contrasts" soon after the war, now became not only more lyrical but more subtle in their effects. Sometimes the gradations in tempo and volume were so slight as to be hardly perceptible. His technique could still "creep up on the most knotted phrase and gobble it up before you know what's happened," as it did when he played Beethoven's *Waldstein* Sonata in Minneapolis. Even so, it was "a technique marvellous not so much for its strength and brilliance . . . but more because of the control of that strength into the finest-spun delicacies and nuance."[8]

Delicacy and nuance—these were the distinctive features of Lhevinne's mature pianism. One of his boldest assertions in *Basic Principles* was this:

> To be able to play with the delicious lightness and beauty of Cluny lace should be the ambition of *all* students. A beautiful lace shawl is the best comparison I know to what I mean by delicacy in playing. There is lightness, fineness, regularity of design, but without weakness or uncertainty[9] (italics added).

To hear Lhevinne's recording of Chopin's *Étude* in Double Thirds is to hear these words come alive in an unforgettable way.

The addition of Debussy's music to his repertoire, and the subtraction of Rubinstein's from it, were only two of the ways in which Lhevinne aimed for increased delicacy and nuance in his recitals. Gradually, he tended to omit the traditional Bach transcription from the beginning of a recital and to plunge directly into the Romantics.[10] His Carnegie Hall program for February 5, 1929, was typical:

Brahms	Two Intermezzos; Capriccio, Op. 76
Schumann	Symphonic Études
Chopin	Scherzo in C-sharp minor
	Impromptu in G-flat
	Mazurkas in A minor and G major
Liszt	Feux Follets
Debussy	La Terrasse des Audiences au Clair de Lune
	Feux d'Artifice
Tausig	Fantasy on Gypsy Airs

By opening with Brahms intermezzos, Lhevinne was not only showing his new taste for more lyrical works. Since returning to America after the war, he had occasionally had difficulty getting into the music at the beginning of a recital. To begin with intermezzos was to challenge himself to bring out his musicality from the first. In later years he went to another extreme—beginning a program with the Schumann Toccata. By opening with it, he hoped to jar himself out of the lassitude that marked the beginning of some of his recitals.

Naturally there were many times when he began a program with a Mozart or a Beethoven sonata and played it with ease and inspiration. But that depended upon his mood—of which he was not always in complete control. In 1929 he wrote nostalgically of his debut with Anton Rubinstein at age fourteen.

> I remember walking on to the platform, dressed in my blue Russian blouse with belt and knickers, and feeling as full of confidence as if the playing of the solo part in a Beethoven concerto was a thing I did every day of my life. The marvellous confidence of youth! I would give everything to have it now![11]

Because his own musical career sometimes seemed a mixed blessing, he was not at all disturbed that his children showed little interest in classical music: he wanted them to have the normal childhood his own precocity had deprived him of. Don was so unmusical that he was actually dismissed from the school chorus in Kew Gardens. Lhevinne admitted that his son enjoyed baseball more than Beethoven, and lovingly referred to him as "the jitterbug" in interviews. Don did like jazz, and his parents must have risen in his esteem when in 1923 they played the first jazz piece ever heard in an Indianapolis concert hall—Edward Burlingame Hill's "Jazz Study" for two pianos.

Rosina could not take so lightly the fact that their son completely ignored the piano. She decided that their daughter should at least be introduced to the instrument—much in the way that other mothers say, "My child can decide later in life whether or not she believes in God, but if I do not take her to church now, she may never have the chance to believe." At first, she taught Marianna herself, but always got this polite reply, "Mother, I don't understand a word that you say." Various students continued the task. Marianna had some talent, but got more pleasure from dancing lessons. Once her father gave her a lesson at the piano, and she remembers having had the temerity to disagree with him.

They got along better with bicycle lessons. "Daddy brought me a bicycle when I was about six, and took me out on a big hill to ride it. He let me get on and try it alone, and I fell. But with his wonderful confidence in me, I soon mastered it." When she was only eleven, he taught her to operate his pride and joy—the automobile. "Josef always thought he was a first-class chauffeur and a second-class pianist," Mme. Lhevinne recalls, "and he was wrong on both counts. We had some beautiful rose bushes on both sides of the driveway, and the number of times he ran into them, it is not to laugh."

There are endless stories about Lhevinne's driving habits, and they can be summed up by contrast with his pianistic skill: there was all of the velocity and little of the nuance. The classical story has a dozen variations. Lhevinne is speeding along at a breathtaking clip, and his mind wanders. The passenger points out the hay truck, girl, red light, or cat he is bearing down upon. He exclaims, "Oh!" and throws his hands high off the wheel—hitting the brake simultaneously.

During the long summer vacations, Lhevinne continued to visit Bonnie Oaks and to teach in Chicago, leaving his wife with the question of how to entertain the children. She wanted to take them somewhere, maybe abroad, but—as in all major domestic decisions—she consulted her doctor. He said the best place for children of their age was home, and he told her to take them swimming.

"Almost every day we would drive to the beach. One year there had been a polio epidemic. When we went to the beach in May it was already over, but there was no vaccine then and the terrible impressions stayed in my mind. I chose a spot far away from the crowd. I did not want the children to worry, so I did not explain why. Gradually one person came near and then another, and I would say, 'You know, I really don't like this place,' and we would move to another spot. Marianna began to notice, and she asked, 'What is the matter? Why do we have to move?' But still I did not want to say why. Maybe if I could have said it in a very simple way, without hysteria, it would have been all right. But I knew that I would say it with such emotion that it would begin to instill fear in them, and knowing how much *I* had suffered in *my* life from this, I wanted to spare them. But in this way I was completely misunderstood." Even today, Don cannot enjoy a simple swim.

During the summer of 1925, Lhevinne taught both in Chicago and at the Master School of Musical Art in California. The latter school was ill-conceived and short-lived, but Lhevinne spent May of that year teaching in its studios in San Francisco and Los Angeles and sitting in on the classes of some of the other teachers, among whom were Felix Salmond and William Henderson (of the *Sun*). A representative of *Musical America* attended Lhevinne's class, and described it with perception:

> Josef Lhevinne is a man of few words. With a gesture he commands that which others use phrases to express. Slow and deliberate, he speaks in a whimsical manner, in a low, musical voice and without hesitancy. The more serious he is—the fewer words he uses. But in a spirit of fun, with his sly humor to the fore, he becomes guilty of surprising loquacity.

When the student begins to play,

> Mr. Lhevinne listens listlessly. The listlessness is an illusion, the listening real. He sings the melody for a few bars. Now and then he waves his hand or beats time with a finger to steady a wavering or indefinite rhythm.

Then he stops the student with his favorite words, "No. No!" Laconic prescriptions follow:

> "It's all right, yet it is bad."
> "Very much wrist work—and STICK-CLOSE-TO-THE-KEYS."
> "That sounds AL-most good."
> "That's not playing. It's only bluffing!"
> "Play with the least possible motion."
> "Hear the melody and the harmony and follow that. Don't just think the *notes*!"
> "Know when to take the pedal OFF!"[12]

In Chicago that summer, Lhevinne had sixty-six students. One of them, Adele Marcus, visited Bonnie Oaks with him. She remembers how relaxed he became there, and the way he would turn commonplace acts into musical metaphors. Peering into an abandoned well, he would say, "Look into this well. It seems dark and lifeless. But when you stick your head in deeper, you see that it is alive, that things are growing there. That is how I feel about this piece of music."[13] Or walking along a trail: "See how this trail goes up and down, twists and turns. So it is with the melodic line. You follow its variations, but you never lose it." As long as he taught or played, Lhevinne stressed the melodic line. To one student, he said, "The longer the line is, the better." To another, "Sing it and see where the phrase goes."

In the classroom Lhevinne often used the same kind of metaphors he used while walking outdoors. One of his favorites dealt with the need to sustain the climax of a musical phrase, which he invariably compared with the peak of a mountain:

"Stay on top—enjoy the view a little more. Especially after having climbed so far."

He once used this image to describe the concept of *rubato*:

"The famous Romantic 'rubato' is simply like water going around a bend. It slows down a little, then makes up for it."

In music, as in life, Lhevinne held out for the importance of silence and restraint:

"After a big stormy passage, wait some for the sound to die out. Make the silence work for you."

He gave this wonderful advice on the use of pianissimo:

"When you whisper, always be sure you have something important to say."

And was equally eloquent on rests:

"*Play* the rests. Play what isn't there!"

Many listeners marveled at the velocity Lhevinne was capable of, but his students learned that he actually achieved the *appearance* of great speed by holding back a bit:

"Don't play *too* fast. You must be able to follow the spokes of the wheel going around. Too fast, means just a blur."[14]

Once he went to a production of *Romeo and Juliet* in which the heroine abused both her voice and the lines. Lhevinne was almost in pain by the time she died. "Why did she have to scream her lines?" he asked. "In Shakespeare, the words are enough by themselves." In music, he often told his students to "save your expression for just the right place. Then give a lot." He gave one student this advice about a Bach partita: "You must not put expression into it; the expression must come out of the structure. Otherwise it sounds like Bach in a silk hat."

There have been many descriptions of Lhevinne's restraint in the concert hall, and this review of a 1927 Chicago recital sums it up as well as any:

> Almost always he throttles himself down to the bottom notch, and because he does, he is frequently more effective and generally more charming than the whole army of thumpsters. . . . It sounds easy as he does it, but that is where Mr. Lhevinne is having his little joke, not to say his little deceit. He is expert at concealment, equally expert at revealment, but he reveals only when he feels like it. In other words, he has brains, not to mention a superb pair of hands.[15]

"You must be magicians," Lhevinne told his students. "What you don't have in one hand, you must have in the other."

In 1927, as the nation was busily running up the mountain of prosperity, unaware of the precipice awaiting it, the Juilliard Graduate School reached the peak of its spendthrift days and gently descended toward fiscal responsibility. Eugene Noble was eased out of the director's chair and was succeeded by John Erskine. Soon the exorbitant hourly rates were done away with, and faculty members were given annual salaries. The blanket fellowships were also eliminated, and students who could afford to pay tuition were asked to do so. These policies curbed some of the school's financial excesses but took away none of its artistic flair. Two venerable Russians were soon added to the staff: Leopold Auer and Alexander Siloti.

While at the St. Petersburg Conservatory before the war, Auer was the world's greatest violin teacher. After following most of his students to America during the war, he made his Carnegie Hall debut in 1924 at age seventy-nine. Three years later, he joined the faculty at Juilliard, where he remained until his death in 1930. He was the only octogenarian on the staff, and it was rumored that he had occasional lapses of attention. Mme. Lhevinne, the only nonagenarian on the Juilliard staff today, recalls that "when Leopold

Auer was making $100 an hour, his students said that during a lesson he would sit in a chair pleasantly dozing. After a while he would wake up and say, 'Don't scratch.' A little later, he would wake up again and say, 'Don't scratch.' The third time he woke up, he moved his hand in the air like a cat's paw, and said, 'Scratch!' "

Alexander Siloti, whom Rosina Bessie had spied on through a keyhole when a student at the Moscow Conservatory, was in his sixties when he arrived at the Vanderbilt Mansion. Still a superb pianist and teacher, Siloti had become increasingly devoted to his memories of Franz Liszt, and claimed to be receiving messages from his deceased master—a fact that gave him a certain notoriety at the school. But Mme. Lhevinne was more impressed with his individuality at the jury examinations.

"We all sat at a long table, and wrote our comments on the student's record sheet as it was passed along. Josef always sat at one end of the table, then Friedberg, Siloti, myself, Mme. Samaroff, Hutcheson, Friskin, and Oscar Wagner (the assistant to Hutcheson, who was dean). Siloti always wrote his remarks in German. And he always disguised his opinion of a student's qualities. A typical comment from him, after an average girl played, was 'Soll heiraten' ('She should marry').

"Although we were not supposed to look at what the other judges wrote, Siloti always insisted that I look at his comments before the card was passed along. One day after a girl played, he wrote, and made me see: 'When she will be married, on the first night she will look at the wall paper to see what design it has.' When I said that he should not write something like that, he took the record back—I thought in order to make a more useful comment. Instead, he wrote, 'Failed to pass the censorship of Rosina Lhevinne,' and insisted that I pass it along. I imagine that card is still in the files somewhere."

James Friskin and Carl Friedberg had joined the Juilliard faculty about the same time Siloti did. All three added to the stature of the school; each gave concerts in addition to teaching. But none played in public as much as Lhevinne, whose tours during the pioneering years of the school did much to spread the name Juilliard. Twice during the late 1920s he crossed the Atlantic.

Shortly before boarding the *Resolute* on September 20, 1926, Lhevinne explained why he had waited so long before returning to Europe: he had been so disillusioned with passports and visas while trying to leave Germany during the war that he had not got up the courage. When asked why his tour was not to include the

Soviet Union, he said he would not go there unless he received guarantees that he would not be killed or imprisoned. He was glad to be returning to Europe for concerts but would not want to live there now: "I feel happier in America," he said. When asked if he looked forward to the wine, beer, and liquor that would be available in Europe, where there was no Prohibition, he said: "I find that we get sufficient here. It is very violent, but it is effective. I shall miss what you call the 'speakeasies.' They are so novel, so unusual, so American."[16] There must have been a "speakeasy" or two on the way to his and Neugebauer's favorite billiard hall, for his wife does not remember ever having been in one.

On his two-month tour of the Continent and the British Isles, Lhevinne played in his favorite prewar cities: Amsterdam, Berlin, Budapest, London, Paris, Vienna. As before, he made the most striking impression upon the Hungarians. A few weeks after playing the Tchaikovsky Concerto with the Berlin Philharmonic, he played it with the Budapest Philharmonic. In praising the pianist's sustained melodic line, *Pester Lloyd* used Lhevinne's favorite image of delicacy: "There are peaks in the noble windings that recall the distinction of old Russian lace." Then came Hungarian rhapsody of a more original sort: "Amongst the imposing walls of rock, rocky reefs and crevices which Lhevinne creates with his dumbfounding technique and his ravishing rhythm, there stalks around something new, like the lightning-like and dazzling dreamy creations of Pushkin."[17] He played the Tchaikovsky again when he returned to Budapest two years later.

His performances in Vienna, Berlin, Amsterdam, and London also assured him of re-engagements. Only in Paris was he not well received. His Salle Gaveau recital on December 15 (the day after a young Russian named Vladimir Horowitz made his debut there, and thirty years after his own Paris debut) was the last he ever gave in France.

When Lhevinne returned to Europe in October 1928, the most interesting reaction to his playing came in Berlin, where his second recital consisted only of short compositions by Brahms, Chopin, Liszt, and Debussy. Such a program—without a red-blooded sonata, and without a work by Bach, Mozart, or Beethoven—was anathema to the Germans, and they gave it this colorful but condescending designation: "klavieristischen Kleinkram" (pianistic trifles).[18] The subtle effects he was after were lost upon Berliners, but when he closed the tour in London, the *Times* printed a perfect tribute to his pianistic restraint: "Speech as forcible as Mr. Lhevinne's rarely needs to raise its voice, and the beauty of the argument is the more clearly revealed by the right distribution of emphasis."[19]

While Lhevinne was overseas, Rosina prepared one of their students for his New York debut. Harold Triggs played at Town Hall in November 1928, three months before his classmate Adele Marcus made her Town Hall debut. During the following year, William Beller and Sascha Gorodnitzki made their first appearances in New York. Since then, hardly a year has gone by without an important debut by a Lhevinne student. (Miss Marcus and Mr. Gorodnitzki later joined the Juilliard faculty, Messrs. Beller and Triggs the piano faculty at Columbia University.)

During the year of Triggs's debut, the Lhevinnes received only one contract from the Juilliard School. But the next year, the contracts—like the teaching—were split between husband and wife. The proportion was three to one in his favor, but that still left her with nearly $5,000 she could count her own. With their Juilliard salaries added to his concert income and his earnings from the American Conservatory, they were doing right well for themselves as the stock market crash approached. But in investing, as in pianism, Lhevinne was a man ahead of his time. Six months before October's Black Thursday, he lost $13,000.

Before leaving for Europe, Lhevinne had entrusted $19,000 in mining stocks to a thirty-two-year-old interior decorator. When he returned, he found that only $6,000 remained. The man had cashed in the rest and invested in bad real estate. Lhevinne's lawyer insisted that he sue, and in May 1929 a magistrate at Manhattan's Tombs Court faced the unlikely prospect of "the red and wooly-pated giant" (as the Minneapolis *Star* once described Lhevinne) standing before him to accuse a man of a crime. A long grand jury proceeding seemed likely, but two weeks later Lhevinne abruptly dropped the charges. Why, no one knows. But Harold Triggs remembers being told of a similar case, in which a man who defrauded the pianist was actually put in jail. Lhevinne had a Carnegie Hall recital coming up, and felt so miserable about having caused another's physical suffering that he was unable to sleep or practice. In that case, too, he dropped the charges.

Among all the confidence men who "took" Lhevinne, the classic operator was one Graf de Shamansky. "This man began to follow Josef," Mme. Lhevinne recalls, "and attended all the concerts he gave in a two-hundred-mile radius. After a while, they even traveled together. Before leaving New York, Shamansky always gave him a little box that contained caviar and various Russian delicacies and a little bottle of champagne. At the bottom, when all was eaten and drunk, was a little golden pencil. Josef would come home from these trips very excited, and would say, 'Look at the devotion of this man.' I would be quiet as a stone, and say that it looked too good to me, what the man was doing. This would surprise Josef, and he would be angry at me for being so suspicious.

"One day Shamansky asked Josef how much insurance he had. When Josef replied that he had $25,000, the man threw his hands in the air and asked: 'How can a man of your importance have so little insurance for your family? You should be insured for at least $200,000. Compared to your income, the premium would be very small. Anyway, everyone knows you're on the "sucker" list all across the country. At least you will put to good use the money you usually give to frauds.'

"That sounded good to Josef, so he arranged to purchase the first year's premium through Shamansky, who happened to be a salesman for one of the reliable insurance firms. Everything worked out fine the first year, and Shamansky continued to come to his concerts. One day Shamansky invited him to lunch, and when the meal was nearly completed he said, 'By the way, Josef, your premium for the second year of insurance is due in a few days, and I know you're very busy. I'm going back to the office after lunch, and will be glad to deliver it for you.'

" 'That's fine,' Josef replied. 'I'll write a check to the company right now.'

" 'Mr. Lhevinne! Can you really insult me so? I cannot believe that you would not trust me after all our years of friendship! As I told you, I am going straightaway to the company, and if you make the check out to me, I'll turn it over to them immediately.'

"So Josef, who was always afraid of giving offense, wrote the check to Graf de Shamansky for $10,000.

"When he came home that night, I could see that something was wrong. He would not admit it, but I knew he was hiding something, and I persisted. When he finally told me what he had done, I nearly lost control of myself, for I was still very impressionable. 'The bank! The check! The ten thousand dollars!' I shouted. 'Gone! They are gone!'

"After I shouted some more, he finally calmed me down. It was already late in the evening, and we realized that we could not do anything until morning. A call to Shamansky's residence only deepened our suspicions, for there was no answer. The next morning, Josef called the bank and told them to stop payment on the check, but of course it was too late. Graf de Shamansky had cashed it the previous afternoon, and further investigation showed that he had fled the country. Neither we nor the insurance company ever heard from him again."

Friends remember that Lhevinne was quite angered by what Shamansky had done, but Marianna remembers his saying, "Yes, it was a terrible thing to do. But he had a wife and children and was in great financial difficulty, and wouldn't have done it otherwise." His temper was like a match: one flicker, and it was out.

On New Year's Day, 1928, Lhevinne finally realized his dream of playing to the nation while sitting in a studio: he was the featured artist on the first program of "The Ampico Hour." Ampico initiated this series because it and other piano-roll manufacturers were beginning to feel threatened by the makers of disc recordings. Only a few months earlier, the Duo-Art company had begun a similar series of radio programs designed to stimulate interest in *its* piano rolls. On Ampico's first program, two of Lhevinne's piano rolls were played, and he gave live performances of Liszt's *Liebestraum* and *La Campanella*. But aside from its historical significance, the program was not very satisfying. Commercial considerations had required that most of the hour be devoted to "vacuous tinklings" from musical comedies, and disgruntled listeners across the land had to "sit through the early banality of the program until the pianist was presented."[20]

A few months after his first network radio broadcast, Lhevinne visited the RCA recording studios in Camden, New Jersey, for the first time. The work he recorded there was the one RCA thought would sell best—the Schulz-Evler arrangement of "The Blue Danube." Because records in those days held only four-plus minutes of music, Lhevinne played an abbreviated version of the work, fitting it onto two sides. A student who accompanied him to the studio remembers that he had difficulty with a certain jump near the end of the work and insisted on recording the second disc twelve separate times (those were the days before technicians could edit sounds into or out of a recording). Fortunately, Lhevinne was satisfied with the twelfth take, and today's reader can listen to the recent Victrola re-issue and discover for himself why audiences were so thrilled by his playing of Strauss's much-abused waltz.[21]

Lhevinne's one recording in the late 1920s and his one network radio broadcast did not, of course, reduce his need to go on tour in order to maintain his reputation. At times, this forced activity irked him. "It was so easy to get to the top, but it is so much work to stay there," he would complain. Certain aspects of traveling, however, excited him. The *National Geographic* was his favorite magazine, and when on tour he usually tried to do some fieldwork of his own. Especially when visiting scenic parts of the country, he tended to give "the Nature"—as he called it—priority over preparation for a recital. Sue Prosser, who was his hostess on one such occasion in 1929, recalls the difficulty his hankering for the outdoors got them into:

> I was married and living in Denver, and we had the privilege and pleasure of entertaining him in our home when he came there for concerts. One of those times was in January and he, being such a lover of nature and the outdoors, always wanted to motor to where he could see the beautiful Rocky Mountains. I was driving, ran into an innocent-looking patch of snow, and the car stopped. We were not near help, so we dug the snow from around the tires with our hands as it stuck and froze; he apparently forgetting that the next day he was to play a concert! Finally, we were able to move, reaching home where he rubbed his hands with what he called "hazel-vitch," and, the next day, he played the concert with no trace of any bad effect on his hands.[22]

That Lhevinne's fingers withstood the cold of the Rocky Mountain snow should not be surprising: Mme. Lhevinne remembers his saying that minutes before his debut with Anton Rubinstein at age fourteen he had thrust his hands into a Moscow snowbank in order to "wake" them. And never during their marriage does she remember his having cold hands before a concert. The only time he put on gloves was when sitting at the wheel of his beloved automobile—a habit having nothing to do with the temperature of his skin.

As the Roaring Twenties came to a close, the Lhevinnes were in their third decade as man and wife. Their first joint musical challenge of the 1930s was a Carnegie Hall recital on February 4, 1930, and they met it by coming up with another new program. Among the pieces they played was Schubert's Fantasie in F minor for four hands at one piano. Their performance of a work from the four-hand repertoire was such a novelty that Oscar Thompson of the *Evening Post* wrote wistfully of the "Golden Age" when it was common for two people to *musizieren* on a single bench.

So delectable were the results of their collaboration that one expects to find all the radios in Kew Gardens out in the street today, and processions of moving vans bringing back pianos, accompanied by benches specifically built for two.

The Lhevinnes had not chosen Schubert's Fantasie because of the novel effect their sitting on the same bench would have. They simply thought it one of the sublime works written for the piano. But for duo-pianists there is always the danger that the furniture —whether two pianos or one bench—will steal the show.

For his solo part of the recital, Lhevinne played an all-Chopin group. At first he seemed to be hiding behind a "veil of diffidence." But what followed prompted Henderson, then the dean of American critics, to review his entire career.

> . . . In his youth he was a virtuoso and a magnificent stormer of the keyboard. He thundered his proclamations and sometimes stunned his hearers by sheer power and irresistible technique. This is not the Lhevinne of today. He is now a ripe and mellowed master who has found all the secrets of tone and who sheds the rays of a refulgent beauty through every composition he plays. . . . He sees laterally across the whole breadth of every composition and perpendicularly down into its depths. He makes the plans of his readings with brains and imagination.

In forty years of reviewing, Henderson had never heard Chopin études played "more poetically, more musically, or with a greater mastery of the instrument for which they were written."[23] Lhevinne was fifty-six years old at the time, and for the rest of his career his Chopin études were in a class of their own.

Carnegie Hall was filled to capacity for the recital, and seats had been placed on stage to handle the overflow. A railing, or fence, separated the onstage onlookers from the two pianos, and at the end of the concert, as the Lhevinnes were playing encores, a strange thing happened. "For some reason, the large audience, stampeding to the stage at the end, showed more curiosity over Mrs. Lhevinne's fleet fingers, and left her gifted husband playing lonely and unobserved until after the third encore, when there was no other place to stand but on his side of the fence."[24]

In one way, it was fitting that she got so much attention. For during the summer, while he taught in Chicago, she temporarily shed her subservient role and took a teaching job of her own. After thirty-two years of marriage, middle-age adjustments were about to begin.

11

Counterpoint

"In 1930, Artie Mason Carter, the founder of the Hollywood Bowl, invited me to teach in Mondsee, a charming little village in Austria. Even though Josef taught that summer in Chicago, I was pleased to accept, and I went abroad with Masha and Marianna.

"Mrs. Carter had the inspiration to take some teachers and students from America and some teachers and students from Austria and to put them together for the summer so they would get to know each other. The school they formed was called the Austro-American Conservatory, and it was housed in the castle of Graf Almeida in Mondsee. Graf Almeida had a three-hundred room *Schloss* but apparently very little money, so he rented the second floor to the Conservatory. Marianna and Masha and I had our bedroom in the library, and in the morning when we wanted to use the bath we had to go down such a long hall that we made a game of it and skipped with the feet like little children do, over the cold stones.

"Mondsee was such a quaint and dainty village that after New York it was like another world. We went swimming and boating and hiking, and Marianna took dancing lessons. We had a wonderful time that summer, and I was re-engaged for the next year."

The Austro-American Conservatory was founded in 1929, a year after the major nations of the world had formally renounced war by signing the Kellog-Briand Pact in Paris. Like the pact itself, the Conservatory was an outgrowth of the hope and expectation —a decade after World War I—of a world without international conflict. The castle in which it was housed had seen more glorious days. A few decades earlier, it had been a favorite haunt of Francis Josef, Emperor of Austria. A century before that, Napoleon had stayed there during his march to Russia. But in the early 1930s the castle's best-known guest was Wilhelm, the former crown prince of Germany, who spent his summers with Graf Almeida and became a fixture at the Conservatory. Wilhelm's favorite occupation was to sit on a windowsill knitting; his favorite diversion was to eye female students through his field glasses to determine which had the prettiest legs (the one whose calves pleased him the most he invited to dine at the village café). His presence was particularly imposing at the Conservatory's parties and dances, where the hard buttons of his military jacket bruised many a tender American breast.

In 1930, the Austro-American Conservatory had twenty-seven students and a handful of teachers, with one American and one Austrian each to teach piano and to teach voice (the Austrian pianist was Paul Weingarten). By 1931, the student body had doubled in size and two Hungarians had joined the faculty: Béla Bartók and Feri Roth. Bartók taught piano and composition, but hardly had enough students to make it worth his while. Both he and Weingarten had to compete with Rosina Lhevinne, who had gained unfair advantage through a devoted but prankish student, Esther Elman, daughter of the violinist, who told every Austrian *fraulein* who came to register to sign up with "the woman from America" because she was a matchmaker. A week after arriving at Mondsee, Bartók wrote these caustic lines:

> I hadn't expected too much of this American school, but it turned out to be a trained-dog show, practically. . . . The Viennese Weingarten went back to Vienna, because not a single pupil showed up for him.—But everybody says that this year the school is excellent, and that it's just beginning to prosper now. Well, I can't imagine what it was like last year, if then it was worse than now.[1]

Bartók stayed at Mondsee for the summer and even returned for the next year's session. But a composition he showed Mme. Lhevinne summed up his ironic distaste for the atmosphere.

"One day he gave me some music and said, 'I would like you to look at this and tell me what you think of it.'

"I looked at it, and it looked horrible to me, so I asked him, 'Mr. Bartók, may I ask you what inspired you to write this piece?'

"And he said, 'You know, the whole night I couldn't sleep on account of the frogs, so in the morning I wrote this little piece.'

"He was a very simple person, and we were good friends and had a good time together, and his second wife was also there, for whom he wrote the Third Piano Concerto."

When Feri Roth joined the faculty of the Conservatory in 1931, he brought with him members of his quartet, including violinist Ferenc Molnar. Roth became Mme. Lhevinne's main chamber-music collaborator at the school; she played sonatas for piano and violin with him, quartets and quintets with his quartet. Chamber music concerts were given in the castle's main dining room, with its wooden paneling and soft red wallpaper. As there was no electricity, the room was illuminated by candlelight. After one evening of chamber music, a banquet was served in honor of the artists. Mme. Lhevinne was given a toast, and she said a few words. Then her collaborator rose to speak. Looking very dignified, he said with strong voice and great assurance, "Friends, I thank you from the heart of my bottom. . . ."

On August 21, 1931, Roth and Mme. Lhevinne played César Franck's Sonata for Violin and Piano. On the same day, out in California, Josef Lhevinne played Rubinstein's Fourth Concerto with Arthur Rodzinski and the Los Angeles Philharmonic. This was Lhevinne's first performance at the Hollywood Bowl, and shortly afterwards his wife and daughter received an ecstatic message: "Enjoyed so much playing for 15,000 people, Saturn, the moon, and the crickets." What opposing pianistic possibilities—playing a suave sonata with a garrulous Hungarian in the candle-lighted room of a cloistered castle versus playing a massive concerto under a moon-lit sky accompanied by the sounds of insects! The former setting was ideal for Rosina Lhevinne; the latter for her husband.

Before returning to America after the summers in Mondsee, Mme. Lhevinne took Marianna to Switzerland and showed her the places she had enjoyed as a child. One year as they were about to sail from France, a telegram arrived from Don, telling them of a polio epidemic in New York. "I am so thankful to Don that he wrote us of that epidemic. It must have been hard for him to do it, because he was educated half by Josef, who didn't give importance to germs, and half by me, who exaggerated them so. At first, Josef was not very concerned, but as the epidemic got worse and worse, even he wrote, 'You had better stay there. I can take care of the students until it is all right.' "

The stranded New Yorkers stayed in the Auteuil suburb of Paris, whose racetracks were favorites of Ernest Hemingway; in whose Bois de Boulogne Josef Lhevinne had lost his stamp book in 1896; and in whose wealthy residential district lived Dr. Goldman, who had assisted with Constantine's birth in 1906. Characteristically, Mme. Lhevinne's memory of the visit is dominated by a single strong impression:

"There was a wonderful park in Auteuil, and every day we rented a bicycle for Marianna. She was allowed to go about thirty yards, and then she had to ride back to Masha and me. She was not learning to ride then, but even so, I didn't want her to go any farther away than that. Once when she went thirty yards, a man with the blackest beard she ever saw stopped his car and said something to her. She started to pedal faster and faster back to us, and he turned the automobile to follow her. When he saw Masha and I were there, he drove on by. But after that, he would follow us. He would drive maybe around the block, and then he would come again. So we told her to ride only fifteen yards. She had to go a few steps and come back—a few steps and come back.

"Then we got more and more worried, because, my goodness, he had the car and he could stop and pick her. We tried to leave the park, but he followed us. Finally we got to a garage, and I said to the man there, 'Can we stay here? There is definitely a man following our little girl, and we don't know what to do.' He was very nice, and it was not far from where we were staying, so he escorted us home. Masha and I had really been afraid the man would grab her. Paris, you know, is absolutely terrible in that way."

Aside from the bearded Parisian, the two summers in Europe were rather idyllic for mother and child. The intervening months, however, were not. For then the Lhevinnes experienced some of their most serious domestic crises. The first involved Marianna's schooling. Taught by tutors to the age of twelve, she had lived an isolated life. She had one friend her own age in the neighborhood, but most of the people she saw were friends and students of her parents, all of whom were much older than she. Her father decided that she would have a more normal life at a boarding school, and enrolled her in one without consulting his wife. Marianna was pleased, her mother angered, by the unilateral decision.

If Lhevinne prevailed with regard to their daughter's schooling, his wife had the final say with regard to their son's. Don, who was twenty-five years old in 1931, had not wanted to go to college immediately after finishing the Kew Forest Private School. He had thought he would prefer to run a service station for automobiles. But his mother had insisted, and he had enrolled at the University of Michigan. When he went through fraternity rush there, he was surprised to find that there were Christian fraternities and Jewish ones, and that the latter wanted him while the former did not. (His parents were as surprised about this as was he, for they, of course, had never been initiated into the social niceties of life on an American campus.) For these and other reasons, Don had not adjusted to life at the university and had left school quite often, only to be urged to return by his mother. When he finally did get the degree, he said to her, with several of his friends and professors standing by, "Mother, this is not my diploma. It is yours. If it were not for your pleading and begging, I would not have it."

Many parents differ about their children's schooling; in this way the Lhevinnes were perhaps not unlike most. But their marital philosophy was unique. It was put to a sharp test shortly before their thirty-third wedding anniversary:

"In my whole life, I did not for a single day love another man than Josef. He, on the other hand, was always a great flirt, and when we married I had said, 'I don't expect you to change your nature. It is as much a part of you as the piano, and you must continue to be the same person. The only thing I wish is a perfect sincerity and honesty in your telling about it and not hiding it.' He agreed.

"As the years went by, he was true to his word and to his nature. He continued to rave about other women as he had before our marriage, and I learned to grade his enthusiasm. Most women, if their husbands flirt, try to do all they can to separate him from the other woman. Not I. I tried to bring the flirtation as close as possible. I always felt it was a great mistake to reprimand the other when something of that sort happens, because forbidden fruit is the most attractive, and to outlaw it usually leads to untruthfulness and hypocrisy. I always said, 'If you find somebody you feel will make you happier, then tell me, and I will not stand in your way.'

"So one year, when I was about fifty, he became very much infatuated with a woman in New York, and I decided to become best friends with her. She was younger than I, and very well educated; she had first been his pupil, and was now a widow. While I was always of a high-strung temperament, she was calm and placid and very poised.

"For many months, I had given the situation great thought, and finally one night I said to Josef and the children, 'Meet me tomorrow in the dining room at eleven o'clock. I have something to say.'

"When the time came and we were all gathered together, I said, 'You know, Josef, I have thought deeply and profoundly about this situation. I have had my time of having you as a husband. I am fifty years old and I think the part to come is not too important. I will give you a divorce and will live on the third floor. You will marry this girl and she will be with you in the bedroom. We will all have meals together and, as she is a poised and cultured person, she will be a good influence on the children and also on me.'

"Silence fell. The children had funny looks, and their foreheads wrinkled. But Josef was flabbergasted. Finally he said, 'Let me think it over.'

"The whole week not a word was said about it. Then one day he asked Don and Marianna and me to come into the dining room. 'I gave it great thought,' he said. 'We are all very fond of her, and I know everything certainly shall continue. But still, you are my wife, and you will stay my wife.' "

With those words, a lasting stalemate was achieved.

In 1931, the Juilliard Graduate School moved from the Vanderbilt Mansion on East 52nd Street to a new building at 122nd Street and Claremont Avenue. This location was adjacent to the Institute of Musical Art, the school with which the Juilliard had cooperated in curricular matters for several years. Given their choice of studios, the Lhevinnes selected Room 412. Reasonably spacious, it faced a small veranda that overlooked the Hudson and could be reached by climbing over a chair and through a window. It was to remain the "Lhevinne studio" until 1969, when the Juilliard School moved back downtown—this time to Lincoln Center.

In moving from the Vanderbilt Mansion to Room 412, the Lhevinnes changed their locale but not their manner of teaching. There were still the discussions in Russian of what a student had played, the sometimes polite disagreements about phrasing and tempo, and the transfer of students from him to her while he was on tour. By and large, the arrangement worked very nicely. "In general, our teaching was a great source of pleasure for us both, and one reason for this was that we were both in some ways quite flexible. For example, one of our principles was always to insist that the student find the long line of the melody and analyze what part of it is the peak, or high point. Josef always had a saying about this: that to have two peaks in the same phrase was like having two heads on one torso. We agreed that each phrase must have one peak—but as to where that peak was, we often felt quite differently.

"Once I gave a certain student a lesson while Josef was on tour. When he came back, he gave the student a lesson, and the student played an important phrase with the peak I had shown him.

" 'What idiot taught you that?' asked Josef.

" 'Mrs. Lhevinne,' replied the student.

"Josef did not tell me about this incident, but later the student told me what he had said, and I had to ask Josef to be a little more careful about the expressions he used. But that was the exception that proved the rule. We did not always agree, but we generally respected the other's opinion. That is the wonderful thing about music, that it is not mathematics, where 'two and two are four' and 'five' is wrong."

There are times, of course, when a musician might wish for an arithmetician's precision: such as when he and his colleagues are attempting to evaluate prospective students. In the early 1930s at Juilliard, the entire piano faculty listened to every piano candidate at entrance examinations. They often disagreed—and not only over Siloti's evaluations of female students. In judging a student's potential, Mmes. Samaroff and Lhevinne tended to be more lenient than their male counterparts. Mme. Samaroff, in her autobiography, made this observation in a general way. Mme. Lhevinne recalls a specific instance.

"There were eight of us on the piano faculty then, and whenever there was a difference of opinion it was discussed. One year a seventeen-year-old boy from Texas took the entrance examination. In general, he played very badly, but his Chopin nocturne was extremely musical and sensitive. The six men voted 'No' for this student and Mme. Samaroff and I voted 'Yes.' The chairman asked us to share with the others what it was we had based our opinion on, so we each said why we thought this student had potential. They asked us both if we would be willing to have him in our class, and we both said yes.

"Finally the boy was accepted, and was assigned to Josef and me. He made wonderful progress that year, and during the jury exams at the end of the term all six men turned to Mme. Samaroff and me and said, 'We were wrong and you two were right.' From that time on, he had a full scholarship." The young Texan was Brooks Smith, later the well-known accompanist to Jascha Heifetz.

When Leopold Auer died in 1930, he was replaced on the Juilliard faculty by Louis Persinger, who had made his pedagogical mark as teacher of Yehudi Menuhin and Ruggiero Ricci. Persinger's wife was a former student of the Lhevinnes, and on Sundays they and the Salmonds often visited Kew Gardens, where Persinger and Salmond played sonatas with the Lhevinnes, who alternated at the piano. Louis Persinger was the first musician other than her husband with whom Rosina Lhevinne performed in public in America. They played together in Town Hall on December 21, 1931, and the highlight of the program was their performance of the *andante* of Mozart's Sonata in B-flat, K. 454. "This movement in itself," Harold Taubman wrote in the *Times,* "should be enough to dispel the delusion, if it still has currency, that Mozart sang only of sunshine and laughter in his music; there are in it thoughts and feelings 'too deep for tears'."[2] Another reviewer, before listing Mme. Lhevinne's "distinguishing pianistic traits," noted that she looked "particularly fashionable and attractive as to gown and appearance."[3] Today she gives as much attention to her students' appearance as she always has to her own.

Persinger was not the only "stranger" she performed with in the early 1930s. One year she played a Bach concerto for two pianos with Carolyn Beebe and the New York Chamber Music Society and also a Bach concerto for three pianos with James Friskin, John Erskine, and the Juilliard Orchestra. (In the latter performance she was impressed that Erskine, a man so outstanding in literature, could play the piano like a professional.) In retrospect, her increasing independence on the concert stage and as a teacher (at Mondsee) might seem to be related to a certain domestic crisis. Still, most of her public appearances, even during this period, were with her husband. As a two-piano team, the Lhevinnes continued to play half a dozen concerts a year. At a performance in 1931, they seemed to one listener to

provide a charming exemplification of the masculine and the feminine in piano playing. Josef Lhevinne, much more the professional, excels in emphasizing the notes that give force and beauty to a phrase and is distinguished for richness of tone and a manner of authority. His wife, thoroughly domesticated, but urged back into the public gaze by César Cui, the composer, and others, has a brightly deft and sensitive way of playing. . . . In the Schumann work husband and wife seemed to be having a tête-à-tête over the keys. . . .[4]

The Schumann work was the Andante and Variations, as the composer had originally scored it (and as it is seldom played): for two pianos, two cellos, and horn. The Lhevinnes, in their continual search for new and better music to play together, had also reached deeper into the four-hand repertoire and come up with Mendelssohn's *Allegro Brilliante* in A major and Mozart's Variations in G major. In addition, they began to play Abram Chasins' two-piano arrangement of the Strauss-Schulz-Evler "Blue Danube." Their performance of that work was popular enough, but was really no improvement on Lhevinne's of the Schulz-Evler alone. Indeed, Mme. Lhevinne now feels "almost guilty" for having joined him at two pianos in a work he could play much more effectively by him-

self. Lhevinne's solo performance of the work was so astonishing
that many who have heard the RCA recording have mistakenly
thought that four hands and two pianos produced the sound.

Lhevinne's solo recitals continued to move in the direction of
polish and refinement, delicacy and nuance. In describing his
artistic goals at this time of his life, he would say, "I like to feel
that I'm not there when I play, that I'm not important. The music
flows through me, and I eliminate myself."[5] After a Carnegie Hall
recital in the early 1930s, the *Times* caught the visual manifestation
of Lhevinne's philosophy in one sentence:

> He sits before the instrument almost motionless and the iridescent tonal
> webs weave themselves beneath a blur of white fingers which he seems
> to observe with the mild interest of a sympathetic but detached ob-
> server.[6]

The reviewer noted that because "the eye so deceivingly supple-
ments the ear, this very immobility tends to make his playing seem
cooler than it actually is." At times, though, Lhevinne's playing not
only seemed but was cool. This was particularly likely to happen
at the beginning of a program. At another Carnegie Hall recital reported by the same reviewer, the pianist negotiated most of the
program with more restraint than fire. Then he came to the last
two numbers—a Scriabin étude and Balakirev's *Islamey*.

> He started the 'Islamey' instead of the Scriabin etude, stopped, bowed to
> the audience, and began the Scriabin. But the incident had disturbed
> the controlled tension an artist brings to his playing, and he forgot the
> piece and had to begin again. Thereupon he played it not only with ex-
> traordinary tonal beauty but with a sharp dramatic modelling that if
> applied earlier would have made the whole recital great as well as ad-
> mirable. The piece received an ovation and had to be repeated, and the
> 'Islamey' which closed the program was electric. If the suggestion were
> not irreverent, one would plead to have something startle Mr. Lhevinne
> at the beginning rather than the end of the concert![7]

At home, as in the concert hall, Lhevinne's great difficulty was
in getting down to work. "In the morning he would sit at the piano,
play for a while, and then get up to see if the furnace was all right.
The furnace was in the basement, and sometimes he went down
there three times a day. Or he would go outside to see whether it
was sunny or cloudy." Once he did get down to work, he could
practice for hours, totally unaware of the passage of time. Those
who overheard him on such occasions say they have never heard
the piano played more beautifully. One curiosity about Lhevinne's

method of practicing was that he never used a metronome (his ears could not tolerate the sound of the thing). In its place, he set his pocket watch on the piano, and measured *tempi* by watching the sweep of the second hand. Lhevinne was rare among concert pianists in that his deepest thoughts and feelings were often too private for public expression. Most pianists as successful as he project the great composers' works outward, adding what they can of their personal selves. Lhevinne, by eliminating himself, magnified the music in reverse.

The summer of 1932 was a watershed for the Lhevinnes—their first summer together since being interned in Germany during the First World War. During the twelve summers following the war, Lhevinne had gone alone to teach at the American Conservatory (whose director, John Hattstaedt, had died in December, 1931); this summer he accepted an invitation to teach at Salzburg's Mozarteum. As Rosina was re-engaged for Mondsee, the Lhevinnes sailed in June with Marianna for Europe. After twelve summers apart, they were destined to spend this and their remaining twelve together.

Lhevinne lived in Salzburg; his wife and daughter in Graf Almeida's castle, thirty miles away. Whenever he or his students gave a recital at the Mozarteum, Mme. Lhevinne chartered a bus and took her students to hear it. Likewise, whenever she or her pupils played at Mondsee, he brought his to listen. Mme. Lhevinne gave two chamber-music performances in July, playing a Beethoven sonata with Feri Roth and a Brahms quartet with his ensemble. Lhevinne played twice in August. His August 7 performance of Carl Maria Von Weber's seldom-heard *Concertstück* with Bruno Walter and the Vienna Philharmonic was one of the fine moments of his career. The audience, wildly demonstrative at the end of the work, broke into near frenzy when a huge laurel wreath was placed over Lhevinne's shoulders. The impression his playing made was so strong that directors of the Salzburg Festival broke a rule against repetitions and invited him to give a solo recital two weeks later; the impression was so indelible that visitors in Salzburg twenty-three years later heard concert buffs there still marveling at his achievement.[8]

One might have hoped that August 7, 1932, was a day of unalloyed joy for Lhevinne. But that, alas, was not the case. Like many of his greatest public performances, this one was accompanied by acute personal agony. But at least on this occasion there was a tangible and quite mundane cause. On the day of the concert, Mme. Lhevinne recalled a few years later,

> I started to unpack his valise. . . . He had insisted on packing for himself. There were a great many things in that valise. There were shirts and sport suits and handkerchiefs and ties. But there was no cutaway suit, and my Josef had to play a concert.
>
> I started to run around town, looking for someone who could lend him a suit. I finally located a singer who was built something like my husband, and borrowed his suit. [They] were built alike when they stood up. But when they sat down it was different. The singer, you see, never sings sitting down, and Josef couldn't play the piano standing up.
>
> So he put on the singer's suit and looked at the pants and said: "I can stand in them, but I can't sit in them." I said: "You'll have to sit in them." My God, how I [suffered] through that concert. I stood off stage and every time he moved I was sure his pants were going to split open down the back. They held, though; I don't know how, but they held.[9]

Getting the singer's pants on her husband was about all that Rosina could manage that day. Joseph Raieff, who studied with Lhevinne in Salzburg that summer, recalls how he was brought into the act: "Just a few minutes before the concert, Rosina brought him into my room and said, 'Joseph, I cannot do anything with him today. Will you get him ready?' So I helped him, and he put his vest on the wrong way and was having a terrible time, and finally he said, just before he went out to play, 'Oh, God, why wasn't I born a bricklayer!' "[10]

That Lhevinne gave such a stupendous performance of the *Concertstück* under those conditions is to be marveled at. It is only a pity that there were so few occasions during his career when he too could fully share the joy he gave others through music.

Because of the strain of playing in public, the summer in Salzburg was not a real vacation for Lhevinne. But he did manage to get in some good fishing and mountain climbing. The peak of the hiking season was reached when the Lhevinnes climbed the Schafberg (5112 feet) with members of the Roth Quartet. As for angling, Lhevinne found trout in abundance right in Lake Mondsee.[11] When classes ended, he stayed in Austria to prepare for an all-Chopin recital in New York. His wife took Marianna and some students on a short trip through Switzerland and Southern Germany. When they arrived in Munich a hotel manager, after hearing the name, advised them to leave the country. He had reason. In the July 31 elections, the Nazi Party had doubled its representation in the Reichstag; four months after Mme. Lhevinne's little entourage left Munich, Adolph Hitler became Chancellor of Germany. None of the Lhevinnes returned to Europe during the next summer and, indeed, Rosina Lhevinne has not been there since. When her husband made one last European tour in 1937, he avoided Germany altogether.

Perhaps it was the rise of Nazism in Germany that finally prodded Lhevinne to take out an American citizenship. On April 11, 1933, the fifty-eight-year-old, five-foot-eight-inch, one-hundred-seventy-two-pound pianist became a naturalized citizen.

The four seasons that followed Lhevinne's return from Salzburg were perhaps the greatest solo years of his life. Each season began with a recital at Carnegie Hall, the successive dates of which, curiously, were October 29, October 28, October 27, October 26. The first two were all-Chopin programs (a novelty in that day), and when Lhevinne was done with them it was clear that his manly approach to the "melancholy" Pole had taken hold—a fact that especially tickled W. J. Henderson. In October 1933, aged seventy-seven, Henderson was still America's most respected critic:

> It causes astonishment to the daily observer of musical doings that a pianist who never created a furore, who used to be regarded as a technician rather than a tone painter, and who approaches Chopin, as he does all other composers, with intellectual grasp and sensitive feeling, but not with throbs and tears, should be selected by the Chopin devotees as one of their high priests. Or does it perhaps mean that the Chopin devotees are acquiring a more correct view of their erotic god?[12]

Elsie Illingworth, who booked Lhevinne for NBC Artists during those years, recalls that "people everywhere wanted him to play Chopin."[13] He gave all-Chopin recitals in Detroit, Chicago, Cincinnati, and numerous smaller cities, and in 1933 added Chopin's F minor Piano Concerto to his active repertoire. The concerto, written during Chopin's nineteenth year, is moody, improvisational, and, some would say, uneven. Few pianists have begun to play it at age fifty-nine; and in Lhevinne's day, few played it at all, as it was not considered dazzling enough for public performance. When Lhevinne first played the concerto—with Bruno Walter and the New York Philharmonic on November 18, 1933—it had not been performed with a major orchestra in New York for seven years. During the following two seasons alone, he played it with the National Symphony (Kindler), the Pittsburgh Symphony (Modarelli), the Denver Symphony (Tureman), and twice with the Chicago Symphony (Stock). His interpretation of the work was restrained: "beautifully wrought and subtle in hue, rather than outspokenly vivid in color."[14] The melodious romanticism of the larghetto was particularly suited to his gifts. When he and Walter performed that movement in New York, with "the orchestra shadowing, rather than echoing, the piano," the themes, according to one observer, had "the translucence which sunlight has, coming through stained glass windows."[15]

It would be misleading, of course, to imply that Lhevinne, at the peak of his powers, played only the music of Chopin. When he and Koussevitzky were reconciled in April 1934, they gave a towering performance of Tchaikovsky's B-flat minor Concerto; two seasons later, he played the Tchaikovsky with Stock in Chicago, Monteux in San Francisco, Cameron in Seattle, and Volpe in Miami. His most impressive sustained achievement of the early 1930s, however, was the series of thirteen weekly radio broadcasts he gave over the NBC network in February, March, April, and May, 1933. The longest series of its kind in radio's then brief history, Lhevinne's weekly half-hour broadcasts each featured one or two movements from a concerto and one or two solo works. Originally scheduled for Thursday nights at 11:30, the program was shifted by popular demand to Wednesday nights at 9:30. Mme. Lhevinne joined him for two of the broadcasts, as indicated by the list of concertos he played:

> Tchaikovsky: B-flat minor
> Beethoven: C major
> Weber: Concertstück
> Rubinstein: D minor
> Mozart: E-flat major (two pianos)

Of the solo works he broadcast, most were by Beethoven, Chopin, Liszt, Brahms, or Debussy.

The NBC Symphony Orchestra, with which Lhevinne played the concertos, was the predecessor of the orchestra with which Toscanini later recorded the Beethoven symphonies. Frank Black, its conductor in 1933, once told Mme. Lhevinne that NBC had begun to make recordings of its broadcasts a year or two after Lhevinne gave his series. What a loss to posterity that they were not made sooner. How revealing it would be to hear Lhevinne's performance of the Tchaikovsky Concerto or the Brahms *Paganini Variations* (both books of which he played during the series). We can only hope that private recordings were taken from the air in 1933 and will someday be discovered.

When interviewed about his weekly radio series, Lhevinne was

willing to admit that it was of some importance. But he showed
as much enthusiasm for other musical broadcasts as for his own.
He was in love with the medium itself, not with his own contribution to it:

> Mr. Lhevinne has not yet, apparently, recovered from the wonder of the
> radio, and before its miracles he is still humble. When it reaches those
> who, because of their remoteness from the activities of cultural centers,
> would otherwise be completely without such experience, the pianist
> finds its greatest service. . . . "I have made many such friends on my fish-
> ing trips to Wisconsin," [he explained], "and I know how much the
> radio can mean to them."[16]

Lhevinne, it seems, was relaxed when playing for the radio. A
former student recalled that "I had the nervous pleasure of turning
pages for [him] and he did nothing but look at his watch! Such
calm nerves! *I* was a wreck!"[17]

The series went so well that NBC wanted to extend it beyond
May 10 (the thirteenth week). But Lhevinne broke it off in order to
go fishing in Wisconsin. Engaged to play the Tchaikovsky in New-
ark on June 21, he wanted a full month at Bonnie Oaks before returning to the metropolitan area. It may have been on this visit
there that he experienced what he called the greatest moment of
his life.

"In the nineteen-thirties, Josef bought a very special fishing rod.
It was of reddish-brown wood, and very light. At Kew Gardens, we
had a big lawn with flowers, and he had the patience to cast for
hours there, trying to land it on the flowers. Sometimes people
would tell us that they had stopped across the street and wondered
what was wrong with that man, that he wanted to catch fish on
the lawn.

"About a year after he got it, we were having lunch somewhere
—Josef and myself and two of his fishing companions—and the
conversation came to fishing rods. I said, 'Josef is so excited about
this beautiful rod, and he paid for it only $25.' The other two did
not say anything, but they exchanged funny looks, so I asked,
'What's the matter?' And Josef said, sheepishly, 'It's not that you
would mind that I spent so much, but I am rather ashamed myself
that I spent, not twenty-five dollars for the rod, but one hundred
and twenty-five.'

"Anyway, the rod was very small and light, and when a big fish
came, the tip bent all the way under water. With that rod, Josef
caught a twenty-five pound muskie. The great art, the great art
there is to it! The moment you feel the fish there, you must let it

go, let it go, otherwise you will lose him. And at the last minute you have to pull very strong, or else he can get away. Josef said there was no concert in his whole life when his heart beat so strongly as the moment he was putting that muskie to shore. No moment of a concert."

After the 1933 month at Bonnie Oaks and the performance in New Jersey, the Lhevinnes began a new summer tradition—master classes in Maine. This year they went to Seal Harbor, where Olga Samaroff, who was in Europe, offered the use of her summer home. It was quite a migration: Josef and Rosina and Marianna, Masha and Sarah, plus the pianist's custom-made Ping-Pong table, which he had carefully removed from the second floor of the house in Kew Gardens and shipped to Seal Harbor in advance. The Lhevinnes had no difficulty attracting students to Maine, and for four consecutive summers taught either in Seal Harbor or Camden. The students, when they were not practicing, could swim in the bay (the water was cold) or play croquet. But aside from piano lessons, they had no musical stimulation. This dilemma Mme. Lhevinne solved in a brilliant way.

"Lea Luboschutz was a violinist who had graduated from the Moscow Conservatory when Josef was teaching there, and he had signed her diploma. She married and had two children, and came to the United States, where she taught at the Curtis Institute. Boris, her son, was a wonderful pianist and he had married a pretty little girl who was an excellent singer, and they were in Maine when we were teaching there.

"When the students arrived for the summer, I felt so sorry for them, for they had come from all parts of the country and had nothing but our lessons for musical stimulation. Boris was an excellent pianist, but I could feel that he was also a brilliant musician, so I had the inspiration to ask him if he woud present six evenings of different operas. As he was interested in opera, I thought he could summarize the plot and play the main theme on the piano and tell us his reactions to the work.

"When I proposed that he do this, he said, 'Mrs. Lhevinne, I would love to do it, but I have never done that sort of thing.'

"And I said, 'But I know you can do it, because you are so clever and you have such a wonderful musical education. Please try, and from our own pocketbook we can pay you $150 for the six lectures.'

"So he worked on it, and every week he presented a different opera. There were thirty-five or forty students, and they appreciated it very much, but I think Josef and I enjoyed it as much as anyone. We knew the operas and we had thought of the idea primarily as a diversion for the students, but still we learned a great deal of information, and we enjoyed tremendously the vividness with which he presented it.

"He enjoyed giving these evenings so much that afterwards he started to do this sort of work on other occasions. Finally, he gained such a reputation that he became official commentator for the Metropolitan Opera House in New York, and now whenever I see Boris Goldovsky he says, 'Mrs. Lhevinne, if it had not been for your encouraging me to give those lectures in your home, I might never have begun to do it.' "

Among the students who formed Boris Goldovsky's first lecture audience was Brooks Smith. He remembers four of the operas that were presented: *Der Rosenkavalier, Die Meistersinger, Pelléas*, and *Carmen*.

For the Lhevinnes, the summers they taught in Maine were also "the summers we spent in the sun with Josef Hofmann." Hofmann had a summer home in Camden, and a sailing yacht that he had converted into a motorboat. He was as proud of his nautical expertise as Lhevinne was of his automotive, and was seldom seen without his captain's hat. He would pilot his boat over to Seal Harbor for lunch with the Lhevinnes, or would ferry them over to his home. These two great masters of Romantic piano playing, each at the peak of his career, sailed together and had wicked Ping-Pong matches, but, as Mme. Lhevinne remembers it, spoke relatively little about music:

"One reason they did not talk much about the piano was that, essentially, Hofmann did not enjoy music as much as his inventions. He once told us that the income from all the concerts he played during the year was like peanuts compared to the royalties he received from his inventions, the most famous of which was the shock absorber. In his music room at Camden, he had a nine-foot piano, but it was covered with green felt, and on top of it were all the toys of his children. He almost never opened it to play. But in the backyard, where he had his workshop, he was totally serious. Sometimes he spent the whole day out there with his mechanical experiments and inventions."

Hofmann and Lhevinne did have a few musical encounters in Maine, each of which was stamped indelibly in the minds of the students fortunate enough to be present. One of the students, Mary Lee Shephard, recalls that during the summer before one of Lhevinne's all-Chopin recitals he and Hofmann sat at opposite pianos playing mazurkas, études, and scherzi. Lhevinne would play a piece his way. Then Hofmann would say, "I always felt it like this," and play it his way. They went through much of the Chopin repertoire in this manner.[18]

Another student remembers a Sunday afternoon when Hofmann and his wife Betty sailed over to Seal Harbor for lunch:

> For some reason Hofmann was greatly preoccupied with the octaves in the downward motion in the Paganini-Brahms Variations. He spent a good part of the lunch demonstrating, on the table, the passage which, though it was faked, sounded as if he played real octaves. He was simply enchanted with his glorious discovery.
>
> At long last, he looked across the table. Josef was preoccupied with the problem of his salad. After a brief silence, Hofmann demanded to know whether Josef had found a better way of solving the problem.
>
> "I play octaves"—was the simple reply.
>
> I still hear the roaring laugh at the table.[19]

Hofmann had chosen the wrong "trick" to show his colleague. Lhevinne not only played the octave glissandos of the *Paganini Variations* from the wrist but took them, as Harold Schonberg has pointed out, "prestissimo, staccato, and pianissimo." No pianist has yet duplicated that technical feat; probably, none ever will. As Schonberg wrote, this was "the utmost Lhevinne would permit himself in the way of outward panache."[20] Likewise, the story of the lunch with Hofmann was one of the few incidents Lhevinne would narrate about himself that was not self-belittling. In later years, he was often heard to repeat it with relish.

During the summer of 1935, Mme. Lhevinne taught the Camden master class almost single-handedly, for her husband taught for part of the summer in Colorado. In October, Betty Hofmann wrote the Lhevinnes from Europe, where her husband was on tour:

> I am almost pleased I was ill this summer as it gave me the opportunity of knowing *well*, hence loving dearly—Rosina! I do wish we could "plant" some interesting fish around Camden so we would have more of your Josef.[21]

In 1935, America had four leading exponents of the "Russian school" of piano playing: Hofmann, Lhevinne, Rachmaninoff, and Vladimir Horowitz (whose American debut in 1928 had been as stunning as Lhevinne's in 1906). After Lhevinne played in Carnegie Hall on October 26, Olin Downes of the *Times* wrote:

> The [Russian] school of piano playing is vanishing, and it is too bad. For if its traditions completely disappear the grand interpretative art of the

pianist will weaken. Then the disposition, not only to disparage exaggeration, which is good, but to disparage grandeur and nobility of utterance in favor of something neater and more puny, which is bad, will vitiate performance. The more is a musician and virtuoso of Mr. Lhevinne's stature welcome when he plays. . . .[22]

Downes must have feared for the life of the Russian school because Gabrilowitsch and Godowsky, though still living, were unable to perform for reasons of health, and because Rachmaninoff, Lhevinne, and Hofmann were aged sixty-two, sixty, and fifty-nine, respectively. As it turned out, the latter three all had excellent years ahead of them, as each played into the early 1940s. Only Hofmann (who lived and played longer than Rachmaninoff and Lhevinne) was to show signs of a serious decline in his powers.

Lhevinne's 1935 recital displayed an increase in the breadth of his powers. Authority for this statement comes not only from Downes but from Lhevinne's most exacting critic but one—his wife. Rosina wrote an account of the recital to Adelaide Salmond, mother of Felix:

Josef played very beautifully—not only with his usual wonderful qualities: the ultimate of pianistic perfection which is not the goal but the means of expression, beautiful velvety tone, forte that is never harsh, lightness and elegance that transfers you to fairy land, and a sharp, poignant rhythm; but this time his playing was unusually colorful and strong.[23]

So colorful and strong was it that the *Sun*'s man, curiously, thought the more lyric variations of Schumann's *Symphonic Études* suffered from "excessive expressiveness"![24]

Even more exacting a critic than his wife was the pianist himself—as his wife recalls. "Sometimes I was not well and could not go to the concert, and I would sleep with one eye open until he came back so I could find out how it had been. He would return and I would say, 'Josef, how was it?' Silence. So I would sit up in bed and ask more emphatically, 'Josef, how was it?' There would be a little silence more, and then would come the answer, which usually was 'Rotten.' The most praise he ever gave himself was 'Well, it was all right.' "

Fortunately we have Lhevinne's recordings for RCA to give the lie to his belittlement of his own playing. Except for the Strauss-Schulz-Evler, all the works on the recently reissued LP were recorded in 1935 and 1936. Included are Schumann's Toccata (with which Lhevinne often opened a recital) and the Schumann-Liszt *Frühlingsnacht* (which he often used as his final encore). According to Igor Kipnis, Lhevinne's performance of the former is "probably the most *musical* account of the Schumann Toccata ever recorded."[25] But Lhevinne's greatest gift to posterity is the Chopin recording he did for RCA—especially the Octave *Étude*, the "Winter Wind" *Étude*, the *Étude* in Double Thirds, and the B-flat Prelude. Kipnis, writing in 1971, used the very words I have overheard myself saying on many occasions: "They would alone entitle Lhevinne to immortality."[26] Anyone wishing to dispute that statement had best hear the recording first.

One wishes Lhevinne had made additional recordings during the last nine years of his life, for advancing age certainly did not dim his pianistic gifts. Nor did it dim his penchant for traveling or his masculine charm. Some pianists in their sixties travel from city to city with barely enough energy for their concerts. Not so Lhevinne. Rosina, knowing this, once made a unique suggestion:

"Once after he returned from San Francisco, he started to describe the concerts and the time he had had. After mentioning some of the more routine facts, he began to get rather excited, and said, 'By the way, I met a woman who is divorced, and who has beautiful hair, face, and complexion, and a most striking figure. She is so interesting, in fact, that she was the high spot of my stay in San Francisco.'

"I was used to this kind of outburst, but with this woman it seemed a little crescendo. So I made a mental note of it.

"Sure enough, he was soon re-engaged for San Francisco, and just before he left, I asked, 'By the way, will you be seeing there Mrs. X?'

" 'Yes, that's the first thing I will do. I was entirely charmed by her, with her many qualities.'

" 'Then will you do me a favor?'

" 'Anything you wish, my darling.'

"So I said, 'Visit her the first day you arrive, but don't telephone her beforehand. Just go to see her at about ten o'clock in the morning. I would like to know your opinion then.'

"He agreed to it, and soon I got this letter as his reply: 'My are you clever! I rang the bell early in the morning, and somebody with terrible hair, a bad complexion, a horrible figure, very poorly dressed, and with glasses opened the door, and I almost said, "Is Mrs. X home?" It was she.' "[27]

Rosina traveled with her husband when she could, but only on short trips. She did go with him to Miami Beach in March 1936, where they played Mozart's E-flat Concerto, but their other performances of that work in the early and middle 1930s were in New

York. Although Marianna was away at boarding school, the school was but a few hours from New York, and her mother was reluctant to be beyond reach for more than a day or two. In September 1936, however, when Marianna was in her senior year at the Baldwin School, Rosina felt freer to travel than before, and NBC Artists was told to arrange, within specified geographical limits, as many two-piano concerts as possible. That fall there were plenty, as the Lhevinnes played together in Carnegie Hall, in Hackensack and Paterson, New Jersey, in Toronto and Poughkeepsie, in Corsicana and Little Rock (where they were the first professional duo-pianists ever heard), and in Pittsburgh (where they substituted on short notice for ailing Vladimir Horowitz).

Continuing their tradition, their duo-concerts were billed as "recitals for one and two pianos." He played the single piano in a series of solo selections; they played the two pianos for the bulk of the recital. At Carnegie Hall, their performances of Mozart's Sonata in D and Debussy's *Fêtes* were well received, but the *Paganini Variations* and solo works by Chopin stole the show. In small towns, on the other hand, the two-piano works most caught the public's ear. Poughkeepsie was typical. In spite of the fact that the Mozart Sonata "proved to be a sleep producer for some of the customers," the duo-recital was preferred to a solo concert Lhevinne had given a few years before. As it takes a fairly sophisticated audience to appreciate the "precision of ensemble" that distinguishes truly first-rate two-piano playing, it would be nice to think it was the Lhevinnes' splendid musicality that made them so popular in America's small towns. But reviews in both Poughkeepsie papers suggest that the theatrical aspect of "two pianos on the same stage" was the major drawing card. Each newspaper gave considerable coverage to the fact that Mme. Lhevinne, finding her seat too low after returning from the intermission, "proceeded to crank it to the proper height, the seat meanwhile emitting a series of rumbling noises. The mishap was accepted by the artists in good grace," and the satisfied customers had a diverting incident to speak about as they left the concert hall.[28]

During the last eight years of his life, Lhevinne played almost twice as many concerts with his wife as he did solo recitals. Early in 1937, however, he made one last grand solo stand. After sailing from New York on the *Île de France* on February 20, he played concerts in Europe for six weeks, before boarding the *Berengaria* on April 7. Lhevinne gave radio concerts in Stockholm, Vienna, and Prague; played with orchestras in Stockholm, Budapest, and Prague; and gave recitals in Budapest, Szeged, and London. He kept a diary while in Europe, and in it are the only written comments we have concerning his own playing. He was spare in praise of himself, though not overly self-critical, and he did take notice of what newspaper critics wrote. Thus in Stockholm, after playing Chopin's F minor Concerto:

Piano was excellent. Played well. Critics are good except for one stupid [one] who said—not young, and without zeal and ardor.[29]

In Budapest, after playing the Tchaikovsky Concerto with the Philharmonic:

Played with *élan*. Was not nervous. Enormous success, and superb critics.

In Prague, for a radio broadcast of the Tchaikovsky:

In the morning terribly disappointed! Learned that the rehearsal was yesterday! The conductor has no idea of the Tchaikovsky Concerto, although I spent with him more than an hour. He buried his nose in the score and did not once look at me or the musicians.

The recital program Lhevinne played in Europe was extremely demanding, not only musically and technically, but physically:

Schumann	Toccata
Beethoven	Rondo in G, Op. 51, No. 2
Beethoven	Sonata, Op. 53 (*Waldstein*)
Brahms	Paganini Variations
Chopin	Ballade in F minor
Liszt	Feux Follets
Scriabin	Étude
Balakirev	Islamey

After playing the recital in Szeged:

Very old Bechstein. Program seemed very difficult physically. At end played with great effort but success was large. Did not consider the Ballade located in a profitable place on the program.

In Budapest:

Hall was full of people but half of them did not have to pay and audience was unattractive. The first group succeeded best of all. Variations went so-so but not badly. In the last group was simply exhausted. Only I played Feux Follets beautifully. Wanted me to repeat it. Islamey could hardly finish and completely without inspiration.

Mass of people left the hall without waiting for encores. Encores: 3

preludes, Chopin; 2 études, one Moszkowski and one Dohnányi; Früh-lingsnacht. Critics superb.

In London:

> I started the concert quietly and well. Rondo I did not give every-where the complete picture of the composition. Consequently uncom-fortable as to sound and balance.
>
> Sonata—much was not clear to myself and did not grasp what I ought to do.
>
> But Brahms Variations I succeeded, especially good in spirit and technique. Aroused great enthusiasm. Came 5 times [for recalls].
>
> The last group, already was as tired as last two times. Islamey went well and clear.
>
> Ballade left me not satisfied.
>
> For encores played 2 preludes [Chopin]; Étude in G minor [Chopin]; Dohnányi [étude]; and Spring Night.

Because Lhevinne was satisfied with his London performance of the *Paganini Variations*, I have included in the notes the *Times*'s review of the recital, which deals almost exclusively with that work and which mentions, in passing, that "physical fatigue does not come into consideration in the case of so perfectly equipped a technician as [Lhevinne] is."[30] He was exhausted, but he did not let his audience know it.

The pianist had more than his playing to make him tired, for he complained throughout the diary of lack of sleep. In nearly every city he stayed up long hours with old friends. In Budapest, he spent considerable time with Gustav Bárczy and Piroska Hevesi (the Hungarians who had, respectively, befriended him and stud-ied with him during the First World War). On the mornings of March 14, 15, and 16, he sat for a sculptor named Hävös, a "very nice and cultured man who loves his work passionately." The re-sulting bust caught, in the eyes and mouth, especially, some out-ward manifestations of Lhevinne's genius.

In Vienna, he spent much of his time with Emil von Sauer and Angelica Morales. He had first met Miss Morales in 1921, when, after one of his concerts in Mexico City, she had auditioned for him at age nine. He had thought her talented, and a letter he wrote to her mother stating that fact was sufficient cause for the Mexi-can government to provide the girl with a fellowship until her piano training was completed. Angelica arrived at Kew Gardens at age sixteen, and after two years with the Lhevinnes made her Car-negie Hall debut in 1929—a glorious formal affair at which both the American and Mexican flags were placed on stage. Following her debut, she went to Europe and studied with Emil von Sauer, who had attended the Moscow Conservatory several years before Lhevinne had, when Nicholas Rubinstein was still alive. After studying with Sauer for several years, Miss Morales married him (he was over seventy at the time), bore him a son, and, after his death in 1942, assumed his chair at the Vienna Conservatory (which she later exchanged for a position at the University of Kansas).

Lhevinne and Sauer struck up a close friendship in Vienna ("He took great fancy to me," the diary says) and reminisced about Safonoff and Anton Rubinstein. When Lhevinne played for Sauer, the older man

was vexed with my timidity, and used many times the same expression Safonoff had used: "I am going to teach you" (the public).

Sauer evidently thought Lhevinne should project the music with more authority. Together, they went to a concert of the Vienna Philharmonic, where Lhevinne was impressed with Wilhelm Furt-wängler's conducting, although "in several places [of Brahms's Second Symphony] he dragged too much." Backstage, they spoke with Furtwängler.

After stops in Prague and Paris, where he visited the Goldmans, Lhevinne turned toward London. Typically, he realized *after* putting all his baggage aboard the boat that would carry him across the Channel that he had forgotten to have his visa approved. He was obliged to disembark, go to the English Consul, and wait five hours for the next boat. In London he stayed at the home of his manager, Wilfred Van Wyck. He was pleased to take note in his diary of Van Wyck's wife's "wonderful vivacious eyes, black and attractive, especially when she is interested in something." But during his first morning in their home he inadvertently brought tears to the eyes he so admired.

I made a terrible "faux pas" by criticizing in a rude way the French people. After that Van Wyck made the remark that his wife is French. She got red to the ears and cried bitterly and then left the room. Afterwards I tried to explain. Now very excited myself. Explained that it was a superficial accusation and had to do only with tourists and taxi-drivers, hotel people and of this type. I said that after that I could not stay at their home and accept their hospitality. Evidently she felt the sincerity in my voice, in my look, and in my behavior. . . . We became very good friends but still I cannot forget that terrible incident.

While Lhevinne was with the Van Wycks, Artur Rubinstein came for lunch.

> Brought [his] new records (proofs) of Nocturnes. Many very wonderful. Afterwards played him my records. Études of Chopin, Schumann Toccata, Fêtes. About the last piece he was in special ecstasy.

The "Fêtes" Rubinstein liked so well was the Lhevinnes' two-piano recording of Ravel's arrangement of Debussey's Nocturne for orchestra, made for RCA in 1935.

On his last day in London, Lhevinne went to Van Wyck's office, where they made plans for another European tour during the following year. Included was a "proposition for Austria in the summer of 1938." Whatever that plan was (perhaps a return to the Mozarteum), Hitler's invasion of Austria in March 1938 scotched it. Lhevinne was to see no more of Europe.

After leaving the office, he treated Van Wyck and his wife to lunch at Simpson's restaurant. From there they took him to the station.

> It was very touching the way they said good-bye. I have a wonderful impression.

The words that follow were among those Lhevinne valued most:

> Hearty, simple, without Chinese ceremony and unnecessary phrase.

12

"Those Who Inhabit Olympus"

MUSICALLY SPEAKING, Lhevinne's European tour was like a bachelor's last fling. For the rest of his life the majority of his musical activities were with his wife. After he returned to New York in mid-April, he and Rosina completed the teaching season at Juilliard, went to RCA's Camden studio to work several days at recording Mozart's D major Sonata, and spent the summer in Colorado, where they taught at Denver and Boulder.

In Boulder he taught at the University of Colorado, where a former student, Mark Wessel, was then head of the piano department. In Denver they both taught at the Lamont School of Music, whose founder they had met at Mondsee in 1932. They spent the remainder of their summers at the two schools and always brought some Juilliard students along to serve as examples to the thirty or forty who came from other parts of the country. The session in Denver usually lasted five weeks and included six public master classes, each of which Mme. Lhevinne opened with a fifteen-minute talk on one aspect of piano-playing: technical problems, tone production, phrasing, pedaling, memorizing, and teaching material. Then students would play and Lhevinne would comment, sometimes demonstrating at the piano. A student could take his private lessons with either of the Lhevinnes, and an accountant might say she was four-fifths the teacher he was. Five private lessons with her cost $107; with him, $132.

During their summers in Colorado the Lhevinnes often spent weekends at the estate of John Rosborough in rarefied Estes Park. Indoors was a spacious cottage with a grand piano and benches and chairs—just as in a concert hall. Outdoors were the mountains and streams. Lhevinne liked to motor on the steep, twisting

235

roads into the Rockies. He got terribly nervous, though, if another person was at the wheel. One former student recalls that whenever she was driving and they would approach a blind turn her distinguished passenger would say, "Katrinka, don't you think you ought to ring your little bell?"—meaning, of course, "honk your horn."[1]

In July of 1937, the Lhevinnes took a short break from the Colorado master class and went to California, where they performed together for the first time on the West Coast. On July 16, at the Hollywood Bowl, with Vladimir Golschmann conducting, they played Mozart's Concerto in E-flat for two pianos and Liszt's in E-flat for one—the same concertos they had first used twenty-five years earlier with Safonoff in St. Petersburg. A strange thing happened at the beginning of the Mozart.

"Amelita Galli-Curci and Homer Samuels lived in Westwood, California, near the Hollywood Bowl, and they invited us to stay with them before our concert there. She drove us to the concert, and we were all very gay, and did not speak a word about what we were going to play, and Josef most of the time stared out the windows at the sky. So we got there and we came on stage, and they made dark the bowl, and the lights were turned on the orchestra and soloists. We sat down opposite each other at the two pianos, and the orchestra began the long tutti of Mozart's Double Concerto. Suddenly Josef caught my eye, and began to move his lips and shake his head violently! I did not know what to think! I looked to see if something was wrong with my dress, but he kept looking to the sky and shaking his head! This continued right up until our cue came and we began to play. After we had finished the concerto, several of our friends rushed backstage and asked me, 'What was Josef denying you?' And I rushed to him, and asked excitedly, 'Josef, what was wrong?'

" 'Oh,' he said calmly, 'I wanted to tell you that above us was not Saturn, like it was the last time I played here, but this time it was Mars.' All the friends had a wonderful time hearing that story, about the telegram he had sent me while I was in Mondsee."

When Lhevinne had played for Saturn and the Moon in 1931, there were 15,000 spectators. Six years later, Mars and the two Lhevinnes drew two-thirds as many. The pianists' performance seemed to have been favorably influenced by the out-of-doors setting; the same cannot be said for that of the critic of the Los Angeles *Evening Herald and Express*. Incredibly, the following three sentences are the *least* star-struck of the ten that made up his review:

Mme. Rosina Lhevinne was seated at the first piano, if one could say that either was first in the rippling exchange between these two very extraordinary geniuses, who are as fluent in their philosophies as they are with finger dexterity.

The light feeling duo rambled flawlessly into ecstasies of a playful appeal, a kind of repartee between the two that was as unusual as it was attention-holding.

After salvos of applause had brought the players back to the footlights many times, Josef Lhevinne seated himself at an 11-foot grand piano and lifted the audience of about 10,000 music lovers into a sparkling effervescence that did not settle back into normal for the rest of the program.[2]

A few months later the Lhevinnes took their concertos to Miami and again ran into astronomical interference. By mistake, the taxi driver let them out at the wrong concert hall. Mme. Lhevinne discovered the error and rushed around until she secured another cab. By then she had lost her husband. She finally found him gazing at a star, and had to push him into the cab so they could be on time for their concert. He had been looking at Canopus, the second brightest star in the heavens.[3] Belonging to the southern constellation Argo, it cannot be seen from the northern or middle parts of the United States. It was of particular interest to astronomers of Lhevinne's day because no suitable parallax had yet been found for it.

The clear view of Canopus was the main reason Lhevinne scheduled concerts in Miami. As long as he lived he remained the young man in the droshky, staring at mosquitos and stars and losing himself in the multiplicity of existence; just as Rosina remained forever his young bride, trying to bring him down to earth, to get him to fix his attention on the here and now. *She* enjoyed the trips to Miami because it was a good place to play golf.

Two days before the concert in Miami, Lhevinne had given a Chopin-Debussy recital at Carnegie Hall. As was her custom, Rosina had sent tickets to certain friends a few months before the recital. Natalie Rachmaninoff wrote to return hers, as she and her husband had tickets already. In a postscript, she relayed a request by Sergei Vassilovich that Lhevinne play as encores two Chopin études—in thirds and in sixths.[4] Lhevinne began the program with the "Schumann Toccata" strategy, opening with Chopin's Impromptu in F-sharp minor, with its flying arabesques in the final section. The major work in the program was Chopin's Sonata in

B minor, and he approached it in a characteristically restrained manner:

> With a fine sense of Chopin's style, the usual avalanches of tone that the majority of pianists believe indispensable in the Sonata's finale were knowingly avoided. There was no punching of tone at the last appearance of the chief theme, and this admirable restraint made it possible to make the great climax with the coda so few interpreters of the work manage to attain. Even nobler was the chaste and sensitively wrought rendition of the largo, which is so seldom perfectly adjusted in matters of tempo.[5]

After the six listed works by Debussy, he played, among others, the encores Rachmaninoff had requested. Some people familiar with most of Lhevinne's career remember this recital as the best he ever gave. He certainly had no difficulty "warming up" that day, and from start to finish was "in the mood."

Lhevinne's fascination with Debussy's music did not stop with his solo playing. He and Rosina began playing Ravel's two-piano arrangements of Debussy's *Fêtes* and *Nuages* so much that these two pieces soon joined Mozart's D major Sonata and Rachmaninoff's Second Suite as staples of their repertoire. Two months after Lhevinne's Chopin-Debussy recital, he and Rosina played the two works at a Town Hall concert in honor of Debussy, who had died twenty years earlier. Their RCA recording of *Fêtes* (which Artur Rubinstein had enjoyed so much in London) achieves such orchestral sonorities that it was submitted along with orchestral recordings of the work at a later event commemorating Debussy in France.[6]

The Lhevinnes always enjoyed playing two pianos at Town Hall because the acoustics were so good. Especially on stage. The articulation was so clean one could hear *exactly* what the other was doing, which is essential for the kind of flexible ensemble they aimed at. "In many compositions for two pianos, first the one piano plays and develops a certain theme and then the second piano takes it up. We did not plan it this way, but our temperaments were so different that quite naturally if one of us played the first theme one way, the other would play it in a different way. We considered this a great deal of fun because we never knew beforehand how the first one was going to announce it."

Sometimes the audience—not the pianists—had the "fun." Veteran Lhevinne-watchers recall with special fondness a Town Hall concert where Chopin's "Minute Waltz" (in Frederick Corder's two-piano arrangement) was played as an encore. *She* played the middle part first, giving the notes all the romantic expressiveness she could muster. Then *he* played them in a manner that could not have been more dry, detached, lackadaisical. For a brief, illuminating moment they were arguing right on stage.

Musical disputes also continued at Kew Gardens and in the studio at Juilliard. One former Juilliard student recalls having to adjudicate a heated argument as to whether in the middle section of Milhaud's *Scaramouche* it was two birds talking or one bird and an echo. At the master classes in Room 412, when students were summoned together to play for their peers and the two Lhevinnes, a student who had prepared his piece with *her* might hear from *him:* "Why so exaggerated?" A student he had prepared might hear from her: "It needs more color." Even their ways of indicating tempo dramatized their differences in approach and temperament. *He* would sit calmly in such a way that his knee was visible to the student who was playing, and would tap the beat lightly with his finger. *She* would take a pencil or a sharp metallic object and tap to be heard, not seen. When really excited about a piece of music, she has been known to stand behind the student and apply the tempo directly to the shoulders, as can be witnessed in the film made of her master class at U.C.L.A. in 1964 (see Filmography).

It would be wrong to imply that the Lhevinnes were always perceived as exemplars of *discordia concors* (harmony through disharmony). On stage, they were seen by some as models of marital charm. At the beginning of a concert, he would follow her on stage, seat her, and see that she was comfortable; afterwards, they would hold hands and bow together while receiving applause. They were often described as the "genial giant" and his "diminutive mate," and the phrases fit them well enough: he husky yet graceful, masculine and immaculately groomed, hair in ordered disarray; she petite, pert, and graciously gowned. After most of their two-piano concerts, she remembers, someone would telephone the next day to tell her how Josef had again been so "chevalieresque."

In the studio, too, the Lhevinnes could betray delicate signs of affection. William Beller recalls a lesson at Kew Gardens: "I was playing a Chopin nocturne for Josef and he was greatly preoccupied with the importance of the left hand. Just as Rosina walked into the room, he said, 'The left hand in Chopin must be like a devoted wife; it must make the other hand feel that it is the most important.'"

In general, Lhevinne's comments about piano playing remained models of simplicity. He would tell a student, when approaching an important phrase, "Lean your body into it, as if you liked it." Or he would say, "*You* push the piano away: *I* say, 'Come to me.' " In teaching a student to sustain a climax, he would say, "Once you get the water boiling, keep it boiling a while." Again, when teaching a work by Debussy, he pulled a handkerchief from his pocket, blew softly so that it floated, and said, "That is how to play it."

His tongue could be as sharp as it was laconic. One thing he could not tolerate was unnecessary hand movement. To one student who liked to finish every phrase about a foot above the keyboard, he said, "You play too much in the air. If you turned the piano upside down, you would be pretty good." Such piercing comments could send a student from the room in tears. But after a few lessons with him, the pupil usually realized the remarks were not meant personally. It was simply that Lhevinne had a high standard for piano playing which he applied impartially to everything he heard (or saw). If this meant that he lacked some flexibility as a teacher in that he was not always successful in adjusting his comments to a particular student's needs, there was compensating virtue in his honesty. And for the student who could understand his comments the rewards were great. Once, discussing a musical phrase, he told a girl, "When you go out at night, you want to have some make-up on!"

Much of Lhevinne's most effective communication was non-verbal. He was best known in this way for his ability to convey a point by demonstrating it at the piano. But that was not all he could do. Brooks Smith remembers a lesson on Debussy's *L'Isle Joyeuse*: "Lhevinne despaired that day of getting me to play the slow middle section correctly, and finally explained to me that the music should move like an Egyptian dancing girl. When still I did not get the idea, he stood up and started doing me a graceful, lazy dance that showed me just what he meant. I wish I'd had a movie camera."[7]

On June 20, 1938, while teaching in Colorado, the Lhevinnes celebrated the fortieth anniversary of their marriage. Three weeks later they headed east in order to play their E-flat concertos with the Philadelphia Orchestra and the New York Philharmonic. At Philadelphia, threatening weather held the crowd at the open-air Robin Hood Dell to a thousand people. When the rain came, it at first threatened to wash pianists, orchestra, and conductor Eugene Goosens right off the stage:

> The storm introduced itself about the Rondo [of the Mozart], but seemed to think better of it and after a preliminary shower held off for another twenty minutes.[8]

The Lhevinnes had time to play three encores after the two-piano concerto, but the second half of the program was sacrificed to the elements.

In New York, the Lhevinnes drew 6,500 persons to Lewisohn Stadium—one of the largest crowds for that summer's outdoor concerts. The evening was unmarred by meteorological disturbance, and with Willem van Hoogstraten conducting, they played the Mozart with "a poise" that "proclaimed the artists of long and common experience."[9] The only aspect of their performance that disturbed some hearers was the use of cadenzas by Leopold Godowsky, the mood and spirit of which were not exactly in keeping with Mozart's style. They stood by the cadenzas, though, and continued to play them, and later gave a spirited defense of them in the New York press.[10]

After the summer anniversary performances, the Lhevinnes took a month's leave from each other: he holing up at Bonnie Oaks; she returning to Denver, where Marianna was, and then going to California, where Don was living. They were now sixty-three and fifty-eight years old. Before leaving New York they were interviewed over lunch at the Russian Tea Room. The reporter found Mme. Lhevinne to be "plumpish, black-haired, dark-eyed and, though she's modishly dressed, she somehow reminds you of a dear mama in a tintype of the Nineties." Her husband had "the brow of a philosopher, the eyes of a poet, the smile of a gentle ironist, and the appetite of a school boy." The highlight of the interview was the Lhevinnes' definitive performance of the "rug story."

Josef, it seems, was walking down Fifth Avenue one day and dropped in at an auction. Rugs were being sold and he bid for the ones he liked. When he got ready to leave, he was told he had bought $2,000 worth, for which he wrote a check. Rosina, counting on that money to pay bills, was furious. She consulted a friend who "knew something about business" and arranged for a refund on half the rugs. But they were left with a huge $1,000 silk Kashan they had no conceivable use for. It came with a certificate that it had once hung in a palace, but at Kew Gardens the only place for it was covering a wall in the sitting room.[11] The rug blocked not only the window that looked out on the garden but also the door that opened out to it, thereby robbing the family of visual and physical access to their beloved flowers.

To many, the purchase of the $1,000 rug seemed just another example of Lhevinne's absent-mindedness. But while his head often *seemed* to be in the clouds, the diffuse facade disguised the workings of a sharp and often practical mind. Rosina liked neither the rug nor his way of acquiring it, and though Josef pretended it was all a "mistake," surely he was delighted with his new possession.

One student remembers Lhevinne as having been "so absent-minded that when he left the house at Kew Gardens we wanted to follow him, for fear he might get lost." One night she accompanied the Lhevinnes to the Russian Tea Room after Josef Hofmann had played a recital at Carnegie Hall. "After the concert we were all having drinks (except for me—I was young then and had a ginger ale). Josef, much to Rosina's consternation, decided to take an extra one. In those days when the circus came to town they unloaded from the train and took the animals down 57th Street on the way to the old Madison Square Garden. When we came out of the Tea Room, there were elephants, lions, and all sorts of other animals on the street. Poor Josef said, 'I think I've had too much to drink.' "[12] Lhevinne *may* have thought he was seeing an alcohol-induced mirage; more likely, "poor Josef" was putting his companions on.

The Lhevinnes' fortieth anniversary as a two-piano team followed their fortieth wedding anniversary by seven months, as had the charity concert arranged by César Cui followed their marriage. They celebrated the occasion with a gala benefit concert at Carnegie Hall on January 14, 1939, the proceeds of which went to the Greenwich Music Settlement House, a school in New York with 450 students ranging in age from six to sixty. The concert was planned in conjunction with the Juilliard Graduate School, where Ernest Hutcheson had succeeded John Erskine as president in 1937. The Lhevinnes played three concertos accompanied by the Juilliard Orchestra—with Albert Stoessel conducting the first two, Hutcheson the third.

When the idea of an anniversary concert was suggested to them, Lhevinne had consented only on the condition that Rosina perform a solo concerto—something she had not done since she played the Henselt with Nikisch in 1902. She had at first said that she did not feel up to it. And he had said, "I know better than yourself what is in your power, and I absolutely insist that you do it." Her condition for agreeing to play was that she first be allowed a "dry run" somewhere out of town.

Appropriately, she chose to play Chopin's E minor Concerto, her only public performance of which, when sixteen in Moscow, had caused Josef to fall in love with her. A concert was arranged upstate. When she arrived for the rehearsal, the conductor said, "Mrs. Lhevinne, there is one thing that I want to ask. Please, never look at me during the concerto, because it would confuse me." They began to rehearse and she tried not to look. But finally she did, and there he was, "with the right hand conducting and with the left hand following what was going on in the score, because if he lost the place he would not be able to find it again." After decades without giving a solo performance, the rehearsal did little for her confidence, but at least she did get the experience of playing the concerto through with an orchestra.

The practice concert had been in December, and as the "real" date got nearer she began to worry more. At the last minute it was arranged for her to play the concerto on January 12, two days before the Carnegie Hall event, with another upstate orchestra (the two cities were Buffalo and Syracuse). That performance went smoothly enough, as did the one with Stoessel and the Juilliard Orchestra, which opened the anniversary program:

> Her reading of each of the three movements of the Chopin concerto was technically immaculate, and her treatment of the romantic music always of utmost refinement. To it she brought a singing tone that was held within a restrained dynamic frame, possibly with the intention of emulating the sounds produced by the French pianos of the composer's day. The interpretation was charmingly poetic, if not particularly impassioned, and brought on the first of the several prolonged ovations of the afternoon.[13]

The next ovation was for Josef Lhevinne alone—for his performance of Tchaikovsky's B-flat minor Concerto. His interpretation of the work "practically exhausted its possibilities," wrote the *Times*. "Never has he played more magnificently or with greater virtuosity and command of tone."

To complete the program, the Lhevinnes, with Hutcheson conducting, played Mozart's E-flat Concerto. Again they used Godowsky's cadenzas, which this time were more warmly received by public and press. Perhaps that was because Godowsky had died in November and his reputation was enjoying a temporary immunity from criticism. At any rate,

Mrs. Lhevinne produced a rounder and fuller tone [in the Mozart] than in the Chopin, the sounds she drew from the instrument being almost identical in quality and volume with those that emanated from under her husband's fingers. The fusion of spirit and uniformity of approach resulted in ensemble of the first order.[14]

After some two-piano encores, the soloists were honored with a party at Mme. Samaroff's Fifth Avenue home, where they were presented with a large cake and two memorabilia of Liszt—the original manuscript of a rather obscure waltz and a letter the composer had written to the mother of a student.

Tributes flowed in from everywhere—from the press, colleagues, students, friends. The Lhevinnes were called the greatest husband-and-wife musical team since Robert and Clara Schumann (a comparison that in one way gets stronger every year now, as Rosina continues to gain on Clara's record for devoted widowhood). Among the countless telegrams they received was one which read as follows:

THAT YOU ARE CELEBRATING YOUR FORTIETH ANNIVERSARY AS MAN AND WIFE AND DUAL PIANISTS IS THRILLING NEWS. BETTY AND I EMBRACE YOU BOTH FOR EACH ONE OF THOSE ACHIEVEMENTS BECAUSE GREAT ACHIEVEMENTS THEY CERTAINLY ARE. OUR BEST LOVE AND EVERY WISH FOR THE NEXT FORTY YEARS. ALWAYS DEVOTEDLY—

JOSEF, THE OTHER.[15]

But the Fortieth Anniversary Concert is memorable more for the music produced that afternoon in Carnegie Hall than for the formal tributes and hoopla. Of all the tributes, the most meaningful was from Alexander Siloti, who was still teaching at Juilliard. "Siloti was a very severe critic—he didn't compliment you just to give you pleasure—and he never ate in the cafeteria. But the next day at the school he came downstairs especially to say, 'I came to tell you that it comes only once in a lifetime that all three concertos were from the first to the last note perfection.' That meant a great deal to us, for he was like Josef in giving praise."

Following the Carnegie Hall concert, the Lhevinnes were honored with appropriate evenings at the Beethoven Association and the Bohemians Club, and in January 1939 appeared on Gabriel Heatter's "We the People" radio program. The interview was so popular it was broadcast again in August. Because Rosina Lhevinne had played a solo concerto for the first time in America, she got a good deal of the attention, and during this brief moment in the national spotlight became an instant authority on marriage, on sharing a career with a husband, on facial creams, and on beauty. Syndicated columns carried her opinions on these and other subjects throughout the land: she must have loved every minute and every line.

In one column she asserts that beauty is more than skin deep because it really consists in "being able to listen to the other person."[16] A quaint concept, perhaps, but one she has lived up to and which has contributed a great deal to her success in life. In "Marriage Is a Bed of Roses" she explains how she and Josef always met their marital problems head on, by arguing, thereby avoiding the kind of tension that comes from harboring secret resentments.[17] Her husband no doubt looked askance at all this printed material (it was the kind of publicity *he* assiduously avoided) and must have wondered how his wife spoke with such authority about cooking—which Sarah and Masha did—and about preparing her own shampoo:

> She makes her own liquid shampoo for her hair, for instance, out of a distillation of flowers, mostly roses, from her own garden, plus castile soap and camomile flowers. And for a hair rinse, the camomile flowers are steeped in boiling water, then strained.[18]

Today Mme. Lhevinne wonders how such nonsense got printed, and hopes no one tried to emulate her alleged technique.

Certainly after forty years during which she had continually pushed her husband into the spotlight she deserved to indulge in *some* publicity. A decade before their fortieth anniversary, Lhevinne said this of her:

> I must tell you what a great inspiration my wife has been to me. When we were married she gave up a great career . . . not only to make me happy, but to improve and develop my artistic soul—which she has done. The most beautiful part of her character is that she always strives for the highest ideals. No one on earth could have inspired me as she has —[while remaining] always, my severest critic.[19]

Rosina Lhevinne brought out the best in her husband in some of the same ways Eleanor Roosevelt did. In each case the mix of diametrically opposed temperaments, aggravating in daily life, led to great achievements in the larger public world. Today Rosina Lhevinne is so aware of the smaller irritations she caused her late husband that she would prefer not to have that loving tribute to her printed. But even if in quantitative terms the irritation had exceeded the inspiration, that would be no reason to deny the inspiration that was there. Just after the fortieth anniversary, *she* described the strength of their relationship to perfection: "It's true that our temperaments are as different as they can be. But bread and butter don't clash and neither do oil and vinegar. In this partnership I am the pepper and he is the salt—the salt of the earth."[20]

If the 1938–39 season was the peak of the Lhevinnes' long musical partnership, the five years that followed were certainly no decline. They might best be termed a nicely sustained plateau. During the season that followed the anniversary, they played more than thirty concerts together, while he gave only ten recitals alone. The interesting thing about their two-piano work is that they did not rest on past laurels. They opened the following season, for example, by adding a new concerto to their repertoire: Mozart's in F major for Three Pianos in the composer's two-piano arrangement. On October 26, 27, and 29, 1939, they played that work with John Barbirolli and the New York Philharmonic. It had previously been played on three pianos in New York, but this was apparently the first public performance of the two-piano version. The Lhevinnes' preparation for the concert was not entirely harmonious.

"Josef and I had a very big argument about this work because the last movement—it was like there *was* no last movement. Mozart had written one, but it was very uninteresting, so I wanted to play it much faster and more brilliant than it was written. But Josef felt we should not change Mozart's intentions, so we did it that way. It was not well received at all."

The last sentence needs qualification, for the *Post*'s critic felt the Lhevinnes' performance "could bear infinite repetition." But the *Sun*'s man, granting that the playing was "musical, polished, and very well unified," pointed out that the "beam of weight and assertiveness tipped to the distaff side." Olin Downes also sensed the tension between the performers. He thought the performance "respectful, almost too respectful, of the music."

During the next season the Lhevinnes returned to their old standby—Mozart's E-flat. But even that work they approached with open minds. On January 8, 1941, they played it with the Women's Symphony Orchestra in Chicago, conducted by young Izler Solomon. Solomon was stunned at the rehearsal. "In the concerto there is a mordent given first by the orchestra in the tutti and then taken up by the piano. I asked the Lhevinnes if they would show me how they liked to do it, so I could do it that way with the orchestra. So he went to the piano and began to demonstrate it. But she said, 'Wait! Wait! Josef! Let's see how he does it. Maybe his way is more beautiful than ours.'

"I tried to get out of it by saying, 'You have been playing this all your lives. Surely your way is more beautiful than mine.' But even he insisted that they wanted to hear it my way."[21]

In characterizing the Lhevinnes' insatiable curiosity about music, Joseph Raieff once put it this way: "She verbalized, he digitalized." She would ask anyone she respected for an opinion about a musical point, as she did Solomon; he would sit at the piano for hours, discover all the possibilities for himself, then decide which he preferred. His students and colleagues could hardly believe how utterly absorbed he was in music he had played for fifty years or more. Once at a summer master class in Denver he began playing "cat and mouse" with Schumann's *Symphonic Études*, repeating phrase after phrase after phrase with only the minutest variation. After he had done this nearly half an hour, completely oblivious to his audience, Rosina had to say from the front of the stage, "Josef, there is not so much time." He replied, "There is all the time in the world," and kept at it.[22]

A more dramatic example of his perfectionism came at a Carnegie Hall concert that a student, Ruth Geiger, attended with Mme. Lhevinne. Leaving Miss Geiger at intermission, Rosina went backstage to see her husband. She returned to the box in an excited state: "I saw Josef backstage and he was practicing—not what he will play in the second half of the program but what he has already played!"[23] His musical and digital curiosity allowed no exceptions. Even his greatest speciality, Chopin's *Étude* in Double Thirds, got overhauled periodically. After years of playing it in such a way that even Horowitz told friends, "No one can match Lhevinne's delicacy in this work," the pianist discovered a new way to finger it. This horrified some of his closest followers, who could not understand why he would tamper with something already "perfect." But Lhevinne had a standard reply, half humorous, half serious, to such queries: "I am the laziest person in the world. I can work harder than anyone else in order to make something easier for myself."

Although he gave more concerts with his wife than alone during the last years of his life, Lhevinne continued to give an annual Carnegie Hall recital. In November 1940, Virgil Thomson wrote what is probably the definitive Lhevinne review. Typical of Thomson, it is an account not of a particular concert but of an artist's musical personality. It deserves to be read in full.

> Mr. Lhevinne seems to have replaced the late Leopold Godowsky as
> the acknowledged master of piano-forte mastery. A full house paid him

homage last night at Carnegie Hall, as he, in turn, paid his audience the honor of executing a distinguished program of the piano's masterworks with authority and no playing down to anybody.

A more satisfactory academism could scarcely be imagined. Mr. Lhevinne's performance, especially of Schumann's Toccata and the Chopin Études, was both a lesson and an inspiration. He made no effort to charm or to seduce or to preach or to impress. He played as if he were expounding to a graduate seminar, "This is the music, and this is the way to play it."

Any authoritative execution derives as much of its excellence from what the artist does not do as from what he does. If he doesn't do anything off color at all, he is correctly said to have taste.

Mr. Lhevinne's taste is as authoritative as his technical method. Not one sectarian interpretation, not one personal fancy, not one stroke below the belt, not a sliver of ham, mars the universal acceptability of his readings. Everything he does is right and clear and complete. Everything he doesn't do is the whole list of all the things that mar the musical executions of lesser men.

This is not to say that tenderness and poetry and personal warmth and fire are faults of musical style, though they frequently do excuse a faulty technique. I am saying that Mr. Lhevinne does not need them. They would mar his style; hence he eschews them. He eschews them because his concept of piano music is an impersonal one. It is norm-centered: it is for all musical men. Any intrusion of the executant's private soul would limit its appeal, diminish its authority.

Thus it is that Mr. Lhevinne's performance is worthy of the honorable word academic. And if he seems to some a little distant, let us remind ourselves that remoteness is, after all, inevitable to those who inhabit Olympus.[24]

Although the Lhevinnes flourished under the challenges of the concert season and the academic year at Juilliard, they came to look forward more and more to the comparatively relaxed summers in Colorado. In 1941, Lawrence Porter, who served as their chauffeur, drove them west in a new Oldsmobile that Lhevinne had purchased about the time of the Thomson review. They stopped in Madison on the way, to see Marianna receive her bachelor's degree from the University of Wisconsin, thereby fulfilling the dream of many American immigrants—a college education for both children. They, too, had garnered some degrees recently. In June 1939, Rosina Lhevinne received an honorary doctorate from the Lamont School (now part of the University of Denver); in August 1940, Josef Lhevinne received his from the University of Colorado at Boulder. Instead of standing to give an address, Lhevinne sat down to play music of Chopin and Debussy.

The Lhevinnes drove west in the summers, but when on tour they had to travel by train, there being no commercial airlines then. As they did not have a private Pullman with a piano as Paderewski had had in his heyday, they liked to pass time and limber the fingers by doing exercises Lhevinne had invented. These consisted of crossing and recrossing the fingers of each hand into intricate, rather ludicrous designs, and had always drawn strange looks from fellow passengers. But there was a new twist when Lhevinne began to wear glasses for the first time. Rosina did not like the way they looked. In addition, she had read that one could eliminate the need for glasses by doing exercises that involved rolling the eyes a certain way. She persuaded him to try it. So in the train's dining car he began to roll his eyes at the same time they did finger exercises together. The car suddenly became silent. Then someone was heard to say, "Good Lord, those poor people! They are not only deaf and dumb, but a little queer, too."

During the fall semester of 1941, the Lhevinnes went twice on tour by train, and Rosina kept a diary of each excursion. In early November they went to Gary, Indiana, via Olean, New York. Her diary comments as much on books she read (Shirer's *Berlin Diary*), things she saw (the library of St. Bonaventure College, the Gary Steel Company plant), and people she met (hosts, former students, taxi drivers, and friends who put slugs in a juke box so it would not play) as on their concerts. Their schedule after returning home was extraordinary. She arrived from Gary early on the morning of November 4, while he had gone to Louisville for a concert. On November 7 he was in Jersey City for a "British Children" benefit. On November 9 the Lhevinnes played together at Centenary College in New Jersey. The day after that they performed at a Carnegie Hall benefit for "Bundles for Britain." The next day they played a concert in Atlantic City. The following day they gave a young boy an audition, and returned to New York.

The day after that, Lhevinne played in East Orange, New Jersey, giving a preview of his Carnegie Hall recital scheduled two days later. Diary entries on the way to Gary had pictured Lhevinne as occasionally "nervous" and "irritable." Felix Salmond went along to East Orange, and Rosina noted in the diary that her husband "played beautifully. Especially the [Chopin] Fantasie." Reviews of the Carnegie Hall concert indicate that he had difficulty getting started: "The sultry afternoon seemed to have conquered the soloist and his audience." But when Lhevinne got to the Chopin things happened.

Three quarters of the way through the recital he suddenly awoke with a titanic bounce and played in a way that few pianists of our time can equal. From the Fantasy to the end of the program, and notably in the encores, Mr. Lhevinne was triumphant.[25]

During the first two weeks of December the Lhevinnes took to the rails again—this time traveling to Ft. Worth via Detroit, Quincy, Illinois, and Tyler, Texas. As part of their two-piano recital in Ft. Worth, Rosina accompanied her husband in the Tchaikovsky Concerto. They also played "The Star-Spangled Banner," which they had memorized that morning in the dining room of Merle Harding, with whom they were staying. That was necessary because three days earlier, when they were riding south from St. Louis in an observation car, the radio had brought news of Pearl Harbor. They returned to New York on December 14, Josef Lhevinne's sixty-seventh birthday.

On the train and in kitchens during the December tour, the Lhevinnes had memorized the latest—and last—major addition to their two-piano repertoire. On January 11, 1942, they played Poulenc's Concerto for Two Pianos with Maurice Abravanel and the City Symphony Orchestra. Mme. Lhevinne recalls that they forgot the Poulenc soon after, but playing it well once was achievement enough. "It is to the credit of Mr. and Mrs. Lhevinne, who are so often associated with nineteenth-century romantic music," wrote the *Tribune*, "that they proved themselves so thoroughly in rapport with this contemporary product."[26]

In the spring of 1942 they went west again, this time for concerts in California, Washington, and North Dakota. By then the war had touched their family directly, for Don was soon to be stationed at the army base in Rapid City. When his Dakota training was complete, he left from California for wartime service that eventually led to a position as a topographer in Europe under Eisenhower's command. Don's mother was in California when he left, and the night of his going-away party remains fixed in her mind. "I was working at the piano in a little annex nearby, and I sent word for him to come from the party to see me. He'd had a little whiskey and was a little gay, and I asked him to open his shirt and I felt his body naked under my hands and hugged it very close and that's a moment I'll never forget as long as I live. I could not believe they were sending him to war, and with my nervous temperament I was really quite out of balance until he came back. But that night I didn't show him how upset I was, and I tried to practice some more after he left." Don's wife, Peggy, whom he had married in October 1940, moved in at Kew Gardens when her husband left for Europe.

The war affected musicians not only by what it did to their families. The Lhevinnes lost many Juilliard students to the war effort. And they now played charity concerts not only for "British Children" and "Bundles for Britain" but for America's "Buy a Bomber" program. Some of these concerts were at their own expense, for the Baldwin company informed them in 1942 that it could no longer supply instruments in towns where it had no offices.[27] Even so, as Miss Illingworth of NBC Artists recalls, "the Lhevinnes very seldom turned down a request for a two-piano appearance. Many times a small civic music organization would request only the Lhevinnes and would not have enough money to meet their fee. Nine times out of ten, they would play anyway." When asked why, they answered sincerely, "To repay America for all it has done for us."

In late May and early June, 1942, Lhevinne spent a month at Bonnie Oaks before meeting Rosina in Denver for another summer of teaching. A number of new students joined them that summer, among them a young man from Kansas named Robert Pace (later the head of the Piano Department at Columbia University's Teachers College). As Pace sat outside the studio waiting for his first audition, the playing he heard inside was so beautiful he thought it must be Lhevinne himself. He was crushed when a nine-year-old boy walked out of the room. When *he* entered, he apologized for not having practiced for several days. Lhevinne replied, "Oh, that's all right. I haven't practiced for years." As Ketchum had in 1914, Pace found Lhevinne to be an incredibly demanding teacher, and felt "clobbered" after each lesson. Being extremely proficient at Ping-Pong, he was *sometimes* able to take revenge at a table in the basement of the Lamont School. But Lhevinne had a wicked left hand, and after losing would keep Pace there until he had reversed the score. Lhevinne showed a like tenacity when playing Ping-Pong with Josef Hofmann—whoever lost would insist on continuing the match until he won.

The nine-year-old who had intimidated Pace was probably the ten-year-old whom Howard Waltz remembers from the Denver class a year later. The boy was playing Mozart with a great deal of tenderness, and Lhevinne said, "That's too sweet." And Rosina said, "But Josef, he loves it so." The boy never knew what Pace had thought, but he never will forget the Lhevinnes playing the

Tchaikovsky Concerto together on two pianos, with Rosina giving her husband a dazzling and powerful accompaniment. The boy was young John Browning.[28]

Another student at Denver was Ruth Geiger, who had come to the Lhevinnes as a fifteen-year-old refugee from Vienna in 1938 and who won the Naumburg Prize after completing her studies with them at Juilliard. She was impressed by what a serious photographer Lhevinne was. He would scale a steep cliff in order to get the right angle on a lake, saying, between breaths, "In my youth I was a mountain goat." She also recalls his elaborate theories on catching fish, none of which brought much in the way of results, so far as she could see. Lhevinne had long been serious about photography: his financial records from Wannsee before World War I show an occasional expenditure for film.

One thing all students remember about summers in Denver is how Lhevinne loathed to practice for his summer engagements. In 1940, 1942, and 1944, he played the Tchaikovsky Concerto with the New York Philharmonic at Lewisohn Stadium. The only time he practiced for these engagements was when someone locked him in the cabin at the Rosboroughs', just as David Shor had had to do when Josef was twelve years old in the Caucasus Mountains. In 1940, Lhevinne's performance of the Tchaikovsky under William Steinberg's baton was the 150th of his career—a fact the heavens saw fit to applaud with several rounds of thunder and lightning. In 1942, Lhevinne, Howard Barlow, and the orchestra were accompanied only by the drone of overhead airplanes. Lhevinne's performance of the Tchaikovsky on July 31, 1944 (two days before this writer was born) was the last concert he ever gave.

During the last two years of his life, Lhevinne showed no outward signs of physical decline. During the 1942–43 season, he and Rosina continued to teach at Juilliard and to tour as duo-pianists, traveling to Texas and Tennessee in November and to Florida in March; in between times they played numerous concerts in the New York area in support of the war effort. Lhevinne's big solo event of the year was an all-Chopin recital at Carnegie Hall, which featured, in the center of the program, the Twenty-four Preludes. One symphonic appearance he had greatly looked forward to that season was to have been with Stock and the Chicago Symphony Orchestra in Milwaukee at the end of February, but Stock died in October at the age of sixty-nine, and Lhevinne had to play the Liszt

Concerto with an unfamiliar conductor. Two weeks after the performance in Milwaukee, Lhevinne learned of Rachmaninoff's death in Los Angeles, of cancer, at the age of seventy-one.

Lhevinne gave a recital at Juilliard that season, curious for what he said afterward. Greeted by a crowd of well-wishers backstage, he said, after being congratulated for his playing, "It was nothing. I just played the notes, some of them loud, some soft." A few people present took his comment as a sign of decline, of a depletion of energy; others found in the remark another of Lhevinne's disarmingly simple statements about the essence of music. Throughout his career, Lhevinne had belittled the importance of his own playing. After one of his block-busting recitals in the mid-twenties, he had played Liszt's *Robert le Diable* as an encore. Backstage, one of his students, Victor Aller, asked, "How can you play such a demanding work after the long program you have already played?" "Victor," Lhevinne replied, "haven't you ever seen a horse that comes in after a hard day's work in the field and then has to go out before it is dark and plow some more?"[29]

Lhevinne's last Carnegie Hall recital was on November 7, 1943. Fittingly, the program included works that spanned his entire career—transcriptions by Liszt and Busoni that he had played at the turn of the century, several works by Chopin, and Debussy pieces he had favored more recently. In Lhevinne's playing of Chopin, one critic pointed with insight to the simultaneous mixture of "suavity and violence."[30] After many encores, the audience demanded "The Blue Danube," the final note of which was the last note he played at Carnegie Hall. After the concert, when a student complimented him on the extraordinary vigor of his performances, he said simply, "I'm getting old." As in London in 1937, his recital had exhausted him; as in London, he had disguised that fact from the audience.

A month later to the day, he played an all-Schumann program at Times Hall on West Forty-fourth Street. The only all-Schumann program of his career (as far as I have discovered), it too spanned the breadth of his career. Included were the *Carnaval* (one of his most successful works in Europe before World War I), four pieces from the *Fantasiestück* (which he had played in the Rubinstein Prize Competition and seldom since), the *Symphonic Études* (played mostly in America after the War), and the Toccata, a favorite during his entire career. As usual, his performance was norm-centered rather than idiosyncratic: Its distinctive feature was the use "of rubato in terms of the traditional and internal demands of the music rather than [in terms] of personal caprice. . . . The literal sense of rubato as 'robbed' was almost always respected."[31]

The Lhevinnes' last two-piano concert in New York was on May 10, 1944, at Town Hall. The program was a benefit for the Bronx Settlement Music School and featured the standard mix of two-piano works plus solos by Lhevinne. The last work they played was Chopin's Rondo for Two Pianos, a particular favorite of Mme. Lhevinne because its close passage work was well suited to her small hands.

As the summer of 1944 approached, there was no reason to fear for Lhevinne's health. One day two or three years before, he had come home and said to Rosina, "Don't be excited, don't worry, but the doctor said my heart is not quite as strong as before." Since then, however, he had had no trouble. He went to Bonnie Oaks that summer, and he and Rosina went to Denver. He returned to New York for the performance of the Tchaikovsky. The *New York Times* reported him "in excellent form," and the audience of six thousand was thrilled by his playing. But Sarah Crump, his housekeeper, thought he looked very tired as he played that day, and never forgot the sight of "Mr. Lhevinne on the stage there, working so hard."

After playing in New York, he went to California to visit Marianna for a short vacation, Rosina staying in Denver. Marianna lived in Los Angeles at the time, where she was a translator at Warner Brothers (she had majored in French). One August day they went to the beach for a swim, and Lhevinne was far from the shore when the waves suddenly got high. The effort it took to swim in was too much for his heart. Marianna took him by ambulance to a hospital and telephoned her mother, who arrived immediately from Denver. Lhevinne recovered slowly and was put in a convalescent home. In September his wife had to return to New York to begin the year at Juilliard. In a few months he decided to return there. But she did not wish him to come until she could find a suitable place for him to stay, for the bedrooms at Kew Gardens were on the second floor, and to climb the stairs would be hazardous before full recovery.

Finding suitable lodgings was not easy. In November of 1944 the soldiers were returning from Europe and the hotels were so crowded, she found, that reservations could be made for three days only. By chance, a Juilliard student was able to help. Her brother had not yet come home from the war, and the mother offered her son's room—on the first floor, a few steps from a park. This would be the perfect place for Josef to recuperate, and Rosina was now eager for her husband's return. The homecoming, however, was marred by Lhevinne's extreme conscientiousness.

"When he arrived from California, I met him. He wore his beautiful tan coat but he looked very worn out. I told him what the woman had offered, and he immediately said, 'Of course, we have to pay.'

"And I said, 'By no means. They are very wealthy and consider it such an honor that you stay there that they don't want to take any money.'

"And he said, 'No, I cannot do it.' He insisted on going home to Kew Gardens. How I wish I'd told a little white lie and made an arrangement with the woman. He would probably still be alive today.

"We spoke a little that night, and he stayed up quite late looking at his papers at the writing desk, for he had been away from home for several months. Later Sarah told me that before going to bed that night he went up to the third floor and climbed a big ladder where all his papers and documents were. He told her he was very pleased that he had found the contract he had made when he bought the house, because without it, it might not be clear that we had paid for all of it.

"The next morning I had to leave for an appointment before he got up. Sarah told me that he had a good breakfast with two eggs and all the rest. Then he said, 'Sarah, I don't feel so well, I think I will go rest a little.' When she didn't hear anything for an hour, she went upstairs and opened the door and saw that he was gone."

Josef Lhevinne died on his bed of a heart attack on December 2, 1944, twelve days before his seventieth birthday. Five days later a memorial service was held at the Juilliard School. Olga Samaroff spoke and Ernest Hutcheson and Sascha Gorodnitzki played compositions by Chopin. Newspapers printed tributes from Lhevinne's colleagues. From the vantage point of the 1970s the most interesting is from Artur Rubinstein:

> With the passing away of Josef Lhevinne the musical world has lost a great artist and one of the greatest pianists of our epoch. His many friends, among whom I proudly count myself, will miss his spirited, heart-warming company; his colleagues and pupils will miss his genuine interest in their work and his ever-ready moral support.
>
> Lhevinne, in my opinion, belonged to the group one could call "aristocrats of the keyboard." Leopold Godowsky and Emil Sauer were "aristocrats," but none came nearer to the ideal than Josef Lhevinne. His playing possessed what the French most love—"éclat," clarity to the

highest degree, the ability to project all the beauty and depth of a musical work with the ease of one who dominates all pianistic difficulties without ever "showing them off." Lhevinne had elegance, and he could also move his listeners to tears by the sheer beauty of his tone.

Yes, he was the last of the "aristocrats."[32]

V

A WORLD RECREATED

13

A New Beginning

ROSINA LHEVINNE "felt completely desperate" after the death of her husband. The children came to comfort her—Marianna for the funeral, Don later, when the Army allowed him to return from Europe. Even so, she was temporarily confined to a hospital. When released, she agreed with the children that the Kew Gardens house must be sold. But when prospective buyers arrived she hid behind the curtains: she could abide no human contact.

At first she had no professional plans. She was certain Juilliard would appoint a famous pianist to fill her late husband's position. She vaguely hoped, and her son agreed, that she might get a job at a settlement school. So when President Hutcheson invited her to visit him at the school she was not expecting much. When he offered her Josef's position she was stunned—and had to sit down. When she collected herself, she said she did not feel capable. He told her to have faith in herself and to try it a year. She said she would, and went home to thumb through the repertoire. Many pieces, of course, were familiar. But she had always worked with Josef. Without him she felt empty, unsure, without ideas. She spent the summer at a Long Island sanatorium.

When the school year began she needed a place to live. Hotels remained overcrowded. She did not want to depend on friends. So she rented a single room on Riverside Drive until the owner's son returned from the war. There was no room for Sarah or Masha, nor did she herself have access to kitchen or dining room. So she took her meals at a small and inexpensive neighborhood restaurant. There began the minor miracles. Because of stomach trouble, she had been on complicated diets all her life. "One doctor would say I should have all meat and no vegetables and another would say all vegetables and no meat. But at this little restaurant I had to eat something, so I had both meat and vegetables and my stomach was better than ever before."

When the apartment owner's son returned, she had to move. She could find nothing. One day at the little restaurant she chanced to meet Lee Thompson, who had studied with the Lhevinnes during their last summer in Denver. Miss Thompson lived with two other girls on Claremont Avenue, just below the school. They invited Mme. Lhevinne to join them. With absolutely nowhere else to go, she accepted. At first she had a bedroom to herself, for two of the girls were able to bundle up every night and go across the street to sleep. When that was no longer possible, they all had to stay in the small one-bedroom apartment. Mme. Lhevinne slept in the bedroom on a cot—separated from two of her roommates by a thin partition. Her third roommate slept on the living-room couch. After years of spacious living in the Chinese House and at Kew Gardens, she somehow thrived on the tight quarters, and remains in the same small apartment today.

At Juilliard she did not at first get many of the best students, for no one knew how good she would be alone. There were enough students, though, for many had returned from the war. Her return to teaching was blessed by the friendship and advice of Felix Salmond. Recently released by the Curtis Institute in Philadelphia, the piano-struck cellist was now in New York with time on his hands. Much of that time he spent observing and commenting on lessons in Room 412. Outspoken and extremely musical, he gave his good friend many suggestions and much courage, and in fact became her musical advisor.

In one important nonmusical matter that year, she herself provided the courage and advice. Masha, then living with friends on Long Island, had become increasingly thin, and Mme. Lhevinne insisted that she see a doctor. It was found that she had cancer of the stomach. Several specialists thought the case hopeless. But Rosina Lhevinne, as her own mother had when she was a child, found a man who would operate. In January 1946, Dr. William C. White removed three-fourths of Masha's stomach plus, in his words, a tumor "the size of a tennis ball."[1] Miraculously, she survived. For many months she was in acute pain while what was left of her stomach stretched and learned to accommodate food. But her ordeal was eased considerably by Mme. Lhevinne, who had managed to sublet an apartment for three months so she could be with Masha and help care for her. When Masha was stronger, she went to California to live with Don and his wife Peggy, who had been a registered nurse.

A few months later Mme. Lhevinne herself arrived in California, where she had been invited to teach for the summer at the Los Angeles Conservatory of Music. As Marianna had been married a few weeks before she arrived, and as Don's house was protected by three-score steep steps, she lacked a place to stay. She was about to take a hotel room when a piano student she had known only by letter invited her to stay in her apartment near the school. So she moved into a rooming house occupied largely by students of the Conservatory. For the next five summers she roomed with one of those students, Salome Ramras, a Juilliard alumnus, who also painted. The apartment was so cluttered with canvases there was hardly room for a "breadcrumb" on the floor. But Mme. Lhevinne was by now used to tight quarters and had only to adjust to her new roommate's debut as a cook. "It was not so bad that Salome would burn the spinach. But in the middle of the night she would have terrible nightmares and scream 'Spinach! Spinach! Spinach!' and I would have to run to the other room, trying not to step on anything, and wake her up so she would stop." Humor and flexibility, combined with Miss Ramras' devotion, turned potential hardship into friendship.

Mme. Lhevinne's first meeting with Dr. Gerry White, President of the Los Angeles Conservatory, like so many events during this period of her life, was slightly bizarre—they met for a picnic in a boat on a lake near the campus. She was not content with teaching during the week only, but conspired with friends and acquaintances to arrange gatherings every Sunday for her class. Sometimes they were merely social affairs; sometimes they were pianistic, such as the afternoon Brooks Smith and Yalli Wagman improvised on the Brahms *Paganini* theme and Wagman was so brilliant that Smith began that summer a disciplined approach to technique. Whether the gathering was social or musical, students were expected to attend. And perhaps it is correct to find here the seeds of what could later be called the Rosina Lhevinne "mystique." This "mystique" has involved close and demanding relationships with the students she has lived with and those she has taught, and it has involved the belief that her piano class is one big family. Like her actual success as a teacher, it has been built upon her ability to adjust to new roommates, new ideas, new ways of living; her ability to admit what she does not know and to rely on others for help; her extreme loyalty to and involvement with those devoted to her; and perhaps above all, her ability to meet adversity with resources previously untapped. In the year and a half following her husband's death, these ingredients for her future success had begun to gather to a head.

During that year and a half, Rosina Lhevinne had turned sixty-six years old. Just as she was beginning a new life, so was the twenty-one-year-old Juilliard Graduate School. Thirty-five-year-old William Schuman had succeeded Ernest Hutcheson as president and had energetically begun to introduce reforms. His first project was to bring about the amalgamation of the Juilliard Graduate School and the Institute of Musical Art—the result being the Juilliard School of Music. In the process, Schuman had to release many teachers. But he did not believe in compulsory retirement. "I pointed out to the board that Mme. Lhevinne was due to retire and that I would like to use her as a test case, because if my judgment was right I thought she had her greatest years ahead of her."[2] The board agreed. When Mme. Lhevinne had her first business meeting with the young president, he told her she would be allowed to teach as long as she felt able.

The piano faculty of the new school included Mmes. Samaroff and Lhevinne from the original 1924 group as well as the most prominent of those who later became Lhevinne's male colleagues: Carl Friedberg and James Friskin (Siloti and Hutcheson had retired). Of these teachers, Mme. Samaroff had by far the strongest reputation. She had stopped performing in the 1930s, but had since developed the popular "Layman's Course" and trained many outstanding pupils, among whom the foremost was William Kapell, whose death in a plane crash in 1953 took away America's first great "home-grown and home-trained" pianistic talent. When Mme. Samaroff herself had died five years earlier, in 1948, dire predictions were heard that Juilliard's piano faculty was "washed up."

Mark Schubart, Dean of the Juilliard School during Schuman's reign, came to the school in 1946. At that time he felt that Mme. Samaroff was clearly the greatest piano teacher there, and that Rosina Lhevinne was just one of the "others." Neither he nor anyone else sensed the degree to which she was soon to assume a leading role. Nor did *she* have any delusions of grandeur about her ability to teach during those first years of going it alone. She had always regarded her husband as the great musician and teacher, and now that he was gone she simply did what she could to "carry on in his tradition." She continued to teach in Room 412, where they had taught together, and beginning in 1946 held an annual reunion on his birthday, December 14, inviting his former pupils to gather and share memories. Because of the population density at the Claremont Avenue apartment, the reunions were held at the Riverside Drive apartment of Joseph Raieff, a former Lhevinne student appointed to the Juilliard faculty in 1946.

In evolving her own teaching style, Mme. Lhevinne continued to count on Felix Salmond for musical advice and, true to character, took musical ideas from as many sources as possible. During her first summer at the Los Angeles Conservatory, she received from Lee Thompson detailed notes from lectures Mme. Samaroff gave in New York, and underlined the parts that seemed to her particularly useful. It is characteristic of Rosina Lhevinne that she would not only wish to make use of another teacher's good ideas but that she would be able to find someone who would go to all the lectures, take notes, and type them up almost verbatim. She was also willing to learn from other teachers' students, and kept up with new approaches to Bach by following the work of Rosalyn Tureck, a student of Mme. Samaroff. Another source of ideas was Isabelle Vengerova, a Russian pianist then teaching at the Curtis Institute in Philadelphia.

"Mme. Vengerova and I were both of the Russian school, but there was some difference because I had studied at Moscow and she at St. Petersburg (with Essipova). Although we both had very little time, we got together once every spring for two hours at the piano. She was an imposing woman and always called me 'my child,' although she was only five years older than I. She always said, 'My child, you are the one I want to know all my secrets,' and the main thing she wanted to show me was her way of getting a beautiful sound. Her way was to 'pull' at the piano, making a down and up motion with the wrists, down and up, and never removing the fingers from the keys, but rather clinging to the keys. She would tell me about a child who had been with her from the age of nine and who never used high fingers, and how her fingers on the piano were like gliding on ice. She would lecture me in this manner and I would patiently listen.

"Then I would say, 'Belochka [diminutive for squirrel], I think it is really wonderful how you do it, so now you play a scale and I play a scale and we'll see how they sound.' Well, she liked my way and I liked hers, but she always said, 'Rosina, I don't understand how it can sound like that the way you do it.' Looking back on it now, I can see that her approach gradually began to have some influence on my teaching, for in certain passages the method of not raising the fingers at all contributes to a wonderful effect of legato."

Rosina Lhevinne responded quickly to the challenge of teaching, but she did not think about returning to the concert stage until the day Victor Babin telephoned and invited her to join him and his wife Vitya Vronsky in Mozart's Triple Concerto at a concert with a new group Thomas Scherman was forming called the Little Orchestra Society. She thanked him but said she could not imagine being on stage with anyone but Josef. He asked her to think it over and said he would call again the next day.

"The same day I went to school to teach, and at lunch I certainly told my friend Felix Salmond what had happened. He listened very quietly, and his eye kept getting smaller and smaller. 'Rosina,' he said, 'if you don't play, I don't know you any more.' So I decided to play."

The first concert ever given by the Little Orchestra Society was in Town Hall on November 17, 1947. (It was repeated the following night at the Brooklyn Academy of Music.) Rosina Lhevinne played the first piano in Mozart's Triple Concerto, Victor Babin played the second, and his wife, Vitya Vronsky, played the third (she said there was so little to do in her part that she was there only for "moral support"). The performance was successful enough, although, as Mme. Lhevinne recalls, "nothing much came of it" in the way of other engagements. Her return to the concert stage was welcomed by the New York press, the *Times* calling her

the guiding light of the ensemble . . . with results which delighted the ear. Her solo performance in the beginning of the slow movement conveyed the unique quality of Mozart's intensity, with mellow tone and graciousness.[3]

Another account noted the way she fixed her "keen eyes" on Babin throughout, in order to assure a unified ensemble. Columbia Records recorded the concerto, and Mme. Lhevinne remembers that one scale for two pianos was difficult to synchronize, so she insisted that Babin play it alone.

It was only after the performance and the recording that someone pointed out to her that she and her husband had played the same F major concerto for two pianos in 1940. Because that experience had been so unpleasant, she had completely blocked it from memory. She told the Babins of how she and Josef had disagreed about that work—and many others. "I told them that even if the performance was successful we would disagree. I would say, 'Look, Josef, we played at my tempo and see what a success it was.' And he would say, 'What do you mean? We played it at *my* tempo and it was successful.' So Vitya said, 'I do it different. When we played at my tempo and it was successful I would tell Victor backstage, 'You see, we played it at your tempo, and look how successful it was.' That was a good lesson for me, but of course it was too late to make use of it."

The performance with Vronsky and Babin signalled Mme. Lhevinne's complete return to the vigorous musical life she had led while her husband was alive. The success of that performance, along with the increasing demand for her teaching at Juilliard and during the summer in Los Angeles, began to restore her confidence in her capabilities and human worth. Her life began to fall into a satisfying pattern. Every winter, under President Schuman's midyear-intersession plan, she spent a month in California with the children and Masha. She enjoyed California's winter sun quite as much as her husband had in 1908–09. Still, there were some strange moments. One year she was late for the train, and leaving Sarah with the suitcases far behind, she got to the gate just as it closed. Pounding on the gate and saying she had to see her children, she not only convinced the conductor to let her on but arranged for a delay in Albany so a second train could bring her luggage. Then there was the Sunday she went to Bear Mountain.

She had gone with Lee Thompson, who was then her assistant, to memorize the concerto she would play with Vronsky and Babin. The three-piano score not being available, Babin had provided a copy from the Library of Congress. She studied it on the boat ride up, but when sitting down for lunch at the inn found the music missing. Panic challenged, then gave way to the near ludicrous: Mme. Lhevinne and Miss Thompson walking in the rain, holding umbrellas in one hand and between them a cardboard sign with REWARD: MUSIC LOST scrawled in lipstick. The park rangers had failed to mobilize ("If the music's so valuable, lady, why'd you bring it here?") and the two women were about ready to give up and reboard the boat when a boy came up to say he had seen something strange below the bridge in the bear pit. They went to look and saw the score. The man who fed the bears was duly dispatched. He soon returned with a pawed-over, sniffed-at, undamaged Mozart concerto. His thoughts as the two women sailed away in a cab for New York are unknown.

After returning from California in January 1949, Mme. Lhevinne had resumed teaching her twenty students at Juilliard and had celebrated her sixty-ninth birthday on March 29. Soon afterwards, she discovered that she had cancer of the breast. On May 9 the malignant tumor, along with a good deal of surrounding tissue, including some under the arm, was removed by Dr. Cushman Haagenson, for whose skill his patient remains ever thankful. Mme. Lhevinne left Columbia-Presbyterian Hospital on May 22, and a month later arrived in Los Angeles to begin her fourth summer master class there. Lee Thompson, because she still lived at the Claremont Avenue apartment, was one of the few people who knew of the pain Rosina had suffered.

One of the most outstanding characteristics of Mme. Lhevinne is her strength of character—her ability to go on in spite of adversity. After this severe operation, she had to do exercises every day in order to regain the use of one of her arms. She never complained, she would stand there doing the exercises sometimes with tears streaming down her face. . . . But she won out, and in a matter of months had resumed her full activities—no one the wiser.[4]

Marianna was amazed that her mother, who reacted in such an exaggerated way to the common cold, could meet major surgery with such courage and fortitude. Strangely enough, it seemed that the operation, rather than tiring Rosina Lhevinne, increased the energy and enthusiasm and sheer indomitability she had shown in her previous seven decades. Somehow the pitiful impressionable girl, the dutiful subservient wife, was becoming a veritable tower of strength.

In October 1949, Rosina Lhevinne gave the convocation address at Juilliard. Her topic was "tempo rubato."

You will find many descriptions of tempo rubato but the one which Mr. Lhevinne and I advocated is the one which tells us that the proper rubato is based on the principle of "give-and-take." It means that if we give more time to certain notes, to compensate we must take away time from others. Since "give-and-take" adds so much warmth and character to the interpretation of music it occurred to me that this idea is not limited to the performance of music.[5]

She then asserted that all human relationships should be based on the principle of "give-and-take" and told the students that "we must start in our homes, we must carry it out in the school and we must certainly practice it in our married life and in our professional life." Applying the principle to the students vis à vis the school, she struck the theme President Kennedy was to stress at his inaugural a decade later:

From my long association with the school I can assure you young people who are fortunate enough to be here that you will find something to take. But ask yourself, "What do I give to the school?" In other words, what do *you* contribute to its success and its pleasant and peaceful atmosphere.

Juilliard students who studied with her were destined to hear the "give-and-take" theme over and over again, for she could be extremely demanding, not only with herself but with them. One has humorously recalled that "she always seemed to stress give-and-take when she wanted some favor from the student, although looking back on it now I see that she really did give an unbelievable amount of herself. On Sundays there were always outings to Bear Mountain or Jones Beach, and she was always after me to get my father's car so more students could go, which I did not appreciate then, but which I do now, in memory. She always involved herself in the minutest details, such as who would go with whom in what car, and of course it was always a great privilege to ride in the car she was in."

When President Schuman had asked her to give the convocation address, she had been quite reluctant to do it, until she woke up one morning knowing what her subject would be. One factor that made her slightly timid about speaking at such an official gathering was her somewhat imperfect command of the English language. Her colorful Russian-accented speech could be vivid and dramatic in the classroom, but she feared it might be inadequate for public address. As soon as the speech was ready, she tried it out on friends. The day before the convocation she read it to Lee Thompson and said, at a crucial point, "Let me disgrace myself" instead of "Let me digress." Though she was not too worried, Miss Thompson was. Unable to sleep, she knocked on the door at midnight and insisted on a correct reading. The next day she coached her—all too conspicuously—from the front row of the auditorium.

Mme. Lhevinne's occasional malapropisms and habitual "Lhevinnese" became legendary at the school, and were widely imitated. Shirley Aronoff, a talented pupil who made an excellent Town Hall debut in 1950, was chief imitator and perpetrator of pranks. "Shirley was a very talented pianist but got more satisfaction by the tricks she played. I would come good-humoredly into the studio and find a frog walking on the floor, and I would scream and she would be happy for the rest of the day. Once I made a mistake with my English and asked her to get me a cup of tea with a meat ball and she went to the counter and said in a loud voice, 'Mme. Lhevinne would like a cup of tea with a meat ball in it.' Another time she advertised that Room 412 was the collection center for gifts for European refugees, and I came to the school to find it filled with boots, gloves, shoes, coats, underwear, and other unimaginable things.

"Then one Christmas she said she had a present for me, and she and a boy came radiant to give it to me. 'It's a record for you,' they said, 'and we've worked on it a whole month.'

" 'Oh, that's wonderful,' I said, and they put it on the machine.

"The record begins and a door opens. A voice with an accent

just like mine says, 'David! David! David! There is a draft! Open the windows a little less!' Then he would say a strange word and she would say that in the whole Lexington of the English language it did not exist. It went on like that for the whole record, and it was horrible the way they copied my Russian accent and my mistakes. They had thought I would be delighted with the record, but as I listened my face got sourer and sourer and I was on the verge of crying. 'If that's how I teach,' I said in a low voice, 'then why do you study with me?'

"They both ran to me and she embraced me and kissed me and said, 'You don't think we would do something like that seriously! We spent so much time and work to give something that would amuse you.'

"I could tell that they were sincere, but still it was many years before I could overcome the hurt I had felt and take that record in the right way. Finally one year when I had a little party for the students at my apartment, I played it, and they all had pleasure, and I myself, too."

Harold Schonberg once wrote that Mme. Lhevinne combines the autocracy of Catherine the Great with the simplicity of the droshky driver.[6] It is a telling observation, and helps explain the paradox of a woman who, seemingly imperious, remains in many ways vulnerable.

Mme. Lhevinne's quaint speech, her vitality and humor, and her uncommon interest in her students' personal lives made her a colorful figure at the school even before her students began walking away with an inordinate number of pianistic prizes. The first public revelation of her unusual success as a teacher came in the early 1950s, when her students began entering the Piano Recording Festival sponsored by the National Guild of Piano Teachers. At the Festival in 1952, her students picked up thirty-two of the forty-five national prizes, and no one was more surprised that the panel of judges, who did not know the names of the competitors (or their teachers) until the winners had been chosen. The contest had been held in Austin, Texas, and candidates entered by sending recordings of their own playing. In 1953, to induce more entries, Irl Allison, president of the Guild, upped the first prize to $1,500 and guaranteed any teacher who entered more than twenty students a cash prize equal to half what his students won.

"At that time I had so many outstanding students that it was not difficult to find twenty, so I called them all together and told them the conditions of the contest. But I said that I wanted them to receive any money that would be due to me. To my great astonishment, my students again won most of the prizes. But the following year I didn't send anyone from my class, because of the discontent I made among my colleagues in various parts of the country. They did not resent so much that so many of my students won. But they did resent that I did not keep my half of the prize money. They felt that if I gave my students all of my prize money, they would have to too, and they did not think that was right after all of the time they spent preparing their students for the competition."

Thirty-three thousand students had entered the 1953 contest for a total of $16,000 in cash awards. Mme. Lhevinne's twenty-two students pulled in $4,120. If she had made her students swear secrecy when she gave them her share of the money, she would have had no difficulty from colleagues across the nation. But her "typically generous gesture" (as a letter one of her winners wrote for publication termed it) was given a great deal of publicity in the trade magazines. This, of course, did put other teachers in a difficult spot. The generous gesture *was* typical. So was the fact that it somehow "leaked" to the press.

The victories of Mme. Lhevinne's students in the National Recording Festival gave a tremendous boost to her reputation among average piano teachers in America but certainly could not have overly impressed her colleagues at Juilliard, many of whom looked down on that kind of competition and did not even enter their students. Those teachers, however, could not help being impressed with the record her students began to compile at Juilliard's own competitions.

Every year at Juilliard there are three or four concerto competitions open to all pianists at the school, with the winner of each being entitled to a performance with the Juilliard Orchestra. For better or worse, there is a tendency to compare teachers on the basis of how many competitions their students win. During the 1949–50 season, when Mme. Lhevinne gave the convocation address, the first two competitions were with Brahms's First Concerto and Beethoven's Second, and the winners were Martin Canin and David Bar-Illan, both members of her class. There were two other competitions that year, and they were won by students of other teachers. As it turned out, this set the proportion for the next twenty years. That is, Rosina Lhevinne's students would win about as many competitions as those of her colleagues combined (31 of 64, according to my count). The record is even more impressive than it appears, because in many of the competitions won by students of other teachers, none of hers had entered.

As the trend became clearer and clearer year after year, her colleagues' reactions ranged from feigned indifference to understandable envy to humorous acceptance: Joseph Raieff announced he would send her no more letters of congratulation because he had ordered cards to be printed up which read 'Congratulations on another victory by one of your students.' In 1954, Dean Schubart wrote her:

> This is getting monotonous, but here I find myself once again writing you a letter of congratulation on the winning of still another prize by a Lhevinne student. I do hope that you are not liable for legal proceedings under the Sherman anti-trust laws for monopolistic practices.[7]

Outside of the school, the big prize in those days was the Leventritt Competition, the winner of which was guaranteed a debut with the New York Philharmonic and several other orchestras (there was a cash award too, but it was not nearly as significant as the concerts that resulted from winning the competition). The terms of the contest stipulate that the prize be awarded only to pianists fully·prepared to begin a professional career, and because of these high standards no prize had been awarded during the competitions from 1949 through 1953. This made it all the more dramatic when two of Mme. Lhevinne's students won it back-to-back in 1954 and 1955: Van Cliburn and John Browning.

Cliburn was twenty years old when he won the Leventritt and had been with Mme. Lhevinne for three years:

"One day as I stepped out of the elevator at the Juilliard School a tall boy standing there said, 'Honey, I came to study with you.' When I replied that my class was already full, he said, 'But Honey, I came all the way from Texas just to study with you.' Some of my students had heard him play, and they urged that I at least give him an audition, and as soon as I heard him play there was no question that I would adore to have such a talent in my class. He had huge hands, just like Josef's. They could span thirteen notes, from C to A.

"Van was seventeen years old then, and until then had studied only with his mother, who was a student of Friedheim (who himself was a student of Liszt). So he already had an excellent training. But seeing how easy bravura pieces were for him, I started to use a great deal of Bach and Mozart and Beethoven. It was a great joy to see how he responded to this music, because he felt it so deeply. Once he was playing a work of Chopin and I showed him something new. After trying it, he got up from the piano and

Rehearsing Dvořák's *Dumka* Quintet with the original members of the Juilliard String Quartet: violinists Robert Koff and Robert Mann, violist Raphael Hillyer, cellist Arthur Winograd. Photo by Graphic House.

Van Cliburn. Photo by Graphic House.

John Browning.

Mme. Lhevinne with some of her students.

Martin Canin, Santos Ojeda, David Bar-Ilan, Jean Geis. Photo by James Abresch.

A summer class at Aspen. Photo by Berko Studio.

With Tony Han. Photo by Berko Studio.

Rosina Lhevinne, in her eighties, rehearsing a Mozart concerto with Robert Blum.

Rehearsing for a solo performance. Photo by Larkin.

Concert at Aspen, Izler Solomon conducting. Photo by Berko Studio.

Eightieth birthday, 1960: with Sarah Crump.

With daughter Marianna Graham. Photo
by Berko Studio.

Eighty-fifth birthday: with Gideon Waldrop, William Schuman,
Peter Mennin, Mark Schubart. Photo by Whitestone Photo.

paced the room, saying, 'It's too beautiful. I can't stand it. I can't stand it.' It is such a pleasure to teach a student who responds to music in this way.

"When a student plays in the Leventritt contest, he has to go home afterward and wait to hear by telephone whether he won. I made it a point never to go to a competition where my student played, so I too had to wait at home to find out how they did. The day Van played in the finals of the Leventritt, it seemed endless, the time that I did not hear from him. I waited there very nervously, and every time the phone rang I thought it was he. Finally the door bell rang very loudly and I went to answer it and he nearly knocked me down, he was so excited. 'I won! I won!' he screamed, and he kissed me and embraced me. Then he sat down on the couch and became quite pensive, and covered his face with his hands, and said, 'What a responsibility! What a responsibility!' That was a remarkable attitude for someone of his age."

During the year that Cliburn won the Leventritt, John Browning won the Steinway Centennial Award, a competition held in celebration of Steinway and Sons' 100th anniversary as piano manufacturers in New York. Browning's victory the next year in the Leventritt came five years after he had begun his adult study with Mme. Lhevinne:

"In 1950, when I went to teach the master class in California, a young man came up to me and said, 'You probably don't remember me, but I studied with you in Denver when I was ten years old.'

"I remembered very well that John had studied with us in Denver, but I didn't know what had happened to him since then. I learned that his parents had moved to Los Angeles and that he had studied with Lee Pattison, formerly of the Maier-Pattison two-piano team, who was an excellent musician. When I heard John play, I found that he too had already become an excellent musician.

"He studied with me during the summer in Los Angeles and wanted to come directly to Juilliard in the fall, but I persuaded him to continue his general education first, by taking a few years of college. He said, 'Well, I'll stay on the condition that when you come to California at Christmas you give me one lesson on the F minor Chopin Concerto.' So John enrolled at Occidental College and I gave him lessons when I went to Los Angeles. He continued to play in my summer master classes, and then in 1953 he came to Juilliard.

"John was always extremely musical and sensitive and showed

a great deal of refinement in his playing. I remember once he was playing a Brahms concerto and I wanted more expression and I held his shoulders and said, 'More! More! More!' and pushed him so hard his nose hit the piano."

When Cliburn and Browning won back-to-back the "Lhevinne-tritt" (as Dean Schubart began to call it), reporters asked Mme. Lhevinne to compare the two pianists. She refused. "A pianist is not like a shoe," she told one, "where you can measure its length and its width." Today the question is still put to her, and her standard laconic answer is, "Take a wonderful apple and a wonderful pear. You cannot compare them."

Refusing to compare her students involves more than tact. For her, the key to teaching piano is to bring out the individuality of each student. Because her students do not fit into a single mold, they are, strictly speaking, incomparable. Her best pupils generally do possess a splendid technique and show an uncommon concern for beauty of tone. But in matters of expression and interpretation they run the gamut. When a student brings her a piece he thinks ready for public performance, she gives her approval on one condition: "The piece must make me enthusiastic. It does not have to be the way I like it. I only insist that it have logic, warmth, purpose, and good taste. If it has all these, then I give my blessing."

Browning recalls several occasions on which he would play a work for her and she would say, "I don't agree. But I won't touch it. I won't change a note." This flexibility, combined with the instinctive judgment needed in order to know when something has "logic, warmth, purpose, and good taste" accounts in large part for her great success as a teacher. Her musical principles are essentially those of her late husband, but her individuality and intuition in applying them have enabled her to carve out a place in the musical world very much her own.

Rosina Lhevinne has always enjoyed big celebrations for birthdays and other anniversaries. For Rosina's seventy-fifth birthday, President Schuman made a proposal that surpassed her greatest expectations. He suggested that the school create a scholarship fund in memory of Josef Lhevinne by holding a benefit concert once each spring for five years, until a sufficient endowment was raised. He invited Mme. Lhevinne to play in each year's concert and to choose the colleagues who would join her. She was both thrilled and honored by the prospect, although "I was not sure God would give me the pleasure of playing for five years, until I was eighty years old." For her part in the first program, she chose to play Dvořák's *Dumka* Quintet, Op. 81, with the Juilliard String Quartet.

The Juilliard String Quartet had been founded in 1947, the year she had played with Vronsky and Babin. Beginning in 1951, she played with the group about once a year for a decade, which made her one of the quartet's chief pianistic collaborators. Their first performance of the Dvořák had been in Los Angeles in 1953, and she had shown a particular flair for meeting the demands of chamber music:

> . . . it was a sheer delight to hear the piano played with such sparkle, such a wide range of expressive nuance, and such unostentatious conformity to the demands of the ensemble.[8]

According to Robert Mann, who has been first violinist of the quartet since its inception, much of her success as a chamber-music player comes from having something he calls a "rarity" even among the very greatest pianists: "a sense for shaping the tone of the piano so it has relation to the sound being produced by stringed instruments."[9]

The first Josef Lhevinne Memorial Scholarship concert was given on March 15, 1955. Dvořák's *Dumka* anchored a program that featured a Haydn quartet and a generous selection of songs by Risë Stevens. The concert was a monetary and musical success. So were the next four. Following the fifth, in March 1959, $25,000 had been raised to establish a permanent scholarship in Josef Lhevinne's name.

One reason Mme. Lhevinne was so thrilled by the memorial concerts is that they focused attention on her husband's art. At the time of his death he had certainly been well known. But her teaching success during the following decade had made her name more familiar than his in some musical circles. He had made so few recordings and been such a retiring personality that people who had not actually heard him play had no way to understand his artistic achievements, and this fact had caused Mme. Lhevinne considerable dismay. There had been a minor flurry of interest in her husband's art when Harry Truman became president, for Truman had been a serious student of piano in his youth and happened to consider Lhevinne "the greatest of them all," a fact he announced publicly at a White House ceremony in 1951 when he was presented with a custom-made spinet.[10] In a letter to Mme. Lhevinne, he expanded his tribute:

I heard Mr. Lhevinne the first time in the early 1900s when he made one of his first tours of the United States. He stopped in Kansas City and I remember very distinctly that Paderewski, Moritz Rosenthal, and Josef Lhevinne all came within about three weeks of each other. . . . That was when I made up my mind that Josef Lhevinne was the greatest of them all. After that I heard him every time he came to town—I expect as much as half a dozen times. I think he had a touch and interpretation that have never been equaled.[11]

A few words from President Truman were gratifying to Mme. Lhevinne, but of course were little use to young pianists who might have been interested in hearing Lhevinne play. By the time of the first anniversary concert, his RCA 78's had long been out of print, and to mark the occasion RCA issued "The Art of Josef Lhevinne," an LP record including all the solo pieces Lhevinne had recorded for the company, plus his and Rosina's two-piano performance of Debussy's *Fêtes*. An LP of Josef Hofmann's playing was released about the same time, and Abram Chasins, writing in the *Saturday Review*, rightly called these two discs "missing links in the evolution of the Romantic approach to the piano."[12] Not only was a scholarship now available in Lhevinne's name but so were samples of his art.

On December 14, 1955, the annual reunion was more joyous than ever before. There was the new RCA disc to be played, there was the success of Cliburn and Browning and other of Mme. Lhevinne's students to be celebrated, and there was the memory of the first memorial concert. In addition, there was the presence of Mme. Lhevinne's current students, who had been invited to join those who had actually known and studied with Josef Lhevinne. The mixture of young and old, too, helped turn what had sometimes been a rather solemn and sad-hearted affair into one of joy and celebration. Sarah prepared a magnificent dinner, and Mme. Lhevinne, as was now customary, delivered a carefully prepared speech about her late husband. It was eleven years since Josef Lhevinne's death, and the influence of his approach to music and to the piano was clearly expanding, not contracting. The same was emphatically true of the life and the art of his wife.

14

Concert Life Begins at Seventy-five

"MACK HARRELL, the famous singer, was on the voice faculty at Juilliard and also taught during the summers at the Aspen Music School. One winter he came into Room 412 and asked me if I would like to teach at Aspen the next summer. I had visited the town once before and had fallen in love with it, so I said I would love to. Then he said that it is customary, but not obligatory, for each member of the faculty to play some concerts during the summer, not only chamber music, but with the festival's orchestra, and he said they would like me to play too.

"At first, this seemed like quite an impossible idea to me, especially the idea of playing with an orchestra alone. I was seventy-five years old then, and ever since I was twenty-two my orchestral appearances had been with Josef. After his death I had played only once with orchestra, and that was with Vronsky and Babin. But Mr. Harrell knew just what to say to me, and he began to speak about what a challenge it would be for me to play. I like challenges, and I agreed on the spot. But I told him, 'I will do it if I can play a Mozart concerto which I have never studied or taught. I want to do something that will be fresh.'

"I had become increasingly fond of Mozart at this stage of my life, and I looked through his concertos to decide which one I would play. They were not played much in public, even in the 1950s, and I chose the C major Concerto (K.467), which I think was not even recorded at the time. I began to study it and was very excited looking forward to playing it in the summer."

Mme. Lhevinne's first visit to Aspen had been in the summer of 1953, when Victor Babin invited her to stop over on her way to the summer master class in California. After a few days there, she was convinced that the town was America's answer to Salzburg, and before leaving she sent her son an ecstatic telegram: "COMING ON PONY EXPRESS TRAIN. . . . HAD WONDERFUL TIME IN ASPEN. . . ."[1] She had returned to the Los Angeles Conservatory during the following two summers, but in 1956 accepted Harrell's invitation.

Aspen sits at a height of 7,900 feet in the Rockies. In the 1880s, when Rosina Bessie entered the Moscow Conservatory, it was a booming mining town. By the end of the 1890s, when Rosina Bessie had just married Josef Lhevinne, it had become more or less of a ghost town, and remained so until shortly after the Second World War, when Walter Paepcke, an American businessman, began to revive it. First he built a ski lift and began turning Aspen into one of the world's fine winter resorts. Then he developed summer programs that were to make Aspen one of America's cultural centers. In 1949 the town was the site of a Bicentennial celebration of Goethe's birth, at which Albert Schweitzer was keynote speaker. The following summer, Paepcke founded the Aspen Music School and Festival as well as the Aspen Institute for Humanistic Studies. And now for more than two decades the town once so rich in silver has been drawing thousands of people with its winter sports and summer culture.

Some relics of the Wild West days remain in Aspen, the most prominent of them being the Wheeler Opera House, which was built in 1887 and was visited by the Metropolitan Opera Company during the town's mining boom. When Rosina Lhevinne had visited Aspen in 1953, she had stayed in a remodeled building that in earlier days had been the town prison. When she arrived for the summer of 1956, she knew only that she would live in a house named the Silver Queen.

"From the outside it seemed to be almost falling apart. But the big shock was when we entered the house, because every room had been redecorated in a pattern of roses. It was in terrible taste and made such a vulgar impression, and the whole house seemed empty except for the roses. Then, a few minutes later, a person walked into the room like a ghost and said, 'I want to introduce myself. I am your decorator.'

"The beds were awful and the furniture was awful and we lived with those roses in every room the whole summer. I had to teach in the living room, because there were no facilities to teach at the school, and three girls who studied with me lived on the top floor. It happened that one girl was more beautiful than the other, and outside there was a big sign in electric lights that advertised the Silver Queen for tourists. Everyone called me Madame, and with those beautiful girls there it left an impression that was not to be forgotten. My mailing address was Madame Lhevinne, Silver Queen, Aspen, Colorado."

Rosina Lhevinne's "solo debut"—her first performance of Mozart's C major Concerto—was not the first concert she played in at Aspen. The Mozart was scheduled for the last week of the summer session, on August 25, 1956, but more than a month before, she had played the *Dumka* Quintet with the Juilliard Quartet. Like all concerts at Aspen, this one took place in the large canvas tent-like amphitheater designed by Eero Saarinen. Mountain showers sometimes fall during concerts there, and such was the case during the *Dumka*, which featured not only thunder and lightning and the drumming of rain on the canvas but actual precipitation, as a leak developed in the canvas almost directly above Mme. Lhevinne and her fellow musicians. They continued to play, and outlasted the storm, and were rewarded with the first standing ovation at Aspen since Schweitzer had spoken in 1949.

Her performance of the Mozart astonished even her deepest admirers. Her warm singing tone and interpretive spontaneity moved not only the audience but the orchestra as well. Conductor Izler Solomon recalls that "Rosina's charisma infused the orchestra the way only the few great artists do. This spirit and vitality permeate everything she does. Everyone in the orchestra outdoes himself and it is not only easier but more of a joy to conduct. Her approach to Mozart was perfect for the composer. It was technically perfect, of course. And it had the experience of having lived so long and developed such musical taste. And it had Rosina's special youthful drive."[2]

A few weeks after the concert, Mme. Lhevinne wrote Dean Schubart a letter which indicated how much Aspen and the concerto had meant to her:

Dear Mark,

It is hard to believe that the 9 weeks in Aspen are over. What a wonderful experience it was!

The highlight of the season was when Marianna and Don came for a few days—just when I played the Concerto with the orchestra. It was so much fun in every respect.

I chose to play Mozart Concerto (K. 467) which I never played or studied and taught it only once in my life. I had a fresh and spontaneous reaction to that magnificent music. The 2d mov. is really heavenly! The response of the audience was most gratifying. I shall tell you all the details about Aspen and the students when I see you. . . .[3]

Because her performance was so gratifying to all concerned, Mme. Lhevinne played solo concertos at Aspen during seven of the following eight summers. "Remarkably captivating" was the way one writer found her at the keyboard. "What she lacks in power of execution from lack of strength," he continued, "she compensates [for] by putting into her art the whole soul of a woman of exquisite refinement and culture, backed by musical education that can hardly be excelled."[4] These words were written not after her 1956 Aspen debut but after the one solo recital she had played in America in 1907. They were even truer fifty years later.

In spite of her long subordination to her husband's career—or possibly because of it—Rosina Lhevinne still had a great deal to give the world as a performer. But she had the wisdom to know with what music and in which performing situations it would be favorably received. She began her "solo career" at seventy-five and continued it to eighty-four, but she always kept it in its proper place—that is, a step behind her teaching.

Tong Il Han's story is a curious footnote to the Cold War. Born in the northern part of Korea, he had begun to play the piano at age three. When he was five, Russians invaded his town and his parents' house, carrying off all movable property, including the piano on which he played. While the Korean war raged, the Hans lived in successive refugee centers and Tong Il suffered from poor health. At the war's end, the family was relocated in Seoul, and Tong Il found a piano he could play in barracks occupied by the United States Air Force, Fifth Division. Some of the men took an interest in the boy's playing, and General Samuel E. Anderson heard him when he visited the base. Anderson was so impressed that he arranged for Tong Il to play concerts at other bases in Korea, Taiwan, and Japan. No admission was charged, but the boy's playing raised $4,300 in donations. This money was put into an educational fund, and finally it was decided that Tong Il would go to the United States to study the piano.

At that time, Tong Il (who had already been nicknamed "Tony") knew nothing about the Juilliard School of Music or Mme. Lhevinne. But some of the soldiers had said that she was one of the world's best piano teachers and that he should study with her. Tony's parents accepted this plan for the education of their son, and in 1954, when the boy was thirteen, he was flown to New York.

Tony had had relatively little piano training in Korea and did not do very well at his entrance examinations. "But he was so small and thin," Mme. Lhevinne remembers, "and he had come all the way from Korea, so I did not have the heart to turn him down." Tony knew so little English that he had to bring an interpreter for his first lessons, from whom Mme. Lhevinne learned the Korean words for "good" and "bad" in order to speed communication with her new charge. The first time she said "Naputa" (no) he jumped up and exclaimed, "You speak Korean!"—which of course she did not. Naturally, as befits the Russian tradition, some of the first *English* words he learned were "scale" and "arpeggio." But he was also introduced to many of the musical masterpieces.

"When I first learned a piece, Mme. Lhevinne would demonstrate, play it through for me, and usually that would be the first time I had heard the work in my life, and I had never heard music of such quality or played so well. That always made things so exciting that I felt, 'Oh boy, I'd love to learn this piece!' "[5]

Tony began studying at Juilliard in the fall of 1954, and the first symphony concert he went to in his life was the one at which Van Cliburn played the Tchaikovsky Concerto with the New York Philharmonic in his debut after winning the Leventritt contest. Tony had never heard the concerto before, but a year and a half later he played its first movement himself with the same orchestra. By winning a competition, he was chosen as soloist for the Philharmonic's Young People's Concert, and although Mme. Lhevinne thought he was too young to play that concerto, she acceded to the demands of Wilfred Pelletier, the conductor, who insisted that he could do it. Tony's performance of the Tchaikovsky justified Pelletier's opinion, and gave another public demonstration of Mme. Lhevinne's efficacy as a teacher. She sat with General Anderson at the concert and was impressed by the American and Korean flags on the stage. A few days later Mme. Lhevinne and Tony were invited by the Korean Ambassador to the Ho-Ho Restaurant, where food was eaten only with chopsticks, and where, "of course, I could not get a single bite into my mouth. So Tony taught me to use chopsticks, just as seriously as I had taught him the piano, and really it is very easy, and very much the same, if you learn to keep the wrist loose."

After playing in the Philharmonic Youth Concert, Tony could certainly have had a career as a *Wunderkind,* but both Mme. Lhevinne and General Anderson agreed that he should play only enough concerts to guarantee the funds needed for his education (Tony's educational fund was administered by the Institute of International Education). Once a year General Anderson came to Mme. Lhevinne's apartment on Claremont Avenue with a portfolio and an adjutant and planned the boy's career with all the seriousness, she says, of deciding whether or not to go to war. The result was that Tony attended private schools in New York, took lessons from Mme. Lhevinne, played a few important recitals each year, and in the summers accompanied Mme. Lhevinne to her master classes, first in Los Angeles and then in Aspen.

"She and I would ride out to Los Angeles on the *California Zephyr* and at night we would sit in the vista dome and she would teach me about the stars. I got an allowance of $2 a week from the I.I.E., and sometimes the money got very low. Once on the trip out West Mme. Lhevinne pulled out a footlocker and reached down into the bottom compartment and drew out ten, twenty, thirty, forty, fifty dollars! And then she gave it to me! I'd never seen so much money in my life.

"She raised me like a child until 1963 and was so much more than a teacher. She was more like a mother, or maybe a grandmother, figure. She would say, 'If you learn such and such a piece well by a certain time, I will take you to the Cinerama.' So we would go together and watch that big screen and there would be some strange effects with unusual camera angles and she would go 'He-he-he' just like a little girl, and we were two children sitting there giggling."

Tony Han was an exception among Mme. Lhevinne's students in that he came to her at such a young age and with relatively little previous training. She was able to teach him the fundamentals of her approach from the very beginning and did not have to worry about how much of a previous teacher's work had to be dismantled, as was the case with many students who came to her at age nineteen or twenty. Another student she was able to train almost from the beginning was Abbott Lee Ruskin, who started with her at an even younger age than Tony.

"In the early 1950s, Dean Schubart and two other men went to many of the important cities in the country to hold auditions for Juilliard. In Minneapolis they heard Abbott Lee and when they came back, Dean Schubart said, 'Rosina, maybe I am a Chinaman, but I think this boy is one of the rare wonderful talents. I will really appreciate it if you will stop there and listen to him.'

"I went to California on the train in the summer and stopped in Chicago, and Abbot Lee's mother brought him down from Minneapolis so I could hear him. He was not yet six years old and he could play thirty pieces of the kind normal children can play only after studying for many years. I told his mother that I was delighted, that he is one of the great talents, but I thought five and a half was a little too tender an age at which to come to New

York. The next two times I went to California I stopped in Chicago to hear him play and then I decided he was ready. He was seven years old, which was the youngest I ever took a student.

"Abbott Lee played on a few television shows (as had Tony) and even played the boy prodigy in a Broadway musical, but mainly he worked in a serious way at the piano. He gave a few recitals and performed with some orchestras, and when he was thirteen he played Kabalevsky's Third (*Youth*) Concerto in the finals of the Merriweather Post Contest in Washington, D.C.

"Half a year later, Kabalevsky came to the United States with five other Russian composers. The National Symphony gave a concert to honor them and the *Youth* Concerto was on the program. It was announced that Kabalevsky would play it himself, but when he arrived he said he would rather conduct, except that in Russia he had never found a youngster who could play it to his satisfaction. Howard Mitchell, conductor of the orchestra, remembered Abbott Lee's performance at the competition, and said that he knew a boy who played it beautifully and that he would get in touch with the boy's teacher if Kabalevsky wished. So two days before the concert, he telephoned me from Washington and asked, 'Will Abbott Lee play the Kabalevsky Concerto with Kabalevsky on the day after tomorrow?'

"Abbott Lee had not woked on the concerto since the competition, but when I asked him he said, 'Of course. Why couldn't I play? I played it once.' Mrs. Ruskin gave her approval, so the next day Abbott Lee and I got on the train to Washington.

"He gave a wonderful performance and made a tremendous impression on Kabalevsky, who conducted the concerto, and an impresario was there and wanted to take Abbott Lee on a European tour. He told him he could name his own price. But Mrs. Ruskin said, 'Why would we need the money? He must continue to study and learn to become a true artist.' And that is really to her credit."

Kabalevsky, Shostakovich, and four other Soviet composers had come to Washington in 1958 as part of the cultural exchange program that was gradually expanding as American-Soviet relations slowly began to thaw. The first important Russian musician to come to the United States after World War II had been Emil Gilels, whose visit in 1955 had created a tremendous stir. While Gilels was in the country, Mme. Lhevinne had received a phone call fom Mme. Vengerova in Philadelphia.

" 'Rosina,' she asked me, 'where are you and all your administrators? Are you all asleep? Gilels comes to America and absolutely conquers the public and we at the Curtis Institute give him a tre-

mendous party and reception. He is from the Moscow Conservatory, like you, and you and your Juilliard, you do nothing.' And of
course she was right.

"So I spoke with President Schuman and he said that it had not
occurred to him that Gilels would accept, but that if I would approach him he would be delighted to plan a luncheon for him.
So I telephoned him, and said, 'This is Rosina Lhevinne. I don't
know if my name is familiar to you.' There was a short silence at
the other end of the phone, and then he said, 'For what reason do
you want to offend me so deeply? Not only I but everybody with
anything to do with music in Russia knows Josef and Rosina Lhevinne. Even now at the Moscow Conservatory when we have a
youngster who plays very well, we say, "Still, he is not a Josef
Lhevinne." '

"This was an auspicious start to the conversation and I asked
him if he would like to come to the school for a luncheon. He
was delighted, but said, 'Of course, you will not mind if I bring my
interpreter'—for this was during the days of Stalin, and a body-
guard, or detective, had to accompany him in the guise of an
interpreter.

"The luncheon was in President Schuman's private office at
Juilliard, and through the interpreter he asked Gilels about the
aims of the Moscow Conservatory and how it was conducted, and
Gilels asked him the same about the Juilliard School. I sat between
them, and was so excited I spoke to Schuman in Russian and Gilels
in English. Gilels came to my class afterwards, and heard Abbott
Lee play, and then he played a short recital for the students. As an
encore he played a very quiet melody that was breathtaking, and
that was a Bach piece arranged by Siloti."

For William Schuman, the highlight of the luncheon at Juilliard was the way Gilels and Mme. Lhevinne first met. "He examined her hands and she examined his," he recalls. Gilels was the
first important Russian she had met for many years. She and Josef
had always remained close to Rachmaninoff and Hofmann and
Gabrilowitsch and other pianists they had known in pre-Revolu-
tionary Russia, but as they never did return to the country after
1914 they failed to have contact with *Soviet* pianists other than
those who, like Horowitz, had moved to the United States before
World War II. The Cold War, of course, had kept Soviet pianists
away from the United States during the decade following Lhevinne's death.

Since meeting Gilels, Mme. Lhevinne has examined the hands
of Sviatoslav Richter, Vladimir Ashkenazy, and Alexander Slo-

bodyanik, to name a few, and while she still has never set foot in the Soviet Union she soon began to send some of her best students as emissaries on her behalf. In these ways she has, since 1955, been able to again touch base with the Russian sources of the pianistic traditions she has devoted the whole of her life to furthering.

While preventing her young students, like Tony Han and Abbott Lee Ruskin, from being unduly exploited on the concert stage, Mme. Lhevinne had been busy encouraging her older, more polished ones to enter competitions where their talents might be recognized. She did this not out of an abstract love for the idea of competitions but because "in America there was no other way for an artist to begin a career. Unlike most other countries, where there is a ministry of art to encourage performance by young musicians, America has been very primitive in this way"—until, one might add, the recent efforts of the National Endowment for the Humanities.

In December 1955, after John Browning won the Leventritt Prize, Mme. Lhevinne suggested that he enter the Queen Elisabeth Contest in Brussels, and spent considerable time helping him prepare. The contest was in May 1956, and she learned of the results before leaving for her first summer at Aspen: Browning had won second place, finishing behind Vladimir Ashkenazy, a nineteen-year-old Russian. Each won a gold medal, but because Ashkenazy had not yet completed his schooling, the Soviet government did not allow him to go on tour. The choice European engagements fell to Browning, who began to build an impressive international reputation.

During the following season, Olegna Fuschi, one of the many talented students to come to Mme. Lhevinne from California, entered a competition in Brazil. She failed to win a prize, but managed to become acquainted with one of the judges, Pavel Seribriakov, from the Soviet Union. He was impressed with her playing and gave her a catalog describing the First International Tchaikovsky Competition, to be held in Moscow the following spring (1958). She brought the catalog back to New York and showed it to her teacher, who was thrilled to discover that an important new competition was to be held in the concert hall of her own alma mater.

"When Olegna showed me the catalog, I told her that although I believed very much in her talent, I thought if anyone from all my class should go, that somebody should be Van. The contest seemed perfectly suited for him. He always had a stong affinity for Russian music, and he had a broad, romantic manner of interpretation. And I knew that not only his playing but his whole personality would be very much appreciated in Russia."

Cliburn's career after his Leventritt victory in 1954 had followed the downward spiral typical of young American prizewinners: many important engagements the year after the contest; some re-engagements the following year; very few the third. At the moment Mme. Lhevinne received the announcement of the Tchaikovsky Competition, Van was not even on tour, but instead was in Texas, helping his mother teach her large piano class. His career was clearly in need of a big shot in the arm—so much so that Mme. Lhevinne felt it was worth the risk of his entering a competition in the Soviet Union.

When her letter proposing that he enter a piano contest in Russia arrived in Kilgore, Texas, some people must have wondered if the seventy-seven-year-old woman had gone off the deep end. Cliburn, his parents, and everyone they asked advice of, thought it would be impossible for an American, a "capitalist," to win a contest held in the Soviet Union. He wrote back to thank her for thinking of him, but said that he saw no use in entering. So she wrote again, and listed four reasons why he should enter.

1. You will work hard to prepare for the competition, which will be good for you no matter what happens.
2. You will learn a good deal of new repertoire.
3. You will meet the cream of your generation's pianists.
4. You might even win.

Even this message failed to convince him, but he did write back to say he would be in New York in a few weeks and that he would stop by to see her.

"Van was in New York in November, and when he came to my apartment I showed him the catalog. The prize money did not impress him at all, but when he saw the gold medal he got very excited. He knew how Mr. Lhevinne and I and Rachmaninoff had won gold medals at the Conservatory and he mistakenly thought this medal was the same one.

"Then he nervously turned the pages and saw what works were required for the competition. 'I'm sorry,' he said, 'but I cannot enter. I can't learn all those pieces.' So I again told him why I thought it would be beneficial for him to prepare for the contest even if he did not decide to enter it, and I said I would help him as much as I could.

"I then had twenty-two students whom I taught without assistants and I said that I did not have any time for him on weekdays but that I would give him my Sundays, which I usually spent with a little group of students at Jones Beach, which was exceedingly refreshing and made it possible for me to work the next week with renewed energy. That I would make a sacrifice of this kind appealed to him, and he decided to come every Sunday to learn the pieces as soon as possible.

"Among the requirements was a 'big' Romantic work, and for that I chose for him to learn the Fantasy of Chopin. But he said, 'Mrs. Lhevinne, that's not a big piece.' So I said that I didn't agree with him, that it was not such a long piece but that it was a very important work in the compositions of Chopin.

"Gilels happened to be playing in New York that winter [on his second American tour] and I heard him and went backstage after his concert because I knew he was the chairman of the committee for the competition. I was extremely impressed with his playing, and among other things I asked him, 'As you will be chairman of the competition, don't you include the Fantasy of Chopin as a big work?'

" 'How can you ask such a question?' he asked. 'Of course.'

"So every Sunday, Van came to play the things he had learned, and his playing was so magnificent and showed so much his great talent that a girl who lived with me at the time, she would fling herself on the floor and say, 'I can't stand it! I can't stand it!'

"In a few weeks was the final date to apply for the competition, and the work was going so well that I advised him not to miss the chance to apply because 'If by the end we see that some pieces are not ready you can always withdraw without disgrace.' So he said, 'All right,' and sent in the applications. I continued to give up my Sunday at Jones Beach and to give Van the whole day. We would work in the afternoon, he would have a big steak, and we would work some more in the evening."

On weekdays, friends remember, Mme. Lhevinne telephoned her charge morning and night to make sure he got enough practice and enough sleep.

As teacher and student were working on preparing the program, Dean Schubart was sounding out the State Department to learn whether it would approve of an American's participation in a Soviet contest, and also seeking funds with which the young pianist could be transported to Russia. The State Department gave its blessing but no funds; but the Martha Baird Rockefeller Foundation and the Institute of International Education, on the condition that the grant be anonymous, came up with the needed money.

"Within a few weeks of the competition, I felt that Van was ready and that he would be a credit to his country if he went [and to his teacher, one might add]. So we decided for sure that he would go. On the day before he left he came and sat on the couch and said, 'I'm afraid. I've never been out of the country. What if I get sick and there are no doctors to treat me?' And I said, 'Believe me, you would have the best doctors in the country because the Russians could not afford *not* to take good care of American visitors.' He left with one suitcase and returned with seventeen."

William Schuman remembers that soon after Cliburn's victory was announced, Mme. Lhevinne rushed into his office at the school and asked if he would call Van in Moscow and tell him not to sign any contracts until he came home. He said he would be glad to, and she left the room, only to return three minutes later to say, "Don't forget to make it person-to-person."

At first, she, like many others, expected that when Van returned from Moscow he would take a good long rest before learning the new repertoire he would need for the engagements in the fall that would certainly result from his victory. But the Cold War, the Russians' having launched the sputnik, Max Frankel's coverage of the competition in the *New York Times*—all of these combined to give the event a national and even international impact no one had dreamed of. The ticker-tape parade in Manhattan, the unprecedented excitement surrounding his Carnegie Hall "homecoming" concert, the interest of taxi drivers, priests, schoolboys, grocery clerks, of all Americans, in Van Cliburn launched the young man on a merry-go-round from which he was loath to step off.

Generously, Van and his mother (who was, of course, his *first* teacher) included Mme. Lhevinne in a few of the celebrations. She was invited to the big reception for the pianist at the Waldorf-Astoria on May 20, 1958, and was presented by Mayor Wagner with the First Annual Music Award of New York City "for outstanding service in cultivating the appreciation and understanding of music among young audiences and students." She saw films of the competition on television, and later learned from Cliburn how her former classmate at the Moscow Conservatory, Alexander Goldenweiser, who was now the director of the Conservatory, had walked down the aisle saying, "A genius! A genius!" after hearing him play. She was also told eventually by her protégé that while a few

Russians had been disappointed that an American had won their most important competition, many took consolation in the fact that he had been trained by a product of their own conservatories. Cliburn has bombarded Mme. Lhevinne with long-distance phone calls, flowers, and fruits from Texas ever since his first trip to Moscow, though of late she has seldom seen him face to face.

While Cliburn got most of the publicity, he was not her only winner in the 1958 Tchaikovsky Competition. Daniel Pollack—who several years earlier had won first prize in the National Piano Guild contest—won ninth place in Moscow and, as a result, received contracts for several recordings and tours in Russia. He had come to Mme. Lhevinne at Juilliard in the early 1950s, and after completing her class had studied in Europe and entered the competition from there. Fourteen years earlier he had been the last person to audition with Josef Lhevinne, having played for him in California when Lhevinne was recovering from the first heart attack. Impressed with the talent of the eight-year-old boy, Lhevinne had arranged for him to study with Lillian Steuber, a former student of his who taught in Los Angeles, both privately and at the University of Southern California. Miss Steuber prepared him for Juilliard, and now Pollack has joined her on the faculty of U.S.C., an appointment he received after assisting Mme. Lhevinne at a 1971 master class there.

The success of Cliburn and Pollack in Moscow was no more outstanding in purely musical terms than Browning's in Brussels in 1956. But because of the international political situation, it caused a phenomenal increase in the number of untutored prospective musicians from the backwoods who wanted Mme. Lhevinne to turn them into "a concert pie-annist." As far as talented pianists go, she could hardly have had more in her class than she did *before* the 1958 Tchaikovsky Competition. The oft-repeated assertion that Cliburn's triumph "made" her as a teacher is ridiculous in light of what she and her students had already achieved before that event. What Cliburn's victory *did* do is greatly increase the publicity she received for her teaching activity. In interview after interview she was asked the secret of her students' success, and she usually replied by saying, "There is no magic pill. It takes talent and hard work to succeed."

Intended to apply to the students, the comment applies equally well to herself. She would teach six days a week and sometimes seven, and in between lessons would be on the phone from morning to night, needling, encouraging, cajoling—doing whatever was needed to get a student to give his best. "She always knew how to make you do what you knew you could not do," almost every former student says. Hour after hour, lesson after lesson, she worked with them in Room 412. If she had a five-minute break before the next student came, and the weather was nice, she would climb up on a chair and step through the window and cross the veranda for a look at the Hudson. But what rejuvenated her the most was the constant exposure to talent: "There are many ways to describe talent, but one way is when you are completely exhausted after a day of teaching and a student comes and plays so beautifully that you feel entirely refreshed."

Such is Mme. Lhevinne's temperament that not only talented students but the repertoire itself keeps her refreshed. Perhaps this is the way she and her husband were most alike—in the regenerative power the great masterworks had for them. Dean Schubart tells of an afternoon when he and Mme. Lhevinne were listening to a student rehearsing Schumann's *Carnaval* in the Juilliard recital hall. "When the piece was over, I turned to Rosina to ask her opinion, and all she could talk about was how beautiful, how marvelous Schumann's music was. Here was this woman who must have been listening to the *Carnaval* for more than sixty years, and it was as if she had heard it for the first time. After raving about the work itself, she then got down to specifics about the student's interpretation: how a dotted note was held here, how there was too much pedal there, and so on."[6]

The fact that Rosina Lhevinne can continue to experience Schumann's *Carnaval* as if hearing it for the first time is certainly related to the "impressionability" she has had from earliest childhood. Her sensory system, which has always reacted so strongly to devils in the opera, to men with crumbling noses, to the eyes of rabid dogs, and to old men spitting tobacco in the park, reacts to music with the same intensity and immediacy. When she says that a student must make her "enthusiastic" with a piece before she approves it for public performance, she means exactly that. The student must make her feel the music, must communicate to her its mood.

For both Josef and Rosina Lhevinne this "emotive" or "affective" approach to interpretation is traceable directly to Anton Rubinstein: to his playing, to the mode of teaching he established at the Moscow Conservatory, to the series of summer auditions he gave Lhevinne in 1892. They both liked to repeat the story Josef Hofmann told of his lessons as a full-time student of Rubinstein. Hofmann would play a piece one way on Wednesday and Rubinstein would love it. When he played it the same way on Sunday, it would leave Rubinstein cold. When Hofmann asked the reason, Rubinstein growled, "It was sunny on Wednesday and it's raining today."

Many students recall similar experiences during their lessons with Mme. Lhevinne. Reacting to a performance in such an intuitive manner is considered old-fashioned in some musical circles today, and there are many teachers who, more systematic and analytical than Mme. Lhevinne, have decided exactly how a piece should sound and measure a student's or colleague's performance by the extent to which it deviates from the "true" pattern. What such an approach gains in consistency it loses in flexibility and immediacy of feeling. But of course to be successful in judging music as Mme. Lhevinne does—by the immediate impact it makes as well as by preconceived standards—requires taste and intuition.

One will sometimes hear people say that Rosina Lhevinne is concerned with only the surface elements of piano playing, that she cares only that her students learn to play cleanly and with precision, because those qualities are the most important ones in winning important international competitions. To anyone who knows her, such an opinion is nonsense. She certainly does give attention to all the details involved in producing a clear sound from the instrument, but her chief goal is that the student be able to do this in order to communicate the emotional content of the music. If she cared only for technical perfection, music would not have the regenerative power it does for her, nor would her teaching have the regenerative power it does for her students.

When Rosina Lhevinne returned to Aspen in the summer of 1958, everyone wanted to hear all about Van Cliburn. There, as at Juilliard, Cliburn's victory did not really improve the quality of her students, for her class was already first-rate, but it did increase the attention given to what she and her students did. Cortland Barnes, President of the Board of Directors there, remembers that from that time on "Rosina's students comprised sort of a school within a school at Aspen."[7] Because the publicity Cliburn received made a piano career seem much more attractive than it ever had to Americans, she had to spend a good deal of her time *discouraging* all but the most talented students from wishing to pursue a full-time career. At the same time, she blithely went on developing her own late-blooming career.

Her major performances during the summer of 1958 included Mozart's B-flat Concerto, K. 595, with Solomon and the Aspen Festival Orchestra, and a Mozart Sonata for Piano and Violin, K.

454, with Eudice Shapiro. The summer before she had played Mozart's G major Concerto, K. 453, with the Orchestra, and Schubert's
Trout Quintet with the Juilliard Quartet, a work she had performed
in the spring with them for the Josef Lhevinne Memorial Scholarship. Harold Taubman was in Aspen to review the concert for the
New York Times and, like so many others, found Rosina Lhevinne
a peerless ensemble player:

> Though she did not seek to dominate in any way, one could not help
> having one's attention centered on Mrs. Lhevinne. The widow of that
> redoubtable pianist, Josef Lhevinne, spends most of her time teaching
> nowadays, and she makes no secret of the fact that she is well into her
> seventies. But she plays with the address and animation of a girl. She
> did nothing out of proportion yesterday, but her playing had a magne-
> tism of its own. Her phrasing had a poetry that comes only from hav-
> ing lived long and perceptively with a work. This was how Schubert
> should sing.[8]

The following summer began with Mme. Lhevinne in customarily high spirits. In early July she played Bach's C major Concerto
for Three Pianos with Babin and Vronsky. Izler Solomon, who
conducted, recalls a trying rehearsal. "Rosina played the first piano,
and there was some difficulty aligning the three instruments on
the stage. Finally, because of the acoustics and the shape of the
stage, we decided to put the pianos in the back. Then there was a
lot of discussion about where hers would be placed. We finally decided on a place and she sat at the piano and tried it. Her students and assistants were watching as she played, and she went
to talk to them for a few minutes. When she came back she said,
'I'm sorry, Izler, but out there they cannot see my hands if I play
here.'

" 'But Rosina, isn't it the music that really matters?'

" 'Yes, of course. But they still like to be able to watch my
fingers.'

"For more than half an hour we horsed around with those pianos until we got them in a position where her friends would be
able to watch her play."

When Rosina Lhevinne is riding high, it is almost impossible
to say no to her. The people who had to "horse" the pianos around
certainly did not appreciate it, but there were those who did. For
watching her septuagenarian fingers was indeed a thrill. Robert
Mann of the Juilliard Quartet feels that even in her late seventies
"she had one of the best finger techniques in the business." Tony
Han, who turned pages for her at Aspen, counts that close observation of her fingers running over the keys as one of the highlights of

his life. The effortlessness of her movements, the economy of motion, the smooth sway of her body as it leans up the keyboard and down—these are precious memories for anyone who has seen her play so much as a scale. As long as she played in public, she practiced a few hours every morning, and always included scales, which she would "shake out of her sleeves" as easily as she had done when studying with Safonoff at the Moscow Conservatory.

Following the performance of the Bach Triple Concerto in 1959, her high spirits took a nose dive. For the first time in a long while, she suffered a sustained period of poor health. As she wrote to Dean Schubart in August, she suffered from "laryngitis, bronchitis and a sore throat which, while it was not of a serious character, kept me under the weather for a great portion of the summer."[9] During this time she was responsible for two chamber-music performances, for public classes on Mozart and Tchaikovsky, and for lessons to thirty-six students. She was able to meet these responsibilities only through the help of a good doctor and a good assistant. The doctor was good, she wrote Schubart, because he was "a good psychologist as well. . . . He insisted on my continuing to give lessons and to give the two classes." The assistant was Jeaneane Dowis, an honor graduate of Juilliard, who had assisted her during her previous Aspen summers, but never on so large a scale. Of the thirty-six students Mme. Lhevinne had accepted that summer, sixteen had come on the condition that they have some of their lessons with Miss Dowis. When Mme. Lhevinne became ill, Miss Dowis took an even greater load.

One would have thought that a seventy-nine-year-old woman who suffered poor health during most of a summer in which she was responsible for thirty-six students would consider reducing her teaching burden for the coming academic year. But in the letter to Dean Schubart in which she described her various illnesses, Mme. Lhevinne asked if she might increase the size of her class at Juilliard so that she could influence as many students as possible in whatever years she might be able to continue teaching. This could be done, she proposed, with the aid of two assistants who could help her at Juilliard the way Miss Dowis had at Aspen. So in the fall, Mme. Lhevinne's class was larger than ever before, and Miss Dowis and Martin Canin (another excellent pianist from her pre-Tchaikovsky Competition class) became her official assistants. Some students continued to have all their lessons with Mme. Lhevinne; others would work on certain pieces with one of the assistants until their playing became polished enough for Mme. Lhevinne to give it the final touches.

That fall, as always, she did much more than give lessons to

her current pupils. Former students preparing to give concerts always found her ready to listen to their programs and make suggestions, and current students occasionally had a public performance to prepare for. In October of that year was the trip to
Washington for Abbott Lee Ruskin's performance with Kabalevsky. In November was the New York debut of Howard Aibel, a
former student who had won the Naumburg Prize and who, ten
years later, was to become one of her assistants. In December, John
Browning gave an important New York recital, which happened
to fall on the day of the Josef Lhevinne reunion.

If the first of the academic year had been highlighted by her
students' concerts, the end of the year featured her own. In March,
to celebrate her eightieth birthday, she played Mozart's C major
Concerto twice—first in Indianapolis and then in New York. The
Indianapolis concert was a month before her birthday and was conducted by Izler Solomon. The New York concert was a day before
the birthday, with Jean Morel conducting the Juilliard Orchestra
before an overflow house at the school. This was the sixth year in
a row she had played at Juilliard in the spring, but the first time
she had played a solo concerto there. After the performance, President Schuman presented her with a special diploma, and she gave
a carefully planned speech typical of her public utterances:

> My heart is so full that I cannot find adequate words to explain my
> feelings, but I want to tell you how thankful I am to Almighty God who
> has given me the great joy to celebrate my eightieth birthday, and al-
> lowed me to play for you today. I hope and pray that I shall be able to
> continue to work, to teach, and to share with you all, my dear young
> people, Mr. Lhevinne's and my experience in music and in life.

Afterwards, she greeted hundreds of well-wishers backstage (and
insisted on shaking hands with each one), took a fifteen-minute
nap, and was taken to dinner at a French restaurant by President
Schuman. Five years earlier, for her seventy-fifth birthday, Schuman had invited her to dinner at an elegant restaurant but she had
wished instead to spend the time in the company of her students.
So he gave her a dinner in the Juilliard cafeteria and invited her
entire class. Mme. Lhevinne likes to see and be seen on such occasions and to touch hands with people she has been sharing
music with. Justly pleased with what she is able to do at her age,
she naturally likes to see that pleasure reflected in the faces of her
numerous well-wishers. A month after her eightieth-birthday celebration, she wrote a student in California: "I accomplished what
I wanted to: to give an example to the young people of what can
be accomplished—even at my age—with work and dedication to

music."[10] A month before her birthday that was the theme of an editorial in the Indianapolis *Times* entitled "Rosina and the Grace of Aging."[11]

Musically, Mme. Lhevinne's performance of the Mozart astounded those New Yorkers who had never heard her play the work outside the city. Columbia Records invited her, Morel, and the Juilliard Orchestra to record the work, which they did successfully on May 6, in spite of some kibitzing by a technician Morel thought was trying to tell him how to conduct his orchestra. The record that resulted is our best evidence on disc of Mme. Lhevinne's warmth of tone and grace in phrasing—qualities that distinguish her playing from the sound most other pianists produce. These qualities are particularly evident in the "dream" andante, which Cuthbert Girdlestone, in writing of all Mozart's concertos, called the "most cantabile of andantes," and which Bo Widerberg selected as the musical counterpart to the youthful romanticism of his film *Elvira Madigan*. Her playing of the andante is distinguished by the purity of the singing tone and the emotion transfused into sound.

One might expect one of her age, experience, and musical taste to play the slow movement of the concerto with such beauty and insight, but the skill and enthusiasm with which she plays the first and third movements is cause for fresh wonder on each hearing. In the opening *allegro maestoso* she negotiates what Girdlestone has called "the thickest scrub of arpeggios and broken octaves Mozart has ever set up before his executants"[12] not only with technical ease but with musical flair. In the concluding *allegro vivace assai* she plays with an animation and vitality that one almost never hears from a young pianist, perhaps because it embodies so perfectly the spirit rather than the actuality of youth.

When first asked to make this recording, Mme. Lhevinne had politely demurred, saying that "since Josef made only one recording, it would be wrong for me to make any." Someone convinced her, though, that that "would make two mistakes instead of one." It actually did take her a while to be persuaded, for the recording was made five weeks after her birthday, and only a few weeks before the students who played in the Juilliard Orchestra would leave New York for summer vacation.

As Cliburn's victory in 1958 brought increased attention to Mme. Lhevinne the teacher, her New York performance of the Mozart at the age of eighty brought increased attention to her as a performer. During the next four seasons, she had a concert schedule many a pianist would be proud of. When reviewing this

part of her life recently, she was surprised to learn that she had
turned down a few engagements, such as an attractive offer to
play Mozart's C major Concerto with the Orchestra of the National Gallery. Before being confronted with that fact, she thought
she had accepted every offer she had received, and now regrets
that she had missed a few.

The concert at the National Gallery would have been in October 1960. At the end of that month, she did play the *Dumka*
Quintet with the Juilliard Quartet at Hyde Park, New York. But
the major event for Lhevinne-watchers that winter was her performance of Chopin's E minor Concerto with John Barnett and the
National Orchestral Association on February 28, 1961. Word had
gotten around town after her Juilliard performance of the Mozart
the previous spring, and many New Yorkers were curious to know
whether the diminutive octogenarian really played as well as reported. When she walked on stage in a creamy white silken gown,
the Hunter College Assembly hall was, in the words of Harold
Schonberg,

> filled with her students, friends, admirers, doubters and well-wishers,
> as well as National Orchestral subscribers and perhaps a geriatrician or
> two. It took Mme. Lhevinne about five minutes to establish the fact that
> she was going to play the concerto and not let the concerto play her. She
> got better as she went along, and ended the presto unisons of the last
> movement with the *brio* of a young virtuoso about to set the world on
> fire.[13]

Her performance of the concerto was in the same restricted dynamic range in which she had played it during her fortieth-anni-
versary concert. Schonberg, as had the *Times* man then, suggested
she may have been trying to imitate the sounds produced on the
instruments of Chopin's day. For Francis Perkins of the *Herald-
Tribune* the significance of her performance was in "its realization
of the essential atmosphere of the music, which is something quite
a few younger pianists find to be elusive. It was an understanding
of an intimate and persuasive kind, which in its pace and phrasing
gave a sense of personality, but not of placing personality in the
foreground."[14] Which sounds like a review of Josef Lhevinne.

After the concert, the only concession the soloist made to her
age was to *sit* while greeting hundreds of admirers. The next day
she taught in Room 412 and thought with pleasure of a bridge
game she had that evening, the arrangements for which she had
made backstage the night before.

Her performance of the Chopin concerto was followed by her

birthday, a feature article in *Newsweek,* a recording of the concerto for Vanguard, honors from various musical associations, and participation in benefit concerts. Amazingly, her health stood up to all the excitement and activity, and her students continued to receive their lessons. This was her second year of teaching with the help of assistants, and the busiest time for her was in the late spring, when she insisted on hearing every piece each of her students planned to play for his final examination. As Safonoff had done, she insisted that the students play their program not only for her but also for their peers, and many former students say that playing for other students in Mme. Lhevinne's class can be more challenging and intimidating than playing on the most important concert stage. There is no audience more "critical" (in both senses of the word) than the constellation of young artists among whom one is wishing to earn a high place.

Mme. Lhevinne has always hoped that her students would form one large and happy family, and has exerted every influence to prevent them from forming personal rivalries among each other. She has no patience for the kind of backbiting endemic to the musical world and severely rebukes any student she overhears making a disparaging remark about a colleague. When she played in public, she always liked to feel that everyone in the audience wished her well, and she helps her students to feel the same way by urging them to avoid petty jealousy. Many promising pianists have wished ill to everyone but themselves, only to find on stage that they could think of nothing but people in the audience with minds as venomous as their own. Such an obsession can lead to a permanent inability to play in public and to the poisoning of a musician's personality. Several of Rosina Lhevinne's better students have told me that before coming to her they had been unable to have generous feelings toward other pianists. Her lack of professional jealousy and her ability to help her students overcome it rank high among her contributions as a teacher. Her class has not always been the happy family she would wish it to be, but ideals are never fully achieved. Her lack of total success in creating a "musical family" only points to the loftiness of the goal.

A further example of her high standards is the way she evaluates her own students in comparison with those of other teachers. One of her colleagues at Juilliard has told me that during jury examinations at the end of the year she is often more liberal in grading other teachers' students than her own. I witnessed this myself when I once attended the finals of an important competition with her. She was not among the jury, but she borrowed my notebook in order to rate the four finalists herself. The first, a student of hers, played beautifully. She was seemingly pleased with his performance, and after each piece nudged me in the ribs so I would clap louder. But after his name she wrote such phrases as "More expression" and "Sing out more here." The other three finalists played well, too, although no better than her student had. But for them she wrote "Beautiful," "Wonderful," "Excellent." In the voting of the judges, the finalists finished in a four-way tie.

Although Rosina Lhevinne's activities in her widowhood were at least as strenuous as Josef Lhevinne's while he was alive, she never felt the need he did to get away for a period of complete rest. She had visited Bonnie Oaks a few times on her way to the Los Angeles Conservatory and each year before going to Aspen stayed for a week or so with the Rosboroughs at Estes Park in order to acclimatize herself to the altitude. But about her vacations she always said, "The first day I am delighted, the second day a little bit restless, and by the third day I cannot wait until the time I start to practice and teach again." Actually, most of her time at Estes Park each June was spent practicing for her summer performances at Aspen.

In the summer of 1961, not knowing what to do with herself during the three weeks between the end of school at Juilliard and the beginning of the Aspen summer session, she taught still another master class: at the University of California at Berkeley (where Pablo Casals had taught the summer before). At Aspen that summer she played Chopin's E minor Concerto, which she had played the summer before. The previous year she had been accompanied by the worst thunderstorm Solomon remembers in his years as a conductor there. "The day after the concert Rosina came to me and said, 'Izler, I played my concerto yesterday but my friends couldn't hear a note. You must let me repeat it next year.' And of course I could not say no, even though she had played five years in a row and this was to have been the last—because not every faculty member could play every year." Her repeat performance in 1961 was attended by the largest audience ever assembled at Aspen, and today she is thankful to the school for having "invited" her to play the concerto again. But "invited" is not quite the right word. "Capitulated" is perhaps too strong, but it is closer to the truth.

The 1961–62 season for Rosina Lhevinne was a high-speed rerun of the previous one. She taught for her thirty-seventh year at Juilliard, her second at Berkeley, and her seventh at Aspen. She played Mozart's C major Concerto (three times), Chopin's E minor Concerto (once), Dvořák's Quintet (twice), and made numerous benefit appearances. She attended the Carnegie Hall debut of James Mathis (a Texan of Cliburn-Browning vintage who had been to Europe on a Fulbright after studying with her) and guided Marek Jablonski and Tony Han to victories in important competitions. Jablonski, an extremely talented Canadian who had first studied with her at Aspen, won the Kosciuszko Paderewski Prize. Tony Han, then seventeen years old, won the Michaels Competition in Chicago.

One of her performances of the Mozart Concerto was with a New York orchestra beginning its first season—the Esterhazy Orchestra, conducted by David Blum. Her performance of the Chopin Concerto was with the Oakland Symphony conducted by Gerhard Samuel, and took place on April 1, following her eighty-second birthday. "I have especially fond memories of that concert because my children were able to come up from Los Angeles to hear it. The Steinway piano I used was the most beautiful I have ever played. There was a big party afterwards with champagne and a cake that weighed seventy-five pounds, almost as much as me."

Her performances of the Dvořák Quintet with the Juilliard Quartet took her to Birmingham, Alabama, in February, and to Carnegie Hall in May. The latter performance was at a benefit concert for Project Hope, and Mme. Lhevinne not only played the piano but sent out hundreds of letters asking for contributions to the charity. Typically, she touched a newspaper man who came to interview her about the concert for a substantial donation. She and her late husband had performed in countless charity concerts during their long career together, but this was the first time she had become actively involved in working for a charity in a non-musical way.

The work for Project Hope was only one of many ways she took up new causes and sought out new experiences at this stage of her life. At age seventy-five, about the time of her first solo concerto at Aspen, she flew for the first time. Since then she has traveled only by jet, and when the 747 entered commercial service she was one of the first to ride it. When the *chemise*, or "sack" dress, had come into fashion, she had been the first woman on the Juilliard faculty to wear it. A few years after that, during the hula-hoop fad, she outdistanced more than a dozen rivals during an informal contest with the plastic ring. And at Aspen, she amazed her colleagues and friends by riding the largest chairlift in the area.

"Normally the chairs run right by, but when an aged person like me comes, they stop it so you can climb in slowly. I appreciated that when I got in, but then they stopped for another elderly person when I was not yet to the top. It felt very strange, with nothing between me and the ground."

Rosina Lhevinne's eightieth year had been a breeze, her eighty-first and eighty-second were a romp. She had entered her ninth decade under a tremendous head of steam.

15

Racing toward
Ninety—and Beyond

IN JANUARY 1962, William Schuman resigned as President of the Juilliard School of Music and became President of Lincoln Center. In June, Mark Schubart resigned as Juilliard's Dean and became executive director of the Lincoln Center Fund. The grand opening of Lincoln Center was during the last week of September 1962, and the first two pianists to play at Philharmonic Hall were Juilliard graduates and pupils of Mme. Lhevinne. On September 25, John Browning gave the world premiere of Samuel Barber's Piano Concerto with Erich Leinsdorf and the Boston Symphony Orchestra. The next day, Van Cliburn played Rachmaninoff's Third Concerto with Eugene Ormandy and the Philadelphia Orchestra.

Four months later, Mme. Lhevinne herself played in Philharmonic Hall. On four memorable days in January 1963, she played "her" Chopin Concerto with Leonard Bernstein and the New York Philharmonic. Josef Lhevinne's greatest moment as a performer had come when he was fifteen years old; Rosina Lhevinne's came when she was eighty-two.

"It all happened so suddenly. Abbott Lee Ruskin, who was still studying with me then, tried out for the Philharmonic Young People's Concerts, and I went to the audition to hear him. Mr. Bernstein was very glad to see me there, and when saying good-bye he said, 'I understand you are playing now. Why haven't you played with the Philharmonic?' And I said, 'Because nobody asked me.' And that was that.

"A few days later, my telephone rang, and it was Carlos Moseley, managing director of the Philharmonic, inviting me to play. I was so thrilled when he asked me that I had to sit down. He said they wanted me to play three days in a row—Thursday, Friday, and Saturday—with a dress rehearsal the day before. I said that I did not feel it was in my power to play so many days. So Mr. Moseley said, 'I will ask Lenny about it.' When he did Lenny said, 'Tell her that after she plays three days she will not know what to do with herself on the fourth, because she will be so eager to play again.' And that was the truth—I *was* eager to play again.

"I chose to play Chopin's E minor Concerto, which I had first played at the Conservatory in Moscow. Lenny asked if he could come up to my studio at Juilliard and accompany me on a second piano in the concerto, so he would know my ideas and it would be easier at the rehearsal. The joy I had when he played the accompaniment is not to be described. When I played the first solo theme he jumped up from his piano and kissed me. He said, 'You know, I generally hate to conduct this concerto, because either you and the soloist feel together or you don't. Either you don't need any rehearsal or you can have ten and it doesn't help.' Then he said that in his whole life he had never heard anyone play the first theme the way I did and that was just the way he liked it himself. From that time on we had a wonderful time.

"After we had played through the rest of the concerto, he asked me if I would be willing to have the dress rehearsal open to the public, because everything was sold out and this was the only way some of my students and his friends would be able to hear the concerto. I thought that was a wonderful idea, so the dress rehearsal was absolutely packed.

"At the performances themselves, for some reason it was very cold in the hall, and I had to wear my green shawl. After we finished, I would bow with Lenny several times and then he told me to bow alone. Sarah was standing by the door in the wings, and he said to her: 'Look at her! It's not only how she plays but how she walks!' "

For those acquainted with Mme. Lhevinne's previous performances of the Chopin, the distinctive feature of the one with Bernstein was the exceedingly slow tempo of both the first and second movements. The Philharmonic program notes suggested that the work should take about thirty-four minutes. The Lhevinne-Bernstein team took forty-three. Some observers quipped that Mme. Lhevinne was playing as slowly as she could because she enjoyed so much being on stage with the Philharmonic and wanted the experience to last as long as possible. *She* says the slow pace of the performance was largely due to Bernstein, who "liked the *tempi* even slower than I did." Whoever was responsible, she and Bernstein took eight minutes more to play the work than she and Barnett had in the recording made a year and a half earlier. The result was a warm, leisurely, spacious reading in which phrasing, nuance, and poetry were foremost. Under the hands of many another conductor and pianist, the concerto would fall apart under such loving attention. But the orchestra's beautiful sound and the soloist's warm sustained tone make the performance a compelling one —even when heard on tape ten years after the event.

The Saturday performance, on January 19, was broadcast nationwide over CBS radio, and the intermission featured an interview of the soloist by James Fassett. Many listeners remember her response when he said how wonderful it was that she could give such a vigorous performance at age eighty-three. "No! No!" she cried. "Eighty-two! Eighty-two! My birthday is not for two months!" Her voice sounded so young and vibrant over the airwaves that people who did not know her could not believe the woman speaking was the age she claimed to be.

One man in Cleveland was so enthralled by her radio personality that he wrote "Madam Rozina Levine" to tell her about it. He had heard a rebroadcast of the concert on his car radio while driving home from work late at night and "in order to hear the entire interview, I drove around the icy wintry streets of my neighborhood till the discussion was completed."[1] A woman in Michigan had tuned in to the broadcast midway through the first movement and did not know who was playing. She was a musical journalist, and by the beginning of the last movement had decided it was a pianist she had never heard before.

> I got my notebook ready to take down the name of the performer . . . so convinced was I by this point . . . that it must be and only could be a very *young* artist to have that unabashed joyousness, that verve, that contemporary sense of accent and rhythm. . . . Madam, I almost wept when I heard your name. How DO you do it?

The phrase by which she characterized the playing was "wine dryness over an undertone of surging warmth."[2]

The New York and national critics naturally made much of the event, and Harold Schonberg pointed out that in the history of music no female pianist (and few male ones) had ever played a major concerto with a major orchestra at the age of eighty-two for one day, much less four. But the greatest tributes to Mme. Lhevinne came from people around the country she had never heard of before. One of the nicest was from a woman in St. Paul who was one month her senior. Anna C. Soucheray had recently broken

her arm in a fall. But with Mme. Lhevinne for inspiration she began to play the piano as soon as the cast was removed, and on her
eighty-third birthday had managed to play a Mendelssohn piece
she had first performed when eighteen.[3]

If the days she played with the Philharmonic were among the
more thrilling of Mme. Lhevinne's long life, the months that preceded and followed them were among the most trying. Her difficulties had begun with an impulsive trip to Fort Worth for the
finals of the First International Van Cliburn Competition. Cliburn
had invited her when he was in New York for the opening of
Lincoln Center, and she had consented even though Ralph Votapek, one of her students, had entered. She had been worried about
how it would look if she went to the competition and Votapek
won, but Cliburn had assured her the contest would be won by
one of two "magnificent" Russians who had entered. He told her
how proud he would be if she were in Texas to telephone the news
to the Soviet Union.

"When I got there and heard the finals, I simply could not understand what Van had been raving about. Neither of the Russians
was so extraordinary, but on the other hand, Ralph Votapek played
beautifully, and it was he who won the competition. I soon learned
what had happened. Every day the Texans gave a grand party for
the few competitors. Votapek would go to each one to show his
gratitude, and eat and drink a little, but would go home after about
ten minutes so he could go early to bed and practice well the next
day. On the other hand, the Russians, who loved parties and good
food but were not accustomed to such quantities of food and
drink at home, enjoyed themselves thoroughly. By the time the
finals came they were not at their best, whereas Votapek played
better that night than I had ever heard him play before. Everyone
agreed that he deserved the prize."

For winning first place, Votapek, a twenty-three-year-old pianist
from Milwaukee, received $10,000. The two Russians, Nikoli Petrov
and Mikhail Voskresenski, finished second and third, respectively.
While in Fort Worth both Votapek and Mme. Lhevinne stayed
with Mrs. Katherine Rich, who had been one of the first pupils to
study with the Lhevinnes at the original Juilliard School in the
Vanderbilt Mansion.

The major difficulty with the trip to Fort Worth was the
weather, which was exceedingly hot and humid, and Mme. Lhevinne was quite exhausted by the time she returned to New York.
Soon after she was home again, a laundry package was delivered

to her apartment. Being alone that afternoon, she tried to shove it with her feet across the room. Life not having prepared her for this kind of task, she did not succeed, and ended up in a painful heap on the floor. Her nerves were badly shaken by the fall, and she sustained several contusions. Her condition worsened, and on October 28 she was admitted to Columbia-Presbyterian Hospital with what was diagnosed as congestive heart failure.

By mid-November her condition had stabilized enough that she could leave the hospital. But such a shake-up is difficult to recover from fully at age eighty-two. She was slow to regain strength, and her doctors doubted that she could maintain her regular teaching activities and still be ready for the Philharmonic appearance in January. They told her that she could practice in the mornings but that she should not attempt to give more than one lesson a day. If she did that for a month, they said, they would then be able to decide whether or not she could play.

The prospect of losing the opportunity to perform with Bernstein and the New York Philharmonic was distressing for obvious reasons of pride and professionalism, but for Mme. Lhevinne it was doubly so, owing to her persistent lifelong aversion to canceling anything already scheduled. She wanted to play, but she knew that if she did she would have to slight her students, who had already missed lessons when she was in the hospital. The situation seemed insoluble and probably would have been so had it not been for Miss Dowis and Mr. Canin, who worked many hours overtime with her students, and for Peter Mennin, Schuman's successor at Juilliard, who allowed her to remain on the faculty at full pay while recuperating and told her to teach as much or as little as she felt able. Because of this, she was able to recover sufficiently to play the Chopin Concerto four days in a row. No one who saw her on the stage of Philharmonic Hall in her creamy white satin gown could have suspected the physical shake-up she had suffered only a few months earlier.

After the series of concerts with the Philharmonic she tried to resume her full-time activities, which were now augmented by the wish to answer considerable fan mail. But in February she got bronchitis, and again it looked as if she might have to cancel a playing engagement—this one with the Fort Worth Symphony in mid-March. The doctors finally allowed her to go, but only on the condition that she completely avoid crowds, for they feared that catching influenza at her age and in her condition might be fatal.

After arriving in Fort Worth, she was virtually quarantined in the Riches' house, and went to not a single party. She even kept her distance from members of the orchestra during rehearsal. During the performance itself, she again felt a strong draft and had to put on her green shawl. She played the Chopin Concerto beautifully, as she had in New York, with no signs on stage of not being in perfect health. But when undergoing a routine medical examination after returning to New York, she was discovered to again have a primary growth of cancer—this time in the other breast. Once more she was hospitalized, this time for much of April and May. Dr. Haagenson performed the operation, as he had in 1949, and medical records show that his patient's body stood up to the ordeal amazingly well. Mme. Lhevinne's blood pressure was constant throughout the operation, and her electrocardiogram readings were extremely steady. To ease the pain following surgery, she needed morphine in smaller amounts and for fewer days than most patients do. Unfortunately, her mind was not able to accommodate the experience as well as her other organs. Before the operation took place she kept fearing it would be canceled (perhaps a reflection of anxiety over her concerts that year). And on the second postoperative day she was not sure the operation had taken place. The greatest strain she felt, though, came from a nurse who told her she did not have long to live, that the operation was likely to prove fatal. The news frightened her so that she kept it within herself for days, suffering intensely, until she finally asked the doctor about it, and was reassured.

Again it took a long while to regain full strength after being hospitalized, and that summer at Aspen she had to cancel a scheduled performance of Mozart's B-flat Concerto, K. 595. She suffered poor health throughout the summer and was able to do little constructive work. At this point it looked as if her age, her lifelong problems with health, and her compulsive need to be active had finally caught up with her. But the next academic year found her teaching at Juilliard and playing in New York (Mozart's B-flat with Blum and the Esterhazy Orchestra) and teaching and playing again at Aspen (her C major Mozart).

As if that were not enough, she taught at U.C.L.A. for two weeks before going to Aspen, and was the subject of a forty-minute film documentary. In the 16-mm feature made by the University of California Humanities Media Extension, she is not only the picture of health and vitality but shows to full advantage her complex combination of charm, severity, and humor. The film must be recommended to anyone interested in her, for the kind of power she exerts and presence she possesses cannot be fully appreciated by anyone who does not know her visually. The sound track picks up both her voice and the playing of her students very well, and the format—a series of student performances commented on by Mme. Lhevinne—allows her to put across many principles of her "Russian School" of piano playing. The film is a great tribute not only to her teaching abilities but to her courage and energy. A year after the tremendous excitement of playing with the New York Philharmonic and the terrible distress of being twice hospitalized, she shows as much vitality and enthusiasm for her work as a squirrel cracking its first nut.

Rosina Lhevinne's record as a public person—her devotion to her husband's career, her own late-blooming solo career, her galaxy of successful students—is well known and easy to admire. But the private woman behind these achievements—with her durability, her stubbornness, and a tenacity that will never let the world wear her down—is perhaps even more deserving of admiration and awe.

In April 1962, a young man wrote Mme. Lhevinne from Kansas, asking what steps he should take to prepare himself for Juilliard. Her answer included a summary of what she had learned more than seventy years before, during her first years at the Moscow Conservatory:

> First of all . . . you must develop a mastery of the instrument. You acquire this by playing daily scales in octaves, thirds, sixths, and tenths; arpeggios in fundamental position, first and second inversions; and some exercises from Dohnányi, Pischna, or Hanon, depending on your level of development. Are you studying theory, harmony, solfeggio, and ear training? Send me your repertoire for the last three or four years. I would be glad to suggest some new material.
>
> Remember that acquiring the mastery of the instrument is not a goal [in itself] but only the way to be able to recreate the music you want to play. . . .[4]

For her, this disciplined approach to a basic mastery of the instrument remains the foundation of the "Russian School" of piano playing. She does not claim that this is the only way to approach the study of the piano, but she does love to remind people that "one cannot deny that since Anton Rubinstein established the Russian School it has produced many of the world's outstanding pianists." In conversations with Vladimir Ashkenazy and others, she has learned that the Russian Conservatories now place less emphasis on scales and arpeggios than when she studied there, and more emphasis on the use of selected exercises, but that the basic

idea of having a perfect knowledge of and command of the instrument remains the same.

This is not the place to try to define "a perfect knowledge of
and command of the instrument," and the reader who is interested
in a technical treatment of the matter would do well to consult
Josef Lhevinne's *Basic Principles in Pianoforte Playing*. But a few
elements of the approach can be suggested here. Essentially, it involves a rather scientific analysis of the piano as a sound-produc-
ing instrument and the adjustment of the artist's physical approach so that it makes full use of the piano's inherent qualities.
This sounds obvious once stated, but is ignored by all too many
pianists and teachers. Take pedaling, for example. Countless students have entered Mme. Lhevinne's class at Juilliard thinking
the pedal has but two levels: "off" and "on." She shows how the
pedal has six or more ranges between these two extremes and how
each of them produces different sound. Then there is the role of
the wrist and the finger in sound-production. If one thinks about
it, it might seem obvious that the pianist wishing to produce an
effective staccato would use a firm wrist and strike the keys with
the rather bony tips of the finger, whereas if trying for singing
legato effects he would use a flexible wrist and "caress" the keys
with the soft "padded" area underneath the finger tip. But many
pianists and teachers do not "think about it," with the result that
many "advanced" students have come to Mme. Lhevinne without being conscious of the close connection between the way one
approaches the piano and the sound that results. Jeffrey Siegel recalls his first lesson with her, in the early 1960s, after winning
several prizes in the Midwest.

"As soon as I had played for her, she said, 'You know, dear,
your tone is not very good. You know, it is not even very pleasant.
You know, dear, your tone is ugly. You are so musical and so well
taught, and yet your tone is bad. You know, dear, God gave us
wrists.'

" 'What?'

" 'Wrists. They allow the hand to move like this,' and she demonstrated. She took everything apart and taught me how to use
a flexible wrist to caress the keys and produce a singing tone, and
now whenever I play I send her the reviews where they speak
about my tone."[5]

In teaching scales and arpeggios, too, Mme. Lhevinne often
stresses elements that other teachers overlook. She never allows a
student to play them mechanically, but instead puts emphasis
on rhythm, tone, and dynamics, much as Safonoff had done in

teaching her. Many times she will ask an advanced student to stop in the middle of a lesson and play a certain scale, and if he is unable to do it to her satisfaction he is certain to get a stern lecture about how such exercises "are the bread, and the rest the butter, and while the butter is very nice, it can't go very well without the bread."[6] Siegel remembers that "she would ask you to play the G-sharp minor cross-hand, and you would get the fingers tied up, and then she would play it beautifully and you would feel so embarrassed to see this eighty-year-old woman doing what you could not do. But she never presented it as only scales. She used it to teach her entire approach to the instrument."

Mme. Lhevinne's lifelong concern with piano playing has led her to formulate certain strong ideas about the ideal posture, wrist position, hand position, and finger positions. One hallmark of a Lhevinne student, for example, is a rigid, absolutely straight little finger when playing octaves. She is not entirely dogmatic about these ideas, however, and if a student can get equally good results with another method she will not insist on a change. Not too long ago, a student came to her who got fine legato effects with fingers that were high and quite stiff, and Mme. Lhevinne left well enough alone. Whenever that student played at a master class, though, she would whisper in a voice meant to be overheard, "I don't know how she does it. Look how she holds the fingers."

The test is never how it looks but how it sounds. Many students recall disputes during which she would turn around in her swivel chair, with her back to the piano, and say, "All right. Play it your way and play it mine. If I cannot tell the difference, you may play it your way." Because so many students come to her with what she considers an imperfect command of the instrument, it is always a challenge to put her point across without seeming to undermine a previous teacher's work. The excellent formula she has developed for this is to say, "There are many ways of approaching the piano, but I must open my heart to you and show you my way." And while she is a strong advocate for her own point of view, she usually will try to see what is good in another's. For all her belief in the "Russian school" of music, it is pure musicianship that impresses her most. This was dramatized when she was hospitalized for her second breast operation, at age eighty-three. Siegel and Ruskin came to visit her at the hospital and she told them, "If anything happens to me and I cannot teach any more, I would like to send you to Serkin. He is a fine musician."[7] A fine musician yes, but not an exemplar of the Russian school.

In matters of interpretation—as opposed to "command of the

instrument"—Mme. Lhevinne's flexibility is equally apparent.
Just as when she and her husband played the Mozart Double Concerto in Chicago and asked a young conductor his opinion of how
a mordent should be played, she in her teaching alone has constantly looked for new ideas. Although Felix Salmond, whom she
had consulted so much during her first years of going it alone, died
in 1962, many other sources for ideas remain. Among them are
recordings made by various artists, suggestions from her colleagues
and assistants, and interpretive ideas of her students—when they
have logic, purpose, warmth, and taste.

The way in which she combines interpretive ideas from various sources can best be described as eclectic rather than dogmatic,
as intuitive rather than systematic. One student remembers how
surprised he was when she introduced him to a new work by playing recordings by both Schnabel and Artur Rubinstein. She pointed
out features in each that were good, saying there was no reason he
could not incorporate a little of this, a little of that. Another student was surprised when, in the middle of a lesson on Bach, Mme.
Lhevinne walked out of Room 412 and down the hall to consult
a colleague she considered an expert on ornamentation. Martin
Canin, who has been her assistant since 1959, feels that from the
very beginning she has treated him more as a colleague than an
"assistant" in terms of consulting him—not only about teaching
but also in regard to her own playing. The year after he began to
assist her with her class, she played a Mendelssohn trio in one of
the Josef Lhevinne Memorial Scholarship Concerts. On the day
of the concert she was having difficulty with the fingering of a
certain passage and asked his advice. He made a suggestion; she
adopted it and used it in performance that very night.

While Mme. Lhevinne's openness to new ideas results in great
flexibility, and in teaching helps a student's performance to grow,
rather than to follow a preset mold, this very flexibility sometimes makes it difficult for a student to say exactly what it is he
gets from a lesson with her. Kun Woo Paik, who came to her in
the early 1960s, has described the dynamics of a lesson with her
very well. "With other teachers who are more systematic you finish a lesson and know exactly what you got—certain ideas about
this, certain ideas about that. But with her it cannot be summa-
rized; it can be a puzzle, a mystery. You would play, and she
would comment—stop you at every note—and after the lesson you
felt that she helped you musically here, technically there, and
pianistically somewhere else. But it was hard to say *exactly* what
she gave. It seems to me that she goes right down to the bottom

of the music—to the note itself. Nothing is added from the outside, no pre-conceptions. You start from the music itself and let it grow out from there."[8] To hear students discuss her way of teaching is to think of a principle central to the Romantic movement in the arts in the nineteenth century—organic form.

One reason why no two students speak of her teaching in exactly the same way is her intuitive rather than systematic approach to music. But it is true that personally as well as pianistically she approaches no two students identically. She strongly feels that the most important part of teaching music is understanding the student's personality, because "what is right for one is completely wrong for another. You must get to know the thoughts and emotions as intimately as possible. This cannot be done simply through giving a sixty-minute lesson every week; so the students that seemed to me the most interesting I would take in a group to Jones Beach on Sundays and we would walk on the boardwalk and I would try to understand their personalities. With others I would try to find the time to go for a walk after their lessons and we would have a conversation on many subjects. In many cases I accredit my achievements as a teacher to this interest in a student's personality."

Cultivating friendships with her students is not only a professional duty but a personal pleasure, for Mme. Lhevinne enjoys being with young people more than with people her own age. This has been true not only in her nineties, when few her own age are left, but also when she was in her sixties and seventies. "I prefer being with young people," she says, "because they live in the present and most people my age always want things the way they were fifty years ago." Whereas Josef Lhevinne always remained "elegantly aloof" (as Arthur Gold put it) from even those students closest to him, Rosina Lhevinne has always tried to be intimately involved.

"I generally try to become not only their teacher but their friend. So they have come to me with many questions that bother them, and they feel they have in me somebody that will really take great interest and give advice. Many times they have spoken about their 'love affairs' and many times they have asked me if I would allow them to bring the person in question. I have always appreciated that and hardly ever refuse."

She claims to be "not exactly a matchmaker," but she is not exactly not one, either. There have been an inordinate number of marriages among her students, and if she has not been the prime mover in every case, she has certainly been an effective catalyst in many. Shortly after winning the Van Cliburn Competition, Ralph Votapek announced to her that he was in love with Albertine Baumgartner, another of her students—at which news Mme. Lhevinne was slightly disappointed because "I had not thought of it first." When she does take the news in stride, she is apt to throw the student by her response. When a male student confided to her that he was madly in love with a fellow pupil, and told her who that pupil was (another pianist from the class, of course), she said, "Thank God it's a girl!"

Mme. Lhevinne prides herself on moving with the times, and even shows a certain amount of tolerance for the increased sexual freedom of the last decade. "So many marriages in my generation were disasters because two people married and found out they were sexually incompatible. In some ways it is a good idea to know someone in that way before marriage." But she has little patience with girls who want to "know in that way" more than one man at a time. In a letter to a friend during a recent winter, she described the week's weather as "changeable and unpleasant, like these new girls."

Year after year her involvement with students would begin early in the morning and go nonstop well into the evening hours. One reason this was possible was that her domestic arrangements were handled so nicely by Sarah, who after the second cancer operation moved into the Claremont Avenue apartment with her. Sarah did all the cooking and shopping and cleaning, and also served as a most efficient memory bank. Astonishingly, she could somehow recognize the face and remember the name of nearly every student who had studied with the Lhevinnes since they first moved to Kew Gardens—a talent that many times saved her employer from embarrassment. With a technique learned from Masha, Sarah prepared *kulich* and *pasha* every Easter, and provided Mme. Lhevinne with eggs to paint in vivid colors, which she has done ever since her childhood. For twenty years, on December 14, Sarah would go over to the Raieffs' apartment early in the day and prepare food and drink for the large group that would come in the evening to remember Josef Lhevinne. "That was always a lot of work," she recalled, "but I loved doing it because it was for him."[9] The last reunion was held in 1965, when Mme. Lhevinne was eighty-five years old, Sarah sixty-five.

In addition to having Sarah's help at home, Mme. Lhevinne has always had a young pianist around the house. Marusha, the girl who left Tiflis in 1902 to live with the Lhevinnes in Moscow, could be called the first of them; since 1945 there have been many, many more. The young woman is usually one of her piano students, often one who is in New York for the first time and needs help with expenses. In exchange for room and board, she provides countless miscellaneous services in addition to filling in for Sarah on weekends. Winthrop Sargeant described the phenomenon quite well in his excellent 1963 *New Yorker* profile:

> Mme. Lhevinne's pupils have learned to recognize the moment when she has reached the point of conferring the signal honor of domestic service on one of them. Her eyes narrow in their peculiarly Oriental fashion, and, with an offhandedness that she affects when contemplating a deep-laid design of any sort, she inquires of no one in particular, 'Do you know a young lady who can type, take shorthand, and answer the telephone, and, preferably, has a knowledge of French, German, Italian, and Russian, and who, perhaps, can cook?' The question brings no rush of volunteers, but there is always somebody who—either out of genuine affection or out of a romanticized idea of continued intimacy with so famous a figure—snatches the bait, although the requirements for the position are never fully met.[10]

A week after Sargeant's article appeared, Mme. Lhevinne received a letter from a fifty-year-old part-time pianist who was working as a secretary in the Pentagon and who wrote: "Incidentally, I would fulfill all the requirements humorously cited in the article. . . ."[11]

After Marusha—an Armenian from Tiflis—the young women who have lived with Mme. Lhevinne have included Caucasians, Negroes, Jews, and Orientals from Oregon, Texas, Alabama, California, New York, Canada, Italy, Greece, France, Russia, Israel, Korea, and Argentina. Several have married students of Mme. Lhevinne. One who did not married Mme. Lhevinne's biographer. A few have bravely remained single.

The young woman's duties, in addition to those listed by Sargeant, include constant communication with members of the class. When a student is at school, unavailable by phone, and Mme. Lhevinne decides a certain sonata needs more work and makes room in her schedule for 3:30 that afternoon, the girl living with her has to find a way to deliver the summons. At the old Juilliard building on Claremont Avenue, this was done by means of a special Lhevinne message board opposite the coat room, which members of the class were expected to check several times a day.

Mme. Lhevinne kept such a demanding pace that students must occasionally have wished she would catch a small cold (not a large one, of course) so they might get a little breathing time. Even colds, though, would not deter her. If she had one herself she would have the student come to the apartment anyway, and would conduct the lesson from her bedroom, tapping the tempo with her pencil loudly enough for the student to hear from the piano in the adjoining room. If the student had a cold, or feigned one in hopes of getting out of a lesson, she would say, "Yes, of course, you must not come. Just put the receiver on the table and play for me there, dear." If he was not calling from a telephone booth, the student would have to play.

Not all pupils thrive under such a demanding teacher. And because she lives and feels life so intensely, Mme. Lhevinne occasionally has breaks with some of her most favored students and companions. Once when one of her best-known students was interviewed for an important radio broadcast, he spoke a great deal about her influence on him—as well as that of a previous teacher. In editing the interview, the technicians cut out his tribute to her because it was too long for the time allowed. She was terribly hurt when she heard the broadcast, assuming that the pianist himself had omitted mention of her. Because she had not kept up with electronic technology, she could not—or would not—understand that his words had been edited out. With time this particular misunderstanding was ironed out. But for much too long her misplaced resentment was fully felt.

One of Isidor Phillip's ten commandments for the piano teacher that Mme. Lhevinne quotes the most is to "expect ingratitude from those you have given the most." Because she has felt the truth of this saying rather sharply in a few instances, she is sometimes quick to see ingratitude where it does not in fact exist. Fortunately, she has been able to develop a mechanism whereby she can forget most such offenses—whether imagined or real. She puts the offending person on what she calls her skunk list, and he will be "skunk number 1" or "skunk number 2" for a while; then all will be forgotten. Even when quite vexed by someone's behavior, she will say, "The worst thing I would wish for him is a hiccup."

Some of the more permanent breaks with people once close have been caused by superstitions and phobias carried from her childhood in Russia. Psychologically speaking, these seem to be beyond her control. Her strongest phobia concerns death—which is particularly unfortunate, since any person who lives more than ninety years has to see much more than his fair share of it. When riding in a car she will often ask the driver to go to great lengths to avoid passing a cemetery, and for many years she refused to ride down a street in Kew Gardens that had a sign advertising a funeral parlor. In all her years of teaching, she has yet to teach Chopin's B-flat minor Sonata, with its funeral march. Martin Luther King's death threw her into a severe depression that incapacitated her for days, and so did Robert Kennedy's. On the other hand, people who know this side of her personality were amazed by the fortitude she showed during the difficult years immediately following her husband's death—when every December she traveled by subway from Manhattan to Queens to visit his grave. That fortitude notwithstanding, if a close friend dies, or a spouse or relative of a friend or student, it is sometimes psychologically impossible for her to acknowledge it, which naturally leads to a serious break in relations with the survivor and to terribly bitter feelings.

Most breaks, though, are temporary, and come about merely because a student who has come to her on the verge of maturity must break away in order to lead an adult life, to make decisions and mistakes on his own. Mme. Lhevinne generally handles this process gracefully, but with her "favorites" it is no easier for her than for a mother to let go of a child and to watch it go unprotected into the world. While it sometimes seems to her that one of her favorites leaves her influence for no reason at all, or for reasons that reflect unfavorably upon her, the opposite is usually the case. One of the young women who had lived with her put it this way:

> I don't know about others but in my own case it was this: one becomes so involved with Rosina's life that you wake up to the fact that you are really not leading your own life, but are much more involved with helping her lead hers. So you pull away in order to renew yourself, reset or re-establish your sense of direction, and get going again. I am sure she is not aware of this, and it is not intentional on her part, it is just something that happens. . . . You have to use sheer force and determination to break away in order to survive.[12]

"Sheer force and determination" is a strong phrase. But Mme. Lhevinne's personality is so strong, the power she exerts so compelling, that the phrase is entirely apt.

The saving grace about this powerful woman is that while having a strong personal influence over so many of her students, she generally refrains from using that influence to the detriment of the student's individuality. She does not push her pupils into a pianistic mold, and she is a master at reading a person's potential and helping him to find it himself. And despite her close personal involvement with many students, she generally knows when to push them out on their own, or into the influence of another teacher for a while. Several times she has sent favorite students to other teachers or to other summer festivals rather than to Aspen with her, and she encourages almost every student—when she feels he has assimilated most of what she has to give—to study a year or two in Europe.

Of course one reason she can afford to let a talented student go is that there is always another waiting to take his place. Mark Schubart was probably the first to refer to those students with her at the moment as the "Lhevinne stable" and those waiting to join her as in the "farm system." Because of her summer teaching in Colorado and California, and because of her numerous former students teaching all across the country, she is assured of a steady flow of fine pianists. This seemingly inexhaustible supply of young American "talents" is something that continues to amaze her, particularly because musical training had been in such a primitive state when she and her husband first visited the country in 1906. Fifty years after that first visit she wrote Schubart incredulously from Aspen: "My [there] are so many talented people. What shall we do with them?"[13]

In this age of mass communication, the "farm system" is no longer limited to the United States. Since Tony Han began to study with her and to return periodically to Korea for tours, she has been very well known in that country, and in each of the last several years has had a handful of Korean students. She has taught students from nearly every Latin American country, including Colombia's Blanca Uribe, Venezuela's Eva Maria Zuk, and Uruguay's Leonidas Lipovetzky. Israeli students have come to her since that country was founded, and she has recently had her first students from Finland, Turkey, and Africa. In recent years she has been surprised to learn from John Browning that South Africans, and from Edward Auer that Australians, are aware of her, and in unguarded moments she has been heard to say, with wonder, "I'm global!"

In spite of the fact that students come from all over the world to study with her, some people say Rosina Lhevinne will "do anything" in order to get a good student away from another teacher. Such charges gained a modicum of respectability when Winthrop Sargeant quoted a student to that effect in his *New Yorker* profile, but they ought not to be taken too seriously, as they are partially the result of the spitefulness of teachers who would like the top-quality students she has. She does not have to run after students—because students run to her. Many times she has bent over backwards *not* to take a student from another teacher. In 1964, Mischa Dichter, an outstanding young pianist from Los Angeles, enrolled in her summer master class at U.C.L.A. He wished to come immediately to Juilliard for further study with her, but she was reluctant to take him, because he was then studying with a Los Angeles teacher she respected who had previously "lost" a talented student to her. She actually refused to accept Dichter until her daughter Marianna insisted, by saying, "Mother, it's not fair to the boy not to take him."

Aside from mere professional jealousy, some of the resentment over Mme. Lhevinne's teaching success can be traced to the days of the Schuman-Schubart administration at Juilliard, when she did receive highly preferential treatment. Dean Schubart's rationale for this was similar to the one Marianna had used: "I always tried to give Rosina the best students I could because I felt she could do more for them than anyone else. I think I was right in that, and if I had to do it over again I would do it the same way. Maybe a few of the other teachers resented it, but I always felt my main responsibility was to the student, not to the teachers."[14]

Peter Mennin's administration, which succeeded Schuman's, has treated Mme. Lhevinne very well, but it has not continued quite the same level of preferential treatment. Even so, she must continue to be very careful, because many students, for whatever motives, wish to study with her after being with another teacher. In some cases, the student may wish to do this only to be able to put Rosina Lhevinne's name on his concert programs a decade hence—a name which, while not an automatic passport to success, might sometimes provide more of a boost to the pianist's career than that of the teacher who has really trained him and been responsible for his musical development. In other cases the student genuinely feels he can learn more from her than from anyone else. Although she tries to handle such situations with tact, Mme. Lhevinne worries about them constantly, always wishing to do what is best for the student while not offending the student's current teacher (sometimes a person dear or once dear to her, who had studied with her or her husband many years earlier and who is him- or herself approaching retirement age, with his or her own teaching reputation to worry about). Like all of us, Mme. Lhevinne has her faults, of which she is only too well aware, but running after students is not one of them. So strongly does she feel on this score that the one paragraph in which Sargeant indirectly attributed that trait to her spoiled for her all pleasure in reading the rest of his extremely perceptive profile.

Into the middle 1960s, Mme. Lhevinne kept a class of twenty to twenty-six students at Juilliard and was assisted by Miss Dowis and Mr. Canin. Her students continued winning prizes both in the school and in the professional world outside, the most notable "outside" victories being those of Tony Han in the 1965 Leventritt Competition, Lois Pachuki (a Silver Queen girl) in the 1965 Vienna Beethoven Competition, and Mischa Dichter's second-place finish in the 1966 Tchaikovsky Competition. Dichter's achievement was particularly dramatic because the Russian audience seemed to prefer his playing to that of the young Russian, Gregory Sokoloff, who won. Dichter returned to the United States with a contract from Sol Hurok and with new reports of how his teacher was revered in her homeland. John Browning, who toured Russia with the Cleveland Orchestra in 1965, brought back more of the same. Rosina Lhevinne has not been in Russia since 1914, but her students have certainly made her presence felt there since 1958.

Dichter attributes much of his success in the Tchaikovsky Competition to the preparation she gave him, especially her work on Schubert's A major posthumous Sonata. With all the other contestants playing flashy virtuoso pieces, he feels he was able to make a much stronger impression as a serious musician with that work. Schubert sonatas were not much played in public during Josef Lhevinne's career, and so far as I have found out he never played one in public. The only pianist of his generation brave enough to play the long, beautiful works for a paying audience was Artur Schnabel. Mme. Lhevinne recalls that Schnabel's performances of Schubert sonatas—especially the slow movements—were among the musical experiences she and her husband valued most. She had begun teaching more and more of Schubert's works in the 1960s, although she still feels that it takes an extraordinarily mature person and musician to play the great sonatas well, and that it takes a very sophisticated audience to appreciate them. One reason she began teaching more Schubert, she admits, was that she was tired of hearing Beethoven sonatas at every Juilliard entrance examination. She had helped to change the requirements, so that a student could play a sonata by either Beethoven or Schubert.

In 1969 the Juilliard School moved from the building on Claremont Avenue to its massive new structure at Lincoln Center. Mme. Lhevinne was asked by the administration if she would like to live near the school, but she preferred to remain in her "unpretentious" apartment on Claremont Avenue, which, out of reverse pride, she likes to describe as being "on a corner of Harlem." Students come to her for lessons, and she goes to her studio at the new school several times a year so they can play before their peers. Like many other faculty members, she was baffled by the labyrinthian corridors of the large building, and enjoys telling of how Marian Szekely-Freschl—the voice teacher who as a student had visited the Lhevinnes in Wannsee during World War I—failed, even with the aid of a large map with which all faculty members were provided, to locate a ladies' room, gave up in disgust, and took a taxi to her nearby home, from which she returned minutes later.

Room 575, Mme. Lhevinne's studio at the new school, is larger than Room 412, and looks out on Broadway rather than on a terrace with a view of the Hudson. Portraits of Josef Lhevinne and Anton Rubinstein hang on its walls, and the room is equipped with two new Steinway grands. Mme. Lhevinne continues to sit in her large green chair, which is another relic from uptown, and to slowly unwrap hard candies while her students play. (She seems to think unwrapping them slowly makes the process harder to hear, but of course it only prolongs the noise. On the other hand, no one really knows whether she does this just because she likes candy or because she wants to inure the student to similar distractions in the concert hall.) Mr. Canin and Howard Aibel (who succeeded Miss Dowis) usually sit near her and she whispers to them and writes comments in the student's score. Seldom at a loss for words at these master classes, she once, when the scheduled performer was late, entertained a room of twenty-five people with an enthusiastic monologue about Linus Pauling's book on Vitamin C and the common cold (1970). Retaining a touching sense of noblesse oblige, she personally distributes green bills every year to elevator operators, coatroom attendants, and other long-time "friends" at the school, though scoffers note that the marks on the bills have not risen enough to offset the drop in a dollar's value since 1924. She also "tipped" the workers who hung the portraits of her husband and Anton Rubinstein on the walls of her new studio.

Soon after the opening of the new building in the fall of 1969, a segment of one of her master classes was broadcast on NBC television. Rosina Lhevinne wore a red dress ("because all those old women in Russia wore black") and played the "Chopin" section of Schumann's *Carnaval*. She rehearsed in the studio before the filming began, and it was inspiring to watch and to listen as her eighty-nine-year-old mind and fingers pressed out the sounds of that beautiful piece, unfazed by the technicians who scurried around the room with cables, lights, reflectors, and other paraphernalia.

The great event of her first year in the new building, though, was the mammoth party given for her on March 31, 1970—two days after her ninetieth birthday. She wore a white dress that night and made a delayed entrance that caused the large crowd "to part like the waters of the Red Sea" when she walked into the lobby on President Mennin's arm.[15] Mennin, tall, straight, and conventionally handsome, and Mme. Lhevinne, diminutive, sparkling, and perfectly groomed, made a memorable pair. There were speeches and awards, but most important for the guest of honor was the opportunity to shake hands and exchange greetings with the hundreds of friends and musical associates who came to pay her their respect. She sat in her green chair while receiving them all, and looked as pleased as a nine-year-old girl having her first big party. The occasion was used to launch a scholarship fund at Juilliard in Mme. Lhevinne's name, and Columbia Records re-issued several thousand copies of her recording of the Mozart Concerto, which were distributed by Juilliard in return for contributions to the fund.

During the summer of 1970 Mme. Lhevinne taught at Aspen for the last time. She had continued to teach there since the last year she had played (1964) and usually she flourished at the 7,900 foot altitude. This year, buoyed by the ninetieth-birthday celebration, she decided she would play again. To consider doing so was courageous, and some thought foolhardy, especially after she was hospitalized for several weeks in May to recover from the birthday excitement. But she bounced out of the hospital full of fire, and every morning played a new Bach prelude and fugue as a way of getting her fingers in shape (she had been inspired to do this while reading Casals' *Joys and Sorrows* in the hospital). The work she had decided to play was her beloved Mozart concerto, K. 467. Early in June she practiced in earnest while staying at the home of her friend and former student, Mary Lee Shephard, in Atherton, California. By the time she arrived in Aspen, she was feeling quite confident. One day, however, after she had been practicing and had given some lessons, the music disappeared. She and Sarah and the girl living with them searched the apartment for weeks, but the music was not to be found. Because of the excitement, because the music included cadenzas by Robert Casadesus difficult to find a copy of, and because of certain suggestions that the music was stolen, not lost, she had to give up the idea of playing the concerto. There were other problems that summer too. The cottonwood trees seemed overfragrant, making it difficult for her and Sarah to breathe. Never one to get in a rut or not receive her due, Mme. Lhevinne accepted for the following summer an offer to give a master class at the University of Southern California.

During the academic year in New York she had another fine season. In October she learned that Garrick Ohlsson had become the first American ever to win the Chopin Prize, awarded every five years at the International Chopin Competition in Warsaw. Ohlsson had been studying with her for two years at the time he won the prize, his previous teachers being Olga Barabini and Sascha Gorodnitzki, a former student of Josef Lhevinne's who became one of the leading teachers at Juilliard. In the finals of the competition, Ohlsson had played a concerto Mme. Lhevinne had devoted a great deal of attention to—Chopin's E minor. He played that work at his Philharmonic Hall debut with the Philadelphia Orchestra, and of course she was there to hear it. Even in her nineties, she has been able to attend numerous concerts each season, and one week went to four in six days. Pianists she hears most often, in addition to students of her own, seem to be the Russians —Gilels, Richter, Ashkenazy, Slobodyanik—though this is by no means exclusively the case.

Not long after the excitement of Ohlsson's victory subsided, another of her students, Kun Woo Paik, won the Naumburg Prize. A few months later Paik also tied for first place in the Leventritt Competition. He had originally come to New York in his early teens, as one of the two Koreans selected to enter the 1961 Mitropoulos Piano Competition. "Kun Woo's only teacher had been his father, who was a professor of painting but not a pianist, so he had taught him to read the notes but no more. In the competition Kun Woo could play the notes of all the works, but still the performances were absolutely monstrous. In spite of that, I could see his great talent, and when they requested that I teach him I was delighted to accept." Paik studied with Mme. Lhevinne throughout the 1960s. A year before winning the Naumburg, he took concurrently some lessons with Ilona Kabos, with whom Mme. Lhevinne agreed to teach a few students in tandem. ("She marks with a red pencil and I use a dark pencil, and I always say to the student, 'If you like the red better than the black, you do it her way'.") Team-teaching is somewhat faddish on college campuses these days, but remains quite rare among higher-echelon piano teachers.

Paik's "Naumburg" debut was in Alice Tully Hall in April 1971, and Mme. Lhevinne was there, commanding the hall from the left loge section. From below she looked like the captain on the bridge of a ship. She was on television twice that month, first on a program called "New Faces" which featured Paik, then in a documentary for German television. The latter was filmed in

Room 575, and before the shooting began she asked, sitting in her green chair, whether it would be in color or black and white. When the director answered "color" she pointed vaguely in the direction of the floor and said "Take that away!" She was wearing blue; at her feet was a brown purse.

In June she and Sarah flew to her new master class at U.S.C. in one of the new Boeing 747s. That summer's class, in which she was assisted by former student Daniel Pollack, was a satisfying experience, but 1972's was hopelessly marred by the illness of Sarah, who halfway through the summer found that she had cancer of the pancreas, and had to fly home to New Jersey, where she died in September. Sarah had been with (or near) Mme. Lhevinne for fifty-one years, and her death was a grievous loss both domestically and personally. Some doubted that Mme. Lhevinne would return to New York and to Juilliard, but such fears proved unfounded. Before leaving California she convinced an able woman she had met only that summer to go to New York and live with her, and in the summers of 1973 and 1974 she flew back to California for her third and fourth summer master classes at U.S.C. After a stroke in November of 1974 she decided to take a summer vacation in 1975—her first since the death of her husband. The next year she returned to Juilliard. At her birthday party in the spring, she was named honorary chairperson of the piano department.

On March 29, 1976, Rosina Lhevinne had her ninety-sixth birthday. After thirty-odd years of devoted widowhood she is steadily gaining on Clara Schumann's musical record in that regard (forty years). She takes it a little easier now than she did a decade ago, teaching only twenty-two students during the school year and half a dozen in the summer. With her two assistants to help her, she seldom gives more than two lessons a day, down from three a day in 1970. The most demanding time for her continues to be late spring, when her goal is always to hear each of her Juilliard students play his full program before the final examinations.

In the fall of 1972, her son Don retired at age sixty-five from his job with the public utility in Los Angeles—which must make her one of the few mothers in history whose son has reached retirement age before she has. Don and his wife celebrated by taking a year-long trip to Europe, to which his mother has not returned since teaching in Mondsee in the summer of 1932. She saw enough of the world in her younger days. Now she is content to look at it through the eyes of her children (Marianna is an insatiable traveler) and her students, much as she used to play on the stage through the fingers of her husband. The girl who had to give up embroidery at age nine because she was entering the Moscow Conservatory still has not found time to take it up again, but she does still teach young pianists the tradition she herself began to assimilate at that age, in the name of the one man in her life, whom she met in that same year.

As each year now goes by, she is more and more amazed by the fact that she, who was always so sickly, has lived so much longer than her husband, who was the paragon of health. In certain moods, she feels her longevity a miracle, and something completely out of her control, and when making plans will say "God willing" or "With God's help" or "God send everything will be all right." The fates have been kind to her, but certainly she herself has done much to contribute to her long-lastingness: the freshness with which she approaches music; her ability to identify with the young and to share in their lives; her simple diet (no fried foods, no coffee or alcohol, no cigarettes); her penchant for exercise (daily walks outside when the weather allows—when it does not, determined striding up and down a twenty-foot "Fifth Avenue" path on her carpet); her ability to surround herself with interesting people and to see the best in others; her total lack of professional jealousy, that poison which eats away at so many musicians' lives.

Perhaps an equally important element is one she does not often reveal: her self-deprecating humor, which at bottom is humility, a quality which for most of her life seemed more a property of her husband's than of hers, but which, through his influence, she finally came to possess. It was a long way from the 1898 summer evening when she was riding in a droshky near Moscow and was so horrified when Josef pointed to the swarm of mosquitoes and said, "You know, Rosina, we are one of them," to the 1970 winter evening when she was sitting with me in her Manhattan apartment working on this book. She was not feeling well that night, so when the telephone rang, I answered it. When an Oriental-sounding voice asked, "Is Mrs. Lhevinne there?" I thought it might be the Chinese husband of a French pianist who had recently been living with her. Wishing to deflect any calls not of the utmost urgency, I asked quite sharply, "Who is this?" The reply, in a mouselike and seemingly apologetic voice, was "Mr. Emil Gilels."

I put Mme. Lhevinne on, and watched her features brighten as she launched into an animated twenty-minute conversation in Russian. When it was over she said, "It's wonderful what he says. He had only now received the invitation to my ninetieth birthday, and he wanted to call to tell me how much he admires me, what a wonderful musician I am, and so on. And just when I was feeling that I didn't know anything. *How do I fool them all!"*

Sarah, who was sitting nearby, began to laugh, and I joined her. Soon it was a trio, with the leading voice joyous, hearty, and, above all, vibrant.

Notes

1. A Girl Meets a Tradition

1. Most Russian Jews had been confined to the Pale since the time of Catherine the Great. At one time, the only way a Jewish family could leave the Pale legally was to be baptized. By the time Rosina was born, Czar Alexander II had granted permission for special categories of Jews—those who were university graduates, merchants of the first class, or foreign-born—to leave the Pale and settle freely in Moscow or St. Petersburg. Jacques Bessie qualified under two of these categories, and evidently was allowed to take his family to Moscow even under the more stringent March Laws of Czar Alexander III.

2. George Eliot, *Daniel Deronda* (New York: Harper and Row, 1966), pp. 179–80.

3. Ibid., p. 191.

2. From Boyhood to Free Artist

1. Josef Lhevinne, "My Early Life," *Gramophone*, October 1929, p. 193.

2. Josef Lhevinne, "Practical Phases of Pianoforte Study," *Etude*, March 1921, p. 151.

3. Ibid. (word order slightly rearranged).

4. Ibid.

5. Lhevinne, "My Early Life," pp. 193–94.

6. Louis Biancolli, "The Great Anton Rubinstein," *New York World-Telegram*, November 25, 1939.

7. Lhevinne, "My Early Life," p. 194.

8. Ibid.

9. *Russkie Vedomosti* (Moscow), November 19, 1890.

10. *Musical Courier* (New York), February 25, 1914.

11. Edward J. Dent, *Ferruccio Busoni* (London: Oxford University Press, 1933), pp. 271–72.

12. Sergei Bertensson and Jay Leyda, *Sergei Rachmaninoff: A Lifetime in Music* (New York: New York University Press, 1956), pp. 27–28.

13. Ibid., p. 41.

14. From Maria Safonoff's unpublished biography of Vassily Safonoff.

3. *From Idolatry to Marriage*

1. Biancolli, "The Great Anton Rubinstein."
2. "Press Material on Josef Lhevinne," National Concert Artists Corporation, 1942–43 season.
3. *Musical Courier*, December 18, 1912.
4. *Musical America* (New York), May 19, 1906.
5. Faubion Bowers, *Scriabin: A Biography of the Russian Composer* (Tokyo and Palo Alto: Kondansha International Ltd., 1969), Vol. I, p. 215.
6. William King, "Forty Years of Marriage and Music Making," *Sun* (New York), January 11, 1939.
7. Tikhomirov's three-volume study entitled *Russia, Political and Social* was published in London in 1888.

4. *Retreat and Rededication*

1. Faubion Bowers, *Scriabin: A Biography of the Russian Composer*, I, 262.
2. "The Piano That Did Not Play Strauss or Offenbach," *Bohemian* (New York), July 1907, pp. 4ff.
3. *Morning Courier* (Warsaw), January 9, 1902.
4. *Le Figaro* (Paris), January 31, 1902.
5. Dr. Paul Ertel, *Künstler Biographieen* (Berlin: Concert Direction Hermann Wolff, 1902), Vol V.

5. *Alma Mater and the New World*

1. *Russkie Vedomosti*, December 11, 1902.
2. Harold C. Schonberg, *The Great Pianists* (New York: Simon and Schuster, 1963), p. 203.
3. *Odessa News* (Ukraine), March 5, 1903.
4. "A Talk with Josef Lhevinne," *New York Times*, March 11, 1906.
5. Lhevinne played in Kazan on March 30/April 11, 1904. The review quoted here is signed with the symbol "X." I have not yet discovered the name of the newspaper in which it appeared.
6. The novels of Mayne Reid (especially *Rifle Rangers* and *Scalp Hunters*) were also favorites of Chaliapin, along with a good many more of the Lhevinnes' Russian contemporaries. Born in England in 1818, Reid lived for much of his life on the American frontier. But his works were never as popular in England or America as in Russia.
7. "Young Pianist Direct from Moscow Tells Story of Bloodshed," *New York Times*, January 21, 1906.
8. "Lhevinne Risked Life in Flight From Moscow," *New York Times*, January 16, 1906.
9. *Musical America*, February 3, 1906.
10. *Evening Post* (New York), January 28, 1906.
11. Letter from Josef Lhevinne to Vassily Safonoff, June 23, 1906 (translated from the Russian by Maria Safonoff).

12. César Cui's Op. 69 (published by Jurgenson) is entitled *Trois Morceaux pour Piano à 4 mains* and is dedicated *à Mme et M Lhevinne*. The three works are labeled *Intermezzo* (D major), *Notturno* (D-flat major), and *Alla marcia* (F major). I have yet to find evidence that the Lhevinnes played them in public.

13. Letter from Josef Lhevinne to Vassily Safonoff, September 12, 1906.

6. *America before the War*

1. *Sun* (New York), November 17, 1906.

2. This version of the Rosenthal story is from Harold Schonberg's article, "In Her Head, a Century of Piano Playing," *New York Times,* March 29, 1970.

3. Faubion Bowers, *Scriabin: A Biography of the Russian Composer,* II, 144.

4. Ibid., II, 149.

5. Charles F. Peters, "Little Glimpses of Famous Musicians," *Bohemian,* May 1907.

6. *Musical America,* February 2, 1907. See also *Musical Leader,* February 7, 1907.

7. Postcard (in Russian) from Rosina Lhevinne to Josef Lhevinne, February 10, 1907, in possession of Marianna Graham.

8. *Chicago Daily Tribune,* February 18, 1907.

9. *New York Times,* March 15, 1907.

10. *Evening Post* (New York), April 6, 1907.

11. *Musical Leader* (Chicago), January 31, 1907.

12. *Musical America,* December 26, 1908. See *Christian Science Monitor* of December 19, 1908, for a more urbane—though equally enthusiastic—account of Lhevinne's debut with the Boston Symphony Orchestra.

13. *Times* (Philadelphia), January 24, 1909, and *Telegraph* (Philadelphia), January 23, 1909.

14. Edward Burlingame Hill, "The Making of a Russian Pianist," *Etude,* October 1906.

15. *El País* (Mexico City), February 21, 1909.

16. *Los Angeles Times,* March 2, 1909.

17. *San Francisco Chronicle,* March 15, 1909.

18. *Seattle Post-Intelligencer,* March 27, 1909.

7. *Europe before the War*

1. A. Herrera y Ogazón, "Una Conversación con Lhevinne," *El Mundo Ilustrado* (Mexico City), January 30, 1910.

2. Josef Lhevinne, "The Playing of Chopin's Étude, Opus 25, No. 10," *Delineator,* November 1909, p. 415.

3. *El País,* January 17, 1910.

4. *Musical Courier,* February 9, 1910.

5. *El País,* January 17, 1910.

6. Herrera y Ogazón, "Una Conversación con Lhevinne."

7. This account of the trip from Troy to Ithaca is from press material released for the 1931–32 season by Lhevinne's managers, NBC Artists. A similar account of the trip was printed in *Musical America*, September 9, 1922.

8. *New York Tribune*, March 7, 1910.

9. *Musical Courier*, April 19, 1911.

10. Herrera y Ogazón, "Una Conversación con Lhevinne."

11. *Messager de Saint-Pétersbourg*, October 28, 1911.

12. Neil S. Graydon and Margaret D. Sizemore, *The Amazing Marriage of Marie Eustis and Josef Hofmann* (Columbia: University of South Carolina Press, 1965), p. 168.

13. The stage was built at Lady Ripon's manor, Coombe, following the London success of the Ballet Russe in 1910. Its permanent setting in blue and green was designed by Léon Bakst. See Tamara Karsavina, *Theatre Street* (London: William Heinemann, 1930), p. 278.

14. *Christian Science Monitor* and *Boston Transcript*, March 4, 1912; *Boston Transcript*, January 5, 1912.

15. Letter from Bassett Hough to Rosina Lhevinne, March 16, 1955.

16. Klindworth and Ertel's comments were printed in *Musical Courier*, June 10, 1914.

17. This and quotations that follow are from J. Davidson Ketchum's unpublished diary, written in Berlin from November 1913 to August 1914.

18. Letter from an unidentified Lhevinne student to Loudon Charlton printed in *Musical America*, May 30, 1914.

19. *Musical Courier*, March 18, 1914.

8. *Enemy Aliens in Berlin*

1. This is Lhevinne's own account of the "Geld-Auto" affair in Wannsee, paraphrased by Ketchum in his diary.

2. The "document from the Kaiser" is no longer extant. Mme. Lhevinne's memory supplies the details given here.

3. *Ruhleben: A Prison Camp Society* (Toronto: University of Toronto Press, 1965). It was while reading the preface of this book that I learned of Ketchum's association with the Lhevinnes.

4. *Musical America*, February 20, 1915.

5. *Musical Courier*, January 6, 1916.

6. *Pesti Naplo* (Budapest), March 13, 1915.

7. Interview with Marian Szekely-Freschl, New York, May 30, 1970.

8. See Edward Willis, *Herbert Hoover and the Russian Prisoners of World War I* (Palo Alto: Stanford University Press, 1951).

9. *Lokal-Anzeiger* (Berlin), September 24, 1919.

10. *Musical Leader*, September 25, 1919.

11. *Musical America*, October 4, 1919.

9. *Kew Gardens and Points West*

1. *Musical America*, November 1, 1919.

2. *New York Tribune*, October 27, 1919.

3. Louis P. Lochner, *Fritz Kreisler* (New York: The Macmillan Company, 1950), p. 187.

4. *Musical America*, January 10, 1920.

5. *Chicago Daily Tribune*, November 1, 1919.

6. *St. Louis Post-Dispatch*, March 6, 1920.

7. *Enquirer* (Cincinnati), March 27, 1920.

8. *Chicago Daily Tribune*, March 31, 1920.

9. *Evening Post* (New York), February 19, 1920.

10. *Sun* (New York), October 18, 1920.

11. *San Francisco Chronicle*, November 29, 1920.

12. *New York American*, December 14, 1922.

13. *Boston Evening Transcript*, February 9, 1920.

14. *New York Times*, May 2, 1971.

15. *St. Louis Post-Dispatch*, March 6, 1920.

16. *Los Angeles News*, November 29, 1923.

17. *Musical Courier*, April 22, 1920.

18. Frieda Schütze, "Reminiscences of Mr. Lhevinne," sent to Rosina Lhevinne on December 5, 1964.

19. Josef Lhevinne, *Basic Principles in Pianoforte Playing* (Philadelphia: Theodore Presser Co., 1924), p. 24.

20. *Musical America*, December 10, 1921.

21. The new Beethoven works included Sonata, Op. 53 (*Waldstein*); Sonata, Op. 109; Sonata, Op. 111; Andante in F major; Fifteen Variations in E-flat; and *Écossaises* (Busoni's transcription). Before the war Lhevinne had played the *Les Adieux*, the *Hammerklavier*, and the so-called "Moonlight" sonatas in America.

22. *Excelsior* (Mexico City), April 17, 19, 23, 28, 1921.

23. *Milwaukee Journal*, February 27, 1922.

24. *Times-Picayune* (New Orleans), February 18, 1923, and *St. Louis Post-Dispatch*, December 3, 1921.

25. *San Antonio Express*, December 4, 1921.

26. *Pittsburgh Post*, April 1, 4, 1922.

27. Rachmaninoff wrote a letter from America after the war with the following sentence: "Here is the program: my first concerto, Beethoven's first concerto (what heavenly music!) and my Rhapsody." See Victor Seroff, *Rachmaninoff* (New York: Simon and Schuster, 1950), p. 222.

28. William J. Shore, "Recollections of Music and Pianists," sent to Rosina Lhevinne on February 7, 1968.

29. Lhevinne, *Basic Principles*, p. 12.

30. Ibid., p. 46.

31. Beethoven, Andante in F; Weber-Tausig, "Invitation to the Dance"; Schubert-Liszt, "The Linden Tree"; Mendelssohn, Presto in E; Chopin, Polonaise in F-sharp minor, Berceuse, and Two Preludes; Ravel, "Une barque sur l'océan"; Schubert-Liszt, "Lorelei"; Tausig, "Fantasy on Gypsy Airs."

32. *Evening Post, New York Times*, and *Sun*, all February 12, 1924.

33. *World* (New York), October 24, 1925.

34. *Diario de la Marina* (Havana), March 19, 1924.

35. *Indianapolis News*, March 9, 1924.

10. *The Juilliard Graduate School*

1. Letter from William Beller to Rosina Lhevinne, March 21, 1955.

2. Lhevinne, *Basic Principles*, p. 27.

3. *New York Times*, November 3, 1924.

4. Ibid., January 13, 1925.

5. The reconciliation came at the Tchaikovsky Festival concert in Boston on April 25, 1934. Actually, Lhevinne had played once before with Koussevitzky in Boston: on April 16, 1926, a month after the inadvertent insult. That concert had been scheduled in advance of the backstage encounter in New York, and while it did take place, the results were unsatisfying for all concerned—according to the Boston press. At the time, of course, Lhevinne did not realize that Koussevitzky had been so offended by the comment.

6. *Basic Principles*, pp. 42–43.

7. *Sun*, January 18, 1926.

8. *Minneapolis Star*, March 7, 1928.

9. *Basic Principles*, p. 26.

10. Until Harold Samuel liberated pure Bach for the piano in the late 1920s, virtuosos customarily began recitals with a Liszt, D'Albert, Tausig, or Busoni transcription of a work by Bach. Lhevinne played many of these early in his career, and later returned to Busoni's transcription of the well-known Chaconne for violin. As for pure Bach, he played works from the Well-Tempered Clavier at home but not in the concert hall. He never did consider himself a Bach specialist, and was not afraid to admit it: he and Rosina could be seen, notebooks in hand, at Samuel's lectures at Town Hall.

11. *Gramophone* (London), October 1929, p. 194.

12. Marjory M. Fisher, "On Tour of Pacific Coast with Master Pianists," *Musical America*, August 15, 1925.

13. Interview with Adele Marcus, New York, June 19, 1970.

14. Most of these comments are taken from notes Harold Triggs kept of his lessons with Lhevinne. A few are from William Beller and Frieda Schütze.

15. *Chicago Daily Tribune*, January 11, 1927.

16. *New York Times*, September 21, 1926.

17. *Pester Lloyd* (Budapest), November 9, 1926.

18. *Deutsche Allgemeine Zeitung* (Berlin), December 4, 1928.

19. *Times* (London), December 3, 1928.

20. *Musical America*, January 7, 1928.

21. Lhevinne's complete performance of the Schulz-Evler arrangement (including the introduction) can be heard on the recent Argo reissue. He cut it on the rolls about the same time he made the disc for Victrola (see Discography).

22. Sue Prosser, "Tribute to Josef Lhevinne," written in April 1959.

23. *Sun*, February 5, 1930. The études Lhevinne played were E-flat major, Op. 10; D-flat major, Op. 25 (in sixths); and G-flat major, Op. 25 (the "Butterfly").

24. *Musical America*, February 25, 1930.

11. *Counterpoint*

1. Letter from Béla Bartók to his Mother and Aunt, July 13, 1931, *Letters of Composers through Six Centuries*, ed. Piero Weiss (Philadelphia: Chilton Book Company, 1967), p. 453.

2. *New York Times*, December 22, 1931.

3. *Musical Courier*, January 2, 1932.

4. *Evening Post*, March 17, 1931.

5. Interview with Sue Prosser, New York, January 7, 1970.

6. *New York Times*, October 29, 1933.

7. February 28, 1932.

8. Letter from Mrs. J. T. Lanman, Jr., to Rosina Lhevinne, March 7, 1955.

9. Eliott Arnold, "Josef Lhevinne Studies His Astronomy as Well as the Music Masters," *New York World-Telegram*, November 20, 1939.

10. Interview with Joseph Raieff, New York, March 31, 1971.

11. See *The Austro-American Artist* (Mondsee, Austria), August 1932.

12. *Sun*, October 30, 1933.

13. Interview with Elsie Illingworth, New York, September 23, 1971.

14. *New York Herald Tribune*, November 20, 1933.

15. *Evening Post*, November 20, 1933.

16. "Lhevinne Discusses Radio," *Musical Courier*, April 8, 1933.

17. Letter from Reah Morton to Rosina Lhevinne, March 1955.

18. Interview with Mary Lee Shephard, Atherton, California, September 3, 1970.

19. Letter from Mrs. J. T. Lanman, Jr., to Rosina Lhevinne, March 7, 1955.

20. Harold Schonberg, *The Great Pianists* (New York: Simon and Schuster, 1963), p. 381.

21. Letter from Betty Hofmann to Josef and Rosina Lhevinne, October 25, 1935.

22. *New York Times*, October 27, 1935.

23. Letter (possibly unsent) to Adelaide Salmond, November 10, 1935.

24. *Sun*, October 28, 1935.

25. *Stereo Review*, March 1971.

26. Ibid.

27. See *New York World-Telegram*, November 20, 1939, for an interview in which both husband and wife speak of this episode.

28. *Poughkeepsie Evening Star* and *Poughkeepsie Eagle News*, both dated November 21, 1936.

29. Josef Lhevinne's unpublished diary, February–April 1937.

30. *Times* (London), April 5, 1937. "The centre-piece of Mr. Josef

Lhevinne's piano recital at Wigmore Hall on Saturday was Brahms's monumental set of Variations on a Theme by Paganini, Op. 35. The programme had begun with Schumann's Toccata in C followed by Beethoven's Rondo in G and the Waldstein Sonata, so the pianist did not save himself for the sustained effort which the two books involve. Indeed, he had no need to, for physical fatigue does not come into consideration in the case of so perfectly equipped a technician as he is. His performance of Brahms showed a wonderful control. The first four variations acquired an almost Mozartian simplicity under his hands; indeed as the first book progressed one began to wonder whether the whole might not be too effortless to convey the intensity of thought which Brahms devotes to Paganini's superficial theme. Variation XIII, with the octave scales played from the wrist instead of *glissando*, was a remarkable technical feat, but one might easily miss the virtuosity that was involved. With that group which forms the final of the first book Mr. Lhevinne added a greater warmth of coloring, the long *poco a poco crescendo* of its coda revealed what seemed an endless increase of tone, and when he plunged into the greater elaborations of the second book one forgot technique in the wealth of the musical invention, and the breadth with which the whole sequence of events was handled. Few pianists have been able to take the measure of this greatest of Brahms's variational works and convey as fully as Mr. Lhevinne does the symphonic design behind all the ingenuity of the structure."

12. *"Those Who Inhabit Olympus"*

1. Interview with Mrs. Katherine Rich, New York, 1970.

2. July 17, 1937.

3. Miami *Herald*, February 13, 1938.

4. Letter from Natalie Rachmaninoff to Rosina Lhevinne, January 6, 1938.

5. *New York Times*, January 16, 1938.

6. I have not yet discovered the French event for which the recording was requested. I rely here on Mme. Lhevinne's memory.

7. Interview with Brooks Smith, New York, October 24, 1971.

8. *Evening Bulletin* (Philadelphia), July 15, 1938.

9. *New York Times*, August 3, 1938.

10. *New York World Telegram*, January 7, 1939.

11. Michel Mok, "The Lhevinnes Love, Honor and Play for 40 Years," *New York Post*, August 4, 1938.

12. Interview with Mary Lee Shephard, Atherton, California, September 3, 1970.

13. *New York Times*, January 15, 1939.

14. Ibid.

15. Telegram from Josef Hofmann to Mr. and Mrs. Josef Lhevinne, November 5, 1938.

16. Antoinette Donnelly, "Trained Listening," *New York Daily News*, February 12, 1939.

17. Alma Archer, "Marriage is a Bed of Roses," Chicago *Daily Mirror,* June 6, 1940.

18. Ibid.

19. Unpublished interview with Josef and Rosina Lhevinne by Beth Levin Siegel, 1927.

20. *New York Post,* August 4, 1938.

21. Interview with Izler Solomon, New York, April 26, 1971.

22. Interview with Joseph Raieff, New York, April 8, 1971.

23. Interview with Ruth Geiger, New York, December 1, 1970.

24. *New York Herald Tribune,* November 19, 1940.

25. Ibid., November 16, 1941.

26. Ibid., January 12, 1942.

27. Letter from H. B. Morse (of the Baldwin Company) to Josef Lhevinne, October 20, 1942.

28. Interviews with Robert Pace, New York, September 28, 1971; with Howard Waltz, Boulder, Colorado, September 18, 1971; with John Browning, New York, November 9, 1970.

29. Interview with Victor Aller, Los Angeles, August 28, 1970.

30. *New York Herald Tribune,* November 8, 1943.

31. *Sun* (New York), December 8, 1943.

32. *New York Herald Tribune,* December 10, 1944.

13. *A New Beginning*

1. Report by W. C. White, M.D., on Maria Alexieff, patient at Roosevelt Hospital, January 25, 1946.

2. Interview with William Schuman, New York, March 2, 1972.

3. *New York Times,* November 18, 1947.

4. Letter from Lee Thompson to Robert K. Wallace, January 23, 1972 (paraphrased slightly).

5. From a copy of the convocation address printed by the Juilliard School.

6. Harold C. Schonberg, "In Her Eighties: Teacher Con Brio," *New York Times,* April 2, 1961.

7. Letter from Mark Schubart to Rosina Lhevinne, May 3, 1954.

8. *Los Angeles Times,* January 19, 1953.

9. Interview with Robert Mann, New York, April 18, 1972.

10. *New York Herald Tribune,* May 10, 1951.

11. Truman's letter, of which I have not found the original, was quoted by Wayne Johnson, "Anniversary of a Virtuoso with Links to Colorado," *Denver Post,* December 13, 1964.

12. Abram Chasins, "The Grand Manner," *Saturday Review,* September 24, 1955.

14. *Concert Life Begins at Seventy-five*

1. July 9, 1953.

2. Interview with Izler Solomon, New York, April 26, 1971.

3. The letter is dated August 12, 1956, but was obviously written on September 12, 1956.

4. Review from *New London* (Conn.) *Telegraph* printed in *Musical Courier*, May 19, 1907.

5. Interview with Tony Han, New York, March 4, 1972.

6. Interview with Mark Schubart, New York, January 9, 1972.

7. Interview with Cortland Barnes, New York, March 27, 1972.

8. *New York Times*, August 12, 1957.

9. Letter from Rosina Lhevinne to Mark Schubart, August 31, 1959.

10. Letter from Rosina Lhevinne to Janet Goodman, April 29, 1960.

11. *Indianapolis Times*, March 2, 1960.

12. Cuthbert Girdlestone, *Mozart and his Piano Concertos* (New York: Dover Publications, 1964), pp. 336, 341.

13. *New York Times*, March 1, 1961.

14. *New York Herald Tribune*, March 1, 1961.

15. *Racing toward Ninety—and Beyond*

1. Letter from Joseph Zelle to Rosina Lhevinne, February 1, 1963.

2. Letter from Mrs. Clair Adler, Ann Arbor, to Rosina Lhevinne, January 20, 1963.

3. Letter from Mrs. H. C. Soucheray to Rosina Lhevinne, February 20, 1963.

4. Letter from Rosina Lhevinne to Ray Allen, Wichita, May 3, 1962.

5. Interview with Jeffrey Siegel, New York, October 19, 1972. One person who spoke of Siegel's tone was Artur Rubinstein, in a letter to the pianist on April 8, 1968. He praised the "simplicity, the tenderness, and the beautiful tone" Siegel had produced in the "lovely Andante" of Schumann's great sonata.

6. Letter from Eva Maria Zuk to Robert K. Wallace, March 11, 1972.

7. Interview with Jeffrey Siegel.

8. Interview with Kun Woo Paik, New York, June 10, 1971.

9. Interview with Sarah Crump, New York, March 2, 1971.

10. Winthrop Sargeant, "Profiles: The Leaves of a Tree," *New Yorker*, January 12, 1963, pp. 40–42.

11. Letter from Mrs. Mary W. Meyer to Rosina Lhevinne, January 14, 1963.

12. Letter from Lee Thompson to Robert K. Wallace, March 9, 1972.

13. Letter from Rosina Lhevinne to Mark Schubart, September 12, 1956.

14. Interview with Mark Schubart, New York, January 9, 1972.

15. Letter from Beulah Bennett to Rosina Lhevinne, April 5, 1970.

Bibliography

This selected bibliography includes the one short book written by Josef Lhevinne and the most important articles written by or about him and his wife.

BOOKS

Lhevinne, Josef. *Basic Principles in Pianoforte Playing*. Philadelphia: Theodore Presser Co., 1924. (Originally published in serial form by *Etude* magazine; reprinted in paperback by Musical Scope Publishers, New York, 1971; reprinted in paperback by Dover Publications, New York, 1972, with a foreword by Rosina Lhevinne.)

ARTICLES BY THE LHEVINNES

Lhevinne, Josef. "The Art of Pianoforte Playing in Russia," *Etude*, March, 1913, pp. 175–76.
———. "Basic Principles in Pianoforte Playing," *Etude*, October, November, December, 1923, pp. 665–66, 747–48, 815–16; January, February, March, 1924, pp. 17–18, 37–38, 157–58.
———. "Good Tone is Born in the Player's Mind" (Transcribed by Harriet Brower), *Musician*, July, 1923, p. 7.
———. "Musical and Personal Reflections," *Ainslee's* (New York), March, 1907, pp. 141–44.
———. "My Early Life," *Gramophone*, October, 1929, pp. 193–94.
———. "Piano Study in Russia." *Great Pianists on Piano Playing*. Edited by James Francis Cooke. Philadelphia: Theodore Presser Co., 1917, pp. 170–79.
———. "The Playing of Chopin's Étude, Opus 25, No. 10," *Delineator*, November, 1909, pp. 415ff.
———. "Practical Phases of Modern Pianoforte Study," *Etude*, March, 1921, pp. 151–52.
———. "Practical Phases of Modern Pianoforte Technique," *Etude*, April, 1921, p. 228.
Lhevinne, Josef and Rosina. "Four Hands That Play as Two" (as told to Ruth Helybut), *Etude*, December, 1933, pp. 809–10.
Lhevinne, Rosina. Foreword to Josef Lhevinne's *Basic Principles in Pianoforte Playing*. New York: Dover Publications, 1972, v–vii.

————. "From Student to Artist," *Music of the West Magazine*, September, 1948, pp. 5ff.

————. "Rubato in Life," *Pan Pipes*, May, 1960, p. 11. (Convocation Address to Students of the Juilliard School of Music, October 4, 1949.)

————. "The Spirit of Ensemble," *Pan Pipes*, February, 1949, pp. 161–63.

ARTICLES ABOUT THE LHEVINNES

Abell, Arthur. "Contest 44 Years Ago," *New York Times*, February 12, 1939.

Arnold, Eliott. "Josef Lhevinne Studies His Astronomy as Well as the Music Masters," *New York World-Telegram*, November 20, 1939.

Biancolli, Louis. "The Great Anton Rubinstein," *New York World-Telegram*, November 25, 1939.

Donelly, Antoinette. "Trained Listening," *New York Daily News*, February 12, 1939.

Farmer, John. "Josef Lhevinne on Ampico Piano Rolls," *Juilliard Review Annual*, 1966–67, pp. 25–35.

Fisher, Marjory M. "On Tour of Pacific Coast with Master Pianists," *Musical America*, August 15, 1925.

Goldberg, Albert. "The Lhevinnes' Impact on the World of Piano Playing," *Los Angeles Times*, November 23, 1969.

"A Great Pianist," *Independent* (New York), February 22, 1906, p. 437.

Henahan, Donal. "Madame Lhevinne Going Strong at 90," *New York Times*, April 1, 1970.

Herrera y Ogazón, A. "Una Conversación con Lhevinne," *El Mundo Ilustrado* (Mexico City), January 30, 1910.

Hill, Edward Burlingame. "The Making of a Russian Pianist: A Talk with Josef Lhevinne," *Etude*, October, 1906, pp. 627–28.

Howard, John Tasker. "Studies in Comparative Interpretations," *Musician*, December, 1924, p. 13.

Jacobson, Robert. "Landmark for Rosina Lhevinne," *Saturday Review*, March 28, 1970, pp. 57ff.

———— (ed.). "The Juilliard School: [An Interview with Rosina Lhevinne]," *Lincoln Center Programs*, March, 1970.

King, William C. "Forty Years of Marriage and Music Making," *New York Sun*, January 11, 1939.

Klein, Howard. "They've Dispelled Those Piano Roll Blues," *New York Times*, October 16, 1966.

"Lhevinne and Rubinstein," *Musician*, September, 1913, p. 595.

"Lhevinne Discusses Preparation of Pianists," *Musical America*, October 25, 1940.

"Lhevinne Discusses Radio," *Musical Courier*, April 8, 1933.

"Lhevinne's First Visit to America," *Musical Leader*, May 7, 1914.

"Mme. Lhevinne's Trials Hunting Apartments," *Musical America*, November 3, 1906.

Mok, Michel. "The Lhevinnes Love, Honor and Play for Forty Years," *New York Post*, August 4, 1938.

Neugebauer, Emil. "Backstage with a Concert Tuner," *Etude*, February, 1948, pp. 67ff.

Peters, Charles. "Little Glimpses of Famous Musicians," *Bohemian* (New York), May, 1907, pp. 655–67.

"The Piano That Did Not Play Strauss or Offenbach," *Bohemian*, July, 1907, pp. 4ff.

Sargeant, Winthrop. "Profiles: The Leaves of a Tree," *New Yorker*, January 12, 1963, pp. 37ff.

Schonberg, Harold C. "In her Eighties, Teacher Con Brio," *New York Times Magazine*, April 2, 1961, pp. 18ff.

————. "In her Head, a Century of Piano Playing," *New York Times*, March 29, 1970.

Schubart, Mark. "A Birthday Greeting to Rosina Lhevinne," *Juilliard Bulletin*, Spring, 1965, pp. 51–52.

"Some New Pieces to Play" (suggested by Josef Lhevinne in an interview with William Armstrong), *Musician*, July, 1906, pp. 235–36.

"A Talk with Josef Lhevinne," *New York Times*, March 11, 1906.

Taubman, H. Howard. "Four Hands that Play as Two," *New York Times*, January 8, 1939.

Wallace, Robert K. "The Lhevinnes' Teaching Legacy," *Piano Quarterly*, Spring, 1974, pp. 7–11.

————. "One Woman's Career: Liberation through Limitation," *American Scholar*, Summer, 1976, pp. 442–47.

"Young Pianist Direct from Moscow Tells Story of Bloodshed," *New York Times*, January 21, 1906.

Discography

I have divided recordings by the Lhevinnes into five categories: Josef Lhevinne: RCA Victor; Josef Lhevinne: Piano Rolls; Josef and Rosina Lhevinne: RCA Victor; Rosina Lhevinne: Vanguard and Columbia; and "Others."

Josef Lhevinne: RCA Victor

In 1928, 1935, and 1936, Lhevinne made recordings at 78 rpm for RCA. All of those recordings were included in "The Art of Josef Lhevinne," an LP album originally released in the 1950s (CAMDEN CAL 265) and re-issued in 1970 as RCA VIC 1544 (in England as VICTROLA VIC 1046). Of all Lhevinne recordings on the market, this is the only one of which we can be sure he would have approved, as it includes all recordings issued with his permission in his lifetime:

RCA VIC 1544

Chopin	Polonaise in A-flat, Op. 53 ("Heroic")
	Étude in A minor, Op. 25, No. 11 ("Winter Wind")
	Étude in E-flat, Op. 10, No. 11
	Étude in G-sharp minor, Op. 25, No. 6 (in Double Thirds)
	Étude in B minor, Op. 25, No. 10 ("Octave")
	Prelude in A-flat, Op. 28, No. 17
	Prelude in B-flat minor, Op. 28, No. 16
Schumann	Toccata in C, Op. 7
Schumann-Liszt	Frühlingsnacht (Spring Night)
Debussy-Ravel	Fêtes (arranged for two pianos) (with Rosina Lhevinne)
Strauss-Schulz-Evler	Blue Danube Waltz

Two of Lhevinne's performances included in RCA VIC 1544 have appeared in other albums released by RCA:

RCA LCT 1038 "Great Pianists of the Past Play Chopin"
Chopin Polonaise in A-flat, Op. 53

337

RCA IM 2585 "Keyboard Giants"
CAMDEN CAL 351
    Strauss-Schulz-Evler   Blue Danube Waltz

For details concerning Lhevinne's recording sessions in the studios of RCA (i.e., dates, number of takes, etc.), see "The Josef Lhevinne Recordings" by Gregor Benko, which is appended to the 1971 reissue of Lhevinne's *Basic Principles in Pianoforte Playing* by Musical Scope Publishers, New York.

Josef Lhevinne: Piano Rolls

Lhevinne made piano rolls for Welte and Sons before the First World War and for the Ampico Corporation after the war. Listed below are the LP recordings that have been made from these rolls. They vary in quality, and only one—ARGO DA 41—can be recommended without reservation. The Argo disc is, by all accounts, a highly lifelike and representative sample of Lhevinne's playing. When released in America in 1966, it was hailed almost universally as the best recording ever made from piano rolls (see Howard Klein, "They've Dispelled Those Piano Roll Blues," *New York Times*, October 16, 1966). Unfortunately, the same cannot be said for the other recordings listed here. Those including Beethoven's *Moonlight* Sonata are particularly suspect: Lhevinne detested his piano-roll performance of that work and refused to listen to it on a player piano. In reviewing KS-104 (see below), Irving Kolodin fittingly called the recording of the *Moonlight* Sonata presented there "a slander on the name of Josef Lhevinne" (*Saturday Review*, October 31, 1970). For the record, however, all long-playing discs made from Lhevinne's piano rolls are listed here:

ARGO DA 41 (11–66) Mono (from Ampico rolls)
Liszt-Busoni	La Campanella
Chopin	Nocturne in B, Op. 9, No. 3
Chopin	Étude in E-flat, Op. 10, No. 11
Chopin	Étude in G-flat, Op. 25, No. 9 ("Butterfly")
Liszt	Gondoliera
Strauss-Schulz-Evler	Blue Danube Waltz
Schubert-Liszt	Soirée de Vienne, No. 6
Cui	Causerie, Op. 40, No. 6
Albeniz	Sevilla (Suite Espagnole)
Mendelssohn-Liszt	On Wings of Song
Tausig	Fantasy on Gypsy Airs

Klavier Keyboard Series KS-104 (12–70) Stereo (from Ampico rolls)
Beethoven	Sonata, Op. 27, No. 2 ("Moonlight")
Liszt-Busoni	La Campanella
Schumann	Papillons, Op. 2
Chopin	Étude, Op. 10, No. 11
Chopin	Étude, Op. 25, No. 9 ("Butterfly")

Klavier Keyboard Series KS-111 (1–71) Stereo (from Ampico rolls)
Mendelssohn-Liszt	On Wings of Song
Schubert-Liszt	Soirée de Vienne, No. 6
Liszt	Liebestraum, No. 3
Rubinstein	Kamennoi-Ostrow
Tausig	Fantasy on Gypsy Airs
Sindig	Frühlingsrauschen (Rustle of Spring)
Schuett	À la bien aimée

Keyboard Immortal Series 4–AO71–S Stereo (from Ampico and Welte rolls)
Beethoven	Sonata, Op. 27, No. 2 ("Moonlight")
Weber	Perpetuum Mobile (from Sonata in C major, Op. 24)
Chopin	Étude in B minor, Op. 25, No. 10
Chopin	Nocturne in B, Op. 9, No. 3
Dohnányi	Étude Caprice in F minor
Rachmaninoff	Prelude in B-flat major, Op. 23, No. 2

Recorded Treasury Album 674 "The Welte Legacy of Piano Treasures"
Chopin	Étude in B minor, Op. 25, No. 10
Schloezer	Étude de Concert in E-flat
Scriabin	Nocturne for the Left Hand, Op. 9, No. 2
Liszt	Die Lorelei
Schubert-Liszt	The Linden Tree
Beethoven-Busoni	Écossaises
Czerny	Octave Study, Op. 740, No. 5
Rubinstein	Prelude, Op. 75, No. 9 (Album de Peterhof)
Sgambati	Veccio Minuetto, Op. 18, No. 2

The Classics Record Library "Legendary Masters of the Piano" includes:
Scriabin	Nocturne for the Left Hand, Op. 9, No. 2
Czerny	Octave Study, Op. 740, No. 5

For a detailed list of the rolls Lhevinne made for Welte and Ampico (and their roll numbers), consult John Farmer's article "Josef Lhevinne on Ampico Piano Rolls," *The Juilliard Review Annual*, 1966–67.

Josef and Rosina Lhevinne: RCA Victor

RCA VIC 1544
  Debussy-Ravel   Fêtes (arranged for two pianos)
RCA LM 2824 "Keyboard Giants, Vol. 2"
  Mozart   Sonata in D major for Two Pianos
The Lhevinnes were not satisfied with their performance of the Mozart Sonata and did not allow it to be released as a 78 rpm disc. The long-playing disc on which it appears was issued after Lhevinne's death.

Rosina Lhevinne: Vanguard and Columbia

COLUMBIA ML–4098 (1948)

    Mozart   Concerto No. 7 in F major for Three Pianos, K. 242

    (with Vitya Vronsky and Victor Babin, pianists, and the Little Symphony Orchestra, conducted by Thomas Scherman)

COLUMBIA ML–5582 Stereo *MS–6182* (1960)

    Mozart   Piano Concerto No. 21 in C major, K. 467

        (with the Juilliard Orchestra, conducted by Jean Morel)

In 1970, a special re-issue of this recording (CSS–1295) was made in connection with Mme. Lhevinne's ninetieth birthday.

VANGUARD VRS–1085 Stereo *VSD–2111* (1962)

    Chopin   Piano Concerto No. 1 in E minor, Op. 11

        (with Alumni of the National Orchestral Association, conducted by John Barnett)

"Others"

In the 1920s Lhevinne recorded four works for Pathe-Marconi which are listed in Benko's previously mentioned article. Two of them (Beethoven-Busoni, *Écossaises*; Rachmaninoff, Prelude in B-flat major) have evidently ended up on the piano-roll discs listed above (see Recorded Treasury Album 674 and Keyboard Immortal Series 4–AO71–S).

One additional Josef Lhevinne recording remains to be listed. It was taken from a radio broadcast of a live performance on November 3, 1935:

VERITAS VM-115 (Produced by the International Piano Library) "The Great Chopin Interpreters"

    Chopin   Polonaise in A-flat, Op. 53

FILMOGRAPHY

A 16-mm, black-and-white, forty-minute film entitled "Mme. Rosina Lhevinne: Pianist and Master Teacher" was made at Mme. Lhevinne's 1964 summer master class at U.C.L.A. It was written and directed by Mark McCarty, Motion Picture Production, University of California Extension Media Center, Los Angeles, and can be highly recommended to anyone interested in Mme. Lhevinne, the piano, or teaching.

Index

Graham, Marianna—*cont.*
  221, 225, 230, 241, 254, 259, 260, 266, 277, 315, 320
Grainger, Percy, 172, 195
Greene, Mildred, 184
Gubert, Alexandra Ivanovna, 23, 27

Haagenson, Dr. Cushman, 265, 304
Hale, Philip, 179
Hambourg, Mark, 134
Hammerstein, Oscar, 102–3
Han, Tong Il (Tony), 278–80, 283, 290, 297, 314, 316
Handel, George Frederick, 34
Hanon, Charles, 305
Harding, Merle, 250
Harding, Warren, 170
Harrell, Mack, 275–76
Haskil, Clara, 172
Hattstaedt, John, 169, 220
Hauptmann, Gerhart, 121
Hävös, sculptor, 232
Haydn, Franz Josef, 77, 273
Heatter, Gabriel, 244
Heifetz, Jascha, 11, 31, 144, 146, 162, 168, 172, 173, 174, 217
Helena Pavlovna, Grand Duchess, 12, 13
Henderson, William J., 91, 92, 101–2, 104, 133, 201, 210, 222
Henschel, William, 101
Henselt, Adolf von, 34, 80; Piano Concerto in F minor, 50, 77–78, 242
Hess, Myra, 172
Hevesi, Piroska, 156, 232
Higginson, Colonel Henry, 172
Hill, David, 121
Hill, Edward Burlingame, "Jazz Study" for Two Pianos, 200
Hilmers, Daphne, 128
Hitler, Adolf, 222, 234
Hofmann, Betty, 227, 244
Hofmann, Josef, 35, 44, 59, 65–66, 69, 80, 83, 87, 114, 115, 126, 129, 133, 144, 168, 172, 173, 174, 226–28, 242, 244, 251, 274, 282, 288–89
Holländer, Gustav, 42, 73, 74
Hollywood Bowl, 213, 236
Holt, Dr., pediatrician, 108, 177
Horowitz, Vladimir, 154, 205, 227, 230, 247, 282
Hough, Basset, 137
Hřimaly, Johann, 49
Hubay, Eugen, 128
Hubbard, W. L., 108–9, 171
Hummel, Johann Nepomuk, 34
Hurok, Sol, 316

Hutcheson, Ernest, 172, 190, 195, 204, 242, 243, 255, 259, 262

Ibach piano, 148, 155, 157
Ibsen, Henrik, 81, 121
Igumnov, Constantine, 42, 43, 51
Illingworth, Elsie, 222, 251
Imperial Russian Conservatory, 11, 13–15. *See also* Moscow Conservatory; Tiflis Conservatory; St. Petersburg Conservatory
Imperial Russian Musical Society (I.R.M.S.) Orchestra: Moscow, 33, 44, 49, 61, 78; St. Petersburg, 129
Institute of International Education, 279, 285
Institute of Musical Art, 216, 262
Ippolitov-Ivanov, Mikhail, 78, 107

Jablonski, Marek, 297
James, Henry, "Great Good Place," 183
Juilliard, Augustus, D., 175, 188, 189; Juilliard Foundation, 175
Juilliard Orchestra, 242–43, 269, 292, 293
Juilliard School of Music (formerly Juilliard Graduate School), 3, 154, 185, 188–91, 193, 195, 203–4, 206, 216–17, 235, 242, 244, 248, 251–55 *passim*, 259–60, 261, 262, 265, 266, 269, 270, 271, 275, 278, 279, 280, 282, 287, 289, 291, 296, 299, 302–6 *passim*, 315–20 *passim*
Juilliard String Quartet, 273, 277, 290, 294, 297

Kabalevsky, Dmitri, 281, 292; Third (*Youth*) Concerto, 281
Kabos, Ilona, 319
Kapell, William, 172, 262
Kardasheva, O., 50, 51
Karsavina, Tamara, 130–31
Kashkin, Nicholas, 28, 43
Katch, Maria. *See* Bessie, Maria
Keneman, Feodor, 42, 43, 51
Kennedy, Robert, 313
Ketchum, J. D., 136–40, 145–46, 150, 158, 251
Khan, the Aga, 131–32
Kindler, Hans, 222
King, Martin Luther, Jr., 313
Kipnis, Igor, 229
Klindworth, Karl, 136
Kneisel Quartet, 133
Kochanski, Paul, 190
Kosciuszko Paderewski Prize, 297